STANDARD EDITION

The BUSINESS GUIDE

OR

Safe Methods of Business

BY

J. L. NICHOLS, A. M.
Late Principal of North-Western Business College
Naperville, Ill.

WITH

AN INTRODUCTION

BY

PRESIDENT DR. L. H. SEAGER

LEGAL DEPARTMENT

EDITED BY

H. H. GOODRICH, A. M.
Attorney at Law and Master in Chancery

Revised and Corrected up to Date

BY

J. L. NICHOLS, A. B.

PUBLISHED BY

J. L. NICHOLS & COMPANY

HOME OFFICE
Naperville, Ill.

BRANCH OFFICE
Atlanta, Ga.

1921

Sold only by subscription and not to be had in bookstores.
Any one desiring a copy should address the publishers.

MORE THAN THREE MILLION COPIES SOLD

PREFACE

The purpose of this book is embraced in its title, The ***Business Guide*** or **Safe Methods of Business.**

The necessity of having a book comprising the practical in business, including forms, points of law, hints and helps in transacting business successfully, together with the most useful tables for rapid computation or for reference, was forcibly impressed upon the mind of the author while acting as principal of a Business College, in which he had ample opportunity to study the needs of our young men before entering the active business world.

After mature thought his purpose to relieve the felt want of business circles and individuals in general took shape in the first edition of the **Business Guide.** That the public has appreciated his efforts is seen in results better than told in words. The many succeeding editions, the large sales, and the interest of the public clearly show that this volume is filling a place that no other fills. Although the author has finished his labors and has passed to his reward, yet **Nichols' Business Guide** is having an ever-increasing educative influence among the masses.

Thirty-five Years have passed since the first edition was published. These have been years of intense activity and of great progress in all lines. Notwithstanding the success that has attended this volume, our constant effort is to keep it an all-around up-to-date book, a book every item of which can be relied upon as correct.

This edition has been rearranged and revised and printed from an entirely new set of plates. We are determined that the **Business Guide** shall continue to be the leading book on practical business. The advice and assistance of able and competent specialists in different lines of business have greatly aided us in making imorovements and in giving accurate and at the same time boiled down statements. All the best and recent volumes on business have been consulted and valuable suggestions taken therefrom. Much of the book has been re-

written, while every part and line has passed under the scrutinizing eye of the critic. All commercial and legal forms are of the very latest. Great pains have been taken to make all illustrations apt and instructive. We are free to say without fear of contradiction that this is decidedly the best book in the market for the money.

The Business Guide is adapted to all classes, not to a certain profession or class of men, but to all who are called upon to do business. And whom does this not include? With the recognition that real merit and true excellence must be depended upon for success, and with the confidence of an appreciation of diligent, painstaking labor and research, this revised edition is sent forth to the millions who may thereby be led to do the right thing, at the right time, in the right place and thus turn defeat, failure, loss of reputation, property, or home into intelligent actions, profitable investments, pleasant homes and prosperous, happy and successful lives.

THE PUBLISHERS.

OUR GUARANTEE.

The Business Guide is sold on the positive guarantee that it must give complete satisfaction or purchase price will be promptly refunded by us. We also agree to furnish free to any owner of the **Business Guide** any new and up-to-date information regarding any subject found in the **Business Guide.** Our advice and help can be had at any time in making wills, deeds, mortgages, or any other papers with which the average person is not familiar.

THE PUBLISHERS.

INTRODUCTION

TO REVISED EDITION.

Never was competition greater than now and never was there a greater demand for business principles applied to daily life than at this present time. The man who knows has his battle half won, while he who is self-satisfied and lags behind is lost.

Every one must largely decide and direct his own course in life, and the only service others can render is to give us data from which we must draw our own conclusions and decide our own course.

I count it a rare privilege to have known the author of this book. I have also been acquainted with the book itself for some years. Wherever it has gone it has blessed mankind. The advice and maxims are the result of expert experience and so plainly written that "he who runs may read." Indeed it would be hard to find a work covering so many subjects and at the same time so entirely free from useless and unpractical matter.

This volume is written for the home, the farm, the office and the shop. Its genius is that of helpfulness, and there would be less friction in the world, less confusion in families, less litigation over wills and legacies, fewer tangles in business and less wear and tear generally if the principles set forth in the "BUSINESS GUIDE" were more closely observed and carefully followed. It has deservedly won its place with the helpful and more popular books of every home and office library.

Naperville, Ill. L. H. SEAGER.

TABLE OF CONTENTS.

SECTION I.

SECTION II.

SECTION III.

SECTION IV.

SECTION VIII.

Points of Law and Legal Forms.

SECTION IX.

SECTION X.

SECTION XI.

SECTION XII.

Parliamentary Laws and Rules.

SECTION XIII.

Counterfeiting, Gambling, Betting and Swindling.

SECTION XIV.

Bookkeeping.

SECTION XV.

Interest Laws and Tables.

SECTION XVI.

SECTION XVII.

SECTION XVIII.

Useful Reference Rules and Items.

SECTION XIX.

Distances, Population, and Trade Facts.

SECTION XX.

PRODUCTION AND WEALTH OF NATION SHOULD INSURE FOOD AND SHELTER TO ALL

DURING THE PAST TWENTY YEARS, from 1900 to 1920, the per capita wealth of the United States has increased from $1,165 to $4,700. Data compiled from the recent census by *Commerce and Finance* presents some interesting information concerning this nation's progress during this period. The bank deposits in the United States exceed by billions the combined bank deposits of the whole world outside of this country. Before the war we owed other nations $5,000,000,000. We have not only paid this debt, but foreign nations now owe us $10,000,000,000, and we hold the largest gold reserves of any nation in the world.

While the United States has only six per cent. of the world's population and only seven per cent. of the globe's land area, we now contribute one-quarter of the world's agricultural supplies, one-third of the mineral products, and one-third of all manufactured goods.

With so much wealth and productivity there should not be a single hungry, shelterless, or ill-clothed individual in this entire country during the winter. There should be no bread lines of the unemployed. The following table gives the best evidence of this:

TWENTY YEARS OF NATIONAL PROGRESS

	1900	*1910*	*1920*
Social			
Continental area	3,026,789	3,026,789	3,026,789
Population	76,303,387	91,972,266	106,650,000
Wealth	$88,517,306,775	$125,000,000,000	$500,000,000,000
Wealth, per capita	1,165	1,360	4,700
Financial			
Gold in circulation	$610,806,472	$592,547,340	$1,225,210,813
Silver in circulation	142,050,335	217,229,937	385,083,071
Circulation of money	2,055,150,998	3,119,753,246	6,084,854,578
Nat. banks, number	3,732	7,145	7,933
Nat. banks, capital	621,536,461	989,567,104	1,182,082,000
Deposits in nat'l banks	2,458,092,758	5,287,216,312	17,155,421,000
Deposits in savings banks	2,389,719,954	4,070,486,247	6,000,000,000
Depositors in savings banks	6,107,083	9,142,708	11,500,000
Bank clearances, U.S.	$84,582,450,081	$169,025,600,000	$417,519,523,388

Commerce and Industry			
Imports, merchandise	$849,941,184	$1,556,947,430	$5,238,621,668
Imports, merchandise, per capita.........	10.88	17.21	49.12
Exports, merchandise	1,394,483,082	1,774,984,720	8,111,039,733
Exports, merchandise, per capita.........	17.96	19.02	76.05
World's gold production.........	262,220,915	454,874,000	380,924,700
World's silver production..........	224,441,200	286,662,700	255,217,648
U. S. bituminous coal output, tons......	172,609,988	420,000,000	458,063,000
U. S. anthracite shipments, tons.........	45,276,622	64,000,000	65,500,000
U. S. petroleum production, gallons....	2,672,062,218	7,469,639,508	14,792,000,000
U. S. pig-iron production, tons.........	13,789,242	27,200,000	30,582,878
U. S. copper production, tons.........	270,588	487,925	639,000
Transportation			
Railroad mileage......	198,964	244,934	260,014
Railroad gross earnings	$1,501,695,378	$2,737,000,000	$5,336,822,558
Post-office receipts....	102,354,579	224,128,637	436,239,126
Agriculture			
Farm animals, value .	$2,228,123,134	$5,138,486,000	$8,566,313,000
Cattle, number.....	43,902,414	69,080,000	68,232,000
Horses, "	13,537,524	20,040,000	21,109,000
Sheep, "	41,883,000	57,216,000	48,615,000
Mules, "	2,086,027	4,123,000	4,995,000
Swine, "	37,079,356	47,782,000	72,909,000
Farm products, value	$3,764,177,706	$8,926,000,000	$16,025,000,000
U. S. wool production, pounds...........	288,636,621	321,362,750	314,239,000
World's wheat crop, bushels............	2,583,389,000	3,590,000,000	2,267,074,000
U. S. wheat crop, bush	522,229,505	695,443,000	794,147,000
U. S. corn crop, bush...	2,105,102,513	3,125,713,000	3,003,322,000
Cotton Production and Consumption			
U. S. cotton crop, val.	$554,000,000	$900,000,000	$2,172,324,368
U. S. commercial cotton crop, bales.. ..	10,383,000	12,000,000	12,443,000
World's cotton consumption, bales....	15,185,000	18,321,000	15,970,000
U. S. consumption of cotton, bales......	3,588,501	4,798,953	6,425,344
World's cotton spindles, number......	106,290,000	134,526,000	150,000,000
U. S. cotton spindles, number...........	19,100,000	29,188,945	34,666,842
U. S. cotton exports, bales..............	6,201,166	6,484,429	6,915,408
U. S. cotton exports, value............	$302,500,000	$460,868,200	$1,381,707,502

IT MAKES THE SPARKS FLY

THE BUSINESS MAN'S CODE.

BUSINESS, ENERGY, PUSH.

Business, in every age of the world, has been the chief pioneer in the march of man's civilization. Blessings everywhere follow its advancing footsteps. We honor and respect our upright, energetic business men. They start every noble project; they build our cities, and rear our manufactories; they whiten the ocean with their sails, and blacken the heavens with the smoke of their steam vessels and furnace fires; they draw treasures from the mines, and give to mankind the various products of every clime and the benefits of skilled labor throughout the world. These results are achieved not by love of ease or idle wish, but by energy that knows no defeat, by that indomitable spirit of push that lays the foundation of true prosperity and builds the structures of success and progress, right over the ruins of defeated projects and apparent failures. The man who was financially ruined by the Chicago fire, but who began his

business at the old stand right in the midst of the burnt district and advertised his goods on a shingle the day after the fire, richly deserved that which he received—the applause of the world and a successful business, with which his former business bore no comparison. Everybody admires the courageous spirit that overcomes difficulties and manages to rise in the world. It is the invincible spirit of "get there" that people like.

HOW SUCCESS IS WON.

Success is a happy word for the average American. To achieve success is the aim of every one. It would more frequently be gained were it not that it is too often wrongly understood to be innate smartness. Young man, the sooner you get rid of the notion that you are smart, the sooner will you win success. You may be a genius of exceeding brilliancy, but the chances are one to one hundred thousand that you are not. It is safer to conclude that you are just a plain ordinary mortal and then set about doing the best you can with the capital nature has given you. You may not soar so high at first, but then, when your balloon of youthful conceit collapses, you will not have so far to fall. Bear in mind that there are thousands who consider themselves exceptionally smart and through a dependence upon that smartness have made an utter failure of life, while on the other hand the apparently dull and stupid youth has by proper means overcome and is enjoying the prosperity that the supposed talented youth has dreamed of.

Success must be won if it is to be enjoyed. The person who waits for it to come along is like a man who waits for the train to arrive before he gets his ticket. To use an ordinary term, both are apt to "get left." Men ordinarily fail to succeed, not because they are naturally destined to fail, but they lack business ability, which is made up of equal parts of business knowledge, sterling integrity, strict economy and everlasting push.

In our day knowledge can be acquired and is in the reach of all who possess the other qualities. The other qualities ought to be in possession of every youth of sound mind. If not, nature can hardly be blamed for the deficiency.

Again, success is the child of confidence and perseverance.

YOUNG LINCOLN CUTTING WOOD FOR HIS MOTHER.

The line between failure and success is so fine that we scarcely know when we pass it, so fine that we are often on the line and do not know it. How many a man has thrown up his hands at a time when a little more effort, a little more patience, would have achieved success. As the tide goes clear out, so it comes clear in. Sometimes business prospects may seem darkest when really they are on the turn. A little more persistence, a little more effort, and what seemed hopeless failure may turn to glorious success. There is no failure except in no longer trying. There is no defeat except from within, no really insurmountable barrier save our own inherent weakness of purpose.

A firm resolution, that barriers shall be surmounted, that difficulties shall be cleared away, goes far toward achieving success. Let us repeat, success must be won. It never comes uninvited, never without effort.

A BUSINESS EDUCATION.

Know Thyself—Is an ancient maxim, but none the less worthy of consideration. Many of the failures of life result from a lack of knowledge of one's self and of adaptations in a business life. There are some farmers who would with credit fill one of the professions; while there are not a few of the professional men who would do themselves credit by seeking the farm, the workshop, or the laborer's task. One of the essentials in starting out in life is to be thoroughly fitted for the position occupied by a proper educational training. First of all the young man should diligently apply himself to an intelligent study of his own adaptations. To have parents or friends say that a young man shall be a lawyer, a doctor, a preacher, or a merchant, without consulting the inclinations and adaptations of the youth and then seek to train him to this end is sheer folly. Success or failure generally hinges on a proper choice of vocation.

Our Educational System.—At the summit of our excellent educational system stands the college and the university. We need not be ashamed of Yale, Harvard and Princeton that compare favorably in scholarship, thoroughness of instruction, and work done with the most honored universities of any land. Our public school and business colleges fit our youth for the practical side of life. Higher education is all very well, but the first and important thing in this practical world is for one to be able to make a good living. A business education fits any one all the better for his calling even though he enters one of the professions.

Practical Education Needed.—Horace Greeley said, many years ago, that he knew of 3,000 college graduates in New York alone that were not able to make a living. The craze to graduate and have a diploma is even greater today. Give these college graduates a thorough practical business education and there will be less of soaring after the infinite and diving after the unfathomable and more of seeking to acquire true success by merit alone.

Importance of Business Education.—A business education is essential to a substantial business career. Not a mere acquaintance with business facts but practical business training is what makes men able to direct successfully the details

THE LATE MARSHALL FIELD.

of large establishments, to control the movements of immense business concerns.

Your Duty.—Study the drift of your mind. Know the current in which your faculties drift the swiftest and the surest, and then lay to the helm, steer so straight a course that neither yourself nor any one else can be mistaken as to the direction or object of your efforts. (They say that there is a place out west where, when the boys wear their breeches threadbare, their mothers just turn them around instead of sewing on a patch, and the result is that when you see those boys out on the road you cannot tell whether they are going to school or coming home.) Young man, let the world know which way you are going.

Certain Prosperity.—Let a man in business be thoroughly fitted for the position he occupies, alert to every opportunity and embracing it to its fullest possibility and he is a success.

Lay a good foundation of business principles and practices. Do a legitimate business. Aim to have a home of your own early in life. Be strictly honest; work hard; be earnest; seek to be an intelligent citizen. Marry a good, healthy, loving girl, keep a clear conscience; fear God and work righteousness, and life's sun will set in tints of gold and splendor.

BUSINESS A PROFESSION.

The occupation of the merchant is now recognized as being as much a profession as that of medicine or theology. To master the intricacies of business and conduct it successfully requires as careful a preparation and training as for any of the professions.

Formerly the particularly bright sons of the family were encouraged by the fond parents to prepare for one of the professions, but those who were not so fortunate were to go into business, on the supposition that it did not require such a high order of ability to make a success. It is not so now. It requires the brightest minds and the strongest intellects to make a success in the fierce competition which rules in every department of business. In this connection the New York Commercial Bulletin says:

"The idea is prevalent that merchandizing is a thing that can be taken up when other vocations fail, and that it only needs a fair degree of push or smartness, or perhaps a genius for speculation which does not hesitate to accept any risk. It need not be said that nothing is further from the truth, and that those who are tempted to accept the delusion are morally certain, sooner or later, to repent of their folly. The mercantile life needs preparation or qualification quite as much as the other professions. We live in an age of extraordinary commercial activity. The world, practically, is today all one market, and the man or people who would handle that market to the best advantage must be well up in the particular kind of knowledge that is requisite to enable them to take advantage of the world-wide methods and to keep pace with their competitors. This cannot be acquired in an offhand, haphazard kind of a way, but by intelligent, painstaking study. Here, if anywhere, knowledge is power."

Hon. John Wanamaker thus expressed himself:

"Let me say to you that a young man who starts in such a field as this (commercial life) will stand but little chance of success without thorough and fruitful business training. The days of chance are gone. The mercantile profession must be studied as one studies law or medicine. There never were so many bids for young men. Banking institutions, business establishments and great importers are calling for young men, but they must be men who have studied, who have applied themselves, who have had training to do the work."

Chauncey M. Depew makes the following statement:

"In the olden time there was no intermediary which taught the young man or young woman the methods of business. To-day the young man who graduates from a literary college and who enters business without going through a business school is enormously hampered in his progress in life."

POOR BOYS AND FAMOUS MEN.

1. **Humble Birth no Barrier to Success.**—In European countries much depends upon one's birth. Class and clan largely control the future, barring out the youth of humble birth from entering upon the avenues open to those through whose veins courses more royal blood.

In America, the land of liberties and opportunities, nature invites all alike to positions of greatness and honor. Here a larger proportion of boys of humble parentage rise to eminence and wealth than in any other country.

2. **Noted Examples.**—Franklin was the son of a tallow-chandler and soap boiler. Daniel Defoe, hostler and son of a butcher. Whitfield the son of an inn-keeper. Shakespeare was the son of a wood stapler. Milton was the son of a money scrivener. Robert Burns was a plowman in Ayrshire. Mohammed, called the prophet, a driver of asses. Madame Bernadotte was a washer-woman of Paris. Napoleon was of an obscure family of Corsica. John Jacob Astor once sold apples on the streets of New York. Catherine, Empress of Russia, was a camp-grisette. Elihu Burritt was a blacksmith. Abraham Lincoln was a rail splitter. Gen. Grant was a tanner.

3. **George Peabody.**—A long time ago, a little boy twelve years old, on his road to Vermont, stopped at a country tavern, and paid for his lodging and breakfast by sawing wood, instead of asking for it as a gift. Fifty years later, the same boy passed that same little inn as George Peabody, the banker, whose name is the synonym of magnificent charities—the honored of two hemispheres.

4. **Cornelius Vanderbilt.**—When Cornelius Vanderbilt was a young man, his mother gave him fifty dollars of her savings to buy a small sail boat, and he engaged in the business of transporting market-gardening from Staten Island to New

York City. When the wind was not favorable he would work his way over the shoals by pushing the boat along by poles, putting his own shoulder to the pole, and was very sure to get his freight in market in season. He accumulated over $20,000,000 during his life.

5. **Stephen Girard.**—Stephen Girard left his native country at the age of ten or twelve years, as a cabin boy on a vessel. He came to New York in that capacity. His deportment was distinguished by such fidelity, industry and temperance that he won the attachment and confidence of his master, who generally bestowed on him the appellation of "My Stephen." When his master gave up business he promoted Girard to the command of a small vessel. Girard was a self-taught man, and the world was his school. It was a favorite theme with him, when he afterwards grew rich, to relate that he commenced life with a sixpence, and to insist that a man's best capital was his industry.

6. **Marshall Field.**—A clerk in a country store in Massachusetts at seventeen; then a foreman in a Chicago dry goods house at twenty-five, a partner in the firm at thirty; the head of the business at forty, and at fifty the owner and director general of a mercantile enterprise doing a business exceeding forty million dollars every year—this is the story of Marshall Field's successful career.

7. **Barefooted Boys.**—The barefooted boy of fifty years ago has been thinking and thinking aright, and thinking with no ordinary mind. He has placed the impression of his character upon the age. His industry, his business habits were developed in round, full and beautiful character. The barefoot boy of fifty years ago is today the prominent millionaire, the prominent business man, the prominent lawyer, the prominent statesman and the prominent philanthropist. It is a common saying that the men who are most successful in business are those who begin the world in their shirt-sleeves; whereas those who begin with fortunes generally lose them. Necessity is always the first stimulus to industry.

OPINIONS OF SUCCESSFUL MEN.

The following gleaned from a letter from Mr. Marshall Field to Dr. Hillis is worthy of every young man's careful perusal:—

"A young man should carefully consider what his natural bent or inclination is, be it business or profession. Then enter upon it with diligence and put into it an energy directed by strong common sense; seek to enhance his own and his employer's interests; choose good companions, and make honesty and devotion to duty his watchword. ECONOMY is one of the most essential elements of success. The average young man is too extravagant and wasteful. In order to acquire the dollars one must take care of the nickels. Begin to save early, be it ever so little. Success in small things is a necessary qualification of controlling a large business and income."

It is a mistake that capital alone is necessary to success. If a man has head and hands suited to his business, it will soon procure him capital.—*John Freedley.*

There is no boy in America, however humble his birth, who, in whatever capacity his lot may be cast, if he have a strong arm, a clear head, brave heart, and honest purpose, may not, by the light of our public schools and the freedom of our laws, rise until he stands foremost in the honor and confidence of the country.—*Congressman Payson, Pontiac, Ill.*

Punctuality is the mother of confidence. Be on time. Be frank. Say what you mean. Do what you say. So shall your friends know and take it for granted, that you mean to do what is just and right.—*John Briggs.*

He that has never known adversity is but half acquainted with others, or with himself, for constant success shows us but one side of the world.—*Colton.*

What though you have found no treasure, nor has any rich relation left you a legacy. Diligence is the mother of good luck, and God gives all things to industry. Then plow deep while the sluggard sleeps, and you shall have corn to sell and to keep. Work while it is called today, for one today is worth two to-morrows.—*Franklin.*

Until men have learned industry, economy and self-control, they cannot be safely intrusted with wealth.—*John Griggs.*

ON BENNETT BEGINNING THE NEW YORK HERALD

SAFE PRINCIPLES AND RULES.

1. Remember that time is gold.
2. True intelligence is always modest.
3. Never covet what is not your own.
4. Don't cultivate a sense of over-smartness.
5. A man of honor respects his word as he does his note.
6. Shun lawsuits, and never take money risks that you can avoid.
7. Endeavor to be perfect in the calling in which you are engaged.
8. Keep your eyes on small expenses. Small leaks sink a great ship.
9. Keep your health good by adopting regular and steady habits.
10. Never forget a favor, for ingratitude is the basest trait of a man's mean character.
11. Remember that the rich are generally plain, while rogues dress well and talk smoothly.
12. Remember that steady, earnest effort alone leads to wealth and high position.
13. Never be afraid to say no. Every successful man must have the backbone to assert his rights.
14. Avoid the tricks of trade; be honest, and never misrepresent an article that you desire to sell.
15. The only safe rule is, never to allow a single year to pass by without laying up something for the future.
16. Remember that trickery, cheating and indolence are never found as attributes of a thrifty and progressive man.
17. Do not be ashamed of hard work. Work for the best salary or wages you can get, but work for anything rather than to be idle.
18. Be not ashamed to work, for it is one of the conditions of our existence. There is no criminal who does not owe his crime to some idle hour.
19. To industry and economy add self-reliance. Do not take too much advice, think for yourself. Independence will add vigor and inspiration to your labors.

GOOD BUSINESS MAXIMS.

1. Goods well bought are half sold.
2. Write a good, plain, legible hand.
3. Keep your word as good as a bank.
4. Goods in store are better than bad debts.
5. Never refuse a choice when you can get it.
6. Never take any chances on another man's game.
7. Never sign a paper without first reading it carefully.
8. Never gamble or take chances on the Board of Trade.
9. Remember that an honest man is the noblest work of God.
10. Your first ambition should be the acquisition of knowledge pertaining to your business.
11. Of two investments, choose that which will best promote your regular business.
12. By prosecuting a useful business energetically, humanity is benefited.
13. Keep accurate accounts, and know the exact condition of your affairs.
14. Be economical; a gain usually requires expense; what is saved is clear.
15. Endeavor to be perfect in the calling in which you are engaged.
16. Never fail to meet a business engagement, however irksome it may be at that moment.
17. Never sign a paper for a stranger. Think nothing insignificant which has a bearing upon your success.
18. Avoid litigation as much as possible, study for yourself the theory of commercial law, and be your own lawyer.
19. Undertake no business without mature reflection, and confine your capital closely to the business you have established.
20. Lead a regular life, avoid display, and choose your associates discreetly, and prefer the society of men of your own type.
21. Be affable, polite, and obliging to everybody; avoid discussions, anger, and pettishness; interfere with no disputes the creation of others.
22. Never misrepresent, falsify, or deceive; have one rule of moral life, never swerve from it, whatever may be the acts or opinions of other men.

23. Make no investments without a full acquaintance with their nature and condition; and select such investments as have intrinsic value.

24. Never run down a neighbor's property or goods and praise up your own. It is a mark of low breeding, and will gain you nothing.

25. Above all things, acquire a good, correct epistolary style, for you are judged by the business world according to the character, expression, and style of your letters.

26. During business hours attend to nothing but business, but be prompt in responding to all communications, and never suffer a letter to remain without an answer.

27. Never form the habit of talking about your neighbors, or repeating things that you hear others say. You will avoid much unpleasantness, and sometimes serious difficulties.

28. Finally, examine carefully every detail of your business. Be prompt in everything. Take time to consider, and then decide positively. Dare to go forward. Bear troubles patiently. Be brave in the struggle of life. Maintain your integrity as a sacred thing. Never tell business lies. Make no useless acquaintances. Never appear something more than you are. Pay your debts promptly. Shun strong liquor. Employ your time well. Never be discouraged. Then work hard and you will succeed.

GENIUS, CAPITAL, SKILL, LABOR.

Here is a comparative table of genius, capital, skill and labor, on the mutual basis of the almighty dollar.

Genius.—The power that enabled Tennyson to take a piece of paper and make it worth sixty-five thousand dollars by writing a poem on it.

Capital.—The ability to write a few words on a sheet of paper and make it worth five million dollars, as a Vanderbilt can do.

Skill.—The ability to take twenty-five cents' worth of steel and make it into watch-springs worth fourteen thousand dollars, as a mechanic can do.

Labor.—The act of working ten hours a day and shoveling three or four tons of earth for $1.50, as the ditcher does.

IF YOU WANT TO CATCH FISH, YOU MUST GO WHERE THEY ARE. THE BOY SEES THE POINT, DO YOU.

BUSINESS FAILURES.

Actual Experience.—It is asserted that at least nine-tenths of those who engage in business pursuits either fail or go out of business after having lost more or less of their capital. The large number of failures is exceedingly discouraging to the young man who may have little or no capital with which to begin business, but when their failures are more closely examined, it is readily seen that they resulted either from a lack of experience or from a yielding to discouraging features, and to difficulties that with perseverance might have been surmounted. Nothing, neither theoretical knowledge nor adaption to the work, can be substituted for actual business experience.

Every young man should avail himself of every opportunity to prepare himself for his work, but let him not attempt to substitute this preparation for actual experience.

No Defeat.—Again, failure, by a determined effort, has often been turned into brilliant and permanent success. It is said that the British have won in many decisive battles, after their enemies believed themselves to be conquerors, simply because they would not acknowledge that they were beaten. Difficulties and apparent failures may become instructors or stepping stones to success, when determined effort will not yield to them.

It is often the case that more may be expected from a man who has failed, yet goes on in spite of his failure, than from the buoyant career of the successful. Many young men have distinguished themselves by brilliant speeches while in college, who were never heard from after leaving college. It may be gratifying but it is seldom beneficial to strike twelve the first time.

Examples.—Examples of success through failure are not wanting. Men are successful in spite of difficulties. It was in the face of many failures that Fulton applied himself to the task of designing a successful steamboat. Hiram Powers, the noted American sculptor, met failure and defeat in a dozen different pursuits before he became established in his chosen profession. Phillips Brooks failed utterly as a teacher in a Boston Latin School, but, undaunted by the predictions of friends and discouraging disappointments, he lived to present to the world one of the richest natures, and noblest preachers of the nineteenth century. Robert Bruce, discouraged and disheartened by repeated defeats, looked to the roof of his cabin and learned a lesson from a spider which after many unsuccessful efforts at last swung itself from one beam of the roof to the other. Stimulated by the success of the spider, Bruce was encouraged to make one more effort for his country, and, as he never before gained a victory, so he never afterward met with any great defeat. If the little ant does not succeed the sixty-ninth time in carrying its food to its home, it makes the seventieth effort. Do not be disheartened at every rebuff. There are few persons who succeed at once. We learn more wisdom from failures than from success.

Causes of Failures.—In answer to the question what causes the numerous failures in life of business and professional men, the following replies from leading men in our country are suggestive and will be helpful to the wide-awake youth:

Alex. H. Stephens.—Want of punctuality, honesty, truth.

Pres. Bartlett.—Lack of principle, of fixed purpose, of perseverance.

Pres. Eliot.—Stupidity, laziness, rashness, dishonesty.

Dr. Dexter.—Want of thoroughness of preparation. Want of fixedness of purpose. Want of faith in the inevitable triumph of right and truth.

Anthony Comstock.—Unholy living and dishonest practices, lust and intemperance, living beyond one's means.

Gen'l. O. O. Howard.—Breaking the Divine laws of the body by vice, those of the mind by overwork and idleness, and those of the heart by making an idol of self.

Prof. Homer Sprague.—Mistakes in choice of employment and lack of persistent and protracted effort. A low ideal, making success to consist in personal aggrandizement, rather than in the training and development of a true and noble character.

Dr. Lyman Abbott.—The combined spirit of laziness and self-conceit that makes a man unwilling to do anything unless he can choose just what he will do.

Marshall Field.—The haste to become rich at the expense of character; want of forethought, idleness, or general shiftlessness; living beyond one's means; outside speculation and gambling; want of proper judgment and overestimating capacity, lack of progressiveness, or, in other words, dying of dry rot.

Joseph Medill, Editor of the Chicago Tribune.—Liquor drinking, gambling, reckless speculation, dishonesty, tricky conduct, cheating, idleness, shirking hard work, frivolous reading, failure to improve opportunities.

A chicken trying to swim with some ducks, complained of the world. "The world is all right," replied the ducks, "if you adjust yourself to it. Keep in your element (the land), and not ours, which is satisfactory to us." Draw your own moral, if you please.

Failure, a Premonition of Success.—Do not by any means court or invite failure, but if it comes look upon it as indicative of success. We owe much of our happiness to our mistakes, and yet it is true that happiness is never found in failure.

Sir Humphry Davy, when shown a dexterously manipulated experiment said, "I thank God I was not made a dexterous manipulator, for the most important of my discoveries have been suggested to me by failures." The very greatest things—great thoughts, great discoveries and inventions have usually been nurtured in hardship, suffering, and poverty, and have not become established before chilly failure seemed to lay its icy hand upon the victim's aching brow. But how often has apparent failure been turned into real success, through the unconquerable courage and will power of the determined spirit.

BUSINESS MANNERS.

Manners are the ornament of action.—Smiles.

Guard manners, if you would protect the morals.—Davidson.

A good name is the best thing in the world; either to get one a good name, or to supply the want of it.—Anonymous.

1. Be cheerful, and show proper civility to all with whom you transact business.

2. There are many who have failed in business because they never learned to respect the feelings or opinions of others.

3. Kindness of manners is the best capital to invest in a business, and will bear a higher rate of interest than any other investment.

4. Be accomplished, polite, refined, civil, affable, well-behaved and well-mannered, and you will never lose by it.

5. Manners make the business man, and give him the art of entertaining and pleasing all with whom he has business relations.

6. If you wish to change a man's views in reference to some business transaction or other negotiations, respect his opinions, and he will be respectful and listen to your arguments.

7. There are a thousand easy, engaging little ways, which we may put on in dealing with others, without running any risk of over-doing it.

8. An old saying, "politeness costs nothing, and accomplishes wonders," is a good one. Of course, politeness without sincerity is simply a refined form of hypocrisy, and sincerity without politeness is but little better. A savage, a barbarian can be honest, but is not likely to be very polite. So politeness of speech and manners is the distinguishing trait between the civilized and the uncivilized.

9. A coarseness and roughness of speech, a studied effort to say things that grate upon or wound the feelings of a person possessing ordinary refinement, is utterly, inexcusably and wholly indefensible.

10. There are many persons, however, who seem to have the idea that because they are honest, sincere and sympathetic, after a fashion, they are excusable for being impolite, and consequently justified in cultivating boorish manners, and indulging in rough speech; but this is a mistake. It pays to regard

the feelings of others, especially when it costs us nothing. It does not follow because a man is polite that he is therefore insincere. Politeness and sincerity can go together, and the man or woman who possesses both will get along much better than the individual who has either without the other.

BUSINESS QUALIFICATIONS.

If your highest ambition is to seek a name for yourself, you need no special qualifications. Thousands of your class have gone deservedly into everlasting desuetude. Aim higher than that, young man.

Many of life's failures are due to attempts of individuals to fill positions for which they lack the proper business qualifications. While the different lines of business require special skill in certain directions, there are other qualifications that are essential in all business pursuits. The choice of a career is by no means of the least importance. This being made there should be an ideal within you that will raise the character and excellence of your work. The qualifications most essential to success are a knowledge of every detail of your business, strict integrity, painstaking economy, and a push that holds high its motto, "This one thing I do," and "keeps everlastingly at it." The world admires the man who does best what multitudes do well. The era of easy money getting is rapidly passing. It is trained ability that makes the business man safe. It is blind recklessness to neglect to acquire, when opportunities present, a skill that may serve well in life's struggle. The world needs you and if you seek the proper qualifications, the world will hear from you.

Horace Mann's Advice.—Follow Horace Mann, the great educator's advice, "Be ashamed to die until you have won some victory for humanity." The stuff is in you to qualify yourself for more than a name, which is the highest ambition of many youth. It is poor advice that makes every life a failure except that which has achieved a great name. The humblest manual laborer, equally with his brother man whose career abounds with the highest achievements of the intellect, whose name is honored among us, is a fellow worker with God.

To Make a Name.—We have taught our American boys that they were cut out for Congressmen instead of carpenters, for Presidents instead of painters and plumbers, for bankers instead of blacksmiths, for a career instead of a calling. These top-lofty notions have been imbibed by our youth until the highest ambition with many is to make a name for themselves. Not one of a thousand acquires a great name. Are the nine hundred and ninety-nine to be failures? Better learn to make a broom handle, a horseshoe, or a loaf of bread. The world needs these vastly more than it does names. This selfish un-Christian ambition for a name stands in the way of the self-denial necessary to real usefulness. It is baneful folly that has kept so many of our American youth out of the humble but happy and useful lives of industry. Not every man is called to preach, but ever man is called to labor in some sphere. Find your place and then seek to qualify yourself for excellence in your work. Aim to stand at the head of your occupation.

TALENT, WILL, PURPOSE.

> **Talk not of talents, is thy duty done?**
> **Thou hast sufficient, were they ten or one.**
> **—Montgomery.**

Talent of Success.—Longfellow once said that the talent of success is nothing more than doing well what you can do, without a thought of fame. This idea of attempting to discover some hidden talent in one's self by which to become distinguished is fraught with much evil to the American youth. What men need most is not talent but purpose, not the power to achieve, but the will to labor through difficulties. Man's real power exhibits itself when enormous obstacles plant themselves right in his track. Success depends more upon ability adapted to work than upon any superior intellectual power.

OVERCOMING CIRCUMSTANCES.
YOUNG PEABODY SAWING WOOD FOR A NIGHT'S LODGING. HE BECAME ONE OF THE FIRST MILLIONAIRES AND PHILANTHROPISTS OF AMERICA.

Circumstances Blamed.—The blaming of circumstances, the shifting of responsibility, is as old as Adam. He blamed the woman. When Moses chided Aaron for making the golden calf, he blamed the people and the circumstances. "The people are set on mischief; we put in the gold and there came out this calf." Just as if he had no responsibility in the matter. Byron, endowed with brilliant talents, was a physical and moral wreck at thirty-five. "What else can we expect from such surroundings? Byron was the victim of circumstances," says his biographer. "Something drove me to it," says the criminal.

Heredity Accountable.—Then again, many charge their sins and failures upon heredity. True, the evil pleasures of one generation become the failures of the next. Napoleon, Byron, Goethe and McCauley demonstrate the laws of heredity. But these physical facts are but half the facts in the case. Man has a body, but he has also a soul. Something within him whispers that he is free. Self-consciousness declares him to be superior to circumstances and heredity. John Bunyan, the offspring of vicious parentage, Jerry McCauley and Marcus Aurelius show clearly that hereditary tendencies can be conquered.

Barriers Broken.—Heredity may modify responsibility, but never destroy it. There is in man that which asserting itself, breaks through all barriers and rises into new realms. We are not waifs and strays with which the winds and currents sport; we are ocean steamers with power to defy the winds and waves, power to mark out our own course, power to determine for ourselves the distant harbor. Every day men fighting and conquering turn their passions into slaves that serve them; every day some tradesman prefers toil to ease, some teacher truth to falsehood, some business man chooses a little honest wealth rather than great treasures by lying methods. To every ambitious and aspiring youth the iron bars of heredity dissolve into smoke at the touch of the aspiring hand. Heredity is not a tyrant over man. Charles Kingsley and Phillips Brooks conquered the stammering tongue and drilled it into eloquence. Huber, through his love of science, triumphed over blindness. Beethoven, despite his deafness, made splendid music. Africanus, a black chief, a cannibal at forty, a colossal lump of depravity, awakened by the teaching and example of Missionary Moffat, took on the aspect of a man; became the emancipator of his race; learned to read and write and speak; learned agriculture and husbandry, and taught farming to his savages; learned the use of the saw and hammer and taught his people to build houses and villages; made himself a scholar and founded schools and churches and Christian homes. At sixty this man stood forth under the aspect of a Christian hero, a veritable Moses for his race. These examples plainly show that birth-gifts are only raw material. The successful man is the architect of his own fortune.

Circumstances and Surroundings.—Neither is it indispensable that man shall be controlled by circumstances and environments. God means man to be the sole proprietor of himself. It was never intended that he should not know what his occupations or beliefs or plans should be until circumstances came together and made up their decisions. A thousand times better be a slave for the meanest man than become the slave for dead circumstances. Uncle Tom's fetters shine like a king's coronet in comparison with the fetters that he must wear who bows to climate, food, and surroundings and asks the weather whether or not he may be happy. It is for a lump of putty to permit things to stamp it, now with this mark and now with that. He who holds circumstances as responsible for his failure or success has made himself a nonentity. When he wakes up in bed at night he can properly reflect, "There is nobody here."

Man a Victor.—As Sampson broke the green withes which bound him, so man by indomitable courage and will may break down the barriers of circumstances that would hinder him. Fred Douglass was born midst such squalor and poverty and wickedness as no tenement house has ever witnessed, and to all this was added slavery. But, unassisted, the black boy learned to read, shook off his slavery, conquered environments, and literally beat his iron fetters into sickles and pruning hooks. Octavio Hill, entering the tenement house district of Whitechapel in London, civilized the entire ward and transformed circumstances of misery and sin into those of happiness and refinement. David Livingstone proved that, instead of circumstances shaping the man, one heaven-endowed man can absolutely create a new social and spiritual climate for a whole continent.

Man is His Own King.—Do not wait for nor dream of talent not in your possession. Use the talent you have. God meant you to be a success. Hold your ground and push hard. Watch opportunities. Be rigidly honest. If you delight to sit around smoking cigarettes and telling shady stories on street corners and lounging counters, it is hardly necessary for you to attempt to learn "how to write a check," for the chances are a thousand to one that you will never have a bank account.

Have a purpose and with a will steer perseveringly in one direction. To the young man who does not succeed at once we would commend the following quaint lines:

"If you strike a thorn or rose,
Keep a-goin'!
If it hails or if it snows,
Keep a-goin'!
'Taint no use to sit and whine
When the fish ain't on your line;
Bait your hook an' keep on tryin'—
Keep a-goin'!"

"DID NOT KNOW HIS SPELLING LESSON."

SPELLING.

It is the fault of the English language that we have so many bad spellers. Beautiful penmanship should never be marred by bad spelling. Rather be a poor penman than a bad speller, but you need not be either. We may not be able to spell correctly the thousands of words in the English language, but it ought to be expected of us to spell correctly the few hundred words in general use. Careful reading will make a good speller. A writer who has at hand a reliable dictionary and makes it a rule never to write a word unless he is positive that it is spelled correctly will in a very short time be a good speller.

Thomas Jefferson in writing to his daughter Martha says, "Take care that you never spell a word wrong. Always before you spell a word, consider how it is spelled, and if you do not remember it, turn to a dictionary. It produces great praise to a lady (or gentleman) to spell well." Your success may depend upon your spelling. During the month of February, 1880, on the floor of the Senate chamber, Senator Gordon of Georgia objected to the confirmation of one of President Hayes' nominees for a marshalship in his State because the applicant had misspelled two words in the letter of application. The nomination was not confirmed. It is better to consult the dictionary for every word than to run the risk of misspelling a single word.

Close and careful reading and writing will always produce good spellers. Today when typewriters are of universal use only good spellers are wanted to fill positions. You may be able to use skillfully the best shorthand method, but if your typewritten copy is disfigured by bad spelling, your position will soon be occupied by another.

Rules for Spelling.

The following rules will aid students somewhat in their knowledge of spelling:

1. Words of one syllable ending in l with a single vowel before it have ll at the close; as mill, sell.
2. Words of one syllable ending in l with a double vowel before it, have only one l at the close; as mail, sail.
3. Words ending in l double that letter in the termination ly.
4. Words ending in e, adding ing, drop the e; as come, coming; divide, dividing.
5. Some words are spelled the same in both the singular and the plural; as deer, sheep.
6. Verbs of one syllable, ending with a single consonant, preceded by a single vowel, and verbs of two or more syllables, ending in the same manner, and having the accent on the last syllable, double the final consonant whenever another syllable is added; as get, getting; omit, omitted.
7. The plural of nouns ending in y, when y is preceded by a consonant, is formed by changing y into i and adding es; as lily, lilies. When y final is preceded by a vowel the plural is formed by adding s; as valley, valleys.
8. Nouns ending in o preceded by another vowel form their plurals regularly by adding s to the singular; as cameo, cameos.
9. Words formed by prefixing one or more syllables to words ending in a double consonant retain both consonants; as, befall, rebuff. The exceptions are, withal, annul, distil, instil, fulfil, until.

THE USE OF CAPITALS.

1. Every entire sentence should begin with a capital.
2. Proper names, and adjectives derived from these, should begin with a capital.
3. All appellations of the Deity should begin with a capital.
4. Official and honorary titles begin with a capital.
5. Every line of poetry should begin with a capital.
6. Titles of books and the heads of their chapters and divisions are printed in capitals.
7. The pronoun, I, and the exclamation, O, are always capitals.
8. The days of the week, and the months of the year, begin with capitals.
9. Every quotation should begin with a capital letter.
10. Names of religious denominations being with capitals.
11. In preparing accounts, each item should begin with a capital.

PUNCTUATION.

Punctuation is a valuable art, easily acquired, yet too frequently neglected by a vast majority of letter-writers. Business men, as a class, seem to despise points as something beneath their notice. Others omit to punctuate through ignorance or carelessness. This is a great mistake, and many mistakes are made on account of this almost universal neglect to give more attention to punctuation.

Importance.—Punctuation is very closely connected with the construction of sentences; so closely that a clear expression in writing is almost an impossibility without it.

Many illustrations might be given to show the importance of punctuation. A young man, writing to a friend, says: "I was married last Sunday night for the first time in five years; the church was full." He intended to say: I was married last Sunday night; for the first time in five years the church was full.

Another:—"Woman, without her, man would be a savage." "Woman, without her man, would be a savage."

The party consisted of Mr. Smith, a merchant, his son, a lawyer, Mr. Jones, a clergyman, his wife, a milliner, and a little child.

Here the party consists of nine persons. Change the punctuation and you have but five. The party consisted of Mr. Smith, a merchant; his son, a lawyer; Mr. Jones, a clergyman; his wife, a milliner; and a little child.

We give another, where both the spelling and the punctuation are defective. A clergyman one Sunday morning received a note from a parishioner, which, in the haste, he read as written, thus:

"Capt. John Smith having gone to see his wife, desires the prayers of the church for his safe return." The note should have been written: 'Capt. John Smith having gone to sea, his wife desires the prayers of the church for his safe return.

These examples strikingly illustrate the importance of punctuation. And while they are of a simple and ridiculous character in a social sense, in a business letter they might be of very grave importance.

General rule: Punctuate where the sense requires it.

The comma (,) is used to mark the smallest degree of separation, the semicolon (;) a greater degree, and the colon (:) the greatest.

The Principal Uses of the Comma.—A comma is generally used before and after a parenthetical expression; after inverted expressions; after each pair of words or phrases, when they are used in pairs; to separate words or phrases that are contrasted with each other; to separate between words or phrases when used in a series, if the conjunction is omitted or used only between the last two; to set off intermediate expressions; to separate dependent and conditional clauses from the rest of the sentence; in the place of a verb that is omitted, and words that are understood; to set off nouns or phrases which are independent by direct address; to set off explanatory words and expressions, and expressions containing the case absolute; and before a short quotation, or an expression resembling a quotation.

The Semicolon.—The semicolon is used to separate the members of a compound sentence, if they are complex, or if they contain commas; to separate short sentences connected in meaning, unless they are *very* short and simple (in which case a comma is used); to separate clauses that have a common dependence upon another clause; also after the main clause if it comes at the beginning of a sentence; to separate an explanatory clause from a complete sentence, when no conjunction is used between them; before the word *as*, when it is used to introduce an example illustrating a rule (in which case, the *as* should be followed by a comma); and to separate explanatory terms from a general term, when the explanatory terms are simple and separated by commas.

The Colon.—The colon is used to separate the members of a compound sentence, if they are subdivided by semicolons; before a clause that is added to a complete sentence, if no connective word is used; to precede a formal quotation; to separate explanatory terms from a general term, when the explanatory terms are complex and separated by semicolons.

The Period (.).—A period is used at the close of a declarative sentence, after every abbreviation, and after Roman numerals.

Interrogation Point (?).—An interrogation point is used after every direct question, and it is sometimes inclosed in parentheses and used after a statement, to express doubt.

Exclamation Point (!).—The exclamation point is used after an expression of strong emotion; after an exclamation; and to express doubt or sarcasm.

O and Oh!—O is employed to express a wish, and it does not take the exclamation point; Oh is an interjection expressing surprise, pain, grief, sorrow, or anxiety, and should be immediately followed by the exclamation point, unless the emotion continues throughout the sentence.

The Dash (—).—The dash is used to mark a sudden change in sentiment and construction; to mark rhetorical pauses and repetitions; to set off a parenthetical expression that has a close connection with the rest of the sentence; and to mark the omission of letters and figures.

Other Marks.—Parentheses ( ) are used to enclose expressions having only a remote connection with the rest of the sentence; and in reports of speeches, to enclose the exclamations from the audience. **Brackets** [ ] are used to enclose words that are entirely independent; as, comments, queries, corrections, etc., inserted by some other person than the original writer or speaker. **Quotation Marks** (" ") are used to enclose direct quotations. In the case of several quoted paragraphs, the marks are used at the beginning of each, but they follow only the last one. Single quotation marks are used to enclose a quotation that is included within another quotation. Quoted titles of books, essays, etc., are enclosed in quotation marks, or else printed in Italics. **The Apostrophe** (') is used to denote the omission of a letter or letters, and as the sign of the possessive case. **The Hyphen** (-) is used to separate the elements of a compound word and to divide a word into syllables. A word may be divided at the end of a line, but only between syllables. **The Ellipsis** (. . . or * * * *) marks an omission. **Reference Marks** (* † ‡ § ‖ ¶) are used to call attention to notes of explanations.

The Possessive Sign.—To denote ownership, kindred, authorship, origin, fitness, time, weights, measure, etc., add the apostrophe (') to plural nouns that end in *s*, and to all other nouns, add the apostrophe and *s* ('s); and if the sound of the added *s* will not unite with the last sound of the word, give to it the sound ĭz. If several possessive nouns are connected by and, and refer to the same noun, the last only takes the possessive sign, otherwise each of the possessives takes the sign. Personal pronouns do not take the apostrophe and *s*.

COMMON FAULTS IN WRITING AND SPEAKING.

"I shall walk no further" should be "I shall walk no farther." "I have no farther use for it" should be "I have no further use for it." Farther refers to distance.

"Is that him?" should be "Is that he?"

"If I was him" should be "If I were he."

"Better than me" should be "Better than I."

"I am very dry" should be "I am very thirsty."

"Both of these men" should be "Both these men."

"He had laid down" should be "He had lain down."

"I have got the book" should be "I have the book."

"If I am not mistaken" should be "If I mistake not."

"It was her who called" should be "It was she who called."

"Lay down or set down" should be "Lie down or sit down."

"When I get off from a car" should be "When I get off a car."

"It spread all over the town" should be "It spread over all the town."

"If I was him I would do it" should be "If I were he I would do it."

"He is down in the basement" should be "He is in the basement."

"I know better; that ain't so" should be "Pardon me, I understand differently."

"I see him every now and then" should be "I see him occasionally."

"I never play if I can help it" should be "I never play if I can avoid it."

"Look out or you'll get hurt" should be "Be careful or you'll get hurt."

"His works are approved of by many" should be "His works are approved by many."

"I went to New York, you know, and when I came back, you see, I commenced attending school," should be "I went to New York, and when I returned I commenced attending school."

"It is me" should be "It is I."

"We enter in" should be "We enter."

"I don't think so" should be "I think not."

"What are the news?" should be "What is the news?"

"He fell on the floor" should be "He fell to the floor."

"He is in under the wall" should be "He is under the wall."

"Two spoonsful of tea" should be "Two spoonfuls of tea."

"A new pair of boots" should be "A pair of new boots."

"I had rather ride" should be "I would rather ride."

"I only want five dollars" should be "I want only five dollars."

"Continue on in this way" should be "Continue in this way."

"Who does this belong to?" should be "Whom does this belong to?"

"I expected to have seen him" should be "I expected to see him."

RESOLUTIONS.

Resolutions on the Departure of a Teacher.

Whereas, Miss Blanche Cooley is about to be removed from our midst and sever her connections with this school, in which she has so long and faithfully labored as teacher; therefore, be it

Resolved, That we deeply regret the necessity of losing her helpful and endearing presence, and most fervently wish for her a future of active usefulness in her chosen field of new associations and interests; ever remembering the good influence of her well ordered life, etc.

ROY WILLIAMSON.	JULIA E. FOSS.
ELLENORE OTTERPOHL.	ERNEST BEMIS.
MARY WOODS.	BERT ROBBINS.
WM. T. WILSON.	WALTER COLLYER.
MARTIN SNODGRASS.	H. E. RENNELS.
EDWIN McNETT.	EMMA B. PADDLEFORD.
VIRGINIA MILLER.	EDWIN WISE.
GEORGE R. RAMSBURG	ERNEST CROWN.
A. A. ALLEN	CORA PECKHAM.
S. M. HEARN.	CARRIE BELDEN.

Resolutions Instructing Members of the Legislature.

Resolved, That we, citizens of the State of New Hampshire, are opposed to the present excessive rates and fares exacted by the Boston & Maine Railroad Company, and we hereby pledge ourselves to vote for no candidate for either house of the Legislature who is not pledged against this extortion of said Company;

Resolved, That the Secretary is instructed to furnish a report of this meeting, together with this resolution, to such papers as will bring the subject most generally before the people.

Resolutions of Thanks to the Officers of a Convention of Business Men, Farmers, Laborers, etc.

Resolved, That the thanks of this Convention are hereby given to the President, for the able, dignified, and impartial manner in which he has presided over its deliberations, and to the other officers for the satisfactory manner in which they have fulfilled the duties assigned them.

N. B. For Death Resolutions, see page 95.

4

PETITIONS.

For Opening a Street.

To the Mayor and Aldermen of the City of Portland, in Common Council Assembled:

Gentlemen:—The undersigned respectfully solicit your honorable body to open and extend Walnut street, which now terminates at Adams street, through blocks Nos. 10 and 12 to Benton street, thereby making Walnut a nearly straight and continuous street for two miles, and greatly accommodating the people in that portion of the city.

Portland, Me., Mar. 12, 1918.

E. E. MILLER.
D. S. GRAY.
FRED FOSTER.
W. R. HOLLOWAY, etc.

To the Legislature of a State.

To the Honorable, the Senate and House of Representatives of the State of Vermont, in General Assembly met:

The petition of the subscribers, citizens of Poultney, in County of Rutland, respectfully showeth (stating the subject of the petition). And your petitioners will ever pray, etc.

F. W. HAUSER,
J. H. FLESSNER, etc.

To Congress of the United States.

To the Honorable, the Senate and House of Representatives of the United States in Congress assembled:

The petition of the subscribers, citizens of Granville, in the State of New York, respectfully showeth: (stating the subject of the petition). And your petitioners will ever pray, etc.

O. B. DAVIS.
W. B. AVERY.
CHAS. HEARN.
M. F. PARSLEY.

To the Executive of a State.

To his Excellency, George A. Foster, Governor of the Commonwealth of Massachusetts:

The petition of, etc. (as foregoing).

AN ITEMIZED BILL.

San Francisco, Cal., June 7, 1918.

H. W. Nehf,

To ABBIE D. MERRILL & CO., *Dr.*

	To 5 yards Silk @ 1 50	7	50		
	" 4 " Lining @ 20		80		
	" 10 " Drilling @ 16	1	60		
	" 3 doz. Buttons @ 20		60		
	" 6 yards Muslin @ 08		48		
	" 5 Spools Thread @ 06		30		
	Paid			11	28
	Abbie D. Merrill & Co.				

AN UNRECEIPTED BILL.

Plainfield, Conn., July 9, 1918.

Mr. B. A. White,

Bought of A. H. SIMPSON,

Terms

June	*1*	*2 doz. Seamless Bags*	*31¢*	7	44		
"	4	*4 lbs. Brown Sugar*	*7¢*		28		
"	*16*	*6 " Rice*	*5¢*		30		
						8	02

CORRECT POSITION AT THE DESK.

"If you can cultivate to perfection some art by which you can gain an independent livelihood, do it, whether there is a necessity for it or not; do it quietly if you will, but do it. There is no telling when or under what circumstances you may need it."—Horace Mann.

Penmanship

A bad handwriting ought never to be forgiven; it is shameful indolence—indeed, sending a badly written letter to a fellow-creature is as impudent an act as I know of.—*Niebuhr*.

The growth of the country, and the consequent increase in trade, commerce and all branches of business, the greater part of which is done through correspondence, requires thousands of good, rapid penmen, where one was formerly needed.

Good writing is a necessity in our day, and yet how few are to be found who write elegant and graceful hands, while with many great patience is required to decipher their writing.

Of the teachers of our country, ninety-nine per cent. are specially incompetent in the matter of writing. Many young men are standing on the street corners or hanging to their fathers' coat tails, waiting for something to turn up, who if they were good penmen might earn a respectable living. The onward march of civilization increasingly demands good writers.

GIVING ORAL ASSISTANCE TO HIS PEN

RULES FOR POSITION AND PRACTICE.

1. Sit in an upright and easy position. It will add to the ease and beauty of your writing. Keep both feet on the floor

2. Hold the pen firmly, but not so tightly as to cramp the fingers.

3. Place the hand on the paper so the top of the holder will always point over the right shoulder. This will cause the points of the pen to press equally on the paper.

4. Keep the wrist from touching the paper or desk, and keep the thumb from bending while writing. Avoid the finger movement. It is not practical.

5. Let every downward stroke of the pen be drawn toward the center of the body, and the writing will have the correct slant.

6. Never practice carelessly. Always practice with a free and quick stroke. Let the movement be bold, free, offhand, resting the pen so lightly that the arm, hand and fingers can move freely together.

7. In making the shades, press on the pen with a gentle, springing movement. It will avoid heavy and irregular strokes.

8. Heavy shading, or shading every downward stroke, never adds beauty nor grace to the writing.

9. The thoughtful student in penmanship, as in other studies, will win. Think and write. Practice with perseverance, and your success will be certain.

10. To make the greatest improvement in the shortest time, practice upon the letters separately until you can make them all correctly.

11. Flourishes, too heavy shading, too large or too small letters, should be carefully avoided.

12. Practice writing by copying business letters, notes, drafts, receipts, etc., and you will improve your knowledge of business as well as your penmanship.

CORRECT POSITION OF THE PEN.

PRINCIPLES OF PENMANSHIP.

Elements and Principles.

Short-Letter Group.

Shaded Group.

Third Principle, or "Loop Group."

Fourth Principle, or "Base Oval" Group.

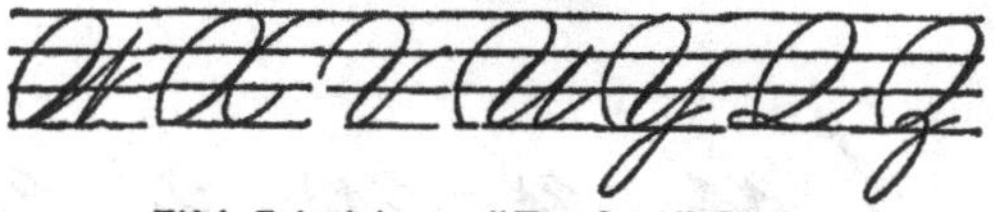

Fifth Principle, or "Top Oval" Group.

Sixth Principle, or "Stem Oval" Group.

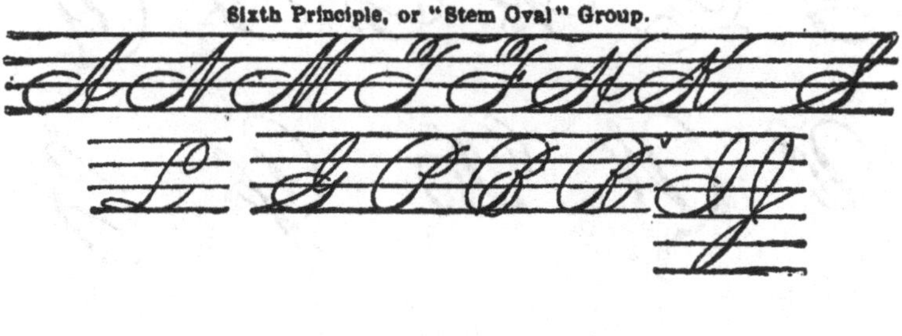

BUSINESS ALPHABET.

CAPITAL LETTERS.

BUSINESS ALPHABET

BUSINESS WRITING.

F. A. Lueben
W. F. Kletzing
A. C. Gegenheimer

A year is a bridge of sand
You tread, and it melts away
To the vast dim void of time
And you call the step "To-day"

A wonderful bridge of sand,
With travelers all a throng,
It runs from the Sunrise Land
To the Valley of Evensong.

And for some the sands are gold,
And for some they are sodden gray,
But none may turn to the Sunrise Land
In the realm of yesterday

PROMISSORY NOTE.

$600.00

Stratford, Apr. 2. 1902.

One year after date, I promise to pay B. G. Browning, or order, the sum of Six Hundred Dollars with interest, value received.

J. B. Bennell.

VERTICAL WRITING.

Count that day lost
Whose low descending sun
Views from thy hand
No worthy action done."

The heights by great men reached and kept,
Were not attained by sudden flight;
But they, while their companions slept,
Were toiling upward in the night."—

PRACTICAL LESSONS IN ORNAMENTAL PENMANSHIP.

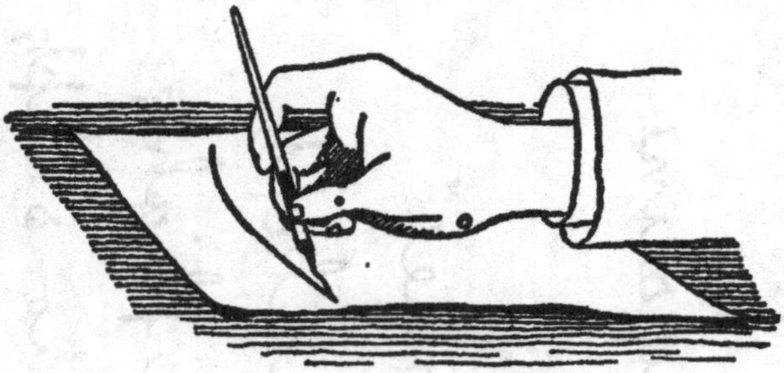

HOW TO HOLD THE PEN FOR ORNAMENTAL WORK.

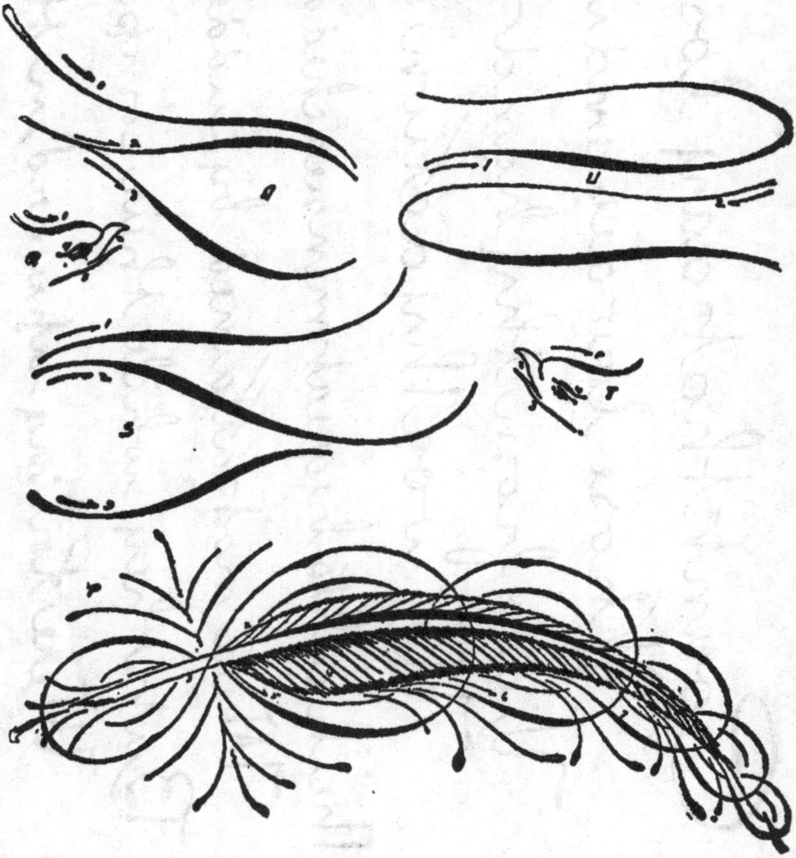

EXERCISES IN ORNAMENTAL PENMANSHIP.

ALPHABET FOR MARKING BOXES AND PACKAGES

ABCDEFGHIJKLMN
OPQRSTUVWXYZ&

a b c d e f g h i j k l m n
o p q r s t u v w x y z

abcdefghijklmnopqrstuvwxyz

Selling Goods Card Marking
At Cost For Packages

THE DEAF AND DUMB ALPHABET

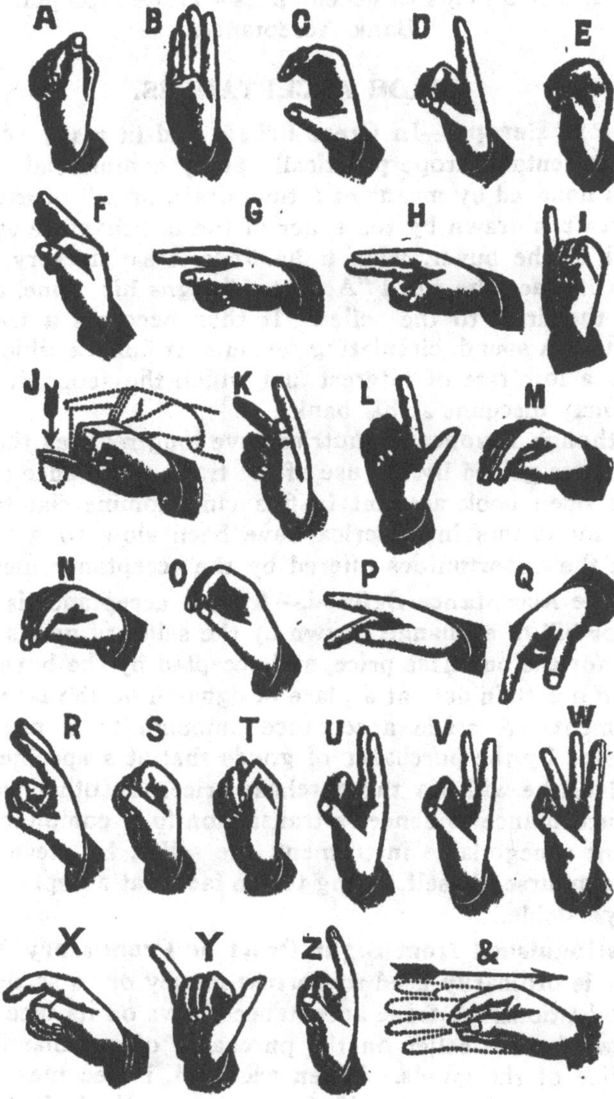

ACCEPTANCES

There are two kinds of acceptances—Trade Acceptances and Bank Acceptances.

TRADE ACCEPTANCES.

Use in Europe.—In Great Britain and in many countries of Continental Europe practically every commercial transaction is financed by means of a time draft, or bill of exchange. The draft is drawn by the seller of the merchandise and presented to the buyer, who, if he finds it satisfactory, writes across its face the word "Accepted," signs his name, and returns the draft to the seller. It then becomes a trade acceptance—a sound, circulating medium of finance which commands a low rate of interest and which the seller, if he desires, may discount at his bank.

Although European countries have long realized the many advantages gained by the use of the trade acceptance in place of the open book account in financing commercial transactions, merchants in America have been slow to grasp and utilize the opportunities offered by the acceptance method.

Trade Acceptance Defined.—A trade acceptance is a time draft or bill of exchange, drawn by the seller of goods on the buyer for the purchase price, and accepted by the buyer, payable on a certain date at a place designated on the face of the instrument. A trade acceptance amounts to a negotiable guarantee by the purchaser of goods that at a specified time and place, he will pay the purchase price. In other words, a trade acceptance evidences a transaction fully completed, and, it being a negotiable instrument, the seller, by means of it, may reimburse himself, owing to the fact that acceptances are readily salable.

Distinguished from Sight Draft or Promissory Note.—A note is ordinarily used to borrow money or to settle overdue obligations. A trade acceptance shows on its face that it is drawn by the seller on the purchaser of merchandise for the price of the goods. When accepted, it becomes a valid promise to pay on a specified date, a negotiable instrument equally as binding upon the person accepting it as his promissory note would be. As a trade acceptance is an obligation of the buyer indorsed by the seller, the bank discounting it is secured by two names instead of by one name paper, as is the case with a promissory note.

BANK ACCEPTANCES.

Trade and Bankers' Acceptances Distinguished.—Some confusion has arisen as to the difference between trade acceptances and bankers' acceptances. The former is the result of a transaction between the buyer and seller; the latter the result of the granting of credit by a banker. In the former case, it is the buyer who accepts the draft; in the latter it is the bank.

Definition.—A banker's acceptance is defined by the Federal Reserve Board as "a bill of exchange of which the acceptor is a bank or trust company, or a firm, person, company or corporation engaged in the business of granting bankers' acceptance credits."

How Acceptance Credit is Extended.—In other words, a bank acceptance consists of the extension of the bank's credit to a customer, wherein the bank, for a consideration, permits the customer to use the bank's credit. This credit may be either secured or unsecured, depending upon the business, character, and financial responsibility of the applicant.

Distinction Between a Bank's Acceptance and its Note.—According to an opinion of the counsel of the Federal Reserve Board, when a member bank of the Federal Reserve System accepts a draft or bill of exchange drawn against it, it enters into a contract substantially similar to that of the maker of a note, so that while the form of the instrument differs, the legal effect is the same. The use of a bank's acceptance, however, differs from the use of its promissory note. When a bank accepts a draft or bill of exchange for one of its customers, it merely lends its credit responsibility to its customer in order that he may procure the funds elsewhere. The holder of a bank's acceptance has the same legal rights against the bank as the holder of its promissory note.

Method of Using.—A bank acceptance may be created as follows:

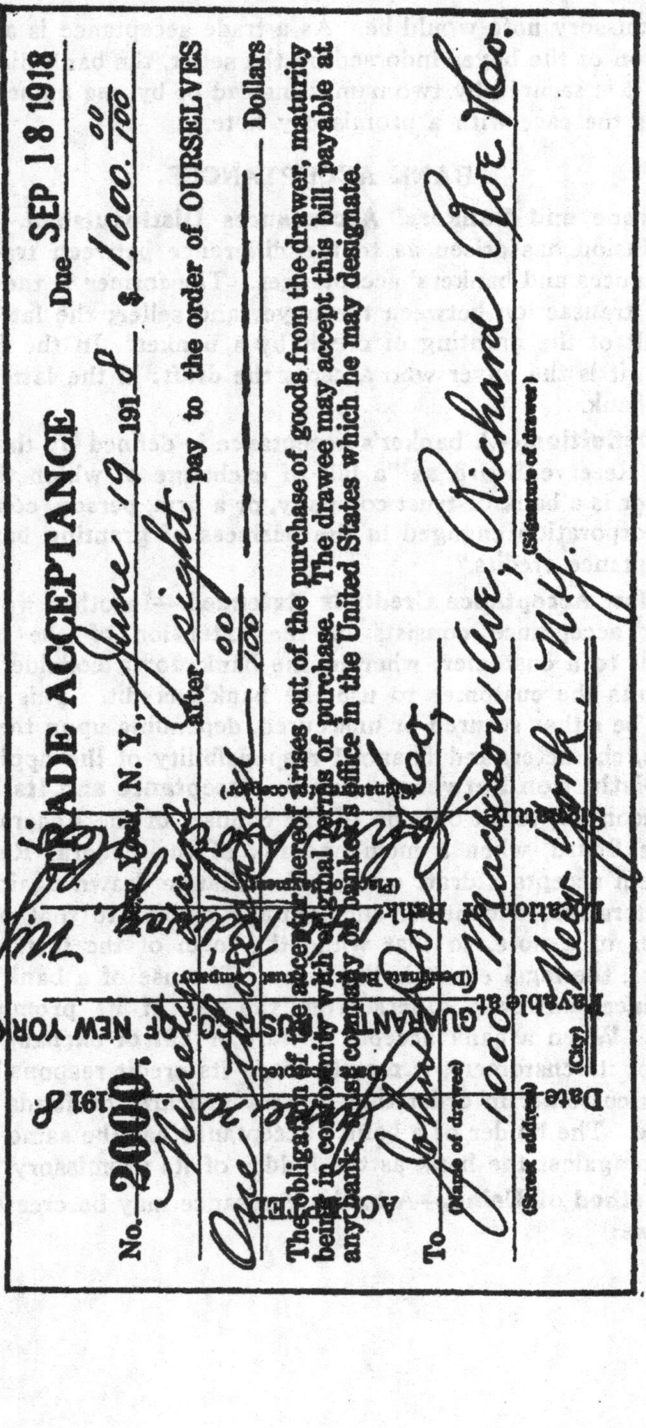

TRADE ACCEPTANCE

No. 2000 New York, N. Y., June 19 1918 Due SEP 18 1918

Ninety days after sight pay to the order of OURSELVES $ 1000.00/100

One thousand 00/100 Dollars

The obligation of the acceptor hereof arises out of the purchase of goods from the drawer, maturity being in conformity with original terms of purchase. The drawee may accept this bill payable at any bank, banker or trust company in the United States which he may designate.

To John Doe & Co. (Name of drawee)

1000 Madison Ave, (Street address)

New York, N.Y. (City)

Richard Roe & Co. (Signature of drawer)

ACCEPTED: Date 1918 (Date accepted)

Payable at GUARANTY TRUST CO. OF NEW YORK (Designate Bank, Banker or Trust Company)

Location of Bank New York (Place of location)

Signature John Doe & Co. (Signature of acceptor)

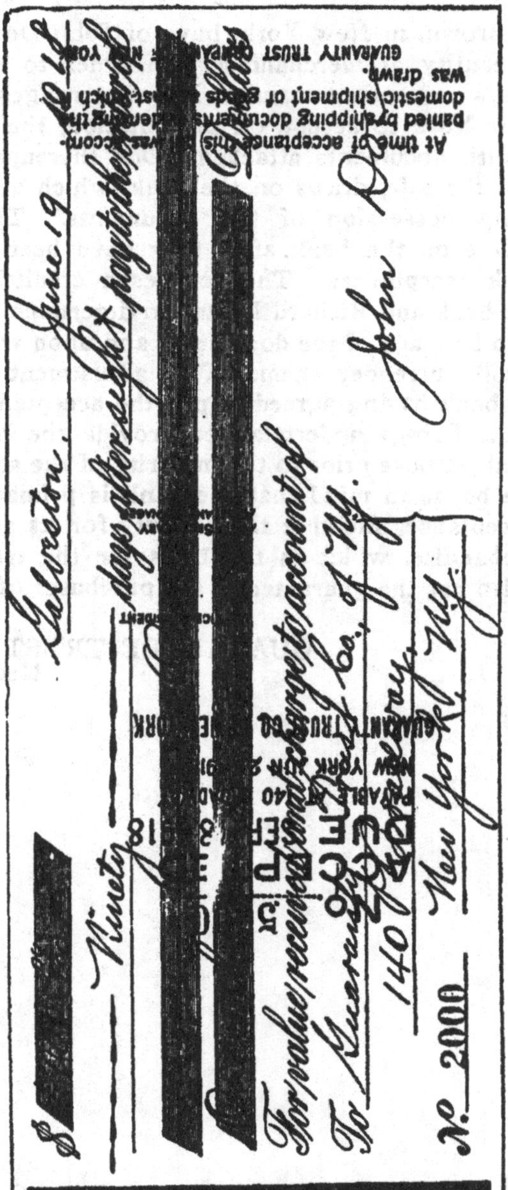
JOHN DOE

No. 2000

Galveston, June 19 1918

$ [redacted]

Ninety days after sight pay to the order of [redacted] Dollars

For value received and charge to account of

To Guaranty Trust Co. of N.Y.
140 Broadway
New York N.Y.

John Doe

At time of acceptance this draft was accompanied by shipping documents covering the domestic shipment of goods against which it was drawn.
GUARANTY TRUST COMPANY OF NEW YORK

Bank Acceptance

Richard Brown, in New York, buys of John Doe, in Galveston, a quantity of merchandise. In order to reimburse John Doe in a convenient manner, Brown arranges with his bank in New York to accept, on presentation, the drafts of John Doe with documents attached. Doe thereupon, under the terms of the sale, draws on the bank, which accepts the drafts, taking possession of the documents. The drafts drawn by Doe on the bank after they have been accepted become bank acceptances. Then ensues a credit operation between the bank and Richard Brown to determine what disposition is to be made of the documents and upon what terms the bank will surrender them. This adjustment is easily made. The bank having agreed to pay the acceptances when they fall due, Brown undertakes to provide the bank with funds for that purpose prior to the maturity of the acceptance. (It must be borne in mind that the bank is primarily liable upon its acceptance, and that the security for its acceptance is the merchandise, which is the basis for the transaction. The bank also has the guarantee of the purchaser of the merchandise.)

GUARANTEE TRUST CO.,
NEW YORK.

Shorthand Writing.

I would advise all parents to have their boys and girls taught shorthand writing and type writing. A shorthand writer who can type write his notes will be safer from poverty than a great Greek scholar.—*Chas. Reade.*

Shorthand is the general term applied to all styles of rapid writing as distinguished from the ordinary method. Many systems of abbreviating writing have been recommended from Socrates and Cicero down to the present day. In the year 380 the Latin poet Ansonius wrote: "Fly, young and famous reporter; prepare the tablets on which you express, with small dots, whole speeches as rapidly as others would trace one single word."

A few of the many names by which these systems were known are Brachygraphy, Tachygraphy, Lemigraphy, Criptography, Bodiography, Polography, Zeitography, Radiography, Tho-ography, and Stenography.

The importance of shorthand need not be argued today. It is used by the author in his study, the clergyman in his library, the editor in his "sanctum," the lawyer in his office, and by business men everywhere, until a modern education almost seems to class among the indispensables a knowledge of shorthand. That there is a great difference in the various systems is seen from the following writing of the Lord's prayer in two different systems. It can readily be seen which is the simpler system.

MUNSON.

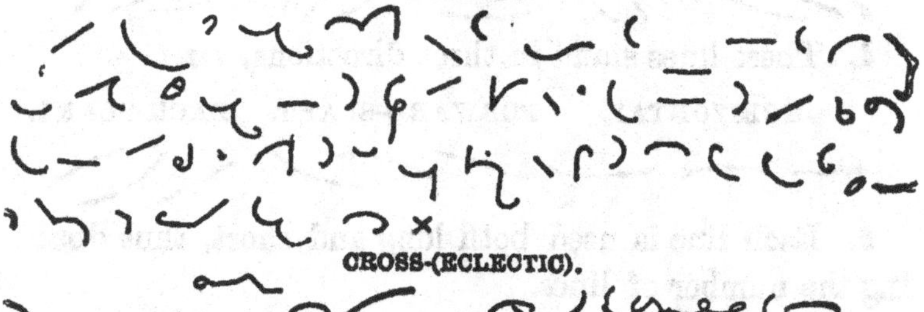

CROSS-(ECLECTIC).

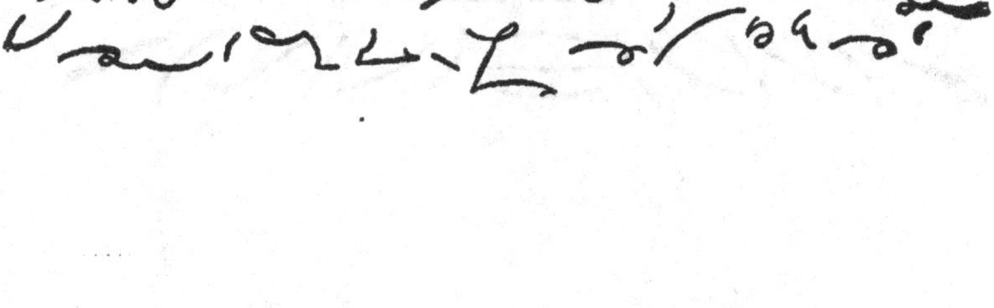

Since the use of shorthand is not confined to any particular science or profession, but is universal, and since any person of ordinary ability who is a good speller may succeed, this art yields remunerative employment to thousands.

By permission of the publishers we present the following pages from Eclectic Shorthand by J. G. Cross, M. A., and published by Scott, Forsman & Co., Chicago, Ill. This system is largely used throughout the country.

CHARACTERS AND THEIR COMBINATIONS.

LESSON I.

1. The alphabetic characters used in this system of shorthand are arcs and chords of the chirographic ellipse.

2. ***The Chirographic Ellipse*** is an ellipse from which are derived the lines of the longhand alphabet.

3. The following figures will serve to show the arcs and chords which are appropriated to the alphabet of this system of shorthand.

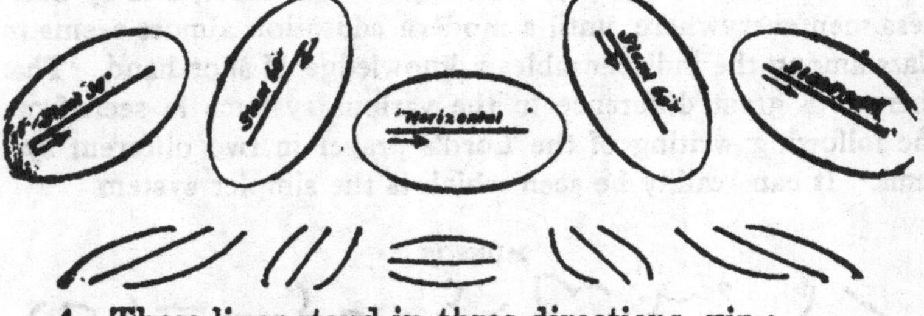

4. These lines stand in three directions, viz.:

HORIZONTAL. FORWARD-SLANT. BACK-SLANT.

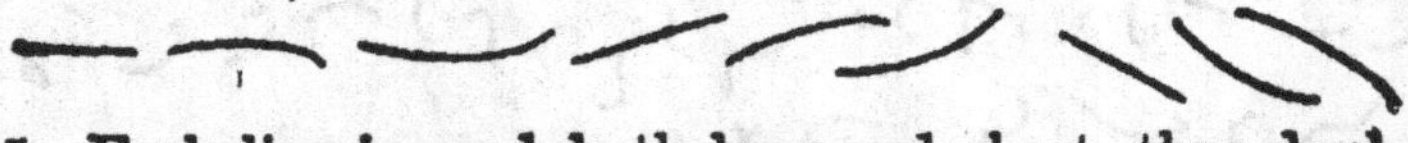

5. Each line is used both long and short, thus doubling the number of lines.

LONG LINES.

SHORT LINES.

6. Each line has three characteristics, viz.: form, direction, length.

7. There are no perpendicular characters, but some are more nearly perpendicular than others. The natural action of the hand in the forward movement draws upward lines at a greater slant than downward lines, and in the back slant characters those drawn by finger movement stand more nearly perpendicular than those drawn by a gliding movement of the hand, as illustrated in the following longhand characters:

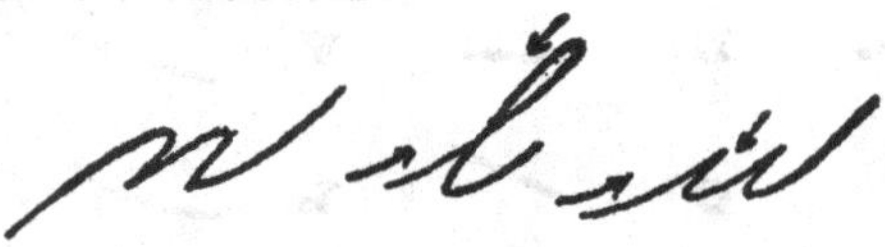

8. The degree of slant of the forward oblique characters when written upwards is about thirty degrees from the horizontal, and when drawn downwards is about thirty degrees from the perpendicular. The slant of the backward oblique characters when drawn by the finger movement is about thirty degrees from the perpendicular, but when made by the hand and arm movement is about thirty degrees from the horizontal, as shown by the following diagrams:

9. This law of movement, adopted from longhand, is peculiar to this system of shorthand, and is important; the motions employed being so similar to those used in longhand, to which, by long practice, we have become accustomed.

THE ALPHABET.

SMALL LETTERS.

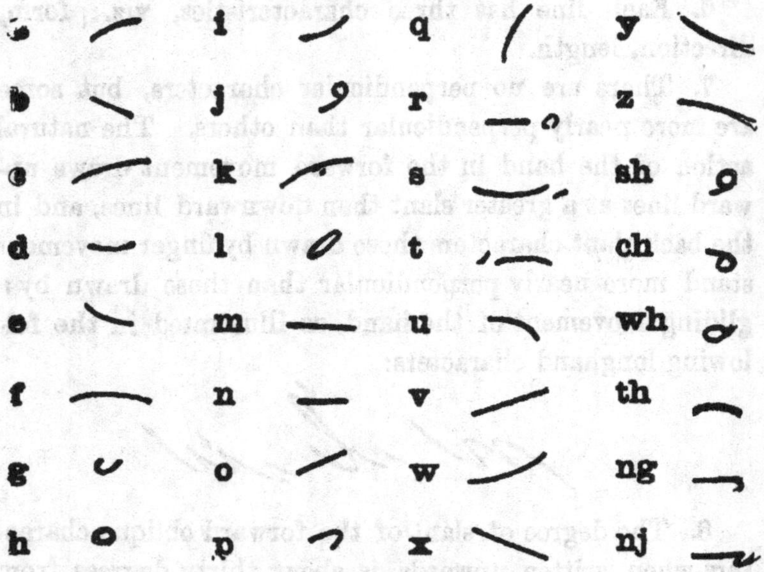

CAPITAL LETTERS.

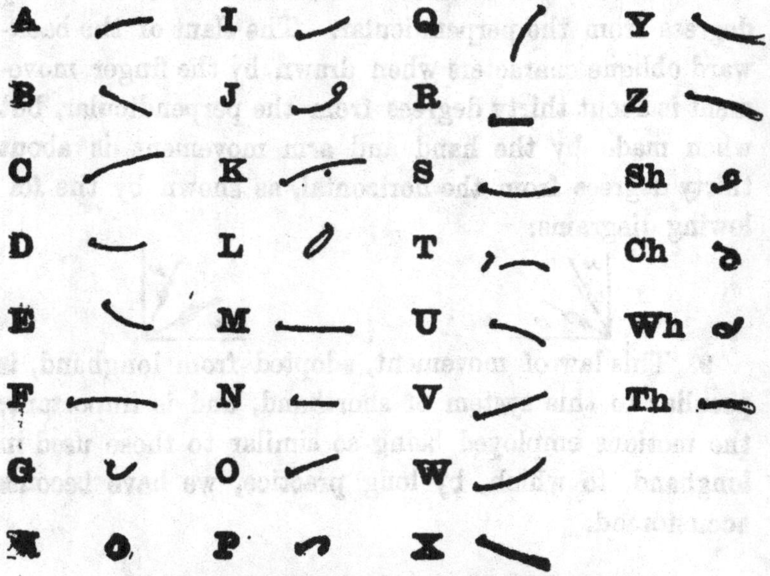

Correspondence.

Letter Writing is the conveying of thoughts through the written page. To be able to write a good letter is a qualification much to be coveted. To depend upon forms will never give that grace and ease that characterizes an appreciated letter. Letter writers are good only in that they give general instructions on the subject. A letter that has no soul or heart in it, but is stiff and formal, is not likely to make a good impression upon the recipient.

Experts.—We may not all become expert penmen, but all can acquire a good legible handwriting and with care can write neat, interesting, and intelligent letters.

Index of Character.—We judge a man by his looks, manners, and words. A letter gives us his words and an illustration of his manners in many ways.

Many a youth has been accepted or rejected because of the manner of his letter. Men judge us by the letters we write. Neatness, order, and the readiness to express one's thoughts or the lack of these qualities, are all photographed on the written page. The character of a man is often determined by the manner and matter of his letters. As the tasty arrangement of dishes adds to the pleasure of the repast, so a neat and well formed letter, with ideas clearly and agreeably expressed, makes a lasting impression upon the mind.

Kinds of Letters.—Letters may be classified as letters of business, letters of courtesy, and letters of friendship. Letters of business include all correspondence relating to business matters; letters of courtesy include invitations and acceptances, letters of introduction and of recommendation, letters of application and of advice, letters of congratulation and of condolence; friendship letters should always be simple and natural. The little things, the incidents of everyday life, the happy relating of the experiences of commonplace and routine occurrences, are what make friendship letters interesting.

Parts of a Letter.—The parts of a letter are the Heading, the Address, the Salutation, the Body of the letter, the Complimentary close and the Signature.

Letter Writing.

HOW TO BEGIN A LETTER.

The Heading consists of place and date. In a city the number and street, city and state should be given.

Arrangement.—The first line on ruled paper is generally about an inch and a half below the top of the page. A letter should never begin much higher than that; but if the letter should be very short, it may begin still lower, so that the spaces above and below the letter would be about equal.

Punctuation.—Always punctuate the parts of the heading as shown in the models.

The Address consists of the name, title and residence (Post Office) of the persons written to. Except in business letters the address is frequently written at the close of a letter.

Salutation is that term of politeness and respect with which we begin a letter; such as Sir, Dear Sir, Dear Friend, etc. In writing to a firm Sirs or Gentlemen should be used. Never use the abbreviations of "Gents" for Gentlemen or "Dr." for Dear or "Sr." for Sir.

In writing to a stranger, he is addressed as "Sir," or "Dear Sir." "My dear Sir" implies very friendly relation. A married lady or a single lady not young, is addressed as "Madam," or "Dear Madam," a young unmarried lady as "Miss," or "Dear Miss," with her last name affixed, and begin your letter without any further introduction. "Rev. Sir," for clergymen; "Esteemed Sir," for formal friends; Judges and legislative officers should be addressed by the title of "Honorable."

Models For Beginning Letters.

Form 1.

Wichita, Kans., Jan. 12, 1918.

Messrs. Hall & West,

Austin, Minn.

Gentlemen: Your favor of 3rd inst. is received, etc.

Form 2.

Naperville, Ills.,
Nov. 25, 1918.

Mr. F. J. Nichols,

Ottawa, Ills.

My dear Sir: Please send by return mail, etc.

Form 3.

229 Madison St., Chicago.
Sept. 12, 1918.

Mrs. B. M. Whiteley,

Atlanta, Ga.

Dear Madam:

Accept thanks for the kindness you have shown me, etc.

Form 4. (Social Form.)

North Western College,
Naperville, Illinois,
Sept. 20, 1918.

Dear Friend:

Your welcome letter arrived to-day, etc.

Form 5.

Cedar Falls, Iowa,

Monday, Sept. 26 1918.

Miss Nellie Reynolds,

Scotland,

Conn.

We acknowledge with pleasure the receipt, etc.

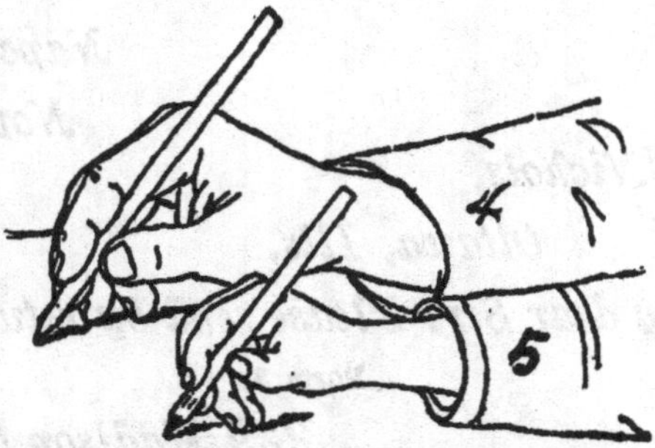

HOW TO IMPROVE YOUR PENMANSHIP IN LETTER WRITING.

1. Never be satisfied with mere legibility; for neatness, elegance and correctness are equally important.

2. Remember, carelessness and too much haste not only fail to improve your penmanship, but actually ruin what progress is already attained.

3. Many persons write letters so hurriedly as to slur over the words, half forming and deforming many of the letters, or making sort of a wavy line to represent a word; this is not only an injury to the writer, but vexatious, unsatisfactory and disrespectful to the reader.

4. Write plainly and neatly as possible, rapidly if you can, slowly if you must. A neat and well worded letter of one page once a month, is better than a slovenly scrawl of four pages once a week.

5. When persons contemplate having a photograph taken, they often bestow much care upon their personal appearance,

in order to heighten the effect of the artist in the presentation of their physical likeness. These same persons, however, will often sit down and write hurriedly an important letter, that from undue haste abounds in blots, illegible writing, erasures, bad spelling, and the wrong use of capital letters; without once thinking they are transmitting to their correspondent a kind of mental photograph of themselves, drawn by their own hand, and one, too, which better indicates their fitness for business or for society than the others.

THE BODY OF THE LETTER.

As letter writing is "speaking with the pen," the language should not be strained but natural and free from all such stereotyped phrases as

"I take my pen in hand to let you know that I am well, and hope you are enjoying the same blessing.'

Originality is the spice of a letter. Do not try to imitate some one else in writing but be yourself; write as you would talk. Do not be afraid to write of little things. Things that are worth talking about are worth writing about. Let your language be pure and chaste and beautiful, always avoiding vulgar and slang expressions. Bear in mind that it is possible to put your letter into print. After writing, think how your letter would read in five years. Has anything been written that might cause the blush of shame.

Letters of friendship and love should reveal the happy mood and cheerful spirit of the writer and should carry hope and happiness to the recipient. A well written letter may gain to you a life-long bosom friend. A careless and foolish letter may forever separate those who might have been dearer to each other than ordinary friends.

THE SUPERSCRIPTION.

The superscription is what is written on the outside of the envelope. In writing the superscription commence the name a little to the left of the center of the envelope, the town or post-office on the line beneath and extending a little to the right of the name. The State next below and still further to the right. In cities the door number and the name of the

street should come on the second line. In the country, the county may be on the same line with the state on the left side of the envelope.

Great care should be exercised in addressing envelopes Thirty thousand misdirected letters reach the dead letter office at Washington daily. Give the full name and title of the person addressed. If abbreviations of States are used, there should be especial care, for N. Y. may easily be taken for N. J.; Pa. for Va.; Me. for Mo. and Cal. for Col. Above all let your penmanship be clear and distinct so that it can be easily read by the postal employes.

Messrs. Wicks & Nichols,
No. 17 Monroe Street,
Chicago,
Ills.

His Excellency,
Governor Wm. McKinley,
Columbus,
Ohio.

HOW TO CLOSE A LETTER.

Never write a letter without signing it and write your name in full if the letter contains important matter.

Write your name plainly. Bad signatures often cause great inconvenience, and many times result in very serious mistakes.

A lady writing to a stranger should sign her name with her proper title, Miss or Mrs.

The complimentary close is written on the next line below the closing sentence, and the signature is written on the next line below the complimentary close.

The closing words of respect, friendship, etc., should be Yours truly, Yours very truly, Yours sincerely, Yours very sincerely, Your affectionate brother, Your loving daughter, etc., etc. A great variety is used.

Models for Closing.

COMMON FORMS.	FORMS WITH ADDRESS.
Yours truly, *R. N. Givler.*	*Please address,* *G. E. Kart,* *Lake Odessa, Mich.*
Yours very truly, *Esther Jaeck.*	*I am,* *Yours truly,* *B. M. Whiteley,* *To C. N. Smith,* *Berlin, Ont.*
I remain, *Yours sincerely,* *L. W. Meyers.*	*We remain,* *Yours very truly,* *J. L. Nichols & Co.*
Sincerely yours, *Mrs. A. S. Barnard.*	

COMMERCIAL CORRESPONDENCE.

Many business houses in writing to their customers always send return envelopes and in order to assist the mail clerk on the cars, and thus facilitate rapid transit of their mail, both outgoing and return, divide the address as shown in the following forms:

6

Stamp.

G. W. Lascell,
41 State Street.

Lynn,
Mass.

Stamp.

Toronto,
Ontario,
Can.

J. L. Nichols & Co.,
33 Richmond Street, W.

It will readily be seen that an address naturally divides itself into two distinct parts concerning two postmasters remote from each other. For example: We mail a letter to G. W. Lascell; the hustling clerks on the mail cars do not care to see anything but Lynn, Mass., and the postal clerks there do not care where the letter was mailed, they are only concerned about its delivery.

The above are valuable only for business houses who have their envelopes printed and properly ruled; we would not recommend them for private correspondence.

Forms of Superscription in Private Correspondence.

Stamp.

To the Governor,
Executive-Department,
Springfield,
Ills.

Stamp.

To the President,
Executive Mansion,
Washington,
D. C.

Stamp.

Miss Ida Best,
99 Ashland Boul.,
Chicago,
Care John Smith, Esq. *Ills.*

Letter sent by a private party.

Mrs. A. G. Hall,
No. 4 Fifth Ave.,
Canton,
By Politeness of *Ohio.*
Mr. J. G. Ash.

TITLES USED IN THE UNITED STATES.

Titles, their use and abuse, might serve as a topic for many pages. The omission of titles of respect and courtesy, professional and official, shows a lack of refinement and gentility. In private correspondence writers should not assume titles. "Let others praise thee, not thine own lips." If, however, it is necessary to inform the person to whom you write, if he is a stranger, then do it with becoming modesty. The young man who starts out attaching Rev., Hon. or Prof. to his name every time that he writes it, is to be pitied for his ignorance. Some writers, when it is desired that the recipient shall understand the office or rank of the writer, inclose the title in parenthesis, thus: (Rev.) Thomas Moore (see page 100).

When it is desired to express the title of the husband, on a letter or note of invitation to the husband and wife, one of the following forms may be used:

His Excellency and Mrs. Grover Cleveland.

Hon. and Mrs. G. M. Wilson.

Rev. and Mrs. W. P. Phillips.

Professor and Mrs. R. A. Gault.

If the lady's husband alone has a title, she is simply addressed as Mrs. Chas. Morton.

HOW TO WRITE A POSTAL CARD.

1. A card should be dated either on the upper right-hand corner, or on the lower left-hand corner.

2. The writer's full name should be signed to it.

3. If an answer is required, the writer's full post-office address should be given, unless it is well known by the person to whom the card is directed.

4. Important matters should not be intrusted to a postal card, as it is open to inspection, and as the law does not provide for its return to the writer in case of failure to reach its destination. Nor is it allowable to use postal cards for notes of invitation, etc., in which society prescribes certain polite forms to be observed.

5. Never write a demand or request for money on a postal card. It is disrespectful to the person receiving it.

Postal cards can be sent to Canada and Mexico.

Business Letters

The essential qualities of a business letter are clearness, neatness and brevity. The writing should be so plain that "he who runs may read." Through a neglect to observe these points serious misunderstandings and mistakes have occurred, often involving great loss to parties concerned. A wealthy gentleman in New York desiring to have two monkeys, wrote his agent in Africa: "Send me too (two) monkeys." The t was not crossed, and the agent was astonished to learn that his principal asked for 100 monkeys. As he was in no way connected with a menagerie the agent was perplexed to know why so large a number of monkeys was desired. After considerable effort he shipped twenty-five monkeys stating that it was impossible to fill the whole order at one time. The New York gentleman was just as much surprised to receive such a large invoice of monkeys at so great an expense and for which he had no use. The fault was his own.

Clearness in expressing the thought or in ordering goods should always be aimed at. The amount, kind, color, quality, shape, size and terms should all be explicitly stated by the order.

Flourishing of penmanship or language is out of place in a business letter.

Prompt replies should characterize all business letters. Neglect in this respect will soon bring a business man into discredit.

Copies of important letters sent and **filing** of letters received for future reference is essential and often prevents litigation and loss.

Ordering a Bill for Goods.

Messrs. L. E. Fiant & Co., Adrian, Mich., Jan. 25, 19 .
414 State Street, Chicago.

Gentlemen:—Please ship me at your earliest convenience, by freight, per C., B. & Q. R. R., the following:

34 brls. Mess Pork,
20 brls. Coffee Sugar,
7 chests Japan Tea,
10 bags Rio Coffee,
3 mats Cinnamon.

Hoping to receive the above order of goods in good condition and without unnecessary delay, I am, Yours truly,

A. C. BROWN.

Order to a Store for Goods.

At Home, Jan. 11.

Mr. J. T. Hearn:
Please deliver to the bearer for me.
22 lbs. Dried Apples,
5 lbs. Best Rice,
$1.00 worth of A Coffee Sugar.
1 bar Rising Sun Stove Polish.
Charge the same to my account, and greatly oblige,

MRS. MATTIE BALLEW.

Requesting Additional Time.

Grand Rapids, Mich., Dec. 17, 19—.

Mr. C. Gilson,
Battle Creek, Mich.

Dear Sir:—You favor of the 15th inst. is received asking for additional time in which to pay your account of $508.75 that became due on the 12th inst. We cannot grant extension of time on regular bills. This would be unfair to our other customers, and the same thing as giving an extra discount to you.

In order to accommodate you we will accept the $300.00 which you can pay now. You may return to us goods to cover the remainder, $208.75. We will then cancel the entire account against you on our books.

Yours very truly,
J. H. PACE & CO.

Sending Draft.

Naperville, Ill., Jan. 15, 19—.

L. Pruitt & Co.,
Chicago, Ill.

Gentlemen:—Inclosed find Chicago draft for $87.77, in payment of Bill for Stationery, dated Jan. 4, 19—.

Please acknowledge receipt, and oblige,

Yours truly,
A. J. WARREN.

Sending Receipt.

Naperville, Ill., Dec. 1, 19—.

Mr. P. S. Kemp,
Marion, Ga.

Dear Sir:—Your favor of Nov. 29, 19—, just received. Inclosed please find receipt. With thanks for your prompt remittance, I am,

Yours very truly,
O. L. NEFF.

A Resignation.

To the Directors of the Joliet Loan Association.

Gentlemen:—I herewith tender my resignation as secretary of your association, for reasons not altogether unknown to you. Same to take effect on the 15th day of April next.

Yours very truly,
March 10, 19—. J. W. JOHNSON.

Advising Receipt of Invoice.

Louisville, Ky., Jan. 14, 19—.

Mr. B. L. Goldsby,
Boston, Mass.

Dear Sir:—Your favor of January 9th, with Invoice, was received in due time. The goods are all that we desired; and for your promptness and care in filling our order, accept our thanks.

Enclosed find in payment Draft on First National Bank of Boston for $1,950.25. Please acknowledge receipt by return mail, and oblige,

Yours truly,
O. P. BALLARD & CO.

Acknowledging Remittance.

New York, Jan. 16, 19—.

Received from Messrs. C. C. Cook & Co., Five Hundred and Fifty Dollars on account.

$550.00 C. W. SADLER.

Letter with Bill of Lading to Bank for Collection.

Atlanta, Ga., Nov. 25, 19—.

First National Bank,
Portland, Ore.

Gentlemen:—Please deliver the enclosed bill of lading to Mr. Charles Stuart, Portland, who will call for same. Kindly notify party of the arrival of this collection, and when paid, remit to us in Chicago or New York Exchange.

IMPORTANT. Exchange or collection charges, if any must be paid by the drawee and the full amount of $56.00 paid in full settlement of this collection. If, for any reason, collection cannot be made as above, kindly notify us and hold bill of lading for further instructions.

Yours truly,
E. J. CHRISTY & CO.

Notice of Non-Payment.

Williams & Fetters,
Chico, Cal.

Gentlemen:—Kindly take notice that a note for $200 signed by John H. Wagner, dated May 29, 1918, due February 6, 1919, and indorsed by you, was duly presented by me, the holder, to the maker for payment and was not paid, and that I shall look to you for payment thereof

Yours truly,
J. S. COMER.

Apologizing for Failure to Pay Promptly.

Memphis, Tenn., July 29, 19—.

Mr. Arthur Green,
Naperville, Ill.

Dear Sir:—I have your request for a prompt settlement of my account and am very sorry indeed that it is impossible for me to send you a remittance at this time.

You can count on receiving payment in full by the 15th of next month.

Hoping my failure to send you a remittance at this time will not inconvenience you in any way, I am,

Yours truly,
H. E. RENNELS.

Requesting Payment.

Naperville, Ill., Jan. 7, 19—.

Messrs. Douglas & Hearth,
St. Louis, Mo.

Dear Sirs:—We are obliged again to ask you for the balance of your account, now four months past due. We are much inconvenienced by your delay, and have waited longer than we think ought to be expected. The account must be speedily settled, and if we do not hear from you by the 15th inst., will draw on you, at five days' sight; if the draft is not protected at maturity, we shall be compelled to adopt some other mode of settlement.

Yours truly,
PAT PICKNEY.

Request for Note in Settlement.

New Orleans, La., July 25, 19—.

Mr. B. M. Whiteley,
Atlanta, Ga.

Dear Sir:—Since you are unable to pay the whole of your account at this time, we will let you settle for part cash and the rest with your personal note bearing interest at 6 per cent. Send us $300, which you can pay now, and the remainder $200 you can send us at the same time by note payable in 60 days. This arrangement will help you over your present difficulty.

Yours truly,
DAVIS FRIERSON.

A Request for Payment of Account.

Chicago, Ill., July 29, 19—.

Mr. C. G. Gates,
McBain, Mich.

Dear Sir:—On May 30th we shipped you goods amounting to $97.50 on thirty days' time. Although the account became due June 30th, and should have been paid at that time, you have failed to send us your check in settlement.

We have been glad to accommodate you by giving you additional time on this account and we feel sure you appreciate it. Won't you show your appreciation in a substantial way by sending us your check for $97.50 by return mail? Yours very truly,

E. G. YORK & CO.

Requesting the Payment of Rent.

Valparaiso, Ind., Aug. 15, 19—.

Mr. C. S. Brown,
Gary, Ind.

Dear Sir:—You will remember that when you rented my house in April it was on the understanding that the rent would be paid at the first of every month. There is now due me $80.00 for four months' rent, and I must ask that you give this your immediate attention.

In case I do not hear from you within the next ten days with remittance for $80.00, I will be obliged to cancel your lease and place the account for collection. Yours truly,

LEON LAICHE.

Letter Complaining of Error in a Bill.

Abbott, Iowa, Aug. 10, 19—.

Messrs. Holmes & Nichols,
Chicago, Ill.

Dear Sirs:—We call your attention to an error of bill of Aug. 4, by which we are charged $45.50 more than the invoice actually amounts to. Please correct the same and oblige,

Yours very truly,

MONROE & HIGGINS.

Answer to Above.

Chicago, Ill., Aug. 12, 19—.

Messrs. Monroe & Higgins,
Abbott, Iowa.

Gentlemen:—We regret that an error was made in bill of Aug. 4. We inclose the corrected bill to you and offer apologies for the error.

Yours truly,

HOLMES & NICHOLS.

Enclosing Note for Discount.

Annapolis, Jan. 14, 19—.

Chas. W. Ward, Esq., Cashier.

Dear Sir:—We offer for discount, enclosed, L. Brown's note, Dec. 20th, at ninety days, for $4,250.75. By discounting the same you will greatly oblige, Yours truly,

E. McNETT.

Letter of Credit.

Naperville, Ill., Feb. 4, 19—.

Messrs. Steiner & Leffler,
New York.

Dear Sirs:—Please allow Mr. J. A. West a credit for such goods as he may select to an amount not exceeding Eight Hundred Dollars ($800.00), for four months. I will become responsible for the payment of the same should Mr. West fail to meet the obligation promptly.

Please inform me of the amount for which you give credit, and in default of payment notify me promptly.

Yours very truly,

(Mr. West's signature, G. E. ALTSTADT.
J. A. West.)

LETTERS OF APPLICATION.

Business men find it profitable at times to advertise for employes. Letters in reply to advertisements should be written at once or it may be too late. Your application should of course be in your own handwriting. From the letter the employer can frequently judge whether the applicant has the necessary qualifications. In replying name the paper in which you saw the advertisement, or better still, paste it at the head of your letter. If you have testimonials, send copies of them, marking them "copy." The original can be used in an interview or held for future use. Do not speak in praise of yourself. You may state your reference, your experience, and your intention of endeavoring to perform the duties required, but let your testimonials state your character and qualifications. In answer to advertisements in the daily paper, business men sometimes receive hundreds of letters. This suggests the importance of the greatest care in the wording as well as the general appearance of the letter. Your letter must represent your abilities and make a favorable impression upon the employer or some one else will fill the place.

Application for a School.

Peru, Ill., Jan. 16, 19—.

Mr. Harry Hyland,
Secretary of School Board,
Yorkville, Ill.

Dear Sir:—I have just learned that there is a vacancy in your school. Kindly consider me as an applicant for the position. I have had four years' experience in teaching and enclose testimonials. I hold a certificate of examination from the superintendents of Kendall and Ogle counties. Should you see fit to engage my services, I will fill the position to the best of my ability, and, I trust, to your entire satisfaction.

Should a personal interview be desired, I shall be glad to present myself at such time and place as may be most convenient to yourself.

Yours truly,
(MISS) MARIE SCHWARTZ.

Application for a Position as Sales Manager.

Naperville, Ill., Nov. 5, 19—.

W. B. Conkey Co.,
Hammond, Ind.

Gentlemen:—I wish to apply for the position of Sales Manager as per your advertisement in Sunday's Daily News. I have had six years' experience as salesman for J. L. Nichols & Company, Publishers, and enclose a letter of endorsement from them.

I also refer you to the First National Bank of this city as to my character, etc.

All I ask is an opportunity to prove my ability to sell your goods.

I shall be glad to call at your office for a personal interview.

Yours very truly,
DELMAR SAYLOR.

From a Boy Applying for a Clerkship.

Chicago, Ill., Jan. 4, 19 .
187 Madison St.

Messrs. A. S. KOCH,
118 Madison Street, Chicago.

Dear Sir:—I notice in this morning's "Clarion" your advertisement of a boy wanted in a grain commission house; for which position I take the first opportunity to apply. I am fourteen years old, have been at school the most of the time, winters, for the past seven years, and understand bookkeeping and conducting correspondence pretty well, having assisted my father much of the time while he was in the coal trade, which was about three years.

I am perfectly willing and ready to take off my coat and go right to work at handling grain or anything else in your line.

I refer you to Mr. George Beldon, Coal Dealer, at 65 State Street, Chicago, who has always known me.

Very respectfully, yours,
GEORGE ARNOLD.

Advertisement.

Wanted—A young man of ability to fill the position of entry-clerk in a dry goods house. One who has had some experience in dry goods business preferred.

Address with reference, X. L. M., Box 1024, P. O.

Reply.

St. Louis, Jan. 13, 19 .

Mr. X. L. M.

Sir:—Consider me an applicant for the position advertised in to-day's Tribune. Am twenty-two years of age, have not handled dry goods, but am thoroughly conversant with the technical terms, abbreviations, and calculations pertaining to the business, having completed a commercial course at North-Western Business College, Naperville, Ill., the professors of which I am at liberty to use as parties of reference.

Respectfully,
E. B. HARDY.

Application for a Situation as Book-keeper.

San Jose, Cal., Feb. 20, 19 .

Messrs. K. K. LANGTON & CO.,
Cincinnati, Ohio.

Gentlemen:—Having learned from Prof. George Sindlinger that you desire the services of a book-keeper, I respectfully offer myself as an applicant for the situation. I have been engaged for two years in the wholesale house of Geo. Reuss & Co., as clerk and assistant book-keeper, and have a good knowledge of accounts. My business acquaintance is extensive in the western part of Kentucky, and I could therefore influence considerable trade. I enclose copy of testimonial from my late employers, and would also respectfully refer you, as to my character and ability, to

S. A. WELTY, Banker, Creston, Ia.
Prof. A. C. GEGENHEIMER, Naperville, Ill.

Any communication which you may be pleased to make, addressed as above, will receive prompt attention.

Very respectfully yours, F. T. GEIST.

Recommendation Enclosed in the Above Copy.

San Jose, Jan. 16, 19 .

The bearer, F. T. Geist, has been in our employ as assistant book-keeper for over two years, and we have always found him to be honest, steady, and correct in his habits and deportment, and well qualified for any position of trust in a counting-house. We cheerfully recommend him as a competent book-keeper and one who will earnestly apply himself to promote the interests of his employers.

Respectfully,
L. H. WERNER & CO.

HOW TO WRITE NOTES OF INVITATION.

1. Notes of invitation differ from ordinary letters in the following ways: 1. More formal; 2. Wholly or partly written in the third person; 3. Date is generally written at the bottom; 4. They are without signature.

2. Materials.—The paper and envelopes used should be of the finest quality.

3. A dinner invitation should be answered immediately, others (if answered at all) not later than the third day.

4. Regrets.—It is more friendly and courteous to state a reason for non-attendance, than to decline without any assigned cause.

After having accepted an invitation, never absent yourself without the strongest reasons.

Birth-Day Celebration.

Mr. and Mrs. H. A. Matthews request the honor of J. A Austin's company to celebrate their son's majority, on Wednesday evening, June tenth, 1901.
1402 Arch St. *R. S. V. P.*

To Meet Visiting Friends.

Mr. and Mrs. C. W. George request the pleasure of W. N. Towner's company, on Friday evening, November 19th, from eight to eleven o'clock, to meet W. A. Womer.
Broad and Walnut Sts., Philadelphia.

Invitation to a Surprise Party.

Dear Grace: We are getting up a surprise party for Lucy; join us and be at Mr. Brown's by 7 p. m., Wednesday evening.
Clara Power.

Evening Parties.

Notes of invitation for evening parties are issued in the name of the lady of the house, as,

AT HOME.

"Mrs. John Bell, Monday evening, June sixteenth, from nine to twelve o'clock. Dancing."

Acceptance.

The reply, if an acceptance, may be as follows:

"Mr. and Mrs. Francis Granger have much pleasure in accepting Mrs. John Bell's kind invitation for Monday evening, the sixteenth of June."

Regrets.

Or, if a regret,

"Mr. and Mrs. Francis Granger regret that a previous engagement deprives them of the pleasure of accepting Mrs. John Bell's kind invitation for Monday evening, June sixteenth."

The above is a courteous form of sending regrets.

The following are not courteous:

"Mr. and Mrs. Howard Smith regret that they cannot accept Mrs. John Bell's invitation for Monday evening."

A still ruder form:

"Mr. and Mrs. Howard Smith decline Mrs. John Bell's invitation for Monday evening."

Dinner Invitations.

Dinner invitations are written or engraved in the name of the husband and wife as follows:

"Mr. and Mrs. Howard Smith request the pleasure of Mr. and Mrs. Willard Scott's company at dinner, on Tuesday, June eighth, at seven o'clock."

If accepted, the answer is as follows:

"Mr. and Mrs. Willard Scott accept with pleasure Mr. and Mrs. Howard Smith's kind invitation to dine with them on Tuesday, the eighth, at seven o'clock."

If a regret, the following is the form that is most frequently used:

"Mr. and Mrs. Willard Scott are not able to accept the kind invitation of Mr. and Mrs. Smith owing to the death of a near relative."

Mr. Walter Hood presents his regards to Miss Jennie Mason, and requests the pleasure of escorting her to the Grand Opera to-morrow evening.

246 Monroe Ave., April 10.

Acceptance.

Miss Jennie Mason presents her compliments to Mr. Hood, and accepts with pleasure his kind invitation to accompany him to the Opera.

April 11th.

Informal Notes.

If the parties are very intimate friends, the formal and ceremonious style may be dropped, and that of a familiar letter adopted, as in the following:—

Saturday Morning, May 10.

Dear Fanny,

We are going to Irving's Cliff this afternoon for wild flowers. Will you oblige us by making one of our little party? If so, we will call for you at two o'clock. Do go.

Yours affectionately,

Libbie.

Please answer by bearer.

My dear Sir,

If you can come next Sunday, we shall be equally glad to see you, but do not trust to any of Martin's appointments in future. Leg of lamb as before, at half-past four, and the heart of Lamb forever.

Yours truly,

C. Lamb.

30th March,

How to Write a Letter of Introduction.

Naperville, Ills., Jan. 7, 1918.

Dear Sir: This will introduce to you my friend, F. D. Vincent, of this city. He intends staying a few days in your city, which he visits on business, and I take the liberty of recommending him to your kind attention.

He is a gentleman of excellent acquirements, and I know him to be responsible to the extent of his engagements. Any attention or favor that you render him will be considered a personal favor, which I shall be happy to reciprocate.

Very sincerely yours,

Jas. F. Holt.

To Jared L. Morton, Esq.

Letter of Introduction.

SHORT FORM.

Dear Friend:—I have the pleasure of introducing to your acquaintance Mr. A. A. Jenkins, whom I commend to your kind attention.

Very respectfully yours,

W. H. BAKER.

To Rev. J. Miller.
Naperville, Ill.

Letter of Apology.

Atlanta, Ga., May 10, 1918.

Mr. A. H. Brown,
Athens.

Dear Sir:—I regret very much that I am compelled to apologize for not meeting you at the Leland Hotel last evening as I had expected and agreed to do. The cause of detention was the sudden and severe illness of my son George, whose life for a time we despaired of. I hope that the arrangements we anticipated can yet be perfected, and shall be pleased to have you kindly inform me when it will be convenient for me to see you.

Very respectfully yours,

E. M. MERRILL.

LETTERS OF RECOMMENDATION.

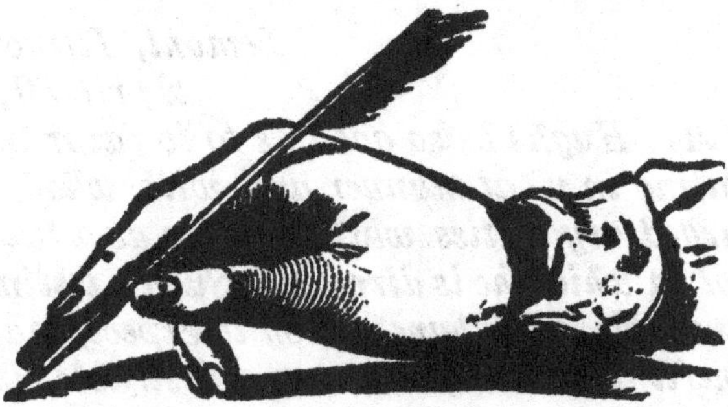

Recommendations are given for the purpose of promoting the benefit, interest, or happiness of another and should be given only when the integrity and uprightness of the individual are known. In a certain sense the individual giving the recommendation is responsible for the character and ability of the person recommended. Great care should be exercised in writing and giving recommendations. It may be hard to refuse a testimonial, but in some cases it may be unjust to give it.

Recommendation to a Young Man.

Joliet, Ill., Feb. 4, 1918.

To Whom It May Concern:—

This is to certify that the bearer, Mr. S. G. Auer, has long been known to me, and that he is a young man of good family, steady habits, and honest and conscientious in the performance of every duty.

He sustains an excellent reputation among his associates and neighbors. He is highly respected by all, and is possessed of a good education. I take pleasure in recommending him to any who may desire the services of an active, competent, and trustworthy young man.

EDWARD LUEBEN.

Recommending a Salesman.

Warren, Oct. 7, 1918.

To Whom It May Concern:—The bearer of this, Mr. J. M. Horton, has been in our employ for three years past as salesman and book-keeper, and we have ever found him diligent and faithful in the discharge of his duties, and one who endeavored to make his employers' interest his own. He is correct and reliable in his accounts, and is well qualified to act as book-keeper or correspondent.

We cheerfully recommend him to any who may require the services of a trustworthy and competent person as accountant.

Very respectfully,
MARSHALL FIELD & CO.

Recommendation for a Farm Laborer.

Sycamore, Ill., Nov. 1, 1918.

To Whom It May Concern:—

This certifies that the bearer, Jno. Jones, has worked for me during the last season upon my farm, and that I have found him steady, reliable, strong and a good workman. I recommend him to any one who wishes help that understands farming, as one who is able and willing to earn good wages.

THOS. HALL.

ASKING FOR A LETTER OF RECOMMENDATION.

Lemont, Illinois.
April 10, 1918

Will Mr. Hughs be so good as to to favor me with a line stating in what manner and with what success I discharged my duties while serving as a teacher in the school in which he is director? Such a testimonial, if as favorable as I have reason to expect, may be of great benefit to me in procuring a desirable situation as teacher.

Hoping that Mr. Hughs will favor me with a reply as soon as convenient, I remain his friend,

Lulu Brown.

To Larry Hughs, Esq.

Business Recommendation.

Winterset, Iowa, May 10, 1918.

To Whom It May Concern:

Having for many years enjoyed the acquaintance and observed the course and conduct of Mr. Dudley Selden, and being also acquainted with his financial circumstances, I do herewith most cheerfully and unhesitatingly express my entire confidence in his integrity as a true Christian gentleman and a trustworthy, reliable business man, bearing a good reputation for honesty and business integrity where best known.

I can conscientiously recommend him as a safe man in any line of business for which he is qualified, being confident that he will not obligate himself beyond his ability to pay.

ALVIN H. BROWN,
Cashier First National Bank.

Recommending a Teacher.

Peoria, Ill., Feb. 16, 1918.

W. G. Brewer, Esq.

Dear Sir:—It gives me pleasure to recommend Miss Lora Minch to the position of teacher of your school. I have known Miss Minch as student and teacher. I most cheerfully bear record to her untiring zeal and close application as a student. As a teacher she has tact, enthusiasm and patience. Her amiable disposition has won to her the hearts of her pupils. She is withal a strict disciplinarian. The two years spent with us have exhibited a marked improvement in our school in every respect.

Very truly yours,
IDA HOFFMAN,
Chairman of School Board.

Declining to Recommend.

W. G. Brown, Esq.

Sir:—I regret that I cannot conscientiously write the testimonial you request of me. I should most gladly do so, if I were not compelled to believe that it would be unjust and an injury to both of us.

I am still your sincere well-wisher,

A. E. JAHN.

LETTERS OF CONGRATULATION.

37. A Letter of Congratulation is a letter written to a friend who has met with some special good fortune or great joy. It should be written in a style suited to the occasion, lively, cheerful and free from all envy or prejudice.

While an abundance of good-natured merriment is permissible, overpraise or exaggeration may create doubt in your friend's mind as to your sincerity. Do not insert any other matter or news in a congratulatory letter.

Congratulating a Friend on Obtaining a Position.

Dear Friend George:—Permit me to congratulate you upon your success in obtaining a good and desirable position. Hoping that it may prove profitable to you and be a stepping stone to even greater prosperity, I am,

Yours truly,
CENTIUS SELDEN.

Letter of Congratulation Upon Marriage.

Naperville, Ill., Jan. 27, 19 .

My Dear Friend James:
Allow me to congratulate you on your marriage, of which I have just heard With all my heart I wish you a long, happy and prosperous life with your helpmeet. May you share with each other many joys and few sorrows.

As ever your friend,
JOHN D. BREWER.

To J. A. Schneider,
Batavia, Ill.

Congratulating a Friend Upon the Birth of a Son.

Peoria, Ill., Jan. 8, 19 .

Dear George:—Accept my warmest congratulations upon the birth of your son. May he always be the source of happiness and comfort to his parents that he now is, and be the pride and help of your old age.
My kindest regards to Mrs. Jackson. I remain,

Faithfully your friend,
H. H. HARDY.

Congratulating a Lady upon her Approaching Marriage.

Dixon, Ill., Feb. 16, 19 .

Dear Anna:—Two beautiful cards on my table advise me of your approaching nuptials. Allow me to congratulate you upon the choice of such a noble man to whom you are to entrust your life's happiness. That the noon and evening of your married life may be as cloudless and beautiful as the morning, is the earnest wish of

Your loving friend,
LUCY SPANGLER.

Congratulating a Friend on Recovering Health

Dear Friend George:—Permit me to offer my heartfelt congratulations on your convalescence from the severe attack of fever. I trust you are again in usual health and hope to see you soon in your usual hopeful and cheerful spirit.

Very truly yours,
H. A. HAGEMEIER.

LETTERS OF SYMPATHY AND CONDOLENCE.

38. A Letter of Condolence is a letter written to some friend who has suffered some grievous loss or bereavement. It should be consoling, comforting and full of sympathy.

Avoid calling up the harrowing details of the sad event, and do not attempt to argue the sufferer out of his (or her) sorrow. The letter should be short, but earnest and sincere. Such letters often afford inexpressible comfort in the hour of affliction.

Letter of Condolence.

Reese, Mich., Jan. 7, 19

Dear Friend Clayton:

With feelings of deepest sorrow I have learned of your recent heavy loss. You have my sincere sympathy in this your affliction. With hope that you may speedily retrieve your loss, I am as ever,

Your friend.

R. R. BARNARD.

To C. H. Wolf.
Naperville, Ill.

A Letter of Condolence on a Child's Death.

Houston, Texas, Jan. 11, 19 .

My Dear Friend:—If anything could have caused me especial pain, it was the news of your sad bereavement. How I remember your dear child! Lovely, lively, intelligent, and affectionate, ever displaying a thoughtfulness beyond her years, and to lose such a promising child truly brings a deep and heavy shadow; but remember that light some time will break through, and there will be a glad and happy reunion in the great beyond.

It has, indeed, been a heavy blow, and I scarcely know how to talk of consolation under so bitter an affliction. But think of One who careth for us all and who loves little children. He has prepared a bright and beautiful home beyond the grave, and the spirit of the dear child will only wait a brief period when in sweetness and love she will meet her mother and father to depart no more.

I can say no more; human consolation is weak. May God bless you in your hour of sorrow, is the wish of Your loving friend,

MARTHA COLE.

To Mrs. Henry Craver.

Lafayette to Jefferson, Announcing the Death of Madame de Lafayette.

Antenil, Jan. 11, 19 .

My Dear Friend:—The constant mourning of your heart will be deepened by the grief I am doomed to impart to you. Who better than you can sympathize for the loss of a beloved wife? The angel who for thirty-four years has blessed my life was to you an affectionate, grateful friend. Pity me, my dear Jefferson, and believe me forever with all my heart,

Yours,

LAFAYETTE.

LETTERS OF FRIENDSHIP.

Friendship letters should be written more frequently. Especially should the young cultivate the art of keeping up an interesting correspondence with friends. Many a friend has been lost through neglect in correspondence. An interesting and lively correspondence will rivet the ties all the closer. You must be governed by circumstances, but an entering into the details of everyday life is often desirable and will interest your friend. Do not be foolish, but be explicit about the happenings of the neighborhood, especially if your friend is acquainted with persons mentioned. If the father were to write more frequently to the son, the son to the father, the husband to the wife, the wife to the husband, the mother to the daughter and the daughter to the mother, home ties would be strengthened and many of our youth would be saved from many evils and in some cases from ruin. Keep home ties closely riveted by frequent correspondence. The same is true with our friends. We may hold our friends, be a blessing to them and they to us by frequent correspondence. At the same time you will be acquiring the art of easy letter writing.

A Student at School.

North-Western College, Oct. 2, 1918.

My Dear Parents:—It will doubtless give you much pleasure to learn that owing to the kind attention of my teachers I have made so satisfactory progress that I have not only been promoted one class higher in the school, but have carried off the first prize in penmanship.

I sincerely hope that I may keep up to all the expectations you have formed of me, and which you have spared no pains or expense to realize.

With feelings of regret at leaving my kind teachers and school-mates, and delight at the prospect of my return home, I remain, my dearest parents, with kindest love to all at home,

Your affectionate child,

ELMER BROWN.

A Letter to a Lady Friend.

Miss NELLIE REYNOLDS, Vicksburg, Miss., Jan. 23, 1918.
Scotland, Conn.

Dear Friend:—It no doubt will be a great surprise to you to receive a letter from a distant friend who has been silent so long. I will venture to try to experiment, hoping you will recover from the shock in season to make an early reply.

How has the world prospered you all these long years since we last met? I hope you are in the full enjoyment of the blessings of good health and find many interesting and profitable enterprises to engage your time and attention.

Where and how are all the good people who used to be our neighbors? Scattered, no doubt, some to distant States, and some to the silent abodes of the village burial ground. And thus, Nellie, does time make its mark, and it writes upon all living the sad, sad words, Passing away.

But I said I would be brief. Please write to me, and tell me all the items of interest. With many kind thoughts, I remain, as ever,

Truly your friend, J. O. EVERETT.

John Quincy Adams, when Seven Years Old, to His Father.

Braintree, Mass., Oct. 13, 1774.

Sir:

I have been trying ever since you went away to write a letter. I shall make poor work of it; but, sir, mamma says you will accept my endeavors, and that my duty to you may be expressed in poor writing as well as good. I hope I grow a better boy, and that you will have no occasion to be ashamed of me when you return. Mr. Thaxter says I learn my books well. He is a very good master. I read my books to mamma. We all love to see you.

I am, sir, your dutiful son,

John Quincy Adams.

Dr. Franklin to His Wife.

"Easton, Nov. 13, 1756.

"My Dear Child:

"I wrote you a few days since, by a special messenger and inclosed letters for all our wives and sweethearts, expecting to hear from you by his return, and to have the northern newspapers and English letters per the packet; but he is just now returned without a scrap for poor us; so I had a good mind not to write to you by this opportunity, but I never can be ill-natured enough, even when there is the most occasion. The messenger says he left the letters at your house, and saw you afterwards at Mr. Duche's and told you when he would go, and that he lodged at Honey's, next door to you, and yet you did not write; so let Goody Smith give me more judgment, and say what should be done to you. I think I won't tell you that we are all well, nor that we expect to return about the middle of the week, nor will I send you a word of news—that's poz.

"My duty to mother, love to children, and to Miss Betsy and Gracy, etc., etc.

"I am your loving husband,

B. FRANKLIN.

"P. S. I have scratched out the loving words, being written in haste by mistake, when I forgot I was angry."

"IN THE MIDST OF LIFE THERE IS DEATH."

HOW TO WRITE RESOLUTIONS.

1. **Resolutions of societies, clubs, or any organization on the death of a member should always be deliberate, concise and consistent.**
2. **Great care should be taken that they are not too brief nor too long, and be careful to avoid excessive exaggerations.**
3. **Resolutions in form are always prefaced with a preamble which should specify the occasion of what shall follow. The preamble should begin with "whereas," and each resolution should begin with "resolved" or "be it resolved."**
4. **When resolutions have been framed by a committee, all their signatures should be annexed to the resolutions.**

Form of Resolutions.

Whereas, The great and supreme Ruler of the universe has in his infinite wisdom removed from among us one of our worthy and esteemed fellow-laborers, Henry A. Harlow; and, whereas, the long and intimate relation held with him in the faithful discharge of his duties in this society makes it eminently befitting that we record our appreciation of him; therefore,

Resolved, That the wisdom and ability which he has exercised in the aid of our organization by service, contributions, and counsel, will be held in grateful remembrance;

Resolved, That the sudden removal of such a life from among our midst leaves a vacancy and a shadow that will be deeply realized by all the members and friends of this organization, and will prove a serious loss to the community and the public.

Resolved, That with deep sympathy with the bereaved relatives of the deceased we express our hope that even so great a loss to us all may be overruled for good by Him who doeth all things well;

Resolved, That a copy of these resolutions be spread upon the records of this organization; a copy printed in the local paper and a copy forwarded to the bereaved family.

Resolutions of Thanks.

Resolved, That the thanks of this convention are hereby given to the president for the able and impartial manner in which he has presided over the deliberations of this body, and to the other officers for the faithful performance of duties fulfilled in so satisfactory a manner.

VISITING AND ADDRESS CARDS.

Uses.—A few of the many uses of cards are, to announce a visitor's name, to make known one's name to a stranger, to serve as credentials or certificates of authority when an indorsement is written upon it.

Kinds.—The business card is valuable for advertising, making known the leading features of the business. The visiting card is used principally by ladies in calling upon acquaintances in the city. The address card is also frequently used for the same purpose. Professional cards are used by professional men. The same card is often used for social purposes.

Cards are of various sizes to suit individual tastes. Ladies' cards are a trifle larger than gentlemen's. The most elegant cards are engraved or written. They should always be in script.

A man and his wife sometimes use a joint card, written Mr. and Mrs. C. J. Lock, but more frequently each have a separate card, the gentleman's card being smaller and delicately engraved in script. Cards should not be "overloaded" with printed matter.

We append a few models, which although diminished in size will give the general form.

George C. Monroe.	*Edith Monroe.*
Mrs. George C. Monroe.	*Mrs. Geo. C. Monroe,* *18 Adams St.*
Miss Edith Monroe, *26 Monroe St.* *1st and 3rd Thursday.*	*Mrs. Geo. C. Monroe,* *Naperville, Ills.*

HELPFUL HINTS TO CORRESPONDENTS.

Abbreviations.—Use abbreviations very sparingly. Be especially careful in using the abbreviations of states. Avoid abbreviations such as "&" for "and," "xRoads" for "Cross Roads," "Balt." for "Baltimore," "Phil." for "Philadelphia," "C'wood" for "Collingwood," "Wmstown" for "Williamstown," "Jno'town" for "Johntown," "ad." for "adv." or "advertisement," etc.

Address.—Write your name and address plainly and in full. N. Y. may look like N. J.

Anonymous Letters.—No gentleman or lady ever writes an anonymous letter.

Application.—Letters of application should be very carefully written in the applicant's own handwriting, modest but self-respectful.

Brevity.—In business letters use as few words as possible.

Business Letters.—Business letters often partake of the nature of contracts, hence they should be clear, brief, direct and without ambiguous terms. Ambiguous language often results in serious loss.

Captain.—When this title is used instead of "Sir" in the salutation or complimentary close, it should not be abbreviated. The same rule applies to "Colonel" and other titles.

Copying Letters.—Copy important business letters and preserve them. A facsimile made with a letter press is a most satisfactory means of preserving a copy of a letter.

Corporations.—A petition or memorial to a Board of Aldermen, or other officers, may begin with "Gentlemen" and close with "All of which is respectfully submitted."

Dear Sir.—This salutation is more intimate than "Sir" and not so officious. It is preferable to "Sir" for ordinary business correspondence.

Degrees.—Scholastic degrees—M. D., D. D., M. A., A. B., etc.—are always abbreviated in addresses. Titular addresses of high rank, however—such as President, Governor, Archbishop, etc.—should never be abbreviated in such use. It is not in good taste to address a man as "Mr. Charles King, M. A.," or "Charles King, Esq., M. D." Titles are multiplied on title-pages and catalogues, but not more than one should appear on letters.

Doctor.—Doctors of Divinity may be addressed "Rev. Dr. or "Rev. —————, D. D." Doctors of medicine may be addressed "A—— B——, M. D.," or "Dr. A—— B——."

Don't.—Don't write illegibly. Don't write crooked. Don't use any other than black ink. Don't write a lettter on foolscap paper. Don't use fancy note paper. Don't grumble on paper. Don't flourish in a business letter. Don't use slang. Don't direct an envelope wrong side up. Don't write "&" for "and." Don't write a letter with a lead pencil. Don't write like Horace Greeley. Don't write "Gents" instead of "Gentlemen." Don't be profuse in apologies.

Envelopes.—In social correspondence, the envelopes, like the paper, should be white and plain, and should correspond to the paper used in size and quality. The square envelope is not used for business correspondence. It is considered bad taste to use colored paper.

Erasures.—Avoid erasures or blots, even if you have to rewrite your letter.

Esquire.—The correct abbreviation is "Esq.," not "Esqr." In addresses this word is accepted as the correct title of a gentleman who has no professional title.

Figures.—Do not use figures in the body of a letter, except in writing dates and sums of money.

Folding.—Fold the letter neatly from the bottom forward and fit it to the size of the envelope. A clumsily folded letter denotes either ignorance or a want of proper respect to the person addressed.

Friendship.—Matters of friendship or private confidence should not be mentioned in business letters.

Hostess.—Be sure to write a friend, or hostess, after making a visit at her house, thanking her for her hospitality. Do not wait several weeks before doing so.

Introduction.—Letters of introduction should be left unsealed and the name of the person introduced should be written on the lower left-hand corner of the envelope, in order that the persons, on meeting, may greet each other without embarrassment.

Margin.—Always leave a margin of a half-inch or more at the left of the page. The margin should correspond to the size of the paper.

Mistakes.—Read your letter carefully when written, and see that you have made no omissions and no mistakes. Examine carefully your envelope when addressed. Millions of letters reach the dead letter office every year because of mistakes in addressing them. In writing a number of letters be careful to enclose them in the proper envelopes. Woeful mistakes have been made this way. Don't make mistakes.

Miss.—This word, unlike Sir, Madam, and General, should never be used alone, hence cannot be used as the salutation of a letter. In addressing a young lady, use the word with the surname, as "Miss Brown." In writing to strangers a woman should in her signature, indicate her sex and also whether she is a "Miss or a "Mrs."

Money.—In sending money, the amount should always be mentioned. Acknowledge the receipt of money promptly.

Nota Bene.—The abbreviation is N. B. and the meaning "note specially." This, like the postscript, follows the completed letter.

Numbers.—Numbers, except dates and sums of money, should be spelled in full, unless exceeding three words in length.

Officials.—In letters to ordinary officials, it is customary to begin with the salutation "Sir," and close with "I have the honor to be, sir, your obedient servant," or "I beg to remain your obedient servant."

Official Letters.—In official correspondence it is better to address the office than the officer, as "To the Minister of Agriculture, etc., Sir," instead of "To the Hon. A—— B——, Minister of Agriculture, etc."

Paper.—Gentlemen should use white paper, ladies may use delicately tinted and perfumed paper. Unruled paper is to be preferred.

Paragraphs.—Letters as well as other compositions should be divided into paragraphs, and a blank margin should always be left on the left-hand side of the page, and not on the right.

Payment.—When it becomes necessary to request payment, it should be done in the most gentlemanly terms. There is more loss than gain in rash and insulting language.

Poor Writing.—It is almost useless for a poor writer to apply for a situation in a business house, for merchants do not wish either the discredit or the inconvenience of bad writing.

Postal Cards.—There is no need of salutation or complimentary close. The economy that resorts to cards need not waste time and two lines on mere civilities.

Postscript.—The abbreviation P. S. is usually made use of. The ordinary use of the postscript is to add some afterthought to the letter. Use sparingly.

Promptness.—Business letters should be promptly answered.

Recommendation.—"It ought to be the pride of every man who writes a letter of recommendation to feel that his letter will have weight, because it is known that he recommends only the deserving and the competent, and recommends truthfully."

Return Stamp.—In writing to others for information a stamp should always be enclosed.

R. S. V. P.—French meaning, "answer if you please." Sometimes written at the lower left hand corner of the invitations.

Sir.—This is used alone while Mr. goes with the name. The plural is "Gentlemen," not the vulgar contraction "Gents."

Social Matters.—Never discuss or refer to social matters in a business letter. If necessary write two letters.

Style.—Let the style be simple, clear and withal forcible In a letter the spirit of the writer should show itself.

Testimonials.—When these are required, and you desire to preserve the original, a copy should be enclosed, and marked "copy" at the top of the page.

Titles.—The principle titles of honor, profession and respect used in the United States are:

His Excellency—President of the United States, Governor of any state, Minister to foreign country.

Honorable—Vice-President, Senators and Representatives of the United States, Lieutenant Governor of a state, State Senators and Representatives, Judges, Consuls, Mayors and heads of Executive Departments of the General Government.

Rev. Joseph Smith, D. D., doctor of divinity.

Rev. Joseph Smith, L.L. D., doctor of laws.

Rev. Joseph Smith, minister of the gospel.

Dr. Joseph Smith, physician or surgeon.

Prof. Joseph Smith, professor or teacher of any art or science.

Joseph Smith, Esq., member of legal fraternity.

Mr. Joseph Smith, non-professional gentleman.

COMMERCIAL FORMS.

Fifty Facts and Principles on Writing, Transferring, Collecting and Paying Notes.

1. Notes are very common, and of great utility in business. At the present time a large proportion of all the business is transacted on credit, that is, a tradesman, instead of paying for his stock when he buys it, promises to pay at some future time; that promise, whether oral or written, is itself property, and may be transferred from one to another.

2. Notes are written and unconditional admission and evidence of a debt and facilitate the use of credit, which is and has been a great factor in the extension of commerce and trade.

3. A note is a simple written promise to pay a certain sum at a certain time, or on demand, or at sight to a person therein named.

The person who promises is called the maker, and the one to whom he promises is called the payee.

4. A protest of a note is a formal statement by a notary public that said note was presented for payment and was refused.

WRITING NOTES.

5. Notes are made payable to bearer or to order.

6. If the words "order" or "bearer" are omitted, the note is not transferable.

7. Negotiable in a commercial sense means transferable. A negotiable note contains the word order or the word bearer. This is the English common law, but in Illinois and some other States the words "order" or "bearer" are not necessary to make a note negotiable.

8. The name of the place and State should be written on the note. It is as important as the date.

9. A note may be written on any kind of paper in ink or in pencil.

10. A note made and issued on Sunday is void.

11. A note negotiable must contain five things: (1) that the date of payment be certain to come; (2) that it have one of the two words, "order" or "bearer"; (3) that the amount be

specified and certain; (4) that it be payable in money only; (5) that it be an unconditional promise. (See 7 above.)

12. A non-negotiable note is payable to a particular person only.

13. The words "without defalcation" must be inserted in Pennsylvania notes.

14. A promissory note does not bear interest until after maturity unless so specified.

15. The signature on a note or bill need not be proven, unless it is first denied under oath.

16. The words "value received" are not legally necessary, although they usually appear on ordinary promissory notes.

17. When several persons unite in a note and say, "we promise" or "we jointly promise," it is a joint liability only, and all must be sued; but if they say we or either of us promise, or "we jointly and severally promise," the liability is both joint and several, and either or all may be sued.

18. When a note says "I promise," but is signed by two or more, each signer is bound for the whole amount, and each or all may be sued.

19. Promissory notes can be transferred after maturity, but are, however, subject to any defense which might have been made against the original payee.

TRANSFERRING NOTES.

20. Paper payable to bearer is transferred by delivery, payable to order by indorsement.

21. An indorser is a person who writes his name on the back of it.

22. Indorsement in blank is writing only the name without the words, "pay to the order of."

23. The indorser is liable for its payment if the maker fails to meet it.

24. An indorser who is compelled to pay a note has a just claim against the maker and against each indorser whose name appears above his own.

25. An indorser to whose order a note is drawn or indorsed, can transfer it without becoming liable for its payment by writing the words "without recourse" over his signature on the back. See Form 3, page 112.

COLLECTING NOTES.

26. A note destroyed by fire can be collected by proof of loss.

27. Money paid under mistake must be refunded.

28. If no time is specified the note is payable on demand.

29. The day of maturity is the day on which a note becomes legally due. In some states three days, called days of grace, are allowed after the expiration of the time given in the note before it becomes legally due.

30. In finding the day of maturity actual days must be counted if the note is drawn days after date, but months are counted when the note is drawn months after date.

31. Days of grace have been abolished in recent years in a number of States. The States still allowing them are: Alabama, Arizona, Arkansas, Indiana, Iowa, Kansas, Kentucky, Maine, Michigan, Minnesota, Mississippi, Nebraska, New Hampshire, North Carolina, Rhode Island, South Carolina, South Dakota, Texas, Washington, West Virginia, Alaska except on demand notes, Colorado, Georgia except on sight paper, Indian Territory, Louisiana except on sight paper, New Mexico, Oklahoma except where expressly waived in the note, Wyoming, West Virginia allows grace where expressly specified in the note.

32. Negotiable paper payable to bearer or indorsed in blank, which has been lost or stolen, cannot be collected by the finder or thief, but a holder who innocently receives it in good faith before maturity for value, can hold it against the owner's claims.

33. A note made in one State, payable in another, must be governed by the laws of that State in which it is to be paid.

34. Demand for payment of a note must be made upon the day of maturity and at the place named. If no place is specified then it is payable at the maker's place of business or at his residence. If it falls due on Sunday, demand must be made on the day previous. In most of the States where note falls due on Sunday or legal holiday, by statute the maker is given until the following day to pay the same.

35. An extension of the time of a note by the holder, releases sureties and indorsers, unless consent to such extension has been given by the indorsers or sureties. In some States this consent may be given verbally, in others it must be in writing. Safety would suggest that it always be given in writing or that a new note be given.

36. Upon presentment for payment and refusal by the maker at maturity, in order to hold the indorser, suit should be immediately instituted upon the note against the maker, and notice of default should be given to the indorser, and in some States the note should be protested by a notary public.

PAYING NOTES.

37. **Indorsers.**—All the parties who have written their names on a note are liable for the amount due; but only one satisfaction can be recovered.

38. **Indorsements.**—Payment made to apply on a note should always be indorsed on the back of the note. The indorsement requires no signature. The usual form is to give the date and write "Received on within note" stating sum paid. It is always well to see that the proper paper is indorsed. All payments of principal and interest must appear as indorsements upon the back of the note. If no indorsement is made and the note passes into innocent hands payment of the face value with interest can be demanded

39. **Cancelled Notes.**—When a number of notes are held by parties and these notes are secured by mortgage it is best to cancel them or mark them paid as soon as they are taken up, but not to destroy or to mutilate them by tearing off signatures. It is important that every note be kept until all are paid and the mortgage discharged.

40. **Payment of Notes at a Distance.**—In the payment of notes where parties live at a distance, it is best to request that the notes be sent to the nearest bank for collection. Payment can then be made and the note received in a safe and business-like way.

41. **Inquiring for Notes at Bank.**—When calling at a bank for your note, always mention the exact day on which it falls due; if the paper belongs to another party, and is held by the bank for collection, then mention also the name of the person to whom it was originally given; if you have received a written notice concerning the note, take this notice with you, for it will tell the whole story. Banks keep their own notes in one place, and those of their customers in another; they also keep each date by itself and can, therefore, find notes more readily if owners' names and date of maturity are given.

PAYMENT DEFEATED.

Many cases occur in which notes are void or in which payment may be defeated especially when held by the original parties. Such are:

42. A note given by one who is not of age, unless the minor ratifies it after becoming of age.

43. A note made by an intoxicated person.

44. A note given by one who cannot write and not witnessed to at the time.

45. A note obtained by duress, in case of compulsion, by fear or illegal imprisonment, or by threats that would lead an ordinary person to fear injury to his person, his reputation or his property. Such defense would be good and would defeat payment.

46. Obtained by fraud or by finding. In these cases the original parties can not collect anything.

47. A note that has been stolen cannot be collected by the party that committed the theft, but if an innocent person buys the note for a consideration, he can collect it.

48. A note given for illegal consideration is illegal everywhere.

49. One who receives a note knowing it to have defects, gets no better right to collect it, than the one from whom he received it had.

50. If a person at the time of taking a note has notice that it is void through fraud, or upon any legal grounds, he cannot collect it.

These defenses would all hold good unless transfer for consideration has been made before maturity in which case some of them would fail.

A TRUST DEED.

A trust deed is a deed to a piece of real estate held by a third party in trust as security for a note. This deed is very extensively used because it takes the place of a mortgage deed and renders the note negotiable.

DIFFERENT FORMS OF NOTES.

Negotiable by Indorsement.

$375.00. Naperville, Ill., Oct. 7, 1918.
One year after date I promise to pay to J. L. Nichols, or order, Three Hundred and Seventy-five Dollars, for value received, with interest at six per cent. J. R. PRICE.

Negotiable without Indorsement.

$100.00. Cleveland, O., Aug. 1, 1918.
Ninety days after date I promise to pay James Jones, or bearer, One Hundred Dollars, value received. E. M. KECK.

Not Negotiable.

$100.00. Chicago, Ill., Dec. 10, 1918.
Sixty days after date I promise to pay Geo. O. Dixon One Hundred Dollars, value received. EUGENE LANSING.

Note Payable in Gold.

$200.00. Sacramento, Cal., June 15, 1918.
One year after date I promise to pay J. G. Snyder, or order, Two Hundred Dollars, in U. S. gold coin, with interest at one per cent. per month in like gold coin until paid. W. F. TEEL.

A Corporation Note.

$200.00. Augusta, Me., Mar. 18, 1918.
Nine months after date, the Granite Stone Company promises to pay S. A. Chilton, or order, Two Hundred Dollars, with interest at seven per cent. Value received. GRANITE STONE COMPANY.
Attest: I. K. Dawes, Secretary.
O. R. Phillips, President.

N. B.—If corporation notes are drawn and signed in the above manner, the officers are not personally liable.

Collaterals.—If a man borrows $2,000 on his personal note and gives twenty shares of bank stock or other notes to be held as security, such shares or notes are called collaterals. They are still the property of the borrower but the lender is responsible for their safe keeping. The lender has power to sell the property if the note is not paid at maturity.

Collateral Note.

$500.00. Mendota, Tex., Sept. 25, 1918.
Sixty days after date I promise to pay to the order of T. J. Boyd, Five Hundred Dollars, without defalcation, for value received. Interest at eight per cent.

Having deposited United States Bonds of the nominal value of Six Hundred Dollars, which I authorize the holder of this Note, upon the non-performance of this promise at maturity, to sell, either at the Brokers' Board or at public or private sale, without demanding payment of this Note, or the debt due thereon, and without further notice, and apply proceeds, or as much thereof as may be necessary to the payment of this Note, and all necessary expenses and charges, holding myself responsible for any deficiency. W. W. STRATTON.

A Judgment Note differs from an ordinary promissory note in having a clause appended giving the holder permission to proceed without delay to sacrifice the property of the debtor to satisfy the debt. This is a very severe form of contract and should be given only under the most extreme conditions.

Judgment Note.

$2,000.00. Philadelphia, Pa., Jan. 4, 1918.

Six months after date I promise to pay J. W. Krasley, or order, Two Thousand Dollars,
value received with interest: And do hereby authorize any attorney of this county or any other county in this state or elsewhere, to enter and confess judgment for the above sum with costs of suit and attorney's commission of five per cent. for collection, release of errors, and without stay of execution, and do waive the right and benefit of any law of this or any other state exempting property, real or personal, from sale, and if levy is made on land, do also waive the right and inquisition and consent to the condemnation thereof, with full liberty to sell the same on *fi. fa.* with release of errors therein. GEO. W. BAIRD.

Payable at Bank.

$440.00. Chicago, Ill., Oct. 10, 1918.

Two years after date, for value received, I promise to pay T. M. Culver, or order, Four Hundred Forty Dollars at Second National Bank, interest at eight per cent. per annum. CHARLES HEARN.

On Demand.

$25.67. Toronto, Ont., Oct. 12, 1918.

On Demand I promise to pay to the order of J. T. Connor, Twenty-Five 67-100 Dollars. Value received, with interest at six per cent.
A. H. SIMPSON.

NOTE.—This note answers the same purpose as a note written one day after date.

Joint Note.

$200.00. Lisle, Ill., Jan. 1, 1918.

One year from date, we promise to pay D. F. Shaw, or order, Two Hundred Dollars. Value received. Interest at six per cent.
J. LEWIS BEAN.
B. A. WHITE.

Joint and Several Note.

$2,000.00. Ottawa, Ont., Nov. 25, 1918.

Ten months after date, we, or either of us, promise to pay Maggie Patterson Two Thousand Dollars, value received. Interest at five per cent.
J. C. HARDY.
R. E. WOOD.

Principal and Surety Note.

$600.00. Montreal, Sept. 21, 1918.

For value received, on or before July 27, 1920, I promise to pay to the order of Grover Cleveland, Six Hundred Dollars. Interest at nine per cent.
W. J. SHAW, Principal.
THOS. RODDEN, Surety.

NOTE.—The general form of a Principal and Surety is for the principal to properly sign the note, and the surety to endorse it.

A Note by One Who Cannot Write.

$49.50. Cleveland, Ohio, Mar. 20, 1918.

One year after date, I promise to pay N. Bowker, or order, Forty-nine 50-100 dollars, with interest at eight per cent. Value received.

his
H. A. Starr, Witness. JOHN x ROURKE.
mark

N. B.—A note made by a person who cannot write should always be witnessed by a disinterested person.

***Iron Clad Form.**

$300.00. Salt Lake City, Utah, May 19, 1918.

Two years after date, for value received, we promise to pay to the order of L. B. Lawson, Three Hundred Dollars, negotiable and payable at the Commercial National Bank of Salt Lake City, Utah, without defalcation or discount, with eight per cent. interest per annum from date until paid, both before and after judgment, payable in U. S. gold coin; and if suit be instituted for the collection of this note, we agree to pay Twenty Dollars attorney's fee. If the interest be not paid as herein stipulated, the legal holder of this note may declare the principal due, and proceed by law to recover both principal and interest.

T. C. HALLETT.
J. T. HALLETT.

A Note by a Married Woman.

$200.00. San Francisco, Cal., June 15, 1918.

Two years after date, I promise to pay Fred Lueben, or order, Two Hundred Dollars, with interest at eight per cent., payable annually. Value received. MRS. MARY CHANDLER.

N. B.—A married woman could formerly incur no liability, but now the statutes of the various States give her more or less freedom to enter into contracts, and consequently her note can be enforced against her. But in most States she cannot be bound by a note given to her husband, nor can he give a note to her. If she lends money to him and takes his note, a court of equity will oblige the husband to pay her, but the court of law will not.

Chattel Note.

$700.00. Earlville, Ill., Aug. 17, 1918.

Thirty days from date, for value received, I promise to pay Walter J. Miller, or order, Seven Hundred Dollars in Warrenville Flour, at the then market rate, the same to be delivered at the option of the owner within the limits of the town of Earlville. C. D. CHAMBERS.

Accommodation Note.

$500.00. Meriden, Vt., March 13, 1918.

Sixty days after date I promise to pay to the order of S. J. Umbreit Five Hundred Dollars, at the Earlville National Bank, without defalcation. Value received. M. SUNDERMAN.

Credit the drawer, S. J. Umbreit.

NOTE.—An accommodation note is where a person gives his note to another person, who is by agreement permitted to take it to the bank and have it discounted. In the hands of the original holder it cannot be collected.

Produce Note.

$37.00. Memphis, Tenn., Nov. 20, 1918.

For value received, I promise to pay to L. L. Orth on demand Thirty-seven Dollars, in goods at our store. J. L. STROHM.

My Own Order.

$200.00. Ottawa, Ont., July 20, 1918.

For value received, I promise to pay, sixty days after date, to my own order, Two Hundred Dollars, with interest at eight per cent.

A. S. BARNARD.

NOTE.—A note may be drawn to the maker's own order, with his indorsement in favor of the creditor. This note then can be transferred without indorsement.

---

*This form is used by bankers and brokers in the Rocky Mountain and Pacific States; it is really a form of Judgment Note.

LET YOUR ACTIONS BE EQUAL TO YOUR PROMISES.

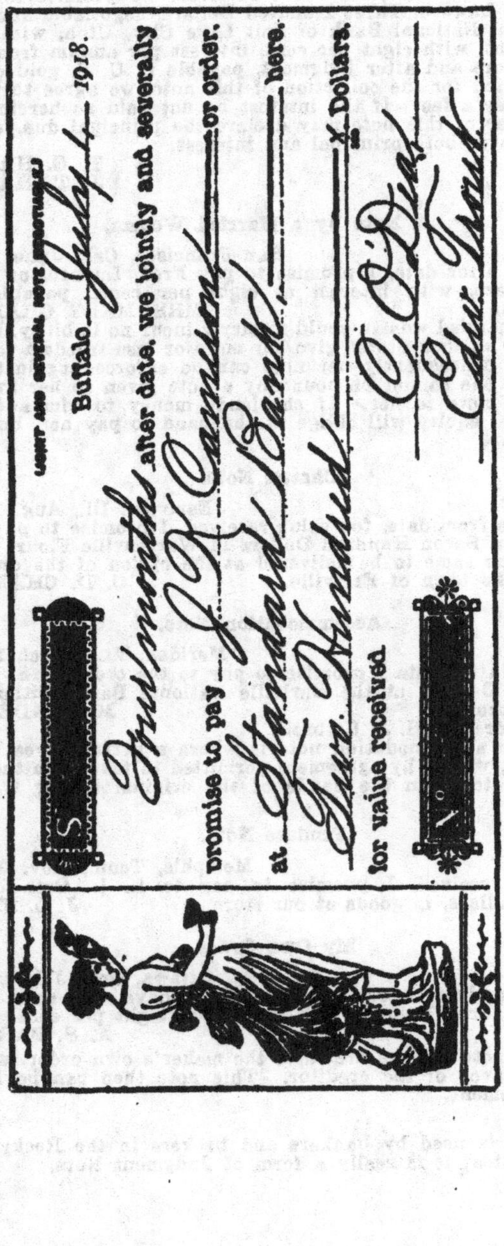

JOINT AND SEVERAL NOTE [illegible]

$ No.

Buffalo July 1, 1918.

Four months after date, we jointly and severally promise to pay J. J. Cameron or order, at Standard Bank here, Two Hundred x Dollars for value received.

C. O. Diaz

Edw. Trout

A Joint and Several Note Transferable.

INDORSEMENTS OF NOTES.

1. The word indorsement signifies a writing on the back of a bill or written instrument.

2. Indorsements are made for the purpose of transferring the title or ownership of notes from one person to another. This quality of transferring negotiable paper gives to it its great value and importance in commerce.

3. The payee of a note may transfer his title to another person by writing across the back of it his own name and then delivering it to the other person.

4. Indorsements are generally made before the maturity of the paper, but they are sometimes made after.

5. When no date is connected with the indorsement the presumption is that it was made before the paper fell due.

6. When the payee of negotiable paper has indorsed a note or bill, he is then called the indorser, and the person to whom he transferred the title is called the indorsee.

7. The indorsement may be on any part of the note, or on a paper annexed to it, in ink or in pencil.

8. When note or bill is drawn payable to a person or his order, it is transferable only by his indorsement. Nothing else in law will hold the parties to a note directly liable to the holder.

9. When money is received on a bill or note, the amount and date of receiving should be plainly written on the back of the paper.

Forms of Indorsements.

1. **Indorsement in Blank.**

John S. Barton.

2. **Indorsement in Full.**

Pay to Jas. Jones, or order.
John S. Barton.

3. **Qualified Indorsement.**

Without recourse.
John S. Barton.

4. **Restrictive Indorsements.**

Pay Robert Hunter, for my use.
John S. Barton.

Pay to Chas. Harrison only.
John S. Barton.

5. **Conditional Indorsement.**

Pay to the order of George Gray, the within, unless before due he receives the amount from my agent.
John S. Barton.

6. **Indorsement by an Agent.**

Howard Chester,
By John S. Barton, his agent.

7. **A Guaranty on a Note.**

For value received in cash, I hereby guarantee the payment of the within note.
John S. Barton.

1.—Blank Indorsement.

A blank indorsement is writing the name of the holder on the back of the note. This, however, is not the best form of indorsement, and should rarely be used.

Form 1 (page 106) is indorsed in blank as follows:

J. L. Nichols

N. B.—This note is now transferable without further indorsement.

2.—Full Indorsement.

When the holder writes upon the back of the note, or bill, the name of the person to whom it is to be paid, and makes it payable to his order, and signs his name below, it is called a full indorsement.

Pay to the order
of J. A. West.
N. A. Lundy

N. B.—This note cannot be sold or transferred without Mr. West's indorsement. Do not write "Pay to J. A. West or order." The word "order" can easily be stricken and "bearer" written over it and then any one holding the note can collect it. Always write "Pay to order of," as in above form.

3.—Qualified Indorsement or, How to Avoid Liability.

This is generally done by inserting the words "without recourse" in the indorsement. It relieves the indorser from all liability to pay, while at the same time it transfers the title perfectly to the one to whom it is sold.

4.—Restrictive Indorsement.

A restrictive indorsement is intended to confine the payment to some particular person or purpose. Form 1 (page 106) is restrictively indorsed as follows:

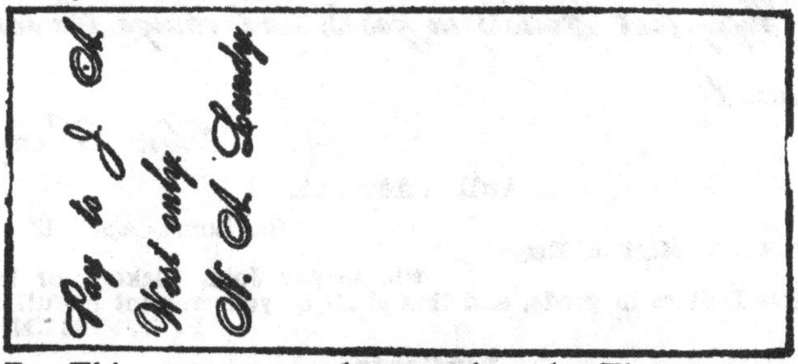

N. B.—This note cannot be transferred. The mere omission of the words "order" or "bearer" in an indorsement on the back of a note or draft does not have the same effect as the omission of the same words in the face of the note or draft. If omitted on the face, it restricts negotiability.

5—Conditional Indorsement.

Neither the original character of the note nor its negotiability is affected by a conditional indorsement. It only affects the title of the one to whom it is transferred.

The Form of a Money Indorsement.

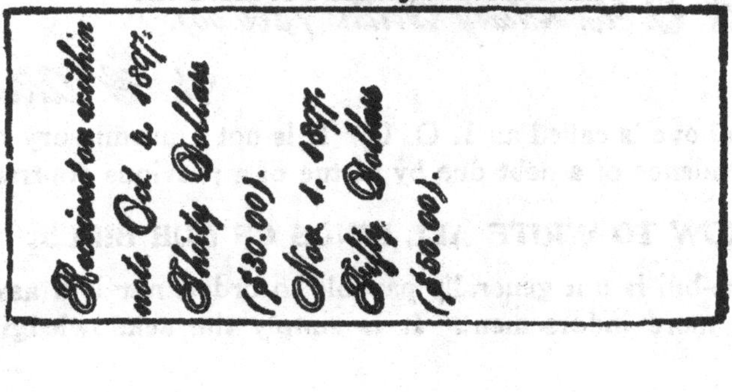

ORDERS.

An order is a written request to deliver money or goods to a person named, or to his order, or to bearer, the same to be charged to the person signing the request.

Orders are negotiable, but the person on whom they are drawn is not under obligation to pay them, unless they have been accepted, for an order partakes of the nature of a draft.

$54.00. Baltimore, Oct. 14. 1918.

Messrs. M. Brown & Co. will please pay to the bearer Fifty-four Dollars in goods, and charge the same to my account.

Clara Powers

In Full of Account.

$25.00. St. Louis, April 13, 1918.

C. A. Mather, Esq.:

Please pay John Rickert, or bearer, Twenty-five Dollars in goods, and this shall be your receipt in full of my account.

P. D. CRIMMINS.

For Goods.

Mr. W. W. Walsworth:

New Orleans, March 4, 1918.

Please send me per bearer ten barrels of Genesee Flour, and oblige,

Yours truly, MINNIE HOWARD.

An "I. O. U."

Chicago, Ills., Dec. 23. 1918.

Mr. A. O. Rogers:

I. O. U. Sixty Dollars ($60.00).

W. G. Allen

The above is called an I. O. U. It is not a promissory note, but is evidence of a debt due by virtue of a previous contract.

HOW TO WRITE ALL KINDS OF DUE BILLS.

A due-bill is not generally payable to order, nor is it assignable by mere indorsement. It is simply the acknowledgment of a debt; yet it may be transferred It may be payable in money or in merchandise.

Due-bills do not draw interest, unless so specified.

$125.00. Chicago, Aug. 14, 1918.

Due Henry Harrington, for value received, One Hundred and Twenty-five Dollars, with interest.

O. Linzer.

On Demand.

$250.00. Naperville, Ill., July 1, 1918.

Due E. E. Miller, on demand, Two Hundred Fifty Dollars in goods from my store, for value received. A. T. HANSON.

In Merchandise.

$1,000.00. Lincoln, Neb., Nov. 1, 1918.

Due R. William, or order, One Thousand Dollars, payable in wheat at market price, on the first day of January next.

CHARLES SCHUERER.

HOW TO WRITE ALL KINDS OF RECEIPTS.

A receipt is an acknowledgment in writing that a certain sum of money or thing has been received by the party giving and signing the same.

1. A complete receipt requires the following statements: That a payment has been received; the date of the payment; the amount or article received; from whom received, and if for another, on whose behalf payment is made; to what debt or purpose it is to be applied; by whom received, and if for another, on whose behalf it was received.

2. If the giving and receiving of receipts were more strictly held to in the transactions of the various kinds of business, less trouble, fewer law-suits, and the saving of thousands of dollars would be the result.

3. If payment is made upon account, upon a special debt, or in full, it should be so stated in the receipt.

4. When an agent signs a receipt, he should sign his principal's name and then write his name underneath as agent.

5. It is not necessary to take a receipt on paying a note, draft, or other instrument indorsed by the payee, because the instrument itself becomes a receipt.

6. If a receipt is obtained through fraud, or given under error or mistake, it is void.

ALL THE DIFFERENT FORMS OF RECEIPTS.

1. **Receipt for Payment on Account.**

$250.00. Naperville, Ills., July 6, 1918.

Received of J. L. Nichols, Two Hundred and Fifty Dollars on account.

J. H. Rohmes.

2. **Receipt for Settlement of an Account.**

Joliet, Ill., March 20, 1918.

Received of Thomas Rourke, Two Hundred and Twenty 14-100 Dollars, in settlement of account to date. C. S. SELBY.

3. **Receipt in Full of All Demands.**

Meriden, Conn., Jan. 14, 1918.

Received of C. F. Hetche, One Thousand Dollars, in full of all demands to date. O. N. OBRIGHT.

4. **Receipt for a Particular Bill.**

Brooklyn, N. Y., Aug. 1, 1918.

Received of Morris Cliggitt, Four Hundred Dollars, in Payment for a bill of Merchandise. R. ZACHMAN.

5. **Receipt for Rent.**

Snyder, Tex., Mar. 20, 1918.

Received of L. Heininger, Forty Dollars, in full for one month's rent, to April 20, for residence at 44 Olive Street.

J. LEWIS BEAN.

6. **Receipt for a Note.**

Rec'd, Buffalo, March 6, 1918, from Messrs. Taylor & Co., their note of this date, at three months, our favor, for Twelve Hundred and Twenty Dollars; which, when paid, will be in full of account rendered to 1st instant.

$1,220.00. C. H. OLIVER.

7. **Receipt for Service.**

Lemont, Ill., July 23, 1918.

Received of Samuel Lynn, Forty-Four Dollars, in full for services to date.

$44.00. DANIEL FURBUSH

8. **Receipt for Money Advanced on a Contract.**

$500.00. Chicago, Ills., May 10, 1918.

Received of Arthur Zahl the sum of Five Hundred Dollars, part payment on contract to build for him a house at No. 1439 Perry St., Chicago.

Carl Dienst.

9. Receipt for the Purchase of a Horse.

$200.00. Omaha, Neb., March 20, 1918.
Received of J. Lerch, Two Hundred Dollars, for a black mare, warranted only six years, sound, free from vice, and quiet to ride and drive.
CHARLES M. SMITH.

10. Indorsement of a Partial Payment of a Note.

Rec'd, March 4, 1901, on account of within note, Three Hundred Dollars.

11. Receipt for Borrowed Money.

$35.00. Naperville, Ills., July 20, 1918.
Borrowed and received from D. B. Givler, Thirty-Five Dollars, which I promise to pay on demand, with interest.
HENRY RAYMER.

12. Receipt for Property.

Rochester, N. Y., April 14, 1918.
Received of Louis Heininger, the following enumerated articles, to be held in trust for him, and returned on his demand: One Gold Watch, two Promissory Notes, each dated March 4, 1901, and signed by Henry Taylor—one for Three Hundred Dollars, and one for Seven Hundred, each due one year from date. WILLIAM PLACE.

13. Receipt for Payment by the Hand of a Third Party.

$450.00. Joliet, Ky., June 4, 1918.
Received of Carl Cook by the hand of Frank Furbush Four Hundred Fifty Dollars, in full for proceeds of sale of stock, sold May 28, 1901.

14. Receipt for a Note of Another Person.

$200.00. Aurora, Ills., May 10, 1918.
Received of Geo. Volk, a note signed by W. W. Paxton for the sum of Two Hundred Dollars, which, when paid, will be in full of all demands to date. WILLIAM KRUGER.

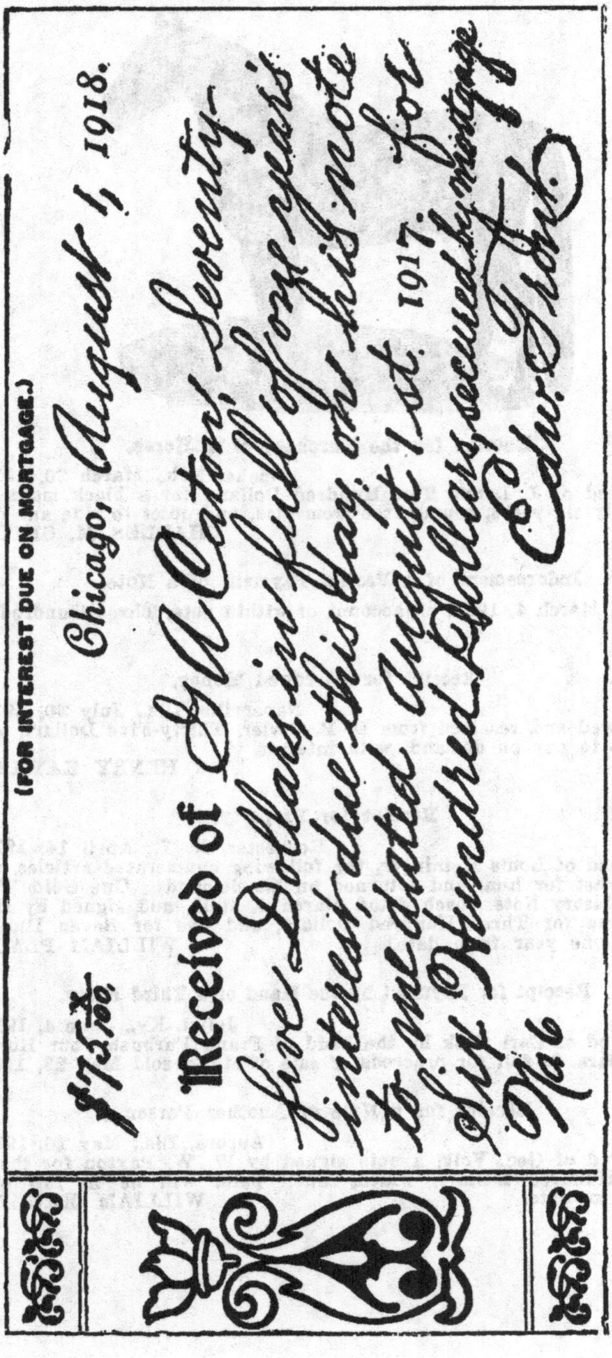

(FOR INTEREST DUE ON MORTGAGE.)

$75 x/100. Chicago, August 1, 1918.

Received of G. A. Caton, Seventy-five Dollars in full of one year's interest, due this day, on his note to me dated August 1st, 1917, for Six Hundred Dollars, secured by mortgage.

No. 6 Edw. Ford.

A Receipt for Interest Due on a Mortgage.

$300.00 Fox Lake, Wis., May 15, 1918.

Received of James H. Blackfoot

Three Hundred Dollars, in full payment for a certain note given by said James H. Blackfoot, dated May 12, 1917, calling for Three Hundred Dollars; which said note is lost, destroyed, or mislaid, and this receipt is a guarantee against future demands on account of said note.

I. M. Trueheart.

N. B.—Better never lose a note.

BANKS AND BANKING.

1. **History.**—The antiquity of banks is very great. Of modern banks the bank of Venice was the first in date. The Bank of England is more than two hundred years old. The first bank in America was the Bank of North America, in Philadelphia, established in 1782.

2. **Value to Business Men.**—Banks are essential for the carrying on of modern commercial enterprises. They provide for the safe-keeping of money and securities, they give business men an opportunity to borrow money, they afford facilities for collection of notes, checks, and drafts.

3. **Custodian of Money.**—A banker is the custodian of the money of other persons. Such is his business, viewed in its simplest aspect. A banker, if he hoarded the money deposited with him, would be simply a cash-keeper to the public; his bank would be literally a bank of deposit. Even were the business of banking limited to the keeping of deposits it would be of no small advantage to society: the depositors would be relieved from the care of their money, and in many cases from the trouble of handing it to those to whom they required to make a payment. If the person to whom the depositor wishes to pay money intends also to deposit it, a transfer in the books of the banker from the one to the other, made on the order or check of the depositor, would effect the payment. The money itself would lie undisturbed.

4. **Loaning It Out.**—But the business of receiving money has almost always been, and is now universally, combined with that of lending it out. A banker does not hoard all the money deposited with him—he gives the greatest portion out in loans. The lending of money is as much a part of his business as the receiving of deposits.

5. **Interest.**—For the money he lends he receives interest from the borrowers; and in this interest he is paid for s trouble in taking care of the deposits, and for his risk of bad debts. The services that a banker performs as the cash-keeper of his depositors are great. In the case of persons not themselves in business it is quite usual for a banker to make all the money payments, beyond their small daily expenditure, and to receive the money payable to them.

6. Discounts.—Banks make their loans chiefly in the form of discounts; that is, upon bills of exchange. Commodities in the wholesale market are generally sold on credit. The buyer promises to pay the amount on a certain date to the seller, and his promise is contained in a bill of exchange. The seller transfers it to a bank, which, on the faith of it, advances the amount in loan to him, less discount, that is, interest of the money till the bill be due. This is called discounting.

7. National Banks.—The system of national banks was established by act of Congress, Feb. 25, 1863. As amended by the act of 1900, national banks may be organized as follows: In towns not exceeding 3,000 in population, with a capital of $25,000; in towns of from 3,000 to 6,000, $50,000 capital; in towns of from 6,000 to 50,000, $100,000 capital; over 50,000, $200,000 capital and upwards. National bank notes must be issued by each national bank to the amount of at least one-quarter of its capital, and such notes may be issued to the full amount of each bank's capital at the option of the directors. These notes are secured by U. S. bonds deposited in the United States Treasury. Only one-third of the notes issued by each bank can be in five dollar bills.

8. Aggregate Circulation.—In 1863 the aggregate circulation allowed was $300,000,000, but an act passed in 1875 repealed all limitation on amount of circulation and made national banking practically free.

9. Safety.—The "National" bank is a private institution, differing from other banks only in this, that bonds have been deposited with the government as security for paper money, which the bank may issue. It is generally supposed that national banks are more secure than others. The examination of these banks by a government inspector has gained the confidence of the public in these institutions. We would not depreciate the necessity or value of these inspections, but that they are no guaranty of safety is seen from the many "National" banks that have gone into bankruptcy.

10. Circulating Notes.—National banks do not always issue the amount of circulating notes permitted by law. When a low rate of interest and a high premium on bonds prevail it does not pay banks to issue currency secured by bonds.

State and private banks do not issue circulating currency, they are usually deposit banks only and carry on a general business of loaning and dealing in money.

FEDERAL RESERVE ACT.

1. **The "Federal Reserve Act"** became operative on the 16th of November, 1914, and provides for the establishment of Federal Reserve Banks, to furnish an elastic currency, to afford means of rediscounting commercial paper, to establish a more effective supervision of banking in the United States, and for other purposes.

2. **Federal Reserve Board.**—The United States, including Alaska, has been divided into twelve districts, each district containing one Federal Reserve city, selected with due regard to the convenience and customary course of business. A Federal Reserve Board of seven members, including the Secretary of the Treasury and the Comptroller of the Currency, and five members selected by the President, has general supervision over the Federal Reserve Banks and in it are vested large powers. Each Federal Reserve Bank is conducted under the general supervision and control of a board of directors, consisting of nine members; three are chosen by and are representatives of stock-holding banks, three shall have been actively engaged in commerce, agriculture or some other industrial pursuit, and three are designated by the Federal Reserve Board.

3. ***Members.***—Every National bank must, and any State bank may, subscribe to the Capital Stock of the Federal Reserve Bank, in a sum equal to six percentum of the paid-up capital stock and surplus of such bank. Each member bank must deposit a portion of its required legal reserve with the Federal Reserve Bank in the district in which it is located. Member banks are to receive an annual dividend of 6% on their paid-up capital stock in the Federal Reserve Bank after all expenses are paid; the balance of net earnings shall go into a surplus fund until it shall aggregate 40% of paid-in capital stock. The remainder to be paid to the United States and to be applied to supplement the gold reserve or to reduce the Government's bonded indebtedness, at the direction of the Secretary of the Treasury.

4. **Operations.**—Upon the endorsement of any of its member banks, a Federal Reserve Bank may discount notes, drafts, and bills of exchange drawn for agriculture, industrial, or commercial purposes. Notes and drafts must have a maturity of not more than ninety days; except that notes, drafts, and bills issued for agricultural purposes based on live stock may have a maturity not exceeding six months. It may engage in open-market operations of the United States, and have power to deal in gold coin and bullion, to buy and sell bonds of the United States, and buy warrants or bonds issued by any State, County, District, or municipality of the United States in anticipation of taxes or revenues. It

may engage in many other financial transactions, subject, however, to carefully defined restrictions. National banks under the act have been granted the privilege to make first mortgage farm land loans for not exceeding a period of five years, limited to 50% of the value of the land; they may also be empowered to act as trustees, executors, administrators or registrators of stocks and bonds, when not in contravention of state or local law.

5. **The United States Treasurer** may deposit funds in any of the Federal Reserve Banks and permit them to be used for commercial or agricultural purposes wherever needed.

HOW TO DO BUSINESS WITH A BANK.

1. In beginning an account with a bank a depositor is required to put on record in the "signature book" his name as he intends to sign it on his checks.

2. Do not wait until you get to the bank to count your money or to indorse your checks.

3. Arrange your deposit at least before you present yourself at the receiving teller's window.

4. Place your bills all one way; right side up.

5. Make your deposits in the bank as early in the day as possible, and never without your bank-book.

6. Always use the deposit tickets furnished by the bank. When checks are deposited, the banks require them to be indorsed, whether drawn to order or not.

7. Keep your check-book under a lock and key.

8. Draw as few checks as possible; when several bills are to be paid, draw the money in one check.

9. Do not allow your bank-book to run too long without balancing. Compare it with the account of the bank.

10. In filling up checks, do not leave space in which the amount may be raised.

11. Write your signature with the usual freedom, and never vary the style of it.

12. The bank is responsible only for the genuineness of the signature and ordinary care in paying the check.

13. Always keep the stub of your check-book, and in issuing a check always fill the stub out first.

14. Never make deposits without your bank-book.

15. Always examine your bank-book after depositing. It is the only receipt you have for money deposited.

DOING BUSINESS WITH A BANK.

DISCOUNTING A NOTE AT THE BANK.

1. Discount is a certain percentage deducted from a note or debt for the payment of same before it is due.

2. Bank discount is simple interest on the principal, taken in advance.

It is the business of a bank to loan money to responsible persons, within reasonable limits. Regular customers receive first consideration. It is proper for you to offer any paper you may wish discounted to your banker. Take it coolly if you are refused, for the banker knows his own business best. The principal profit in banking is discounting notes, which is simply loaning money and receiving the interest in advance.

3. In discounting a note which is drawing interest, the discount must be reckoned on the amount or value of the note when due. (The interest for the full time must be first added to the face of the note before computing the discount.)

Example.—Robert F. May, on May 2d, offered the following note properly indorsed, for discount:

$525. Philadelphia, March 29, 1918.

Sixty days after date, we promise to pay to Robert F. May, or order, at the Union National Bank, Five Hundred and Twenty-Five Dollars, without defalcation. Value received. R. J. BIRNEY & CO.

How much will he receive as the net proceeds of the above note?

Sixty days from March 29th is May 28th. From May 2d to May 28th, including the day of discount, is 27 days.

Interest on $525 for 27 days—2.36 discount.

525—2.36—522.64 net proceeds.

9

VITAL POINTS ON CHECKS.

1. A check is a simple order on a bank by one who has funds in the bank, for the immediate payment of a certain sum of money.

2. A bank can stamp a check good, or certify it, and thus become responsible to the holder for the amount.

3. In sending a check away from your own town or locality it should always be certified, as in the above.

4. A check is not due until presented. It is negotiable. It has no days of grace.

5. Giving a check is no payment of an indebtedness, unless the check is paid.

6. The death of the maker of the check before presentment to the bank renders the check null and void.

7. A forged check paid by the bank is the bank's loss, and not the depositor's.

8. Payment of a check may be stopped by subsequent order to bank by maker before presentment of check.

9. The amount of the check should always be written out in words.

10. Every holder of a check is liable to a subsequent holder only for the time for which he would be held, if originally liable.

11. It is the safest rule always to act with diligence in presenting checks for payment.

12. If a raised check is paid by the bank, it can only charge the depositor the amount for which he drew, unless the raising of the check was made possible by the carelessness of the maker. In that case the maker would be responsible for the loss.

13. If you have money in a bank and you wish to draw out a certain sum, write "Pay to myself," instead of writing your name in the body of the check, and then sign it.

14. Banks of this country do not cash a check drawn payable to order unless the person presenting the check is known to the bank.

15. If you write a check for a stranger who needs identification at your bank, have him indorse the check in your presence and under his indorsement write "Indorsement above guaranteed," signing your name. He can then draw the check without further identification by signing his name again in the

presence of the banker. Another method is to write "Pay to Cash."

16. Do not draw a check unless you have the money on deposit or in your possession to deposit. Do not presume on the generosity of your bank by drawing a sum larger than your balance.

HOW TO INDORSE A CHECK.

1. The check is the most common commercial paper in use, and it is astonishing to see how many intelligent and educated people lack the necessary information on this subject.

2. Write across the back (not lengthwise) near the left end.

3. Simply writing your name on the back is a blank indorsement, and signifies that it has passed through your hands, and is payable to bearer.

4. If you wish to make the check payable to some particular person, write: Pay to the order of (person's name), and then sign your name below.

5. Always indorse a check just as it appears on the face. If a check is payable to F. Block, it cannot be indorsed Frank Block. If the spelling of the name on the face of the check is wrong, indorse first as the name appears on the face, and below this first indorsement write your name correctly.

6. If the name on the face of the check is written Rev. W. A. Schutte, it must be so written in the indorsement.

7. If you wish to deposit a check, write: "For Deposit," and below this your name. This is not necessary if you take the check to the bank yourself.

8. Do not write any unnecessary information on the back of your check. A story is told of a woman who received a check from her husband, and when cashing it wrote "Your loving wife" above her name on the check.

Form of an Indorsement When Transferred.

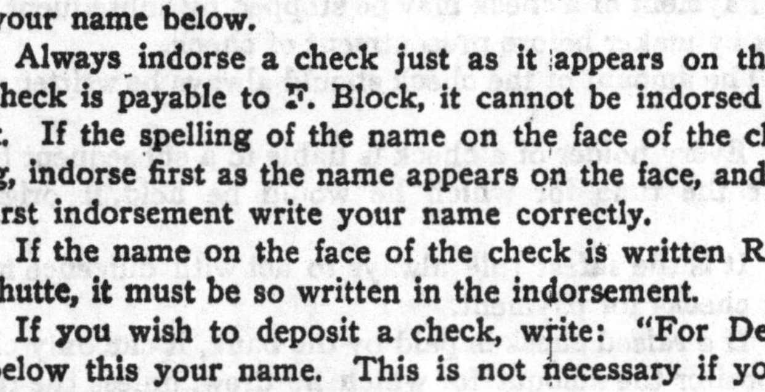

CERTIFICATE OF DEPOSIT.

Certificates of deposit are used when money is deposited for a short time, and no regular bank account is kept. They can be used the same as a certified check.

In issuing certificates of deposit to strangers banks usually take their signatures upon the margin of the certificate book, so that the signatures may be compared to avoid fraud.

Form of Certificate of Deposit.

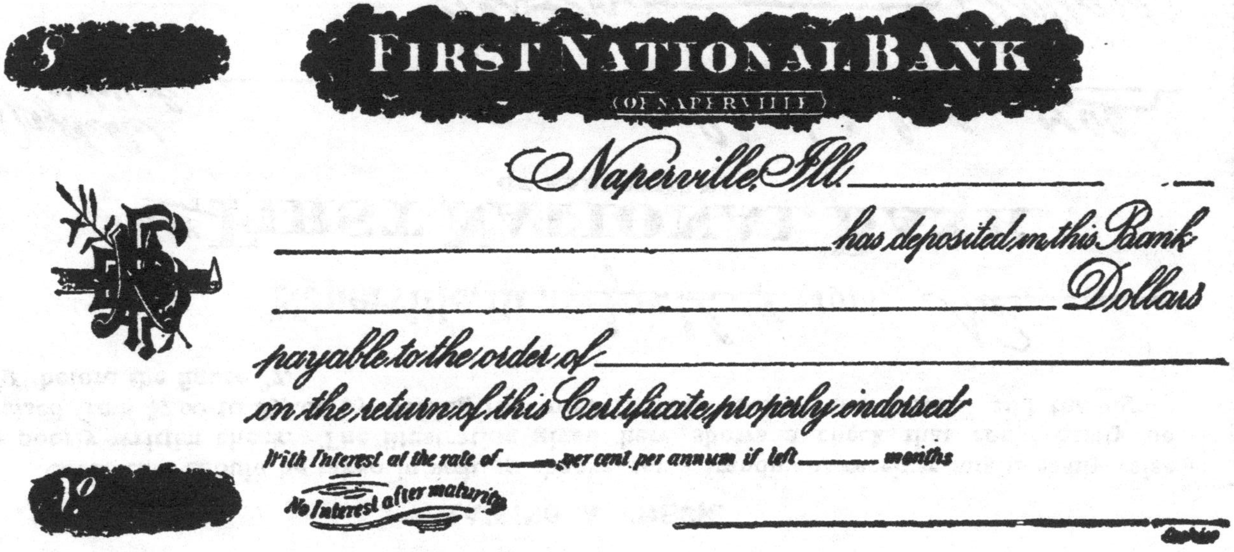

FIRST NATIONAL BANK
(OF NAPERVILLE)

Naperville, Ill. ______________

______________ has deposited in this Bank

______________ Dollars

payable to the order of ______________

on the return of this Certificate properly indorsed

With Interest at the rate of ____ per cent. per annum if left ____ months

No Interest after maturity

______________ Cashier

RAISING A CHECK.

Great care should be taken in writing checks, for a fraudulent receiver might easily raise a poorly written check. The illustration given here shows a check that could easily be raised from $7.00 to $97.00 by writing the word "ninety" before the "seven" and the figure "9" before the figure "7."

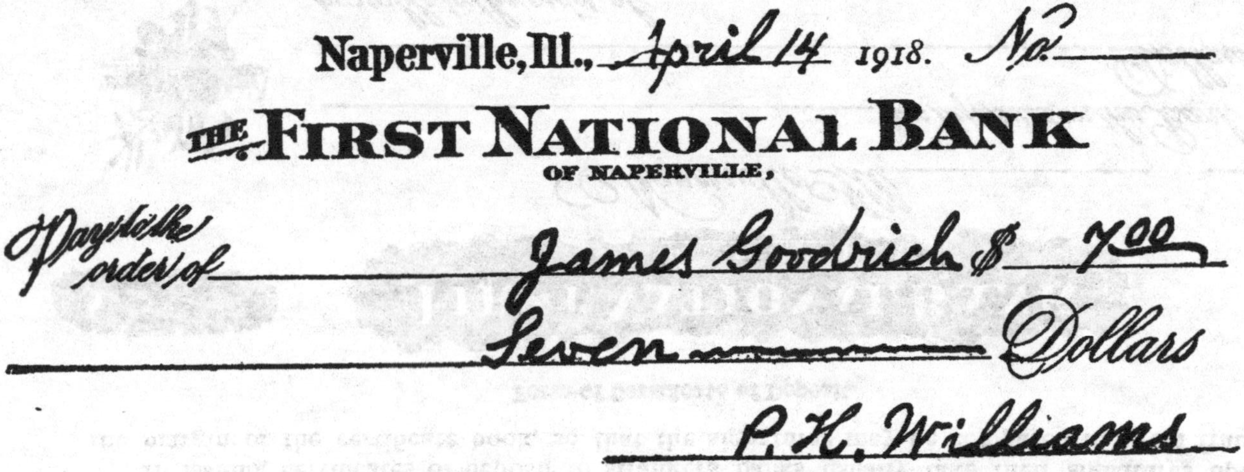

Naperville, Ill., April 14 1918. No. ______

THE FIRST NATIONAL BANK

OF NAPERVILLE,

Pay to the order of James Goodrich $ 7.00

Seven ——— Dollars

P. H. Williams

In such case it would be exceedingly difficult to hold a bank responsible for your own carelessness. A check for $100 could easily be raised to $160 by writing the words "and sixty" after the words "one hundred" and changing one of the ciphers to a 6.

CHECK PAYABLE TO ORDER.

The following form of a check payable to order is the form generally used:

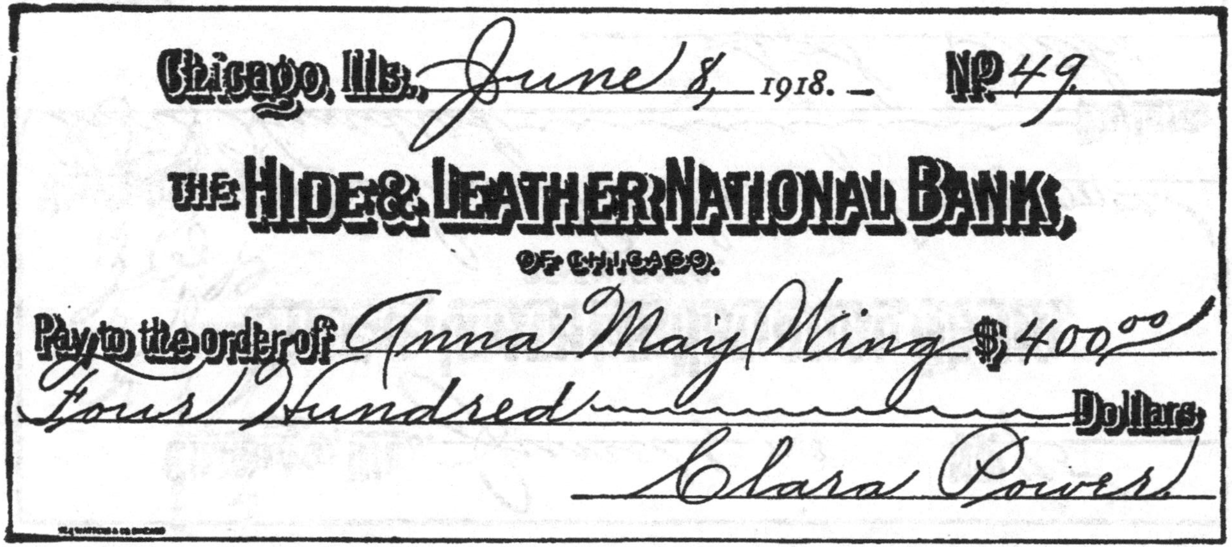
Chicago, Ills., June 8, 1918. — No. 49

THE HIDE & LEATHER NATIONAL BANK, OF CHICAGO.

Pay to the order of Anna May Wing $400.00

Four Hundred Dollars.

Clara Powers

In writing in the amount begin at the extreme left of the line. After the amount in words a running line should always be drawn, as shown in the above. If necessary to write a check for less than a dollar, as 56 cents, write "Fifty-six cents," and draw your pen through the printed word "Dollars."

A CERTIFIED CHECK.—A man may offer you a check on the bank and still have no deposit there. It is best never to accept a check from a stranger unless it is certified by the bank.

Form of Certified Check.

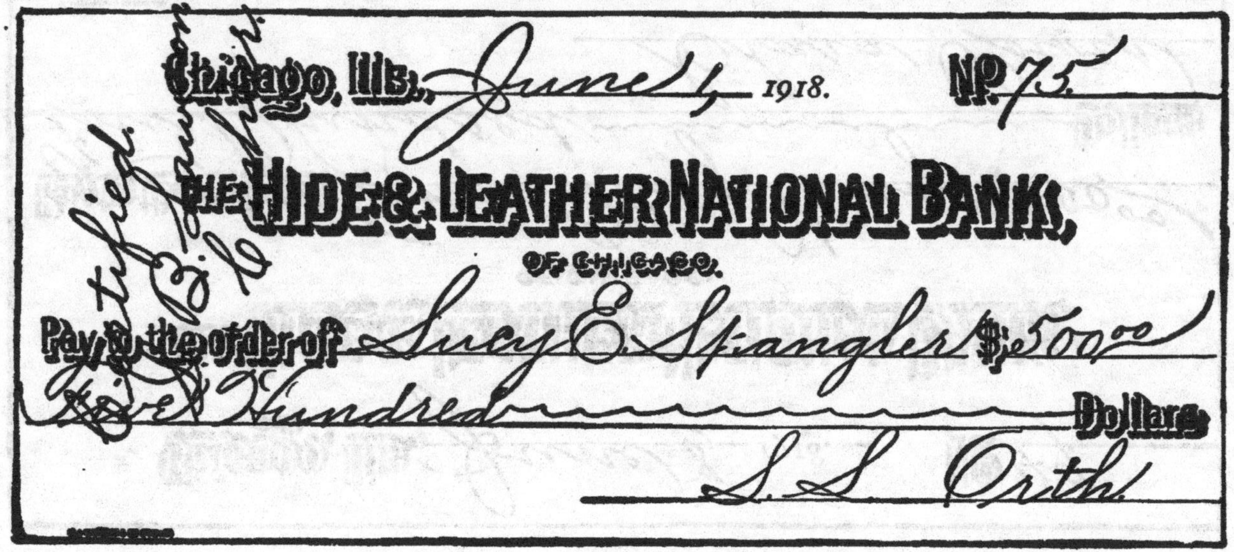

The above is a form of check sometimes used, but it is better to use the form on page 128. In this case the word "order" can easily be stricken and "bearer" written above. If the words, "Pay to order of," as on page 128, are used, the change cannot easily be made.

How to Fill Out Blank Checks, Notes, etc., and Keep the Stubs

No. 1.
Feb. 2d, 1918.
Wm. F. Barker,
for Merchandise.
$300.

300

STAMP.

No. 1. *Naperville, Ill., Feb. 2, 1918.*

National Exchange Bank,

Pay to.........Wm. F. Barker,..........or Bearer,

Three Hundred .... $\frac{00}{100}$ *Dollars.*

$300. *F. A. Maurer.*

$240.40
To *C. C. Mumm.*
For *Merchandise.*
Date *March 3, 1918.*
Time *One year.*
Due *March 3, 1919.*
No. 1.

$240.40 *Naperville, Ills., March 3, 1918.*

One year....after date....I ....promise to pay to

the order of...................C. C. Mumm,.........

Two Hundred Forty.............................. $\frac{40}{100}$ **Dollars,**

at...six per cent. interest. *Value received.*

No. 1. Due............ *H. A. Thoburn.*

HINTS AND HELPS FOR WRITING, ACCEPTING, AND TRANSFERRING ALL KINDS OF DRAFTS.

1. A draft is a written order by one person on another for the payment of a specified sum of money.

2. The one who writes the draft is called the "drawer," the one on whom it is written the "drawee," and the one to whom it is to be paid the "payee."

3. Drafts may be made payable at sight, on demand, or at a certain time after date, or after sight.

4. The person drawn upon is under no obligation to the holder of the draft unless he accepts it.

5. The usual method of writing an acceptance is, to write across the face of the draft, with red ink, the word "Accepted," following with date and signature.

6. When acceptance or payment is refused the draft is protested.

7. A protest is a formal declaration made by a notary public, under his hand and seal, at the request of the holder, for non-acceptance or non-payment, and the parties liable are formally notified.

8. Drafts are negotiable both before and after acceptance.

9. Drafts drawn at sight or on demand are not presented for acceptance, but for payment only.

10. Drafts may be drawn to one's own order, and then indorsed in favor of the party to whom they are to be sent.

11. In buying a draft at the bank, it is always best to have it made payable to yourself, and then indorse it in favor of the party to whom you intend to transfer it. This gives you a good receipt for the money.

12. A promise to accept a draft will be equivalent to an acceptance if it has given credit to the bill.

13. Should the person upon whom the draft is drawn die before it was accepted, it should be presented for acceptance to his legal representatives.

14. Any material alteration of a draft after it has been drawn or accepted makes it valueless.

15. A draft made by one bank upon another is called a bank draft.

FORMS OF DRAFTS.

There are four kinds of drafts:—Bank Draft, On-Demand Draft, Sight Draft, and Time Draft. The Bank Draft is most frequently used. An On-Demand Draft is payable at once, while a Sight Draft is allowed three days of grace in some States.

1. **Bank Draft.**

$100. State of Illinois, May 10, 1918.
The first National Bank of Naperville. Pay to the order of F. A. Lueben One Hundred Dollars.
To Union National Bank, W. L. HETZ, Cashier.
Chicago, Ill.
No. 46.

2. **On-Demand Draft.**

$100. Troy Grove, Ill., Aug. 1, 1918.
On demand pay to the order of Frank Myers at the Mendota First National Bank, One Hundred Dollars.
Value received. A. S. HUDSON.
To Charles Lerch,
Mendota, Ill.

3. **Sight Draft.**

$500. Naperville, Tenn., July 10, 1918.
At sight pay to the order of C. Parman, Five Hundred Dollars, and charge to the account of
To Jesse Lerch, H. H. ZEMMER.
Meriden, Ill.

4. **Time Draft.**

$450.30. Ottawa, Fla., July 5, 1918.
Ten days from date pay to J. L. Nichols, or order, Four Hundred Fifty 30-100 Dollars. Value received.
To Alvin Brown, C. E. LAMALE.
Ottawa, Fla.

6. **Accepted Draft.**

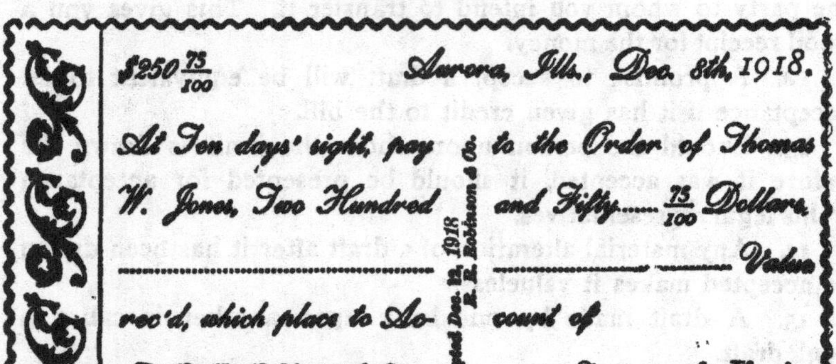
$250 75/100 Aurora, Ills., Dec. 8th, 1918.
At Ten days' sight, pay to the Order of Thomas W. Jones, Two Hundred and Fifty...... 75/100 Dollars.
.... Value rec'd, which place to Account of
To R. R. Robinson & Co., Wilmington, Del.
Samuel Kain
Accepted Dec. 18, 1918 R. R. Robinson & Co.

BILLS OF EXCHANGE.

Drafts on foreign countries are usually drawn in sets of three, each one referring to the other two, in order to prevent loss in transmission. They are sent by different routes, and the payment of one of them cancels the three.

These are used by travelers who are thereby saved the trouble and risk of carrying large amounts of money with them. The principal use, however, is by merchants engaged in foreign trade, who make all their payments through them. The following is a form:

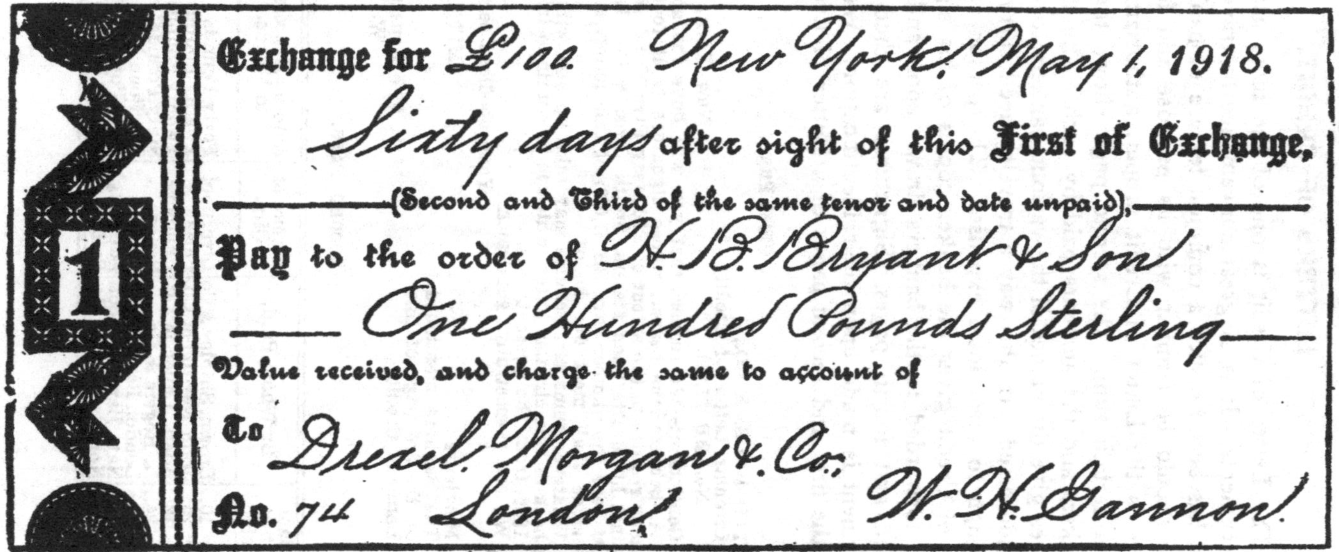

Exchange for £100. New York, May 1, 1918.

Sixty days after sight of this First of Exchange,

(Second and Third of the same tenor and date unpaid),

Pay to the order of H. B. Bryant & Son

One Hundred Pounds Sterling

Value received, and charge the same to account of

To Drexel, Morgan & Co.,

No. 74 London. W. H. Gannon.

A Foreign Draft, or Bill of Exchange.

LETTERS OF CREDIT.

The Letter of Credit is one of the most useful of banking instruments. It is of great convenience to travelers in Europe and has become such a common feature of banking that every one should be familiar with its purpose and form. The first page is the Letter of Credit proper, authorizing the payment of a certain sum. The second page shows the names of the bankers and the amounts paid by each. The third and fourth pages give the names of the various bankers to whom the letter is addressed. In this way a traveler need carry with him only enough to meet local expenses. The person receiving a Letter of Credit gives the banker copies of his signature. These are forwarded to the bankers drawn upon and named on the third and fourth pages. Signatures are then compared and payment is made upon their identification. We append forms of the first and second pages of a Letter of Credit:

First Page.

SMITH BROS. & CO.,
Circular Letter of Credit,
No. BB 27,049. New York, May 10, 1918.

Gentlemen:—We request that you will have the goodness to furnish W. A. Schutte, the bearer, whose signature is at foot, with any funds he may require to the extent of £500 (say Five Hundred Pounds Sterling) against his drafts upon Messrs. Smith Bros. & Co., London; each draft must bear the number (No. BB 27,049) of this letter, and we engage that the same shall meet due honor.

Whatever sums Mr. Schutte may take up you will please indorse on the back of this circular letter, which is to continue in force until March 15, 1919, from the present date.

We are respectfully, gentlemen,
Your obedient servants,
SMITH BROS. & CO.

To Messieurs
The Bankers mentioned
on the 3rd page of this
Letter of Credit.

The signature of
W. A. SCHUTTE.

Second Page.

Date when paid.	By Whom Paid.	Name of City.	Amount Expressed in Words.	Amount in Figures.		
July 10..	Brown, Shipley & Co	Liverpool	Forty Pounds	£40	0	0
July 25..	John Newton & Co.	Paris	Twenty Pounds	20	0	0
Aug. 12..	Koch, Lauer & Co.	Hamburg	Twenty Pounds	20	0	0
Aug. 24..	L. Rogers & Co.	Geneva	Sixty Pounds	60	0	0
Sept. 1...	London Banking Co.	London	Ten Pounds	10	0	0
Sept. 10..	Nat. Bank of Scot.	Edinburgh	Fifty Pounds	50	0	0
Sept. 24..	North'n Bank'g Co.	Belfast	Twenty Pounds	20	0	0

THE CLEARING-HOUSE SYSTEM.

Almost every business and professional man in the country keeps all the money which he does not need for casual personal expenses on deposit in a bank; he pays nearly all his bills by means of checks; and consequently he receives payments for the most part in checks drawn by those who owed him; he does not, on receiving a check, go or send to the bank to procure the money, but deposits it to his credit in his own bank; and there are many banks in every large city.

Now a wholesale merchant may receive each day a large number of checks, some on one bank, some on another. Of course his own bank, in which he deposits these checks, properly endorsed, desires to collect the money upon them at once, because its profits are made by lending at interest the money entrusted to it by depositors.

But in a city where there are twenty or forty or more banks, it would be a great waste of time and labor, besides being hazardous, for each one to send around a messenger to each bank to collect what is due. To avoid this the clearing-house has been devised.

At a certain hour on every business day a messenger from each bank goes to "the clearing," carrying all the checks against any and every other bank in the city taken during the previous twenty-four hours. The checks are made up into separate packages, and each has a statement of the aggregate amount due from the bank.

All the rest is a mere matter of addition and subtraction, which is done by the clearing-house clerks. The First National Bank has brought in checks against other banks to the amount of fifty thousand dollars; other banks have brought in checks against the First National to the amount of fifty-one thousand dollars. Then the First National is debtor to the clearing-house in the sum of one thousand dollars.

Other banks are creditors. Of course the debits and credits balance each other to a cent. The debtor banks must immediately pay, in money, whatever they each owe to the clearing-house; the whole sum is at once divided among the creditor banks, and the "clearing" is over.

Thus the claims by each bank against every other bank

in the city have been adjusted at very little expense of time and labor, and with the use of a small amount of actual money. The checks and drafts settled are called "exchanges," and the money necessary to complete the settlement is the "balance."

London originated the clearing-house. In times of money panics the clearing-house has been of great service to banks and communities. In good years the exchanges at the New York clearing-house reach nearly forty thousand million dollars a year, or about one hundred and twenty-five millions on every bank day. These vast accounts are settled by the shifting about, from day to day, of not more than ten million dollars.

This shows what an immense saving in the use of money the clearing-house makes. The principle is applied to other things besides banking. At New York and also at Boston the brokers have a stock clearing-house. Certificates of stock take the place of checks. The broker who has bought five thousand shares and sold four thousand of "Northwest" receives one thousand shares from the clearing-house and pays the money balance due on all his transactions.

But although the clearing-house principle is capable of wide application, it is chiefly employed in the bankers' clearing-houses of this country to the number of about sixty in the chief cities from Maine to Washington.

CLEARING-HOUSE MANAGEMENT.

In a clearing-house where a very slight error may postpone the settlement of all the banks of the city, it is necessary that the rules be strict and rigidly enforced. The clerks employed are experts in their work. Disorderly conduct and errors are subject to a fine. A committee is empowered to remove any one when the interests of the Association require it. Should any bank fail to pay the balance due from it at the proper hour, the balances due must be paid by the remaining banks in proportion to the respective balances against the defaulting bank.

DEPOSITING CHECKS.

A business man, receiving a check in the course of trade, seldom thinks of sending it to the bank on which it is drawn, but deposits it in the bank with which he keeps his account.

FEDERAL TAXES

Estimated Expenditures for Certain Articles Upon Which Federal Taxes Are Now Levied.

Admissions and dues	$ 800,000,000
Art works	15,000,000
Automobiles and parts	2,000,000,000
Candy	1,000,000,000
Cakes, confections, etc.	350,000,000
Carpets, rugs, and wearing apparel (on excesses over stated prices)	1,500,000,000
Cereal beverages	230,000,000
Chewing gum	50,000,000
Cigar and cigaret holders	1,000,000
Cigarets	800,000,000
Cigars	510,000,000
Electric fans, portable	8,000,000
Firearms and shells	50,000,000
Fur articles	300,000,000
Hunting and shooting garments	7,000,000
Ice cream	250,000,000
Jewelry	500,000,000
Liveries	3,000,000
Luxuries in hotels and restaurants	750,000,000
Luxurious food, etc.	5,000,000,000
Luxurious services	3,000,000,000
Other luxuries—joy-riding, pleasure resorts, races, etc.	3,000,000,000
Perfumery and cosmetics	750,000,000
Pianos, organs, victrolas, etc.	250,000,000
Soft drinks, including ice cream and soda	350,000,000
Sporting goods	25,000,000
Tobacco and snuff	800,000,000
Toilet soaps, etc.	400,000,000
Yachts	1,000,000
Total estimated expenditures	$22,700,000,000

PRACTICAL INFORMATION FOR BUSINESS MEN.

TRANSFERRING COMMERCIAL PAPERS.

1. A Legal Transfer.—A legal transfer of commercial paper is usually made before it matures, and the law protects the innocent holder of it in his possession. Even if he buys it from the thief who stole it, or from the party who found it or got it by fraud, it belongs to him, if he knew nothing of the illegal transactions and acted without knowledge of the theft or fraud.

2. Usual Form.—Paper is usually transferred by indorsement (the seller placing his name on the back of the note or bill). Thus the indorser agrees to pay the amount if the maker does not, and he is therefore responsible, if properly notified when the paper is due and is not paid.

3. Blank Indorsement.—A blank indorsement most commonly used in business is simply writing the name on the back of the note or bill, and after the first indorsement it may be transferred by delivery the same as a government bond or bank bill.

4. Peculiar Sacredness of Commercial Paper.—The law protects the holder of negotiable paper in his possession of it, when it would not protect him in the possession of any other kind of property, for there is a peculiar sacredness attached to paper. Thus: If A had stolen a horse from B and sold it to C, the law would not protect C, but would allow B to take the horse. Whereas in case of a note, the law would protect C in his ownership of the note and he could hold the maker for the amount, if C was innocent and knew nothing of the way in which A got possession of the note.

5. The Purchaser.—If the purchaser is aware that there are any defects about a note or bill, or if there is anything suspicious, he buys it at his own risk.

6. Transferring Found or Stolen Paper.—Should A lose his note for $300 and B find it, the latter could not compel A to pay it, unless he could prove that he came fairly into possession of it. No thief could collect a note himself which he had stolen if the fact of this theft could be proved, but if the note had a blank indorsement on the back of it, he could transfer or sell the note to an innocent party who could collect the note if he can show he made the purchase in good faith.

7. **Void Paper.**—Paper void where made is everywhere void. Even in case of void paper, a party who indorses it over to an innocent holder would be bound by his indorsement, because he made a new contract to pay it when he indorsed it.

8. **Indorsement of a Note Before it is Made.**—When a party indorses a note before it is made, and it is afterwards made for a larger amount than was agreed, he cannot escape his liability to an innocent holder by pleading that fact. The rule is the same when a party accepts a blank draft.

9. **Avoiding Liability.**—An indorser can avoid liability by writing the words "without recourse," or, "without recourse to me." He can also specify what use is to be made of the funds when the paper is made, as for instance: "Pay Irving Taylor, or order, for credit of my account."

10. **After Maturity.**—Paper can be transferred after maturity and usually no difficulty will arise over it, but the maker of the note may make any defense against the assignee possible had the note not been transferred.

11. **An Innocent Holder.**—An innocent holder of paper, having paid value for it before maturity, can hold both the maker and indorser responsible for payment.

12. **General Rule.**—In the transfer of commercial paper the indorser is held equally responsible for payment with the maker, and it is a safe rule to require the indorsement of the party who holds the paper before accepting it. An indorser who has paid a note can afterwards sell it. In the case of accommodation paper, however, when the payee has once paid it the paper is canceled, and cannot again be transferred so as to give the holder a right of action against any one, except the party who paid and then transferred it.

DEMAND OF PAYMENT.

1. **Time and Place.**—Demand should always be made at the proper time and place. If the name of a bank or any other place is mentioned in the paper, it should be made there.

2. **Insolvency.**—If the debtor is bankrupt, it is no reason why a demand should not be made on him.

3. **In Person.** Demand must be made in person, and it cannot legally be made by mail.

4. **Possession of Paper.**—The party making the demand must have possession of the paper, for the debtor can insist on having it delivered to him when paid.

5. **Lost Paper.**—In case the paper is lost, a bond of indemnity must be made and tendered to the debtor, as protection in case it is ever found.

6. **Refused Payment.**—If demand is legally made and it is refused, the paper must be protested and the proper parties notified. This is usually the work of a notary public.

THE CREDIT SYSTEM—ADVANTAGES AND DISADVANTAGES.

1. There are many good reasons why people should pay cash for everything purchased. Hopeful people will always buy more freely if they can get it on credit, and are never anxious for pay day to come around.

2. Remember that those who sell on credit must charge from 10 to 15 per cent. more for goods in order to cover the interest and risks. It has been found that from 7 to 10 per cent. of trusted out accounts become worthless.

3. It is always uncertain which of the trusted persons will fail to pay his account, and consequently all persons buying on credit have to share the extra prices, in order to meet the losses which all business men sustain that do a credit business.

4. Remember, the man who can pay cash for goods, or whatever purchases he may make, can always secure a better bargain than the man who buys on credit. It therefore would be a great saving if every one could manage, by rigid economy, if necessary, to pay cash for everything he buys.

5. Persons who buy real estate, or merchants who buy large quantities of goods, may often find it necessary to buy on credit. Many of our wealthiest farmers and business men made their money largely in having the benefit of credit, but, at the same time, if cash could be paid for everything purchased, whether real estate or other articles, it would be a great saving to the purchaser.

6. Keep your word as good as a bank and you will always have credit when you desire it, and friends when you need them.

"HIS BURDEN OF DEBT HE BORE TO THE GRAVE."

HOW TO COLLECT DEBTS.

While most debts are paid voluntarily, yet many men have been ruined by the failures of others to pay their debts. This suggests caution on the part of all who give credit or make loans. The earnings of a life time may soon be swallowed up by unworthy and dishonest creditors.

1. Settlement. It is, however, necessary to extend credit to others, and with the greatest of precaution those who can not or will not pay their debts sometimes become our debtors. When this is the case the best method is to attempt an adjustment by mutual agreement. If your debtor is honest and still by some unfortunate circumstance is unable to pay his debts, it is best to treat him with respect and kindness. The law of kindness has affected the payment of many debts where legal measures would have wholly failed. Every effort possible should be made to effect a settlement by mutual agreement. Rather suffer and lose what may belong to you than seek an adjustment by law.

2. **Expense.**—Litigation is always expensive and also uncertain. Avoid it if possible. Settle without consulting a lawyer if possible. Go to law as a last resort.

3. **Collection.**—If it is impossible for you to secure a settlement, then, if the case demands, it may be necessary to place the account with a lawyer for collection.

4. **Arrest.**—The arrest of the debtor can only be made to secure the person of the debtor (or defendant) while the suit for debt is pending, or to force him to give security for his appearance after judgment, but in some States no arrests are allowed, except in criminal cases.

5. **Attachment.**—This is a writ issued by the Justice of the Peace or Judge, or some other officer having jurisdiction, commanding the sheriff or constable to attach the property of the debtor, to satisfy the demands of the creditor. This writ may be issued at the beginning or during the suit. In some States, Alabama, Illinois, Louisiana, Mississippi, Missouri and others, the debtor may retain possession of the property and give a bond as a guaranty that the property will be held for the debt in case he is defeated in the suit. All attachments lose their validity in case the debtor (or defendant) wins the suit.

6. **Judgment and Execution.**—A suit is ended by the courts giving a judgment, either in favor of the debtor or the creditor. If the judgment is in favor of the plaintiff and the defendant refuses to pay the amount of the judgment, an execution is issued by the court which commands the sheriff to take sufficient property of the defendant, if it can be found, to satisfy the judgment. The sheriff may also seize the person of the defendant and imprison him until he pays judgment or the same is discharged by judicial decision of insolvency. Real estate, however, cannot be sold on execution in some States, unless a jury should find that the profits in rents, etc., will not pay the judgment within the limit of seven years, or some other time fixed by law.

7. **Garnishment.** After judgment has been rendered, the money or goods due the defendant, if in the hands of a third person, may be attached to pay the plaintiff. The person in whose hands the money or goods attached are, is known in law as the garnishee or trustee.

HOW TO OBTAIN WEALTH.

It matters not what a man's income is, reckless extravagance and waste will sooner or later bring him to ruin. The average young man of today when he begins to earn is soon inclined to habits of extravagance and wastefulness. The five, ten or fifteen cents a day that is squandered, while a mere trifle apparently, if saved, would in a few years amount to thousands of dollars and go far towards establishing the foundation of a future career. In order to acquire the dollars one must take care of the dimes and nickels. It is not what a man earns but what he saves that makes him rich. John Jacob Astor said that the saving of the first thousand dollars cost him the hardest struggle. It is the duty of every young man to begin to save from the moment he commences to earn, be it ever so little. This habit will not only aid in acquiring wealth, but will give a fitness for larger duties. He who is not able to manage a small income is not competent to have charge of a larger one.

The way to make money is to save it. Always remember and practice the maxim, "A dollar saved, a dollar earned."

A small sum of money saved daily for fifty years will grow at the following rate:

Daily Savings.

One Cent	$ 950	Fifty Cents	$47,520
Ten Cents	9,504	Sixty Cents	57,024
Twenty Cents	19,006	Seventy Cents	66,528
Thirty Cents	28,515	Eighty Cents	76,032
Forty Cents	38,015	Ninety Cents	85,537

One Dollar $95,040

HOW TO MAKE CHANGE QUICKLY.

1. Consider the amount of the purchase as money already counted out; for example, if the purchase amounts to 46 cents, and you are handed a $2.00 bill in payment, count out 4 cents to make it 50 cents, then count out the other $1.50.

2. Should the purchase amount to $2.54, and you are handed $10.00, count out 46 cents to make it $3.00, then count out even dollars to make the $10.00, and your change is correct.

3. Always count your change after receiving, and see that it is correct.

"MY SON, YOU SHALL HAVE A HOME WHILE I LIVE. BUT I CANNOT DEED YOU MY FARM; IT IS ALL I HAVE TO SUPPORT ME IN MY OLD AGE."

DO NOT GIVE AWAY YOUR PROPERTY IN OLD AGE.

Many persons, as they advance in years, make the fatal mistake of giving away their property to children and then depend upon them for support.

How many old persons have gone to their graves broken-hearted and suffering for the necessaries of life, because they desired to help their children, and gave them their property.

If the weight of years becomes heavy and there is plenty of property, a portion may be safely divided among the children, but the major portion should always be held and controlled directly or indirectly by the old couple.

1. It will insure good care and plenty of the necessaries of life

2. The devotion and love of children will never grow cold while there is something in store for them.

It was the writer's experience in his boyhood to board in a family where the father in his old age had bequeathed his entire property to his children. When the same was divided between them their aged father became a burden, and he was sent from daughter to son, as they had all obligated themselves to care in turn for their aged father. But he never entered the home of a son or daughter, where he was a welcome guest. In the family, where the writer boarded, where the aged father was then, if there was a cup of coffee short in the morning, it was the old man's cup that was not filled; if meat or other food was short, it was the old man's plate that indicated the shortage; if the pie was somewhat deficient, it was the old man's piece that was cut in two, and he was compelled to sleep in a cold garret at night, alone and deserted, and when the broken-hearted old man passed away, no doubt every child felt delight instead of sorrow in his heart.

Every man should make a will in favor of his wife, so that in her old age she shall not become dependent.

TEACHING BUSINESS TO WIVES AND DAUGHTERS.

Women are too frequently ridiculed because of their ignorance of business matters. How can they understand business and business methods, if they have never had an opportunity to learn and transact business? Every husband should teach his wife some of the more important ways of business. He should interest her in his financial affairs, and show her some of the business forms and business documents which form a part of his business transactions. It is a great advantage for a wife to be familiar with her husband's business, as she is liable to be called upon at any time to settle his estate.

How many burdens are annually thrust upon widows, and at what a disadvantage they are in managing the business affairs of the family! Then why not make the path straighter and smoother by beginning now, by teaching your wives and daughters practical business methods?

For family instruction we would suggest the following rules:

1. Assist your wife or daughter in drawing up notes, and

teach her not only the correct form, but give her some of the laws bearing upon the legal relations of both debtor and creditor.

2. Make various indorsements upon the notes which have been thus written for copy. Write a note for each indorsement and explain it. This is a very easy and simple lesson and can be mastered in a very few evenings.

3. Teach the forms of receipts. Write receipts for rent, for money paid on account, for money to be paid a third party, etc. This will be found a very interesting exercise.

4. Checks and drafts will form the same interesting exercise.

5. The next step will be to secure a few blank forms of notes, checks, drafts, deeds, leases, etc., and any husband will be surprised what progress his wife will make in a few lessons in filling out these business documents.

6. If you carry out this plan your wife or daughter will become interested in your business, and will understand the different forms of paper and will soon be able to give you considerable assistance as well as safe counsel.

HOW TO TEACH BUSINESS TO CHILDREN.

Give your sons and daughters some familiarity with the customs of the business world. Let them learn while young how to transact the ordinary forms of business. It is probably best to give them opportunities for earning a little money and try to teach them its value in disposing of same.

It is best to buy them a little account book, and make them have an account of all the money they receive, and the disposition they make of it. Teach them how to make such entries, and always insist upon their keeping a correct record of all the money they receive, and upon giving an account of the money they pay out, always showing a correct, itemized account.

In this way they may receive a degree of benefit which will insure their business success during life. This learned early in life will always produce an abiding and substantial benefit, and no doubt give birth to many practical ideas of business.

POINTS OF LAW AND LEGAL FORMS.

It must be admitted that legal and business forms, together with the important points of law on these subjects, are essential and should be in the reach of all. A knowledge of these rules and principles would prevent many mistakes and losses. The following pages contain all the principal and important forms ordinarily in use in business.

AFFIDAVITS.

An affidavit is an oath or affirmation made in writing, sworn to or affirmed, before an officer empowered to administer the same. Affidavits are not testimony in courts of law, because the makers are not cross-examined; but a false affiant may be punished for perjury.

The following is a common form, and with certain modifications can be made to apply to almost any case:

Common Form of Affidavit.

STATE OF ILLINOIS, }
COUNTY OF HENRY, } ss.

John Jones being duly sworn on his oath states that he is well acquainted with the handwriting of Daniel Seitz, one of the subscribing witnesses to the deed hereto attached; that affiant has frequently seen him write and knows his signature; that he believes that the name of the said Daniel Seitz, signed in the said deed, is in the handwriting of the said Daniel Seitz, and further affiant says not.

Subscribed and sworn to before me this 28th day of February, A. D. 1918,
E. M. SCHWARTZ,
Notary Public.
(Signed) JOHN JONES.

A Form attached to a Declaration of any kind.

STATE OF ILLINOIS. }
COUNTY OF COOK. } ss.
Chicago, Nov. 10, 1918

The above named John Saylor personally appeared before me and made oath that the following declaration by him subscribed is true.

L. B. LAWSON, Justice of the Peace.

HOW TO SETTLE DIFFICULTIES BY ARBITRATION.

Arbitration is an agreement by parties who have a controversy or difference to submit the question to the decision of a third party instead of appealing to law.

Arbitration is one of the highest courts for the settlement of personal differences, and if people would only learn more of its benefits and advantages, lawyers by the thousands would not thrive and fatten upon the earnings of those who could make better use of their money.

When the matters in difference are simply those of fact, it is often more satisfactory to submit them to the decision of mutual friends, each contending party choosing one, and the two arbitrators thus chosen, choosing the third, and the three parties thus chosen constituting the court.

The decision of the arbitrators is called an award.

The award should be specific and distinct, containing the decision of the arbitrators in as clear and concise language as possible.

Form of Submission to Arbitration.

KNOW ALL MEN, That we, the undersigned, hereby mutually agree to submit all questions and claims between us (or a specific claim or question) to the determination and award of (here name the arbitrators), whose decision and award shall be final and binding on us. In case of disagreement, the decision and award of a majority of said arbitrators shall be final and conclusive. The said arbitrators shall make their award in writing on or before July 10, 19 .

Done at Aurora, Ill., June 4, 19

JOHN GLOVER, P. C. JONES,	} Witnesses.	THOMAS ELLIS, J. C. TETER,

Form of Arbitrator's Oath.

The following oath should be taken by the persons chosen to act as arbitrators or referees before entering upon the examination of the matters in dispute: We, the undersigned arbitrators, appointed by and between Henry Smith and Richard Brown, do swear fairly and faithfully to hear and examine the matters in controversy between said Henry Smith and Richard Brown, and to make a just award, according to the best of our understanding.

Sworn to this 26th day of May, A. D. 19 , before me.
D. B. GIVELER,
Justice of the Peace.

P. D. CRIMMINS,
J. O. EVERETT,
O. M. POWERS.

Oath.

To be administered to a witness by the arbitrators: You do solemnly swear, that the evidence you shall give to the arbitrators here present in a certain controversy submitted to them by and between Henry Smith and Richard Brown, shall be the truth, and nothing but the truth, so help you God.

ARBITRATION PREFERABLE TO LITIGATION.

Arbitration is always preferable to litigation. It is not only the easiest, quickest and cheapest way to settle disagreements, but saves much vexation and subsequent dissension. Were individuals, corporations and nations to arrange their disputes by arbitration, instead of resorting to litigation and warfare, the people would be saved millions of treasure, and the world spared much shedding of blood. A peaceful settlement of difficulties is usually followed by prosperity, while "going to law" or war usually results in loss and suffering to both contestants. Indeed, litigation and warfare are twin relics of the dark ages, and so long as they continue in vogue we may look in vain for harbingers of the promised millennium. Of all classes, farmers should, so far as possible, avoid entering into litigation; for whether they win or lose, they are proverbially worsted, the lawyers usually taking the cream, and leaving only the skim-milk for the winning contestant. Truly, there is neither glory nor honor, profit nor pleasure in litigation, and the less people who profess to live "on the square," and according to the Commandments, have to do therewith, the better it will be for both their present and future peace and prosperity. Even in the most aggravating case of trespass, and the like, no good citizen should resort to the law, until all amicable attempts at settlement have failed. Indeed, and finally, whatever may be the provocation, don't get mad and impulsively prosecute your neighbor, but keep your temper.

HON. WILLIAM McKINLEY, THIRD MARTYRED PRESIDENT.

HOW TO DO BUSINESS WITH AN AGENT.

1. Agency.—Agency is one of the most important relations which exist in the transaction of the ordinary business affairs of life.

2. Implied Agency.—Agency may be implied from previous dealing and transaction between the parties. If the principal has held a person out as an agent he will be bound by his acts, even though as a matter of fact the agent had no authority to represent him.

3. Agents.—An agent is defined to be one who is authorized to represent another, who is called the principal, and when so authorized acts for and in the place and stead of the principal. A man may do through his agent whatever he may lawfully do for himself. Persons not of age, married women and aliens may act as agents for others. Factors, brokers, attorneys, etc., are but agents in a business sense. The acts of the agent, if exercised within the powers delegated, bind the principal and become the latter's acts and deeds, but the agent's authority may be revoked by the principal at any time. Authority given to two persons must be executed by both to be binding on the principal.

4. **Special Agent.**—A special agent is one authorized to do one or more special things in pursuance of particular instructions, or within restrictions necessarily implied from the act to be done.

5. **General Agent.**—A general agent is one authorized to transact all his principal's business, or all his business of some particular kind, or at some particular place. If an agency is proved without its extent being shown, it will be presumed to be a general agency. The acts of a general agent will bind the principal, even though he had no authority to do them, provided he acts in the general scope of the business which he was authorized to transact.

6. **Authority of Agent.**—If a special agent exceeds his authority, the principal is not bound, but if a general agent exceeds his authority the principal is bound, provided the agent acted within the ordinary and usual scope of the business he was authorized to transact, and the party dealing with him did not know he was exceeding his authority.

7. **Authority, How Given.**—The authority of an agent may be constituted in three ways: By deed under seal, by writing, or by mere word. Express authority is given to an agent by what is called a power of attorney. If the authority is to execute a writing under seal and acknowledged, the power of attorney must be likewise under seal and acknowledged. An agent to sell land, or to do any important business, where he is required to make contracts, draw or sign notes, drafts or checks, should be appointed by "power of attorney."

8. **Agent's Acts Ratified.**—The acts or contracts of an agent made beyond the scope of his authority may be ratified by the principal, and when so ratified are binding on the latter.

9. **Agent's Responsibility.**—An agent concealing his principal is himself responsible, and if acting fraudulently or

deceitfully is himself responsible to third parties. He cannot appoint a substitute or delegate his authority to another, **without consent of his principal. If an agent embezzles his principal's property it may be reclaimed if it can be identified or distinctly traced.**

10. Agent Restricted.—An agent employed to sell property cannot buy it himself, or if employed to purchase property, cannot buy from himself.

11. Principal's Liability.—The principal is liable to the third person for the negligence or unskillfulness of the agent, when he is acting in the fulfillment of the agency business. The principal is liable for all acts of his agent within the scope of his agency, but money paid by an agent can be recovered by the principal, if it has been paid by mistake. The knowledge of the agent relating to the business of the agency is binding upon the principal, and notice to an agent as to matters relating to the agency is notice to the principal.

12. Authority May Be Revoked.—The authority of an agent may be determined: First, by the express revocation thereof by the principal. Second, by renunciation of such power by the agent. Third, by the death of the principal, which also revokes the agency. Fourth, by the expiration of the time within which the agent was to perform the acts which were to be done by him, or by him, having completed and fully performed the commission and closed the business which he was to transact. Fifth, by the sale of the subject matter of the agency.

13. Revocation Takes Effect When.—A revocation of authority takes effect, so far as the agent is concerned, when he receives notice thereof; so far as third persons are concerned, when they receive notice of such revocation. Personal notice or its equivalent is required, and is sufficient to those who have dealt with the agent. Advertising the fact would be sufficient as to all others. Without a sufficient notice of the revocation, a contract made in good faith with the agent after revocation will bind the principal the same as before.

14. **Caution.**—Persons dealing with agents who are strangers should be very careful to ascertain that the agent has authority to transact the business in hand. In all trans-

actions in regard to real estate the authority of the agent should be in writing, signed by the owner of the property, in order to be binding upon him. In all cases of doubt as to the authority of an agent or the extent of his authority, it would be wise to require of the agent a written proof of his agency and the extent of his authority.

15. Power of Attorney.—To delegate to an agent the power to sign notes, checks, and other legal documents, as well as to transact any business where such documents are necessary, is called power of attorney—that is, the power to be attorney for you. Such power or authority should be given in writing. It should be witnessed to and should state clearly what the attorney has power to do.

Power of Attorney, General Form.

KNOW ALL MEN BY THESE PRESENTS, That I, James L. Binton, of Naperville, County of Du Page, and State of Illinois, have made, constituted and appointed, and BY THESE PRESENTS do make, constitute and appoint, Chas. A. Lerch true and lawful attorney for me and in my name, place and stead, [here state the purpose for which the power is given], giving and granting unto my said attorney full power and authority to do and perform all and every act and thing whatsoever, requisite and necessary to be done in and about the premises, as fully, to all intents and purposes, as I might or could do if personally present, with all power of substitution and revocation, hereby ratifying and confirming all that my said attorney or his substitute shall lawfully do or cause to be done by virtue thereof.

IN WITNESS WHEREOF, I have hereunto set my hand and seal the 2nd day of January, one thousand nine hundred.

Signed, Sealed and Delivered in Presence of } JAMES L. BINTON. (Seal.)

....

To be properly acknowledged before an officer, the same as a deed, according to the law of the State.

Proxy or Power of Attorney to Vote.

Know all men by these presents: That I, David E. Hughes, do hereby constitute and appoint C. A. Brown my true and lawful attorney, for me and in my name, place and stead, to vote as my proxy and representative at the..........................meeting of the stockholders of the......................................, a corporation, and at any adjournment of said meeting, all of the..............shares of the capital stock of said corporation standing on the books of said corporation, as fully and amply as I could or might do were I personally present; with full power of substitution and revocation.

Witness my hand and seal at Aurora, Illinois, this 26th day of June, A. D. 1900. E. R. ZEMMER. (Seal.)

N. B. A seal is an impression, or writing (seal), placed at the right of signature confirming authority of same.

Revoking of Power of Attorney.

Whereas, I, Sylvester Jones of Aurora, County of Kane, and State of Illinois, did on the tenth day of June, 1901, by my letter or power of attorney appoint John C. Cook of Chicago my true and lawful attorney, for me and in my name to [here state in precise language what he was authorized to do] as by the said power of attorney, reference thereunto being had, will fully appear;

Therefore, know all men by these presents, That I, Sylvester Jones, aforesaid, have revoked and recalled the said letter of attorney, and by these presents do revoke and recall all power and authority thereby given to the said John C. Cook.

Given this tenth day of October, 1902.

Signed and sealed in presence of............................ SYLVESTER JONES. (Seal.)

16. **Brokers** are agents who buy and sell real estate, notes, stock, bonds, mortgages, etc., or who make contracts for their principals and in their names. They are often employed to transact business or to negotiate bargains between different individuals. Their attention being given to one class of business, they acquire a knowledge and skill that an average merchant does not possess. It is often advantageous for large firms to employ brokers to buy their raw material. In our large cities brokers in anything and everything that is bought and sold in large quantities are extensively employed.

17. **Commission Merchants** are agents in large cities who sell goods on commission for fruit raisers, farmers, and manufacturers.

APPRENTICESHIP.

1. **Definition.**—This is a contract by which one person who understands some art, trade, or business, and who is called the master, undertakes to teach the same to another person, a minor, who is called an apprentice. The latter is bound to serve the master during the period fixed by the contract in such art, trade, or business. This method of binding minors out for the purpose of learning different trades and callings was formerly very common, but late years, and particularly in the United States, it has fallen into disuse, and is a form of contract very seldom used.

2. **Duties of the Master.**—To instruct the apprentice in the art or trade which he has undertaken to teach him. It is his duty also to watch over his conduct, giving him prudent advice, setting him a good example, and virtually exer-

cising over him the rights, duties, and obligations of the parent. He had no right to dismiss the apprentice except by consent of all the parties, or to remove him from the State unless such removal was authorized in the contract.

3. Duties of Apprentice.—He is bound to obey his master in all lawful commands, to take care of his property, to endeavor to the best of his ability to learn the trade, business or occupation to which he was apprenticed, and to perform all the covenants contained in his contract. He was originally required to assent to the contract by signing the same.

Form.

This indenture made this 14th day of July, 1901, between John Smith of the city of Naperville, County of Du Page, and State of Illinois, party of the first part, with whom joins George Smith, minor, son of said John Smith, for the purpose of showing his assent to this article of agreement, and Charles Jones of the same place, party of the second part, Witnesseth: That the said party of the first part does hereby bind and apprentice unto the party of the second part the said George Smith, age 10 years, for and during and until the said George Smith shall attain to the age of sixteen years to learn the art and trade of a barber; and the said party of the first part hereby covenants and agrees that the said George Smith shall faithfully serve the said party of the second part and that he shall obey all the lawful commands of the said party of the second part and preserve and care for his property and use all diligence to learn the said art and trade of a barber for and during the term aforesaid; that he will not use intoxicating liquors or tobacco in any of its forms during the said term, and shall in all things properly conduct himself. And the said party of the second part hereby agrees that he will teach and instruct the said George Smith in said art and trade; that he will during the term of his apprenticeship furnish him with board and lodging and suitable clothing, washing, medicine, and other necessaries suitable to the condition of life of said minor; that he will teach or cause to be taught to the said George Smith reading and writing and the ground rules of arithmetic; and also that he will at the expiration of said term give to said apprentice a new Bible, two complete new suits of wearing apparel suitable to his condition in life and twenty dollars in money.

In testimony whereof the parties hereto have hereunto set their hands and seals the day and year above written; and the said George Smith has signed these premises for the purpose of showing his assent thereto.

JOHN SMITH. (Seal.)
CHARLES JONES. (Seal.)
GEORGE SMITH.

4. Dissolution.—The articles of apprenticeship may be canceled by the mutual consent and agreement of all the parties. The better way would be to have such cancellation made in writing. Any form of contract clearly showing the intentions of the parties to dissolve the articles of agreement, and signed by the parties to the original contract, would be sufficient. The contract of dissolution might well be written on the back of original contract.

AGREEMENTS AND CONTRACTS.

1. A contract is a mutual agreement between two competent parties for a valuable consideration to do or not to do a particular thing.

2. It must have, 1. Parties; 2. Subject Matter; 3. Consideration; 4. Assent of the parties. There cannot be a contract when any of these are wanting.

IT TAKES TWO TO MAKE A CONTRACT.

HOW TO WRITE A CONTRACT.

1. The parties to a contract are taken in the order in which they are written and referred to as "the party of the first part," "the party of the second part," without repeating their names. It matters not which name is written first.

2. After writing the date, names of the parties and their places of residence, state fully all that the first party agrees to do, and then state all that the second party agrees to do.

3. Next state the penalties or forfeitures in case either party does not faithfully and fully perform, or offer to perform, his part of the agreement.

4. Finally, the closing clause, the signatures and seals, the signatures of witnesses are written. (A seal is simply the mark of a pen around the word "seal," written after the signature.)

5. No particular form of legal language is necessary. Use your own words and state in a plain way just what you want done. Any one who can write a letter and express his desire in an intelligent manner can write a contract.

6. Errors in grammar or spelling do not affect the legality of the agreement.

7. If the language should be obscure on certain points, the "court" will always interpret the intent of the parties, when they entered into the agreement, provided the intent can be gathered from the terms of the instrument itself.

8. When an agreement is written it must all be in writing. It cannot be partly written and partly oral.

THE VITAL PART OF A CONTRACT—CONSIDERATION.

1. **Definition.**—A consideration is the thing which induces parties to make a contract. It is the substantial cause or reason moving parties to enter into an agreement.

2. **A Sufficient Consideration.**—The law does not require that the consideration should be a good or bad bargain. As long as something is done or suffered by either party, the consideration is good. The smallest consideration is sufficient to make it legal. The value of the consideration is unimportant. For instance: $10,000 worth of property can be sold for $1.

3. **Promise of Marriage.**—If a man promises a woman any certain sum of money if she would agree to marry him, he can be made to fulfill his promise, and the court will hold that the promise of marriage was a sufficient consideration for the money. Marriage contracts may be entered into under age.

4. **A Valuable Consideration.**—A valuable consideration is one which is equal to money or may be changed into money.

5. **A Good Consideration.**—A good consideration is one which is based upon love, gratitude or esteem, or blood relationship. But in order to make a good consideration legal, the agreement has to be performed by one or both parties. For instance: If a man should promise to give a lady $500 because he loved her, it could not be collected, but if the money was once paid to the woman it could not be recovered.

6. **Gratuitous Consideration.**—A gratuitous consideration is a consideration where something is done or money promised on account of some affection or charity, and like a good consideration the act must be performed in order to hold the party. For instance: If a father gives his son a note

on account of his affection for him, the son cannot force the father to pay it; so also if a person subscribes for a church or charitable society he cannot be compelled to pay it, unless the church or charitable society can show that it depended upon that money when it entered upon some contract, or assumed some obligation on account of it.

7. **Immoral Consideration.**—All considerations which are immoral are consequently illegal.

8. **Impossible Consideration.**—If a man should promise to cross the ocean in one day, or walk from Philadelphia to New York in two hours or any consideration of such an impossible character, is illegal and void.

THE LAW GOVERNING ALL KINDS OF CONTRACTS.

1. An alteration of a contract in a material part, after its execution, renders it void.

2. A contract made by a minor, a lunatic, or an idiot is not binding upon him, yet he can hold the party with whom he contracts, to all the conditions of the contract.

3. A fraudulent contract may be binding on the party guilty of fraud, although not laying any obligation on the part of the party acting in good faith.

4. A contract for the sale or purchase of personal property over a certain amount—ranging from $30 to $100 in the different States—must be in writing.

5. A contract which cannot be performed within a year must be in writing.

6. If no time of payment is stated in the contract, payment must be made on the delivery of the goods.

7. A contract totally restraining the exercise of a man's trade or profession is void, but one restraining him in any particular place is not void.

8. An offer or proposal, which includes the essential parts of a contract, becomes a contract as soon as accepted.

9. A contract required by law to be in writing cannot be dissolved by verbal agreement.

10. A contract cannot be partly written and partly verbal. It must be wholly written or wholly verbal.

11. A contract cannot be rescinded except by consent of both parties.

12. An oral contract must be proved by evidence.

13. A contract binding in the place where it is made is binding everywhere.

14. Each party to an agreement or contract should retain a copy.

15. While signatures or contracts written with a pencil are good in law, it is always safer to write them in ink.

JUSTICE.

CONTRACTS THAT ARE NOT LAWFUL.

1. A contract to commit a breach of peace.
2. Contracts made on Sunday, are, in most of the States, now held to be legal and binding.
3. An agreement for immoral purposes.
4. All agreements in which there is fraud.
5. An agreement made by threats or violence.
6. Wagers or bets cannot be collected by law.
7. More than legal interest cannot be collected.
8. If any part of a contract is illegal, the whole is illegal.
9. A contract with an intoxicated person, lunatic, or minor.
10. A contract in violation of a statute in the State in which it is made.

11. An agreement to prevent competition on a sale under an execution.

12. An agreement to prohibit the carrying on of a trade throughout the State.

13. A contract impossible in its nature; such as crossing the ocean in one day, is void.

14. Where consent to an agreement is given by mistake, it cannot become a contract.

15. The right to vote or hold office, etc., cannot be sold by contract.

16. Contract without a consideration; such as a promise to make a gift, cannot be enforced.

17. Two or more persons cannot intentionally make a contract to the injury of a third person.

18. Contracts for concealing felony or violating public trust, for bribery and extortion, are prohibited.

19. Useless things cannot become the subject of a contract; such as agreeing not to go out of the house for a month.

20. Money borrowed for the purpose of betting, the lender knowing it to be for that purpose, cannot be collected.

21. A verbal release without payment or satisfaction for the debt is not good. Release must be under seal.

22. If there are two parts to a contract, and one conflicts with the other, the first part holds good in preference to the last.

23. Contracts in which there is misrepresentation or concealment of material facts cannot be enforced. It is fraud to conceal a fraud.

24. If a thing contracted for was not in existence at the time of making the contract, such as buying a horse and not knowing that he was dead at the time, is not good.

25. If a person agrees to serve as a laborer or clerk, he cannot be compelled to fulfill his agreement; damages, however, can be recovered for a failure to perform.

26. An agreement with a thief to drop a criminal prosecution, by his bringing back the goods and paying all damages, is not good, and will be no bar to a future prosecution.

27. Guardians, Trustees, Executors, Administrators or Attorneys cannot take advantage of those for whom they act by becoming parties to contracts in which their wards are interested.

DAMAGES FOR VIOLATION OF CONTRACT.

1. It is the very essence of a contract that some penalty attaches to its violation. Otherwise it is no contract at all. Herein an agreement resembles a law. A statute which provides no penalties for the law-breaker is merely the expression of a wish, or the giving of advice. The contract that binds must be binding on both parties. This element of mutual obligation is also the very essence of a contract.

2. Where no actual loss has been sustained by the violation of a contract, the plaintiff is entitled to nominal damages only.

3. Actual expenditures under the contract may be recovered.

4. Expected profits or speculations in real property cannot be recovered in case of a violation of contract.

5. Failure to convey real estate according to covenant entitles plaintiff to the value of the land at the time the transfer was to be made.

6. Failure to deliver property at the time and place named in the contract entitles the plaintiff to the value of the property at the time and place fixed for deliverance.

7. In loss of goods by common carrier the plaintiff is entitled to the value of the goods where they were to be delivered, less the freight on such goods.

A Broken Contract.

Parent:—You have violated my command.
Small Boy:—I should think you would be ashamed to strike me when my back is turned toward you.

8. If a party contracts to employ another for a certain time, at a specified compensation, and discharges him, without cause, before the expiration of time, the plaintiff can obtain judgment

for full amount of wages for the whole time, provided he does not engage in any other business.

9. In Illinois the penalty for a railroad for the killing of a passenger is fixed by statute at $5,000, and the only question that is allowed to arise in such a case is whether the railroad company was at all responsible for the disaster.

10. To prevent lawsuits and disputes the amount of damages for the violation of contracts is sometimes fixed by inserting in the contract the following clause:

And it is further agreed that the party that shall fail to perform this agreement on his part shall pay to the other the full sum of [here state amount], as liquidated, fixed, and settled charges.

General Form of Agreement.

This agreement, made the tenth day of June, 19—, between Clarence Ranck of Aurora, County of Kane, State of Illinois, of the first part, and Charles Vandersall of Columbus, Ohio, of the second part: Witnesseth, that the said Clarence Ranck, in consideration of the agreement of the party of the second part hereinafter contained, contracts and agrees to and with the said Charles Vandersall, that [here insert the agreement of Clarence Ranck]. And the said Charles Vandersall in consideration of the fulfillment of this contract on the part of the party of the first part, contracts and agrees with the said Clarence Ranck [here insert the agreement on the part of Charles Vandersall].

In case of failure of agreement by either of the parties hereto it is hereby stipulated and agreed that the party so failing shall pay to the other Two Hundred Dollars as fixed and settled damages.

In witness whereof, we have hereunto set our hands and seals, the day and year first above mentioned.

Signed and sealed
in presence of
John Rutter.

CLARENCE RANCK.
CHARLES VANDERSALL.

Contract for Sale of Land.

This agreement, made this first day of June, A. D. 19 , between John Brown, of the City of Dunkirk, in the State of New York, party of the first part, and Norman C. Stull, of the City of Buffalo, of the same State, party of the second part, Witnesseth, That if the said party of the second part shall make the payments and perform the covenants hereinafter mentioned on his part the said party of the first part hereby agrees to convey and assure to the said party of the second part in fee simple, clear of all incumbrances whatsoever, by a good and sufficient warranty deed the following described premises to wit: [Here describe property to be conveyed], and the said party of the second part covenants and agrees to pay to the said party of the first part the sum of two thousand ($2,000.) dollars as follows:

Five hundred ($500) dollars cash in hand paid, the receipt whereof is hereby acknowledged, balance on March 1, 1902, with interest at the rate of 6 per cent. per annum, payable annually after the date hereof, and all taxes and assessments legally levied or imposed upon said land subsequent to the year 1899. A complete abstract of title brought down to date to be furnished by said party of the first part on or before thirty days from the date hereof. In case title, on examination, should prove to be defective, then the said party of the first part agrees to perfect the same within a reasonable time, and in case of failure so to do, or in case said title cannot be perfected, the cash paid hereon shall be refunded and this contract shall become null and void. Deed to be delivered March 1, 1901, deferred payments to be secured by note and first mortgage by the party of the second part on the premises hereby sold. This contract shall extend to, and be obligatory upon, the heirs, administrators, executors, and assigns of the respective parties.

In testimony whereof the parties have hereunto set their hands and seals the day and year first above written.

(Signed) JOHN BROWN, (Seal.)
NORMAN C. STULL. (Seal.)

Witness: Richard Peck.

An Agreement to Build a House.

This agreement, made this 16th day of July, 19 , between John Reid, of Lisle, Illinois, party of the first part, and C. Cooper, of Naperville, Illinois, party of the second part, Witnesseth: That the said party of the second part for and in consideration of the sum of fifteen hundred ($1,500) dollars, to be paid as hereinafter stated, covenants and agrees with the party of the first part that he will within the space of six months from the date hereof in a good substantial and workmanlike manner erect, build, and finish on Lot Two (2) in Block Three (3) of Park Addition to Naperville, Illinois, a dwelling house in accordance with the plans and specifications hereunto annexed and made a part hereof.

It is further agreed that the party of the first part shall at all times furnish to the said party of the second part all such stone, brick, lime, cement, lumber, and such other materials as may be required by him for the construction of said house, and such lumber and materials to be delivered upon said lot from time to time as required by said party of the second part. Said party of the first part agrees to pay the said party of the second part the sum of five hundred ($500) dollars when the building is enclosed and the roof is on. Five hundred ($500) dollars when the house is plastered and the chimneys erected, and the remainder upon the completion of the contract.

In witness whereof the parties have hereunto set their hands and seals the day and year first above written.

(Signed) JOHN REID. (Seal.)
C. COOPER. (Seal.)

A Contract for Hiring a Farm Hand.

KNOW ALL MEN BY THESE PRESENTS:

That Fred J. Dolan agrees to work faithfully for G. J. Keller, as a general laborer on his farm, and to do any work that he may be called upon to do in connection therewith, in the township of Freedom, County of La Salle, and State of Illinois, for the period of one year, beginning the first day of March next, 1918, for the sum of Twenty Dollars per month.

In consideration of the services to be performed, the said G. J. Keller agrees to pay Fred J. Dolan, Twenty Dollars per month.

IN WITNESS WHEREOF, the said parties have hereunto set their hands this first day of January, 1918.

FRED J. DOLAN.
G. J. KELLER.

Agreement for the Hiring of a Clerk.

THIS AGREEMENT, made this twenty-eighth day of June, one thousand nine hundred and eighteen, between John Smith, of the Town of Naperville, in the County of Du Page, and State of Illinois, of the first part, and Richard Brown, of the City of Chicago, in the County of Cook, State of Illinois, of the second part, Witnesseth:

That the said John Smith has agreed to enter the service of the said Richard Brown as clerk, and covenants and agrees to and with the said Richard Brown that he will faithfully, honestly and diligently

apply himself and perform the duties of a clerk in the store of the said Richard Brown, and faithfully obey all the reasonable wishes and commands of the said Richard Brown, for and during the space of one year from the thirtieth day of May next for the compensation of Six Hundred Dollars ($600) per annum, payable monthly.

And the said Richard Brown covenants with the said John Smith that he will receive him as his clerk for the term of one year aforesaid and will pay him for his services as such clerk the sum of Six Hundred Dollars ($600) annually, in monthly payments.

In witness whereof, we have hereunto set our hands and seals, this twenty-eighth day of June, A. D. 1918.

JOHN SMITH. (Seal.)
RICHARD BROWN. (Seal.)
JOHN H. WAGNER.

A Contract for Laying Tile or Building Fence.

This agreement, made this first day of July, 19 , between W. J. Shaw, of the first part, and A. N. Jenkins, of the second part, Witnesseth: That the said party of the first part agrees to lay upon the farm of the said party of the second part, of Naperville Township, Du Page County, Illinois, 120 rods of six-inch tile at such places on said farm as the said party of the first part may designate for the sum of forty cents per rod, said tile to be so laid that there shall be sufficient fall to properly drain the land through which the same is laid. And all ditches to be properly filled by the party of the first part; and the said party of the second part agrees to pay said party of the first part one-half the consideration above expressed when he has laid 60 rods of said tiling and the remainder on completion of the contract.

Witness the hands of the parties hereto the day and year above written. (Signed) W. J. SHAW,
A. N. JENKINS.

A Contract for the Sale of Horses, Cattle, or other Personal Property.

This agreement, between A. B. Johnson and C. D. Coddington, made this nineteenth day of October, 19 , witnesseth:

That said A. B. Johnson, for the consideration hereinafter mentioned, shall sell and deliver on the first day of November next to said C. D. Coddington at his residence, One Double Wagon, Two Four-Year-Old Colts and Six Yearling Heifers.

That said C. D. Coddington, in consideration thereof, shall pay said A. B. Johnson Three Hundred Dollars, upon the delivery of said property.

In witness whereof we have this day set our hands and seal.

A. B. JOHNSON,
C. D. CODDINGTON.

Estray Notice.

Take Notice!—On the 3rd day of June, 19 , there strayed onto my inclosed land in the town of Van Wert, County of Du Page: One two-year-old colt, a dark bay, with small star in the forehead, and left hind foot white; and one dark-brown calf, with black spots on each side. Any one claiming the above-described animals can obtain possession of same by furnishing sufficient proof of ownership, and paying all expense and cost. R. ZACHMAN.

1. The above notice may be printed in the local paper, or written out, and tacked up in three or four prominent places in the vicinity where the stray animal was taken up.

2. No one can claim a stray without advertising the same, and giving the proper notice, such as the statutes of the State require.

3. If the stray is not redeemed by the owner, it may be sold at public auction to pay cost and expense.

PROPERTY, REAL AND PERSONAL.

Property is either **Real Estate** or **Personal Property.**

Real Estate is fixed property, such as houses and lands.

Personal Property consists of all movable material, such as horses, cattle, furniture, merchandise, notes, cash, mortgages, etc. The capital stock of corporations is personal property.

Personal property may become real estate by being attached to the ground, and real estate can be made personal property; as coal taken from a mine or trees that have been cut down.

THE LAW GOVERNING THE SALE AND TRANSFER OF PROPERTY.

1. A sale is the exchange of property for money, which is either paid at once or is to be paid in the future. An agreement to sell at a future date is not a sale.

2. There are many complicated things pertaining to the sale of property which every thoughtful man should understand.

3. The thing sold must either exist at the time of the sale or there must be a well-founded reason that it will be in existence and in possession of the seller. For example: If a man sold a horse for $100 and it transpires that the horse died before the actual time of the sale the transaction would not be a sale, otherwise it would.

4. Grain or other produce not yet sowed or planted can be sold because the seller may reasonably expect a crop. Machinery or other manufactured goods may be sold before they are made and the seller can be held to perform his part of the contract the same as though the articles actually existed at the time of the sale.

5. The thing sold must be specified and set apart as the property of the buyer. For example: The sale of ten bushels of wheat from a certain bin would not be a sale unless the grain was measured and set apart.

6. The price must be fixed by mutual consent, or be understood by the terms of the sale.

7. Any defects which can be seen in property or in animals when sold do not relieve the buyer from meeting his contract though he claims that he did not see the defects. The law does not furnish eyes for the purchaser of property.

8. But defects in property or animals which cannot be seen and of which the seller makes no statement, but recommends is as good or sound, relieves the buyer from his contract.

9. When nothing is said as to the time of payment when the sale is made the law presumes that the property must be paid for before the purchaser can secure possession. If credit is agreed upon the buyer is entitled to immediate possession.

10. The purchaser, in order to make good his bargain, should always advance a small amount, to bind the seller to the bargain.

Form of Bill of Sale.

KNOW ALL MEN BY THESE PRESENTS, That I, Jared K. Long, of Aurora, Kane County, Illinois, in consideration of six hundred ($600) dollars to me in hand paid by F. A. Lueben, of the same place, the receipt of which is hereby acknowledged, do hereby grant, sell, assign, transfer and deliver unto the said F. A. Lueben, his heirs and assigns, the following goods and chattels, to wit:

Four Oxen, at $50.00 each	$200.00
30 head of Sheep, at $4.00 each	120.00
Five sets of Harness, at $20.00 each	100.00
Two Farm Wagons, at $35.00 each	70.00
One Corn Planter, at $20.00	20.00
Six Plows, at $15.00 each	90.00

To have and to hold all of the said goods and chattels to the said F. A. Lueben, his heirs and assigns forever. And I do hereby covenant to and with the said F. A. Lueben that I am the legal owner of said goods and chattels; that they are free and clear from all other and prior sales and incumbrances; that I have good right to sell and convey the same as aforesaid, and that in the peaceable possession of the said F. A. Lueben I will forever warrant and defend the same against the lawful claims and demands of all persons whomsoever.

In witness whereof I have hereunto set my hand and seal this 29th day of June, A. D. 1918. (Signed) J. K. LONG. [Seal.]
In the presence of
Jacob Damm.

Bill of Sale. Special Form for the West.

KNOW ALL MEN BY THESE PRESENTS, That I, James C. Smith, of Great Falls, County of Cascade, and State Montana, in consideration of eighty dollars to me in hand paid by D. C. Robert of the same place the receipt of which is hereby acknowledged, do hereby grant, sell, transfer and deliver unto the said D. C. Robert, his heirs and assigns, the following chattels, to wit:

One Black Mare, warranted only four years old, sound and gentle, branded (X)............$60.00
One Red Heifer, branded (L).................... 20.00

And I hereby guarantee these chattels to be in every way as above described; that they are my lawful property, free from all incumbrances, and that I have a good right to sell and convey the same as aforesaid; and further, that I will defend the same against all claims whatsoever.

In witness whereof I have hereunto set my hand and seal this 19th day of June, A. D. 1900. (Signed) JAMES C. SMITH. [Seal.]
In the presence of
Walter J. Miller.

BANKRUPTCY.

1. **A Bankruptcy Act** was passed by Congress and went into force July 1, 1898, which virtually supersedes and does away with all state insolvency laws and proceedings. While this act is in force, all such acts are suspended.

2. **Courts.**—The courts having jurisdiction in bankruptcy cases are the District Courts of the United States, in the several States and Territories, and the Supreme Court of the District of Columbia.

3. **Acts of Bankruptcy.**—(*a*) Acts of bankruptcy by a person consist of fraudulently conveying, transferring, concealing, or removing property with intent to hinder, delay, or defraud creditors. (*b*) Making transfers of property when a person is insolvent. (*c*) Suffering a creditor to obtain a preference when the debtor is insolvent. (*d*) General assignment for the benefit of creditors. (*e*) Admitting in writing inability to pay debts.

4. **Bankrupts.**—Bankrupts are of two kinds, voluntary and involuntary. Involuntary bankrupts are those declared bankrupts by the proper courts on petition of creditors who have committed one or more of the acts of bankruptcy hereinbefore specified. Voluntary bankrupts are those who are declared to be bankrupts on their own motion or petition. Any person who owes debts, except a corporation, may become a voluntary bank-

rupt. Any person, except a wage-earner, farmer, any unincorporated company and any corporation engaged in manufacturing, trading, printing, publishing or mercantile proceedings owing debts to the amount of One Thousand Dollars or over and private bankers, may be declared involuntary bankrupts.

5. **Exemptions.**—Bankrupts are allowed the same exemptions as against executions or attachments.

6. **Discharges in Bankruptcy,** which protect persons from all debts except those hereinafter mentioned, may be secured on petition to the proper court after the expiration of one month and within twelve months after being adjudged a bankrupt. Such discharge releases a bankrupt from all of his debts, except taxes, judgments for fraud, debts not scheduled, debts created by embezzlement, misappropriation or defalcation.

7. **Officers in Bankruptcy.**—The principal officers in bankruptcy proceedings are the referee and trustee. The referees are appointed by the District Judge, hold their terms for two years, and are practically assistant judges to the court, and have general charge of bankruptcy proceedings. Their number is determined by the amount of business, and is largely discretionary with the United States District Judge. Their fee is Ten Dollars, which must be paid when the proceedings are commenced. The trustee is appointed by the creditors at their first meeting after the person has been declared a bankrupt, and their duties are largely the same as those of receivers or assignees in insolvency proceedings. Both referees and trustees are required to give bond.

8. **Meetings of Creditors.**—After the party has been adjudged a bankrupt, a meeting of all creditors must be called not less than ten days nor more than thirty days after such adjudication, at the county seat of the county where the bankrupt has his principal place of business or resides. At the first meeting of the creditors, the referee presides, allows or disallows claims of creditors, and may publicly examine the bankrupt. At this meeting the trustee is appointed. All claims must be presented under oath in writing, setting forth his claim to the referee.

9. **Notices.**—Ten days' notice by mail of all the principal proceedings in bankruptcy are given to creditors by the referee.

10. **How Commenced.**—Proceedings in involuntary bankruptcy are commenced by filing a petition with the Clerk of the

District Court, setting forth the name and residence of the bankrupt, an accurate list of all his property, and a schedule of all his debts, giving the name and address of all his creditors. The time is then fixed by the court for a hearing upon said petition, due notice thereof being given. On such hearing, the question of whether the person is entitled to the benefits of the act is decided, and the judgment of the court declares the person a bankrupt or not, as the case requires, and then the proceedings take the usual course under rules which have been adopted by the Supreme Court of the United States. These rules are too numerous and extensive to be recited here.

COAL LANDS.

1. **Application for Entry.**—Every person above the age of twenty-one years, who is a citizen of the United States or who has declared his intention to become such, or any association of persons severally qualified as above, shall, upon application to the Register of the proper Land Office, have the right to enter by legal subdivisions any quantity of vacant coal land of the United States, not otherwise appropriated or reserved by competent authority, not exceeding one hundred sixty acres to each individual or person, or three hundred twenty acres to such association, upon payment to the receiver of not less than Ten Dollars ($10.00) per acre for such land where the same shall be situated more than fifteen miles from any completed railroad, and not less than Twenty Dollars ($20.00) per acre for such land as shall be within fifteen miles of such road.

2. **Settlers Preferred.**—Any person or association of persons, severally qualified as above provided, who have opened and improved, or shall hereafter open and improve, any coal mine or mines upon public lands. and shall be in actual possession of the same, shall be entitled to a preference-right of entry, under the preceding section, of mines so opened and improved, provided, that when any association of no less than four persons severally qualified as above provided, shall have expended not less than Five Thousand Dollars ($5,000.00) in working or improving any such mine or mines, such association may enter not exceeding six hundred forty acres, including such mining improvements.

3. **Land Office Proceedings.**—All claims under the preceding sections must be presented to the Register of the proper land district within sixty days after the date of actual possession, and the commencement of improvements on the land by the filing of a declaratory statement therefor; but when the township plat is not on file at the date of such improvement, filing must be made within sixty days from the receipt of such plat from the Land Office.

4. **Entry Limited.**—The three preceding sections shall be held to authorize only one entry by the same person or association of persons, and no association of persons, any member of which shall have taken the benefit of such sections, either as an individual or as a member of any other association, shall enter or hold any other lands under the provision thereof, and no member of any association, which shall have taken the benefit of such sections, shall enter or hold any other lands under their provisions, and all persons claiming under Section 1 shall be required to prove their respective rights and pay for the lands filed upon, within one year from the time prescribed for filing their respective claims, and upon failure to file the proper notice or to pay for the land within the required period, the same shall be subject to entry by any other qualified applicant.

5. **Conflicting Claims.**—In case of conflicting claims upon coal lands where improvement shall be commenced, priority of possession and improvements, followed by proper filing and continued good faith, shall determine the preference-right to purchase. The Commissioner of the General Land Office is authorized to issue all needful rules and regulations for carrying into effect the provisions of this and the four preceding sections.

NOTE.—The proceedings to enter coal lands under the above sections are regulated by a circular of the General Land Office.

NORTHWESTERN COLLEGE, NAPERVILLE, ILL.

Proposal to Erect a Public Building.

To the Directors of School District No. 7, Township of Milton, Du Page County, Illinois:

We propose to erect, complete and finish, on the lots owned by you in your district, a schoolhouse according to plans, specifications and details this day furnished to us, and from which these estimates are prepared, and upon which they are based.

We propose to furnish all materials of every kind and character required to be used in the construction and the completion of said building, and we agree that the work, when completed, and all materials, shall fully and strictly comply with the plans and specifications hereinbefore mentioned, and that said building shall be completed and ready for occupancy on or before six months from the date hereof.

We propose to construct said building and complete it in accordance with the foregoing proposition for the sum of ten thousand ($10,000) dollars, payable as follows: $5,000.00 when the walls are up and roof is on; $2,000.00 when the plastering is completed, and the remainder on completion of the building.

We hope this proposition may be accepted by your honorable board.

Dated this 13th day of May, 1918. JAMES HARRIS & CO.

HOW TO SECURE A LIEN ON PROPERTY.

1. **A Lien** is a legal claim. It includes every case in which either real or personal property is charged with any debt or duty. In other words, it is the right to hold possession of property until some claim against it has been satisfied.

2. **Possession** is always necessary to create a lien except in case of mortgages. The lien simply extends to the right

of holding the property until the debt is satisfied. The property cannot be sold without the consent of the owner, except by order of the court.

3. **Law.**—The existence of a lien does not prevent the party entitled to it from collecting the debt or claim by taking it into court.

4. **Parties Entitled to Liens.**—Warehouse men, carpenters, tailors, dyers, millers, printers, etc., or any persons who perform labor or advance money on property or goods of another have a lien on same until all charges are paid.

5. **Hotel Keepers** have a lien upon the baggage of their guests, whom they have accommodated.

6. **Common Carriers** have a lien on goods carried for transportation charges.

7. **Agents** have a lien on goods of their principals for money advanced.

8. **How to Hold the Lien.**—Never give up possession of the property until the debt is paid.

9. **Real Property.**—If the debt is on a house, barn or other real property, file a lien on the whole property, and have it recorded in the County Recorder's office. The claim then partakes of the nature of a mortgage.

10. **Mechanic's Lien.**—Nearly all the States have enacted special laws to protect mechanics and material men, who may furnish material and labor for the erection, construction, repair and improvement of buildings situated thereon. The method of securing these liens and enforcing them in the different States varies so widely that it is almost impossible to give such a statement as will cover all States. The courts have construed such laws very strictly and in order to entitle a person to such lien the provisions of the law granting the same must be strictly complied with. Mechanics and material men desiring to avail themselves of these statutes would better consult some good lawyer and have him prepare the necessary papers. The following form is the one commonly in use in the State of Illinois:

Form of Mechanic's Lien.

STATE OF ILLINOIS, DU PAGE COUNTY. } ss. In the Circuit Court, Du Page County.

JULIUS WARREN, vs. MARTIN SMITH. } Claim for Lien.

Julius Warren, being first duly sworn, on oath, says that he is the claimant above named, and that the attached "Exhibit A," is a just and true statement of the account due him from said Martin Smith for labor and materials furnished said Martin Smith at the times in said statement mentioned, which various amounts are due and payable to him from and after the respective dates thereof; and affiant says that the labor and materials in said statement mentioned were used in the construction and improvement of a two-story frame building situate upon the following described premises in the County of Du Page and State of Illinois, to wit: Lot two (2), in Block three (3), of the original town of Hinsdale.

And affiant says that there is now due and owing to said Julius Warren from said Martin Smith, at whose request said material and labor was furnished as aforesaid, after allowing to him all just credits, deductions, and set-offs, the sum of $500, for which amount said Julius Warren claims a lien upon the above described premises.

Subscribed and sworn to before me this 29th day of February, A. D. 1918.
JOHN SMITH,
Notary Public.

JULIUS WARREN.

N. B.—The foregoing statement should be signed and sworn to before some officer authorized to administer oaths, and filed with the Clerk of the Circuit Court of the County where the real estate is situated, and a suit to enforce the same must be begun within two years from the date of the completion of the contract.

LAW ON GUARANTEES.

1. A guarantee (also spelled guaranty) is a written promise that a person will perform some duty or answer for the payment of some debt, in case of the failure of another person.

2. The person who guarantees the faithfulness of another is called the guarantor.

3. The guarantee is the person to whom the pledge is made.

4. All guarantees must be in writing.

5. A guarantee, to be binding, must be for a consideration. The consideration should be named or expressed as "for value received."

6. A mere accommodation or overture is not sufficient to hold a guarantor.

7. A guarantee must be accepted to make it a contract, and the guarantor must have notice of its acceptance within a reasonable time.

8. A guarantor, after paying the debt, has the right to substitute himself in place of the creditor.

9. Guarantees of commission merchants binding them to warrant the solvency of the purchaser of goods they sell on credit, need not be in writing.

10. The terms of the contract of guarantee are to be strictly construed.

11. In the sale of a horse the purchaser can only hold the guarantor for defects of the horse when sold.

12. In case of a cough the horse must have been heard to cough previous to the purchase. If lame, the lameness must be proved to arise from a cause that could not have occurred after the purchase. A guarantee after the sale of the horse is of no effect.

FORMS OF GUARANTEES.

A Guarantee for the Purchase of a Horse.

Osage, Kansas, June 30, 1918.

In consideration of One Hundred and Fifty Dollars, for a bay mare, I hereby guarantee her to be only six years old, sound, free from vice and quiet to ride or drive.
RALPH GOOD.

N. B.—This guarantee embraces every cause of unsoundness that can be detected, and the seller will be held for all the defects in the animal at the time of sale. This is the only safe and satisfactory way for a man to purchase a horse who is not an experienced judge of horses.

Guarantee on Back of a Note.

For value received, I hereby guarantee the payment of the within note.
JAMES GLOVER.

Fort Scott, Kansas, Oct. 12, 1918.

Guarantee for Payment of a Bill.

W. Reinke, Esq. Dayton, Ohio, Aug. 30, 1918.

Dear Sir:—I hereby guarantee the payment of any bill or bills of merchandise Mr. John A. Dahlem may purchase from you, the amount of this guarantee not to exceed five hundred dollars ($500), and to expire at the end of three months from date.
Respectfully yours,
CHAS. ADAMS.

Guarantee of a Debt Already Incurred.

St. Louis, Mo., July 10, 1918.

Messrs. H. E. Bechtel & Co., West Salem.

Gentlemen:—In consideration of one dollar paid me by yourselves, the receipt of which I hereby acknowledge, I guarantee that the debt of four hundred dollars now owing to you by Ira J. Ferry shall be paid at maturity.
Very respectfully yours,
W. A. PIPER.

LANDLORD AND TENANT.

1. **Definition.**—This is a term used to denote the relation which exists by virtue of a contract expressed or implied between two or more persons for the possession or occupation of lands or tenements either for a definite period of life or at will.

The LANDLORD is the person who lets the premises. The TENANT is the one who occupies the land or premises in subordination to the Landlord only. The contract between the two is called a LEASE. The party granting the possession and profit is called the LESSOR, and the party to whom the grant is made is called the LESSEE. The most common forms of tenancy are for life or for a definite term. Either so many years, so many months, or so many weeks.

2. **Leases.**—Leases which are to run for more than a year or which are not to be performed within a year must be in writing, or they are absolutely void. Leases for a year or less and which can be performed within a year are valid if not in writing. To avoid misunderstandings, disputes, and possible litigation it is always best that the Lease be in writing and signed by both parties.

3. **Leases** for life are those which are terminated either by death of the Lessee or of some other person living at the date of the Lease. Unless such Leases contain covenants to the contrary the life Tenant or the Lessee is required to pay all taxes on the premises and keep the same in repair.

4. **Leases for Years.**—The Lessor, unless it is otherwise expressly provided in the Lease, is under obligations to put the Tenant in possession and see that his possession is not disturbed by any title paramount to his Landlord's. He is not required to make repairs unless he so stipulates in the Lease, nor is there an implied contract on his part that the premises are fit for the purpose for which they are let. He must pay all taxes regularly levied and assessed against said premises and keep the buildings on said premises insured at his own expense if he desires to carry insurance.

5. **Implied Agreement by Tenant.**—Where there is no agreement to the contrary, the Tenant is bound to take possession of the premises, take ordinary care of the same, keep them in a tenantable condition, and make repairs made necessary by his negligence, except injuries resulting from wear and tear and inevitable accident.

If the premises leased be a farm, he is also required to cultivate the same in the manner required of good husbandry. He must not commit waste, alter buildings or fences, and must surrender up the premises at the end of his term in as good condition as when entered upon originally, wear and tear excepted. He is not required to pay taxes or keep buildings insured, and must pay the stipulated rent at the time it becomes due by the terms of his Lease. If no time is specified in his Lease, then the rent is due at the end of the term. He may underlet the premises or assign the Lease unless his Lease contains covenants to the contrary.

If he places permanent improvements upon the premises which are so attached to the buildings or land that they cannot be removed without injury, he has no right to remove the same unless his Lease so provides. He may remove trade fixtures if the same are removed from the premises before the expiration of his Lease.

6. Special Covenants.—The usual covenants contained in the ordinary Lease provide for the yielding up of the possession of the premises at the end of the term without notice, in as good condition as when the same were entered upon by the Lessee, loss by fire, inevitable accident and ordinary wear excepted. There is also usually a covenant providing against underletting or assigning the Lease, and a covenant that in case of non-payment of rent, or failure to perform any of the covenants of the Lease the Lessor shall have the right to determine said Lease and recover possession of the premises.

Farm leases usually provide, in addition to the covenant above mentioned, that the Tenant shall keep the fruit and ornamental trees, vines and shrubbery, free from injury of stock and from plowing or otherwise; that the Lessee will draw out the manure and spread it on the premises; that no straw shall be sold and removed from the premises during the term or at its termination; that the Tenant will keep the buildings and fences in repairs, the Landlord to furnish necessary material; that the Landlord may do fall plowing on the stubble ground after the grain has been removed therefrom, and that he may enter for the purpose of making repairs, viewing the premises and sowing timothy seed.

Sometimes the Landlord covenants to make all new fences, to furnish water and many other provisions which may be inserted as the occasion may require.

A Lease for Renting a House.

KNOW ALL MEN BY THESE PRESENTS:

That I have, this sixth day of September, 1901, let and rented unto Andrew Jay my house and premises, number 142 on Archer Street, in the town of Livermore, and State of Iowa, with the sole and uninterrupted use and occupation thereof for one year, to commence the first day of May next, at the monthly rent of twenty dollars, payable in advance.

Witness my hand and seal,

J. W. GLASGOW. (Seal.)

Short Form of Lease.

John Parks leases to J. B. Moulton [description of premises] for a erm of..........upon the payment of..........Dollars.

Dated this 1st day of August, 1901. J. K. MILLER.

The following is a form of Lease in common use for bot' city and country property:

THIS INDENTURE, Made this 15th day of July, A. D. 1901, betwe.n John Doe of Decatur, Ill., party of the first part, and Richard Roe of the same place, party of the second part, Witnesseth, That the party of the first part, in consideration of the covenants of the party of the second part, hereinafter set forth, does by these Presents, lease to the party of the second part the following described property, to wit: Lot one (1) in Block Ten in the original Town of Decatur in the City of Decatur and State of Illinois, TO HAVE AND TO HOLD THE SAME, To the party of the second part, from the 15th day of July, 1901, to the 15th day of January, 1902. And the party of the second part, in consideration of the leasing the premises as above set forth, covenants and agrees with the party of the first part to pay the party of the first part, at First National Bank, Decatur, as rent for the same, the sum of Sixty Dollars, payable as follows, to wit: $10 on the 15th day of each and every month during the term commencing on the date hereof.

AND THE PARTY OF THE SECOND PART covenants with the party of the first part, that at the expiration of the term of this lease ....he....will yield up the premises to the party of the first part, without further notice, in as good condition as when the same were entered upon by the party of the second part, loss by fire or inevitable accident and ordinary wear excepted.

IT IS FURTHER AGREED by the party of the second part, that neither........he........nor his legal representatives will underlet said premises or any part thereof, or assign this lease without the written assent of the party of the first part first had thereto.

AND IT IS FURTHER EXPRESSLY AGREED between the parties hereto, that if default shall be made in the payment of the rent above reserved, or any part thereof, or any of the covenants or agreements herein contained to be kept by the party of the second part, it shall be lawful for the party of the first part or his legal representatives, into and upon said premises or any part thereof, either with or without process of law, to re-enter and re-possess the same at the election of the party of the first part, and to distrain for any rent that may be due thereon upon any property belonging to the party of the second part. And in order to enforce a forfeiture for non-payment of rent it shall not be necessary to make a demand on the same day the rent shall become due, but a failure to pay the same at the place aforesaid or a demand and a refusal to pay on the same day, or at any time on any subsequent day, shall be sufficient; and after such default shall be made, the party of the second part and all persons in possession under him shall be deemed guilty of a forcible detainer of said premises under the statute.

AND IT IS FURTHER COVENANTED AND AGREED between the parties aforesaid, ...

....

The covenants herein shall extend to and be binding upon the heirs, executors and administrators of the parties to this Lease.

WITNESS THE HANDS AND SEALS of the parties aforesaid, the day d year first above written.

JOHN DOE. (Seal.)

RICHARD ROE. (Seal.)

Farm Lease, Money Rent.

The following form for farm lease, money rent, is a good one and contains the usual special covenants required under ordinary circumstances:

THIS INDENTURE, Made this second day of April, in the year of our Lord one thousand eight hundred and ninety-seven, between Henry Williams of the Town of Milton, in the County of Du Page and State of Illinois, party of the first part, and John Carter of the same place, party of the second part, WITNESSETH, That the said party of the first part for and in consideration of the covenants and agreements hereinafter mentioned, to be kept and performed by the said party of the second part, his executors, administrators and assigns, has demised and leased to the said party of the second part all those premises situate, lying and being in the Town of Milton, County of Du Page, State of Illinois, known and described as follows, to wit: The North West quarter of Section ten (10) in Township 39, north range 10, east of the 3d principal meridian.

TO HAVE AND TO HOLD the said above described premises, with the appurtenances, unto the said party of the second part, his executors, administrators and assigns, from the 2d day of April, in the year of our Lord one thousand eight hundred and ninety-seven, for and during and until the 2d day of April, in the year of our Lord one thousand nine hundred, yielding possession and paying rent therefor as hereinafter stated.

And the said party of the second part, in consideration of the leasing of the premises aforesaid by the said party of the first part to the said party of the second part, does covenant and agree with the said party of the first part, his heirs, executors, administrators and assigns, to pay the said party of the first part, as rent for the said demised premises the sum of fifteen hundred dollars, as follows: $200 on the 1st day of October, 1897, $300 Jan. 1, 1898, $200 Oct. 1, 1898, $300 Jan. 1, 1899, $200 Oct. 1, 1899, $300 Jan. 1, 1900, payable at the First National Bank, Naperville, Ill.

And the said party of the second part agrees to preserve and keep the fruit and ornamental trees, vines and shrubbery, that now are or shall be planted on the premises, from injury by plowing, or from cattle, horses, sheep or otherwise.

To scatter and expend upon said premises all the manure and compost, suitable to be used; such manure as is unfit for use to leave upon said premises for future use thereon; and not to burn any stalks or straw or stubble on said premises. No straw to be sold or removed from said premises or at its termination.

To keep said premises, including the hedges and fences, in proper and necessary repair, provided that, if necessary, the landlord.. shall furnish such materials as shall be needful to repair the fences within a reasonable time of being notified of its want.

And the said party of the second part further covenants with the said party of the first part that, at the expiration of the time in this lease mentioned, he will yield up the said demised premises to the said party of the first part in as good condition as when the same were entered upon by the said party of the second part, loss by fire or inevitable accident and ordinary wear excepted.

It is further agreed by the said party of the second part, that neither he nor his legal representatives will underlet said premises, or any part thereof, or assign this lease without the written assent of said party of the first part had and obtained thereto.

The said party of the first part reserves the privilege of plowing the stubble ground when the said party of the second part may have secured the grain grown thereon. The said party of the second part agrees to keep said premises free from burs, and to keep all necessary ditches and drains plowed out during this lease. Also agrees that the said party of the first part may enter said premises for the purpose of viewing and sowing timothy seed and making repairs.

IT IS EXPRESSLY UNDERSTOOD AND AGREED by and between the parties aforesaid, that if the rent above reserved, or any part thereof, shall be behind or unpaid on the day and at the place of payment whereon the same ought to be paid, as aforesaid, or if default shall be made in any of the covenants herein contained, to be kept by the said party of the second part, his executors, administrators or assigns, it shall and may be lawful for the said party of the first part, his heirs, executors, administrators, agent, attorney or assigns, at his election, to declare said term ended, and the said demised premises, or any part thereof, either with or without process of law, to re-enter, and the said party of the second part, or any other person or persons occupying, in or upon the same, to expel, remove and put out, using such force as may be necessary in so doing, and the said premises again to re-possess and enjoy, as in his first and former estate; and it shall be the duty of the said party of the second part, his executors, administrators or assigns, to be and appear at the said place above specified for the payment of said rent, and then and there tender and pay the same as the same shall fall due from time to time, as above, to the said party of the first part, his agent or assigns; or in his absence, if he shall offer to pay the same then and there, such offer shall prevent said forfeiture.

And it is expressly understood that it shall not be necessary, in any event, for the party of the first part, or his assigns, to go on or near the said demised premises to demand said rent, or elsewhere than at the place aforesaid. And in the event of any rent being due and unpaid, whether before or after such forfeiture declared, to distrain for any rent that may be due thereon, upon any property belonging to the said party of the second part. And if at any time said term shall be ended at such election of said party of the first part, his heirs, executors, administrators or assigns, as aforesaid or in any other way, the said party of the second part, his executors, administrators or assigns, do hereby covenant, promise and agree to surrender up and deliver said above described premises and property peaceably to the said party of the first part, his heirs, executors, administrators or assigns, immediately upon the determination of said term as aforesaid; and if he shall remain in the possession of the same five days after notice of such default, or after the termination of this lease, in any of the ways above named, he shall be deemed guilty of a forcible detainer of said demised premises, under the statute, and shall be subject to all the conditions and provisions above named, and to eviction and removal, forcibly or otherwise, with or without process of law, as above stated.

And it is further covenanted and agreed by and between the parties, that the party of the second part shall pay and discharge all costs and attorney's fees and expenses that shall arise from enforcing the covenants of this indenture by the party of the first part.

IN TESTIMONY WHEREOF, The said parties have hereunto set hands and seals the day and year first above written in duplicate.

In presence of — HENRY WILLIAMS. (Seal.)
Centius Seldon. — JOHN CARTER. (Seal.)

7. Termination of Lease.—Under the strict rules of the common law the Landlord might terminate the lease for non-payment of rent, but in order to do so it was necessary for him to go upon the premises and make a demand for the exact amount of rent due upon the very day that the rent came due, and a failure to do this waived the right to declare forfeiture. This strict rule of the common law has been modified in nearly all the States so that it is no longer necessary to make a demand for the rent on the day the rent comes due. Instead of this most of the States provide that before the Landlord shall declare a forfeiture a demand in writing, for the amount of rent due, shall be served upon the Tenant, and he be notified that in case he fails to pay the same within a fixed time, generally five or ten days, the Landlord will elect to terminate his lease; in such cases the Tenant has until the end of the last day fixed in the notice to pay the rent and save the forfeiture.

The statutes of the various States also provide that in case of breaches of other covenants contained in the lease, notice of such breach and intention of the Landlord to declare forfeiture of the same shall be served upon the Tenant to quit and deliver up possession of said premises within a time, generally not less than ten days.

The following are the forms of notices above referred to in common use:

Landlord's Five Day Notice.

To John Doe:

YOU ARE HEREBY NOTIFIED that there is now due me the sum of One Hundred Dollars and....................Cents, being rent for the premises situated in the City of Chicago, in Cook County, in the State of Illinois, and known and described as follows, viz: Lot one (1) in Block two (2) of the Original Town of Chicago.

And you are further notified that payment of said sum, so due, has been demanded of you, and that unless payment thereof is made on or before the 21st day of July, A. D. 1918, your lease of said premises will be terminated. Richard Roe is hereby authorized to receive said rent so due, for me.

Dated this 15th day of July, 1918. JAMES SMITH,
Landlord.

Ten Days' Notice to Quit.

To John Doe:—You are hereby notified that in consequence of your default in payment of rent and also to keep the buildings and fences on the premises hereinafter described in proper repair, being Lot One in Block Ten of the original town of Aurora, Kane County, Illinois, I have elected to terminate your lease, and you are hereby notified to quit and deliver up possession of the said premises to me within ten days of this date.

Dated this 21st day of July, 1918.
(Signed) RICHARD ROE,
Landlord.

8. Termination of Tenancy from Year to Year and Month to Month.—Where a Tenant has a Lease for a year of premises with annual rent, and at the end of his term holds over without a new agreement, the law construes this to be a leasing from year to year, and such tenancy at common law could only be terminated by either party giving the other six months notice prior to the end of any year.

This notice has been changed by a statute in Illinois to sixty days prior to the end of any year, and a shorter time has also been fixed in many other States.

A Tenant who has a Lease of property for one or more months with monthly rent, who holds over after the termination of his Lease, it termed a Tenant from month to month, and such relation can only be terminated by either party giving the other thirty days' notice of his intention to terminate the tenancy. Such notice to be given thirty days prior to the end of any month.

9. **Demand.**—It is a general rule, subject to few exceptions, that in order to get possession of property where the inception of the Tenant was lawful, either a notice to quit or a demand for possession is necessary on the part of the owner before commencing proceedings to get possession.

10. **Securing Possession.**—When a Lease has been terminated either by its term or by notice, and the Landlord is entitled to possession, the most common method of recovering possession is to commence an action of forcible entry and detainer against the Tenant for the possession of the premises. This may be done before a Justice of the Peace by filing a complaint and having a summons issued. If the possession of the Tenant was lawful in its inception the Landlord has no right to forcibly dispossess him, and if he does so it is at his peril. Taking possession by force subjects the Landlord to an action for heavy damages.

Leases sometimes contain clauses that where a forfeiture has taken place the Landlord shall have the right to take possession of the premises leased by force if necessary. Such covenants, however, cannot be enforced and do not justify the Landlord in using force, and the only course to pursue is to begin an action and recover a judgment for possession and have the constable or sheriff legally put the Landlord in possession.

DISTRESS FOR RENT.

1. The usual and most effective method of collecting rent is by distress warrant. This is a warrant issued by the Landlord to some third person, authorizing and empowering such third person to levy said warrant upon any property of the Tenant

for the satisfaction of the rent. This remedy is the most common and effective, as it enables the Landlord to get a lien upon the property of the Tenant without delay, and the process is of very ancient origin.

The statutes of most of the States provide for this remedy and the mode of procedure after the levy of the warrant is generally prescribed by the statute. In general it is the duty of the officer, as soon as the levy is made, to file an inventory of the property levied upon with some court together with a copy of his warrant, and usually a summons from said court is issued against the Tenant in favor of the Landlord and the suit then proceeds much after the manner of suits in attachment.

2. Time of Levy.—Under the Common Law the Tenant had all of the day on which the rent came due within which to pay the same and a distress could not be levied until the day after the rent came due. In Illinois, however, in case the Tenant sells or attempts to dispose of the crop grown upon the premises so as to endanger the Landlord's lien for his rent, a distress warrant may be levied before the rent comes due. Many of the statutes of the other States contain provisions of a similar character. The person making the levy should be careful not to levy on more property than is necessary in order to satisfy the rent due, otherwise he will be liable to the Tenant for making an excessive levy.

LANDLORD'S LIEN.

Under the Common Law the Landlord had no lien upon the property of the tenant until a distress warrant was actually levied upon the property of the Tenant. Most of the States, however, now provide that the Landlord shall have a lien upon all the crops grown upon the leased premises until the rent of the year in which said crop was grown has been paid, and this lien is ahead of all other liens; even though an execution may have been levied upon such crops, the Landlord's lien is paramount until his rent is satisfied. The usual method of enforcing the lien of the Landlord is by distress warrant levied in the manner hereinbefore described.

DEEDS, HOW WRITTEN, AND LAWS GOVERNING THEM.

1. Deeds must be written or printed on paper or parchment.

2. The names of the parties and places of residence are written first.

3. The property must be fully described. The description should be by bounds, or by divisions of United States surveys, or by subdivisions into blocks and lots, as shown on the records.

4. The deed must express a consideration, also a covenant to "warrant and defend," and be signed and sealed by the grantor or grantors. A deed without consideration is void.

5. Deeds must be completely written before delivery.

6. Numbers should always be written in words followed by figures in parentheses.

7. If the grantor is married both he and his wife should join in the grant and in the execution of the deed, signing and acknowledging.

8. Where forms are prescribed by the statutes of a State, they must be followed.

9. The acknowledgment of a deed can be made only before certain persons authorized to take the same, such as justices of the peace, notaries, masters in chancery, judges and clerks of the courts, commissioners of deeds, etc.

10. Any person of legal age, competent to transact business and owning real estate, may convey it by deed.

11. The deed takes effect upon its delivery to the person authorized to receive it, and should be recorded at once.

12. After the acknowledgment of a deed the parties have no right to make the slightest alteration.

13. The person making the deed is called the grantor, the person to whom the deed is delivered is called grantee.

14. **A Warranty Deed.**—The grantor warrants the title to be good, and agrees to defend the same against all persons.

15. **A Quitclaim Deed** releases only what interest the grantor has in the property.

16. Never purchase real estate without a careful examination of the title, either by yourself or a trusty attorney.

17. Always procure an abstract of title before advancing money or signing contract for purchase of land or lots.

18. The deed of a corporation must be signed by an agent or attorney and should be carefully executed. The seal is properly a piece of paper wafered on, or sealing wax pressed on. In the Eastern States nothing else satisfies the legal requirement of the seal. In other States the word "seal" inclosed in a square or any line drawn around it is regarded in law as a seal.

19. The execution of a deed is generally attested by witnesses. In many States two witnesses are required. In New York one is sufficient. In some States a witness is not required by law but it is always safer to have witnesses.

20. To have full effect a deed should be acknowledged and recorded. It is considered recorded as soon as it reaches the recording officer, who generally notes upon it the day, hour, and minute when it was received.

21. If the land is a gift and no price is paid for it, it is customary to insert "in consideration of one dollar paid me, the receipt of which I acknowledge."

22. Deeds are of a great variety. The forms vary greatly in the different States.

23. Forms of acknowledgments also differ greatly. The fuller forms are generally safer. For Forms of Acknowledgment see page 196.

Warranty Deed.—Long Form.

This Indenture, made this second day of March, in the year of our Lord one thousand nine hundred and eighteen, between Andrew Samson and Polly Ann Samson, his wife, of the Village of Naperville, in the County of Du Page and State of Illinois, party of the first part, and Ebenezer P. Stought, of the City of Chicago, in the County of Cook and State of Illinois, party of the second part:

Witnesseth, That the said party of the first part, for and in consideration of the sum of ten thousand eight hundred and ninety ($10,890) dollars, in hand paid by the said party of the second part, the receipt whereof is hereby acknowledged, and the said party of the first part forever released and discharged therefrom, have granted, bargained, sold, remised, released, conveyed, aliened and confirmed, and by these presents do grant, bargain, sell, remise, release, convey, alien, and confirm unto the said party of the second part, and to his heirs and assigns, forever, all the following described lots, pieces, or parcel of land, situated in the County of Du Page, and State of Illinois, and known and described as follows, to-wit:

The northwest quarter of Section thirty-six (36) in Township thirty-eight (38), North of Range eleven (11), East of the Third Principal Meridian, containing one hundred and sixty acres by Government survey. Also, an equal undivided one-half interest in lot number one (1) in block number three (3) of Smith's subdivision of Schuyler's addition to the Village of Naperville, in the County and State aforesaid.

Together with all and singular the hereditaments and appurtenances thereunto belonging, or in any wise appertaining, and the reversion and reversions, remainder and remainders, rents, issues, and profits thereof;

and all of the estate, right, title, interest, claim, or demand whatsoever, of the said party of the first part, either in law or in equity, of, in, and to the above bargained premises, with the hereditaments and appurtenances: To have and to hold the said premises above bargained and described, with the appurtenances, unto the said party of the second part, his heirs and assigns forever.

And the said Andrew Samson and Polly Ann Samson, his wife, party of the first part, for themselves and their heirs, executors and administrators, do covenant, grant, bargain, and agree to and with the said party of the second part, his heirs and assigns, that at the time of the ensealing and delivery of these presents, they are well seized of the premises above conveyed, as of a good, sure, perfect, absolute and indefeasible estate of inheritance in law, in fee simple, and have good right, full power, and lawful authority to grant, bargain, sell and convey the same in manner and form aforesaid, and that the same are free and clear from all former and other grants, bargains, sales, liens, taxes, assessments, and encumbrances, of what kind or nature soever; and the above bargained premises, in the quiet and peaceable possession of the said party of the second part, his heirs and assigns, against all and every other person or persons lawfully claiming or to claim the whole or any part thereof, the said party of the first part shall and will Warrant and Defend.

And the said party of the first part hereby expressly waive and release any and all right, benefit, privilege, advantage and exemption, under or by virtue of any and all Statutes of the State of Illinois, providing for the exemption of homesteads from sale on execution or otherwise.

In witness whereof, the said party of the first part have hereunto set their hands and seals the day and year first above written.

Signed, Sealed and Delivered in the Presence of SALAMANDER S. STONE.

ANDREW SAMSON. [Seal.]
POLLY ANN SAMSON. [Seal.]

Quitclaim Deed.

This Indenture, made the 18th day of August, in the year of our Lord one thousand nine hundred and one, between Bay Scott and his wife, Lizzie E. Scott, of the City of San Francisco, in the State of California, party of the first part, and Timothy H. Barnard, of the Town of Chico, County of Butte, in the State of California, the party of the second part, Witnesseth: That the said party of the first part, for and in consideration of the sum of nine thousand ($9,000) dollars, currency of the United States of America, to us in hand paid by the said party of the second part, the receipt whereof is hereby acknowledged, do by these presents remise, release, and forever Quitclaim unto the said party of the second part, and to his heirs and assigns forever, all the certain lots, pieces or parcels of land, situated in the said Town of Chico, County of Butte and State of California, and bounded and particularly described as follows, to-wit:

Lot number three (3), in block number six (6), in the Town of Chico, and County of Butte, State of California. Also the northwest quarter of Section thirty-seven (37), in the Town of Chico, County of Butte and State of California, containing one hundred and sixty acres, more or less, according to United States surveys.

Together with all and singular the tenements, hereditaments and appurtenances thereunto belonging, or in anywise appertaining, and the reversion and reversions, remainder and remainders, rents, issues and profits thereof.

To have and to hold, all and singular, the said premises, together with the appurtenances, unto the said party of the second part, and to his heirs and assigns forever.

In witness whereof, the said party of the first part have hereunto set their hands and seals the day and year first above written.

Signed, Sealed and Delivered in the Presence of KATIE BURKE, R. O. HALL.

BAY SCOTT. [Seal.]
LIZZIE O. SCOTT. [Seal.]

N. B. For certificate of acknowledgment see Form 3, page 196.

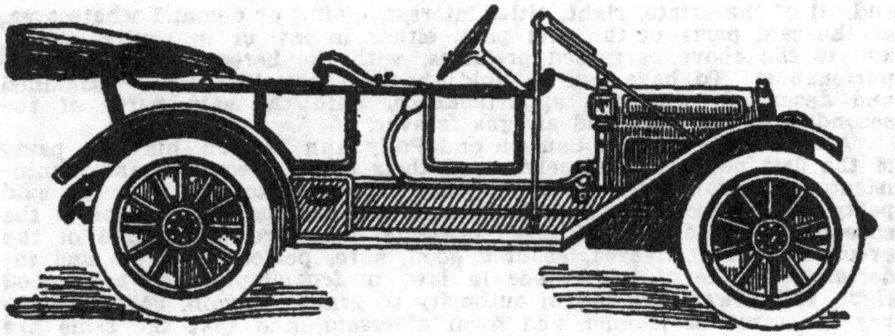

LEGAL POINTS FOR AUTO OWNERS.

When a man buys a car for the use of his family and authorizes his son to drive same, the son is the servant or agent of the father and the latter is liable for the negligent acts of the son. When the son takes the car without the authority of the father, the father is not liable.

Drivers of automobiles have an equal right on the highways with other vehicles, but they do not have any greater right. It is the duty of the driver to keep his car under control at all times. When approaching corners, or when seeing that his machine is frightening a horse, the motorist must slow down, or if necessary stop his car.

The driver of an unregistered car is a trespasser on the highway.

If the owner lends his car with a chauffeur, he will be held liable for the negligent acts of the chauffeur. This does not apply if the car is loaned without the chauffeur.

In the absence of statutory regulation an automobile may be left at the side of the road after shutting off the power and setting the brakes.

A person who drives his car at night without lights will be held to have acted in a negligent manner at common law.

Automobiles and pedestrians have equal rights upon the streets.

In case of accident due to a defective part, the owner will as a rule have an action against the manufacturer.

Criminal liability is attached to the unlawful use of another's automobile.

A garage keeper is a bailee for hire and hence liable for the proper care and protection of the machine.

If one willfully or negligently drives a car on a street or road at an unlawful speed, thereby killing another, he may be guilty of homicide.

A MORTGAGE SALE.
They mortgaged their farm to start their son in business.
"Now over the hill to the poor-house."

MORTGAGES AND LAWS GOVERNING THEM.

1. Mortgages are conditioned conveyances of estates or property by way of pledge to secure a debt.

2. All mortgages must be in writing, and be signed and sealed. They must be acknowledged and recorded.

3. There are two kinds of mortgages; a real estate mortgage, and a chattel mortgage. The former is a mortgage on real estate, the latter a mortgage on personal property.

4. A mortgagor is one who gives a mortgage and a mortgagee one to whom it is given.

5. A mortgagee may sell or transfer his mortgage to another party.

6. Mortgages given with the intent to defraud creditors are void, as to all persons knowing of the fraudulent intent.

7. When the debt is paid for which the mortgage was given, the mortgage is void.

8. A foreclosure is the legal proceeding to sell the mortgaged property to satisfy the debt.

9. In writing mortgages always insert the same description of land and lots as given in the deeds of same property.

10. Mortgages should be recorded with promptness after their execution. The first mortgage on record is the first lien on the property, notwithstanding another mortgage was given first, as to all persons not aware of that fact.

11. Formerly, a mortgagor could redeem his land only before or when the debt became due, but further time is now given. This right to redeem is called a right in equity to redeem or an equity of redemption. This time to redeem varies in different States but is usually three years.

12. This right to redeem is considered of so much importance that no party is permitted to lose it even by his own agreement. Even though the mortgagor agrees in the most positive terms to forfeit his equity of redemption, the law sets aside such agreement and gives the debtor full time to redeem his property.

13. The only way to set aside this time to redeem is to give the mortgagee permission or authority to sell the property and thus to secure himself.

14. If a mortgagor erects buildings on mortgaged land and the mortgage is foreclosed, the mortgagee in taking possession gets all these additions.

15. If the mortgagee erects buildings and the mortgagor thereafter redeems his land, he gets the buildings without paying for them.

16. Notes secured by mortgage must in some States show upon their face that they are so secured.

17. The mortgage, or mortgage deed as it is usually called, gives the mortgagee the right to take immediate possession of the property, unless the mortgage deed contains a clause to the effect that the mortgagor may retain possession as long as he meets his payments.

THE MAN WHO PAYS HIS MORTGAGE AT THE DAY OF MATURITY.

Mortgage to Secure a Debt, with Power of Sale—Short Form.

This Indenture, made the......day of.........in the year one thousand nine hundred and ......, between (name, residence and occupation of mortgagor) party of the first part, and (name, residence and occupation of mortgagee) party of the second part, witnesseth, that the said party of the first part, in consideration of the sum of (the amount of the debt) to him duly paid before the delivery thereof, has bargained and sold, and by these presents does grant and convey to the said party of the second part, and his heirs and assigns forever, all (here describe the premises) with the appurtenances, and all the estate, right, title, and interest of the said party of the first part therein.

This grant is intended as a security for the payment of (here describe the debt), which payments, if duly made, will render this conveyance void. And if default shall be made in the payment of the principal or interest above mentioned, then the said party of the second part, or his executors, administrators, or assigns, are hereby authorized to sell the premises above granted, or so much thereof as will be necessary to satisfy the amount then due, with the cost and expenses allowed by law.

In witness whereof, the said party of the first part has hereunto set his hand and seal the day and year first above written.

Sealed and Delivered in
the Presence of
....

Mortgage on Real Estate—Long Form, with Insurance Clause.

THIS INDENTURE WITNESSETH, That the mortgagor, F. A. Reik, and Fanny E. Reik, his wife, of the Town of Naperville, in the County of Du Page and State of Illinois, mortgage and warrant to C. E. Meyers, of the City of LaCrosse, County of LaCrosse and State of Wisconsin, to secure the payment of a certain promissory note executed by F. A. Reik, bearing even date herewith, payable to the order or said C. E. Meyers, for the sum of eight hundred dollars payable four years from the date thereof, with interest at the rate of seven (7) per cent. per annum, payable annually, the following described real estate to-wit: The southeast quarter (S. E. ¼) of section number twenty-five (25), in township number forty (40), north of range number fifteen (15), east of fourth principal meridian. Also: Lots numbers one (1) and two (2), in block number nineteen (19), of Park addition to the town of Naperville, situated in the County of Du Page, in the State of Illinois, hereby releasing and waiving all rights under and by virtue of the homestead exemption laws of the State of Illinois,

THE MAN WHO NEVER PAYS A MORTGAGE.

and all rights to retain possession of said premises, after any default in payment or breach of any of the covenants or agreements herein contained.

BUT IT IS EXPRESSLY PROVIDED AND AGREED, That if default be made in the payment of the said Promissory Note, or any part thereof, or the interest thereon, or any part thereof, at the time and in the manner above specified for the payment thereof, or in case of waste or non-payment of taxes or assessments on said premises, or of a breach of any of the covenants or agreements herein contained, then and in such case the whole of said principal sum and interest, secured by the said Promissory Note in this Mortgage mentioned, shall thereupon, at the option of the said Mortgagee or his heirs, executors, administrators, attorneys or assigns, become immediately due and payable; and this Mortgage may be immediately foreclosed to pay the same by said Mortgagee, or his heirs, executors, administrators, attorneys or assigns; and it shall be lawful for the said Mortgagee, or his heirs, executors, administrators, attorneys or assigns, to enter into and upon the premises hereby granted, or any part thereof, and to receive and collect all rents, issues and profits thereof.

UPON THE FILING OF ANY BILL to foreclose this Mortgage in any court having jurisdiction thereof, such court may appoint any attorney or any proper person Receiver, with power to collect the rents, issues and profits arising out of said premises during the pendency of such foreclosure suit and until the time to redeem the same from any sale that may be made under any decree foreclosing this Mortgage shall expire; and such rents, issues and profits when collected may be applied toward the payment of the indebtedness and costs herein mentioned and described. And upon the foreclosure and sale of said premises, there shall be first paid out of the proceeds of such sale, all expenses of advertisement, selling and conveying said premises, and fifty dollars attorney's or solicitor's fees, to be included in the decree, and all moneys advanced for taxes, assessments and other liens; then there shall be paid the principal of said Note, whether due and payable by the terms thereof or not, and the interest thereon.

THE SAID MORTGAGOR covenants and agrees that he will keep all buildings that may at any time be upon said premises insured in such companies as the holder of said Note shall direct, for their full insurable value, and make the loss, if any, payable to, and deposit the Policies of Insurance with, the party of the second part, or his assigns, as further security for the indebtedness aforesaid.

DATED this Third day of March, A. D., 19—.

F. A. REIK. (Seal.)
FANNY E. REIK. (Seal.)

For forms of Certificate of Acknowledgment see page 196.

Mortgage on Personal Property.

KNOW ALL MEN BY THESE PRESENTS, That E. L. Gattshall, of the Town of Ottawa, in the County of La Salle, and State of Illinois, in consideration of seven hundred dollars, to him paid by George Henry Raynor, of the County of La Salle, and State of Illinois, the receipt whereof is hereby acknowledged, does hereby grant, bargain, and sell unto the said Geo. H. Raynor, and to his heirs and assigns forever, the following goods and chattels, to-wit:

One Pitts' Thrashing Machine; One Romeo Steam Engine; Two Bay Mares, six years old; Four Pair of Double Harnesses; Five White Chester Hogs (black and white); One Bay Gelding, seven years old; One Black and White Cow, four years old.

To have and to hold all and singular the goods and chattels unto the said Mortgagee herein, and his heirs and assigns, to their sole use and behoof forever. And the Mortgagor herein, for him and for his heirs and executors and administrators, does hereby covenant to and with the said Mortgagee and his heirs and assigns, that the said Mortgagor is being lawfully possessed of the said goods and chattels as of his own property; that the same are free from all incumbrances, and that he will warrant and defend the same to him the said Mortgagee, and his heirs and assigns, against the lawful claims and demands of all persons.

Provided, nevertheless, that if the said Mortgagor shall pay a certain promissory note of seven hundred dollars, bearing even date with the above, given for one year, at eight per cent. interest, then this mortgage to be void, otherwise to remain in full force and effect.

And provided further, that until default be made by the said Mortgagor in one performance of the condition aforesaid, it shall and may be lawful for him to retain the possession of said goods and chattels, and to use and enjoy the same; but if the same, or any part thereof, shall be attached or claimed by any other person or persons, at any time before payment, or the said Mortgagor, or any person or persons whatever, upon any pretense, shall attempt to carry off, conceal, make way with, sell or in any manner dispose of the same, or any part thereof, without the authority and permission of the said Mortgagee, or his heirs, executors, administrators or assigns, in writing expressed, then it shall and may be lawful for the said Mortgagee, with or without assistance, or his agent or attorney or heirs, executors or administrators, to take possession of said goods and chattels, by entering upon any premises wherever the same may be, whether in this County or State or elsewhere, to and for the use of said Mortgagee, his heirs and assigns. And if the moneys hereby secured, or the matters to be done or performed at the time and according to the conditions above set forth, then the said Mortgagee, or his attorney or agent, or his heirs, executors, administrators or assigns, may, by virtue thereof, and without any suit or process, immediately enter and take possession of said goods and chattels, and sell and dispose of the same at public or private sale, and after satisfying the amount due, and all expenses, the surplus, if any remain, shall be paid over to said Mortgagor, or his heirs and assigns. The exhibition of this Mortgage shall be sufficient proof that any person claiming to act for the Mortgagee is duly made, constituted and appointed agent and attorney to do whatever is above authorized.

In witness whereof, the said Mortgagor has hereunto set his hand and seal, this eighteenth day of January, in the year of our Lord one thousand nine hundred.

Signed, Sealed and Delivered in Presence of
HENRY BROOKS.

E. L. GATTSHALL.

For form of acknowledgment see page 196.

ASSIGNMENT OF MORTGAGE.

The indorsement and transfer of a note secured by a mortgage transfers the security also, but in order to prevent the mortgagee from releasing to the prejudice of the assignee of the note it is always safest to have a written assignment of the mortgage made and recorded. In some States the assignment can be made upon the back of the mortgage and recorded. For such States the following assignment is the usual form. See Form 1.

In other States, such as Illinois, the assignment should be by formal separate instrument, duly executed and acknowledged in the same manner as mortgages and the same filed for record. Form 2 is the usual form for such assignments.

Form 1.

KNOW ALL MEN BY THESE PRESENTS, That I, Henry Betzold, the within named Mortgagee for a consideration of eight hundred dollars ($800), hereby assign, transfer, and set over unto E. B. Neeman, his heirs and assigns, the within named instrument of mortgage, and all the real estate, with appurtenances therein mentioned and described, to have and to hold the same forever. Subject nevertheless to the equity and right of redemption of the within named A. Meyer, his heirs and assigns therein.

In witness whereof the party of the first part has hereunto set his hand and seal this third day of March, in the year of our Lord nineteen hundred and one.

Sealed and Delivered in the Presence of E. E. HAWTHORN. } HENRY BETZOLD. [Seal.]

Form 2.

KNOW ALL MEN BY THESE PRESENTS, That I, James Y. Scammon, of Chicago, Cook County, Illinois, party of the first part, in consideration of fifteen hundred ($1,500) dollars, lawful money of the United States, to me in hand paid by Henry Jones, of the same place, party of the second part, do hereby sell, assign, and transfer unto the said party of the second part, his heirs, executors, administrators, and assigns, a certain indenture of mortgage bearing date the first day of January, 1897, made by Samuel P. Smith, and Sarah E. Smith, his wife, and all my right, title and interest in and to the premises therein described as follows, to-wit: The southwest quarter of Section 21, Township No. 38, north, Range 11 east, of the 3d Principal Meridian; also lots Nos. 1, 3 and 5, in Block No. 19, in Scofield's Addition to the Village of Naperville, situated in the County of Du Page, and State of Illinois, which said mortgage is recorded in the Recorder's office of Du Page County, Illinois, in book 25 of mortgages, on page 100, together with notes therein described, and the money to come due thereon with all interest thereon.

To have and to hold the same unto the party of the second part, his executors, administrators, and assigns forever, subject only to the proviso in said indenture mortgage contained. And I do for myself, and my heirs, executors, and administrators, covenant with the party of the second part that there is now actually due and owing on said note and mortgage on principal and interest the sum of sixteen hundred ($1,600) dollars, and that I have a good right to assign the same, and I do hereby constitute and appoint the said party of the second part my true and lawful attorney irrevocably in my name or otherwise, but at his own proper costs and charges to have, use, and take all lawful ways and means for the recovery of said money and interest, and in case of payment to discharge the same as fully as I might or could do if these presents were not made.

In witness whereof I have hereunto set my hand and seal this 13th day of May, A. D. 1901. JAMES Y. SCAMMON. [Seal.]

RELEASE.

A mortgage on real estate is released by deed of a lease under seal, and acknowledged, or receipt of satisfaction of the debt entered upon the margin of the record of mortgage by mortgagee.

Whenever a mortgage is paid a proper release thereof should be made, signed and acknowledged by the mortgagee and the same recorded. In some States the indorsement of satisfaction and cancellation on the face of the mortgage authorizes the recorder or register of deeds to enter satisfaction thereof upon the records; in others a formal release must be executed and acknowledged by the mortgagee and recorded, or a release may be entered upon the margin of the record of the mortgage in the recorder's office. The important thing, however, is to see that the record in the proper office shows the satisfaction of the mortgage. The methods of so doing differ in the various States, but the general rule is as above stated.

The following form of a release of mortgage is the one commonly in use in Illinois, and is a form which will effectually release a mortgage in any State, although more formal than those required by some of the States:

Form of Release.

KNOW ALL MEN BY THESE PRESENTS, That I, James Y. Scammon, of the County of Cook, and State of Illinois, for and in consideration of one dollar, to me in hand paid, and for other good and valuable considerations, the receipt whereof is hereby confessed, do hereby grant, bargain, remise, convey, release and quitclaim unto Samuel P. Smith and Sarah E. Smith, of the County of Du Page and State of Illinois, all the right, title, interest, claim or demand whatsoever I may have acquired in, through or by a certain indenture or mortgage deed, bearing date the first day of January, A. D. 1901, and recorded in the Recorder's office of Du Page County, Illinois, in book 25 of mortgages, page 100, to the premises therein described, and which said deed was made to secure two certain promissory notes, bearing even date with said deed, for the sum of twenty-five hundred dollars.

Witness my hand and seal this 28th day of February, A. D. 1901.

JAMES Y. SCAMMON. [Seal.]

FORECLOSURE OF MORTGAGE.

In case the mortgagor fails to meet the conditions of the mortgage, the mortgagee to secure his interests may foreclose the mortgage; that is, cut off the mortgagee from redeeming the mortgaged property by a judgment of court.

Methods of foreclosure vary in different States, but the general features are: Application to court of chancery for authority to foreclose; notifying of the mortgagor; hearing the parties; reference to a master in chancery; advertising the property; selling it to the highest bidder at the specified time; deeding it to the purchaser, and paying over any surplus funds to the mortgagor.

CERTIFICATE OF ACKNOWLEDGMENT.

For Deeds, Mortgages, Assignments of Mortgages and Releases.

Deeds, mortgages, assignments of mortgages, and releases must all be acknowledged before a proper officer. The certificate must be made by both man and wife when married.

Form 1, for Chattel Mortgages.

STATE OF ILLINOIS, } ss.
KANE COUNTY. }

I, John Richard, a Justice of the Peace in the Town of Dundee, in and for the said County, do hereby certify that this mortgage was duly acknowledged before me by the above named ————, the grantor therein named, and entered by me this 17th day of July, 1918.

Witness my hand and seal.

(Seal.) JOHN RICHARD,
Justice of the Peace.

Form 2, for Assignments and Releases.

STATE OF ILLINOIS, } ss.
COUNTY OF DU PAGE. }

I, John Smith, a Notary Public in and for said County, and in the State aforesaid, do hereby certify that James Y. Scammon, who is personally known to me to be the same person whose name is subscribed to the foregoing instrument, appeared before me this day in person and acknowledged that he signed, sealed and delivered the said instrument as his free and voluntary act for the uses and purposes therein set forth.

Given under my hand and Notarial Seal this 13th day of May, 1918.

(Notarial Seal.) JOHN SMITH,
Notary Public.

Form 3, for Mortgages and Deeds.

STATE OF ILLINOIS, } ss.
COUNTY OF DU PAGE. }

I, John Smith, a Notary Public in and for said County in the State aforesaid, do hereby certify that Samuel P. Smith and Sarah E.

Smith, his wife, who are personally known to me to be the same persons whose names are subscribed to the foregoing instrument, appeared before me this day in person and acknowledged that they signed, sealed, and delivered said instrument as their free and voluntary act for the uses and purposes therein set forth, including a release and waiver of all rights under and by virtue of the homestead exemption laws of this State.

Given under my hand and Notarial Seal this first day of January, A. D. 1901.
JOHN SMITH,
(Notarial Seal.) Notary Public.

Form 4, General and Short Form.

STATE OF ———————, }
COUNTY OF ———————. } ss.

On the ——— day of ——————— in the year one thousand nine hundred and ———, before me personally came (name of both parties), who are known to me to be the individuals described in, and who executed the foregoing instrument, and acknowledged that they executed the same. (Signature.)

BAIL.

1. Bail means sureties who bind themselves either to satisfy the plaintiff, his debt and costs, or to surrender the defendant into custody, provided judgment is rendered against him in the action. The above definition applies to civil action. In criminal cases bail means the sureties who bind themselves to have the prisoner present in court when required for trial. In ordinary parlance the word bail is used as synonymous with the word surety and practically means the same thing. We shall treat the subject in its relation to civil matters under the law of suretyship. In criminal matters the subject not being germain to the purpose of this book is not further discussed.

BONDS.

1. A bond is defined to be an obligation in writing under seal. It is a form of contract which is almost infinite in variety. The parties to the bond are the obligor and the obligee, the former being the one who makes the promise and the latter the person to whom the promise is made.

A simple bond is an instrument for the payment of money at a certain time, and generally bears interest at the rate specified in the bond. Nearly all corporate and municipal bonds are of this character and contain no condition except for the payment of the amount of the bond at a certain time and place with a certain specified rate of interest. Frequently interest coupons are attached to the original bond providing for the payments of several installments of interest as they come due.

The following is the form commonly in use for such bonds:

UNITED STATES OF AMERICA.
JEFFERSON CITY, STATE OF MISSOURI.
RENEWAL SCHOOL BOND.
INTEREST 5 PER CENT., PAYABLE SEMI-ANNUALLY.

The Board of Education of the City of Jefferson, County of Cole, and State of Missouri, being legally organized under and pursuant to an act of the General Assembly of the State of Missouri entitled "An act to revise and amend the Laws in relation to Public Schools in Cities, Towns and Villages," approved April 26th, 1877, for value received promise to pay to the bearer ten years after the date hereof ONE THOUSAND DOLLARS, at the St. Louis National Bank, in the City of St. Louis, Missouri, and interest thereon at the rate of Five per centum per annum from the date hereof, which interest shall be payable semi-annually at said St. Louis National Bank in the City of St. Louis, Missouri, on the surrender of the proper interest coupons hereto attached. This bond shall be redeemable at the pleasure of the said Board of Education of the City of Jefferson at any time after the expiration of Five years from the date hereof, and is issued under and pursuant to an act of the General Assembly of the State of Missouri, entitled "An Act to authorize Board of Education to issue renewal funding School Bonds to be sold or exchanged for the purpose of meeting and paying matured or maturing bonded indebtedness of school districts, and for levying special tax to pay the bonded indebtedness of school districts," approved April 11th, 1877.

In Testimony Whereof: the said Board of Education has caused this bond to be signed by the President, countersigned by the Secretary, authenticated by the seal of said Board of Education and attested by the Clerk of the County Court of said County of Cole, with the seal of said Court affixed this First day of July, 1901.

JOHN JONES, President.
WM. SMITH, Secretary.
GEO. SMILEY, Clerk County Court.

2. Bonds of Public Officials conditioned for the faithful performance of certain things are almost of infinite variety and in common use. All State, county, town and city officers having in their hands moneys or funds of any character belonging to said corporation are required to give bonds for the proper performance of the duties of their office. The following form of a bond of city treasurer can be used with few slight changes for almost any office:

KNOW ALL MEN BY THESE PRESENTS, That we, John Jones, Henry Smith, and Charles Marshall of the City of Naperville, County of Du Page, and State of Illinois, are held and firmly bound unto the City of Naperville in the penal sum of Twenty Thousand ($20,000) Dollars, for the payment of which, well and truly to be made, we bind ourselves, our heirs, executors, and administrators jointly and firmly by these presents.

Witness our hands and seals this 14th day of July, 1900.

The condition of the above obligation is such that whereas the above bounden John Jones has been duly elected to the office of City Treasurer of the City of Naperville, Now if the said John Jones shall faithfully perform all the duties of said office and shall account for and pay over all moneys that may come into his hands as such Treasurer, according to law, and the ordinances of said City and the order and direction of the city council of said City, then this obligation to be void, otherwise to remain in full force and effect.

JOHN JONES, (Seal.)
HENRY SMITH, (Seal.)
CHARLES MARSHALL. (Seal.)

3. **Officers of Corporation** are generally required to give bonds for the faithful performance of their duties. The following form can be used for nearly all such bonds:

KNOW ALL MEN BY THESE PRESENTS, That we, James Lord, John Williams, and Charles Smith, are held and firmly bound unto the Naperville Manufacturing Company, a corporation duly organized under the laws of the State of Illinois, in the penal sum of Ten Thousand ($10,000) Dollars, good and lawful money of the United States for the payment of which, well and truly to be made for said corporation or its assigns, we bind ourselves jointly and severally by these presents.

Witness our hands and seals this 14th day of July, 1901.

The condition of the above obligation is such that whereas the above bounden has been elected President of the Naperville Manufacturing Company; Now Therefore, if the said James Lord shall well and truly perform the duties of his said office and shall account for and pay over all moneys that shall come into his hands as such President, according to the rules of said corporation and the order and direction of the board of directors thereof, then this obligation shall be void, otherwise to remain in full force and effect.

JAMES LORD, (Seal.)
JOHN WILLIAMS, (Seal.)
CHARLES SMITH, (Seal.)

4. **Indemnifying Bonds.**—Bonds are also frequently given to indemnify persons who incur liability for another in nearly all the walks of life. The following form may be used:

KNOW ALL MEN BY THESE PRESENTS, That William Marsh, Principal, and John Henry, Surety, are held and firmly bound unto John Jones in the penal sum of One Hundred ($100) Dollars lawful money of the United States, for the payment of which, well and truly to be made, we bind ourselves, our heirs, executors, and administrators, jointly, severally and firmly by these presents.

Witness our hands and seals this 1st day of June, A. D. 1901.

The condition of the above obligation is such that whereas the said John Jones has been surety for the above bounden William Marsh on his note for One Hundred ($100) Dollars, payable to the order of Charles William, due on one year from the date hereof, with interest at the rate of 6 per cent. per annum.

Now, Therefore, if the said William Marsh shall well and truly pay the said note with all interest thereon when the same comes due and shall from time to time and at all times hereafter save, keep harmless and indemnify the said John Jones of and from all actions, suits, costs, charges, damages, and expenses whatsoever, including attorney's fees which shall or may at any time hereafter happen or come to him for any reason, by reason of his becoming surety on said note, then this obligation to be void, otherwise to remain in full force and effect.

WILLIAM MARSH, (Seal.)
JOHN HENRY. (Seal.)

5. **Executor's Bond.**—Executors, administrators, guardians and conservators are required to enter into bonds to be approved by the proper court before they are allowed to enter upon their duties as such. The forms for such bonds, however, vary in the different States.

WILLS AND LAWS OF WILLS.

1. A will is a legal statement of what a person determines to have done with his property after his death.

2. The maker of a will is called a testator; if female, testatrix.

3. There are two kinds of wills, written and verbal or nuncupative.

4. Nuncupative wills depend upon proof of persons hearing the same. They are usually unsafe and are now obsolete.

5. The wishes of the testator should be fully and clearly expressed in a written will.

6. No exact form of words is necessary to make a will.

7. In writing wills simple language should be used. Statements concerning every provision or condition of the will should be fully and plainly made.

8. All persons of sound mind and memory, of lawful age, freely exercising their own will, may dispose of their property by will. In some States a married woman cannot make a will without consent of her husband.

9. "Lawful age" is in most States twenty-one years, in both male and female; in some States a female is of lawful age when eighteen years old; in some States persons may dispose of personal property by will at the age of seventeen.

10. A will has no force or effect until after testator's death.

11. The last will annuls all former wills.

12. A wife cannot be deprived of her dower, which is a life interest in one-third of her husband's real estate, by will, but in some States taking any interest in her husband's property by virtue of his will bars her dower.

13. Subsequent marriage by female revokes will made while single in some States.

14. Testator's property is primarily liable for testator's debts and funeral expenses, which must be paid before any part of it can be distributed to legatees.

15. A will is good, though written with a lead pencil.

16. A person who is competent to make a will can appoint his own executor. If the person so appointed is legally competent to transact business, the probate court will confirm the ap-

pointment. The person so appointed is not obliged to serve.

17. It is not necessary that the witnesses should know the contents of the will. It is generally necessary that testator acknowledge to them that it is his will, sign it in their presence, or acknowledge the signature already signed to be his, and request them to sign as witnesses; they should sign as witnesses in the presence of each other.

18. Testator should write his own name in full. If unable to do so, his hand should be guided by another, and his name written, or a mark made near his name.

The following is the usual form where testator signs by mark.

his
John X Smith.
mark.

19. An addition to an executed will is called a codicil.

20. The same essentials apply to a codicil as to a will.

21. Legacies to subscribing witnesses are generally declared void by the statute.

22. To convey real estate by will, it must be done in accordance with the law of the State where such land is located.

23. Personal property may be conveyed in accordance with the law where the testator resides.

24. An executor is a person named in the will of a deceased person to settle his or her estate; there may be one or more.

25. An administrator is one appointed by the court to settle the estate of a deceased person.

The Form of a Will.

I, John Smith, of the Village of Naperville, County of Du Page, and State of Illinois, being of sound mind and memory, do make, publish and declare this to be my last will and testament, to-wit:

First—All my just debts and funeral expenses shall be first duly paid.

Second—I give, devise and bequeath all the rest, residue and remainder of my estate, both real and personal, to my beloved wife, Susie E. Smith, to have and to hold to her, my said wife, and to her heirs and assigns forever.

Third—I nominate and appoint my said wife, Susie E. Smith, to be the executor of this my last will and testament, hereby revoking all former wills by me made.

In witness whereof I have hereunto set my hand and seal this 15th day of November, A. D. 1902. JOHN SMITH. (Seal.)

Signed, sealed, published and declared as and for his last will and testament by the above named testator, in our presence, who have, at his request, and in his presence, and in the presence of each other, signed our names as witnesses thereto.

Most States require two witnesses. A. B.
Some States require three. C. D.
E. F.

INFORMATION FOR EXECUTORS AND ADMINISTRATORS.

An executor is named in a will to execute that will and settle the estate. If the will does not name an executor, or if named, he will or can not act, the Probate Court (some states Surrogate, others Orphans' Court) appoints an "administrator with the will annexed." If a person dies without leaving a will the court appoints an administrator, whose duty is the same as that of an executor, except that he, having no will of the deceased, distributes the property as the law directs.

The duties of an executor are: *First.* To see that the deceased is suitably buried, avoiding unreasonable expense if the estate is insolvent. *Second.* To offer the will for probate, or proving; to conform to the laws of his state and rules of the court, the clerk of which will give full instructions. *Third.* To make and return to the court within required time an inventory of the property. "Real estate lying in another state need not be inventoried, for that must be administered upon in the state where it lies; but personal property situated in another state should be inventoried." If the real estate is encumbered, it should be described. *Fourth.* To collect the property, pay the debts and dispose of the remainder as the law and will, or either, directs. Generally the debts should be paid as follows: 1. Funeral expenses. 2. Expenses of last sickness. 3. Debts due the United States. 4. Debts due the state. 5. Claims of creditors. *Fifth.* To render the accounts as directed by the court.

Commissioners are generally appointed to hear the claims of all within a limited time. An appeal from their action may be taken to the court. If no appeal, the executor pays the legacies, etc., makes final accounts which are submitted to a hearing, and if no objection, the estate is closed. If the executor dies before the estate is closed, his executor has no authority over the first estate. Anothet is appointed to complete the execution.

The law provides that the widow of the intestate shall be first entitled to act as administrator; next, the nearest of kin who are competent; next, any creditor who will accept the trust; and lastly, any other suitable person.

Executors and administrators are required to take an official oath; also to give a bond, which is usually for double the amount of the estate.

EXECUTOR'S OR ADMINISTRATOR'S BOND.

KNOW ALL MEN BY THESE PRESENTS, That I, Charles D. Mann of Ira in the County of Rutland and State of Vermont, as principal, and Benj. E. Merrill of Poultney and N. Wright Emerson of Wells in the County of Rutland aforesaid, as sureties, are holden and firmly bound unto the Probate Court for the District of Rutland (in some states, unto the People of the State of————), in the sum of Eight Thousand Dollars, to be paid unto the said Probate Court, to the which payment well and truly to be made, we bind ourselves, and each of our heirs, executors and administrators, jointly and severally, firmly be these presents, signed with our hands and sealed with our seals.

Dated at Rutland, in said District, this fifteenth day of September, A. D., 1906.

The condition of the above obligation is such, That if the above bounden Charles D. Mann, Executor of the last Will and Testament of John I. Merritt late of Fair Haven in the County of Rutland and State of Vermont, deceased, shall make and return to the Probate Court within three months a true and perfect inventory of all the goods, chattels, rights, credits, and estate of said deceased, which shall come to his possession or knowledge, or to the possession of any other person for him; and also all other goods, chattels, rights, credits and estate of said deceased, which shall any time after come to his possession, or the possession of any other person for him; and shall well and truly administer the same and pay and discharge all debts, legacies and charges chargeable thereon, or such dividends thereon as shall be ordered and decreed by said Probate Court; render a true and just account of his administration to said Court, within one year, and at any other time when required by said Court, and perform all orders and decrees of said Probate Court by Executor to be performed in the premises—then the above obligation is void, otherwise in force.

Signed, sealed and delivered in presence of H. MAX WEBBER, Clerk of County Court.	CHARLES D. MANN.	(L. S.)
	BENJ. E. MERRILL.	(L. S.)
	N. WRIGHT EMERSON.	(L. S.)

Some States require acknowledgment as below.

RUTLAND COUNTY, ss.

At the session of Probate Court in and for said County, holden at Rutland, on the eighteenth day of September, A. D., 1906, I have examined and do approve of the foregoing bond, and order the same to be filed and recorded in the Probate Office of said County.

M. T. GUTELIUS,
Judge of Probate.

LEAVING FOR AMERICA.

NATURALIZATION.

1. Definition.—Naturalization is the act by which an alien is made a citizen of the United States.

2. How Secured.—An alien to become a citizen of the United States must have resided therein five years before making his final application. At least two years before his admission he must declare on oath before the clerk of some court of record in the State in which he resides his bona fide intention to become a citizen of the United States and renounce forever all allegiance and fidelity to any foreign Prince, Potentate, State, or Sovereignty, and particularly by name to Prince, Potentate, State, and Sovereignty of which the alien may be at the time a citizen and subject.

3. Final Papers.—At the time of securing his final papers he must declare on oath before some court of record having common law jurisdiction that he will support the Constitution of the United States; that he absolutely and entirely renounces and abjures all allegiance and fidelity to every foreign Prince, Potentate, State, and Sovereignty of which he was a citizen and a subject.

4. Residence.—It must also be made to appear to the

satisfaction of said court that he has resided within the United States five years at least, and within the State where such court is at the time of application one year at least, and that during all that time he has behaved himself as a man of good moral character in accordance with the principles of the Constitution of the United States, and well disposed to the good order and happiness of the same. This last proof is usually made by the affidavit of two witnesses who have known the applicant for at least five years prior to the time of such application.

5. **Hereditary Title.**—In case the applicant has borne any hereditary title or been of any of the orders of nobility in the kingdom or state from which he came, he must, in connection with the above requirements, make an express renunciation of his title or order of nobility in the court in which his application is made.

6. **Signed Petition Required.**—Before an applicant can secure his final papers he must make and file in duplicate a petition in writing *signed by himself* and duly verified in which he shall state his full name, place of residence, occupation, etc. Such petition must be filed not less than two nor more than seven years after the declaration of intention.

7. **Must be Able to Speak the English Language.**—An alien to be admitted as a citizen of the U. S. must be able to speak the English language. This requirement does not apply to those who are physically unable to comply therewith, nor to such who declare their intention to become citizens and who make homestead entries upon the public lands of the U. S. and comply with the laws governing same.

8. **Enemies of Government.**—Anarchists, polygamists, and all other enemies of organized government can not be naturalized or become citizens of the U. S.

9. **Declaration of Intention under Old Law.**—Aliens who made declaration of intention prior to Sept. 27, 1906, but were not naturalized before that date under the old law must comply with the requirements of the new law in regard to the filing of petition for naturalization and furnishing proof except that they will not be required to speak the English language or to sign petition in their own handwriting.

10. **Fees.**—For receiving and filing a declaration of intention and issuing a duplicate, $1.00. For making, filing and docketing the petition for admission as a citizen, $2.00. For entering the long order and issuing certificate of citizenship, $2.00.

QUALIFICATIONS FOR SUFFRAGE, VOTING, ETC.

Requirements for Citizenship and for Voting.

States.	Requirements as to Citizenship.	Residence in		
		State.	County	Precinct.
Alabama (a)	Citizen or declared intent	2 yr...	1 yr...	3 mo..
Alaska	Citizen	1 yr...	....	30 days.
Arizona	Citizen or declared intent	1 yr...	30 days.	30 days.
Arkansas (c)	Citizen or declared intent	1 yr...	6 mo..	1 mo..
Califor'a (h)(i)(a)	Actual citizens	1 yr...	90 days.	30 days.
Colorado (b)	Citizen or declared intent	1 yr...	90 days.	10 days.
Connecticut (o)(a)	Actual citizens	1 yr...	6 mo..	6 mo..
Delaware (a)	Actual county taxpayers.	1 yr...	3 mo..	30 days.
Florida (b)	Citizen	1 yr...	6 mo..	30 days.
Georgia (o)(a) ...	Actual citizens	1 yr...	6 mo..	30 days.
Idaho (÷)(a)......	Actual citizens	6 mo..	30 days.	10 days.
Illinois (a)	Actual citizens	1 yr...	90 days.	30 days.
Indiana (e)	Citizen or declared intent	6 mo..	60 days.	30 days.
Iowa (d)	Actual citizens	6 mo..	60 days.	10 days.
Kansas (d)........	Citizen or declared intent	6 mo..	30 days.	10 days.
Kentucky (d)	Actual citizens	1 yr...	6 mo..	60 days.
Louisiana (o)(a)..	Citizen	2 yr...	1 yr...	6 mo..
Maine (a)	Actual citizens	3 mo..	3 mo..	3 mo..
Maryland (o) (b).	Actual citizens	1 yr...	6 mo..	1 day..
Massachus'ts (o)(a)	Citizen	1 yr...	6 mo..	6 mo..
Michigan (a)......	Citizen or declared intent	6 mo..	20 days.	20 days.
Minnesota (a)	Citizen	6 mo..	30 days.	30 days.
Mississippi (‖)(b).	Actual citizens	2 yr...	1 yr...	1 yr...
Missouri (b)	Citizen or declared intent	1 yr...	60 days.	60 days.
Montana (a)	Citizen	1 yr...	30 days.	30 days.
Nebraska (a)	Citizen or declared intent	6 mo..	10 days.	10 days.
Nevada (b)	Citizen or declared intent	6 mo..	30 days.	30 days.
N. Hampshire (a).	Actual citizens	6 mo..	6 mo..	6 mo..
New Jersey (a)...	Actual citizens	1 yr...	5 mo...	....
New Mexico (a)...	Actual citizens	1 yr...	90 days.	30 days.
New York (d).....	Actual citizens	1 yr...	4 mo..	30 days.
N. Carolina (o)(b)	Actual citizens	2 yr...	6 mo...	4 mo...
North Dakota (d).	Citizen or declared intent	1 yr...	6 mo...	90 days.
Ohio (d)	Actual citizens	1 yr...	30 days.	20 days.
Oklahoma (a) ...	Actual citizens	1 yr...	6 mo..	30 days.
Oregon (e)	Citizen or declared intent	6 mo..	....	....
Pennsylvania (b)..	Actual citizens	1 yr...	....	2 mo..
Rhode Island (a)	Actual citizens	2 yr...	....	6 mo..
S. Carolina (‖)(b).	Actual citizens	2 yr...	1 yr...	4 mo..
South Dakota (a).	Citizen or declared intent	6 mo..	30 days.	10 days.
Tennessee (d)	Actual citizens	1 yr...	6 mo..	....
Texas (d)	Citizen or declared intent	1 yr...	6 mo..	6 mo..
Utah (b)	Citizen	1 yr...	4 mo..	60 days.
Vermont (a)	Actual citizens	1 yr...	3 mo..	3 mo..
Virginia (o)(a)...	Actual citizens	2 yr...	1 yr...	30 days.
Washington (a)...	Citizen or declared intent	1 yr...	90 days.	30 days.
West Virginia (c).	Actual citizens	1 yr...	60 days.	10 days.
Wisconsin (d)	Citizen or declared intent	1 yr...	10 days.	10 days.
Wyoming (a)	Citizen	1 yr...	60 days.	10 days.

(a) Registration required by law. (b) Required by constitution. (c) Prohibited by constitution. (d) Required in large cities. (e) No registration required. (x) Mayor and city council have power to require registration. (o) Educational qualification (read the constitution in the English language), or own property assessed for not less than $300, or voter on Jan. 1, 1867, or descendant of such voter, or a foreigner naturalized prior to Jan. 1, 1898. (h) Citizen 90 days before election. (÷) Bigamists disqualified. (i) Native of China disqualified. (‖) Educational qualification by which voter is required to read and understand constitution.

The year 1920 brought the passage of the nineteenth amendment to the constitution of the United States granting women complete suffrage in all the states.

PASSPORTS.

Passports are permissions granted by the Government to its citizens, commending them to the protection of foreign countries which they may visit. They are issued only by the Secretary of State.

To Whom Granted.—They are issued only to citizens of the United States on written application. Blank forms of application can be secured by applying to the Secretary of State, Washington, D. C.

Wife, Minor Children, and Servants of an American citizen may all be included in the citizen's passport. Any other person requires a separate passport.

Applications.—A citizen of the United States desiring to procure a passport must make a written application in the form of an affidavit to the Secretary of State.

Naturalized Citizens.—A naturalized citizen must transmit his certificate of naturalization, or a duly certified copy of the court record thereof, with his application. He must state in his affidavit when and from what port he emigrated, what ship he sailed in, and where he has lived since his arrival in the United States.

Professional Titles are not allowed in passports.

Expiration.—A passport expires two years from the date of its issuance. A new one can be obtained upon a new application.

Fee.—A fee of $1 is required to be collected for every citizen's passport, and must be paid in currency or postal money order. Drafts or checks will not be received.

Blank Forms will be furnished on application if it is stated whether they are for native or for naturalized citizens.

Address all communications to "Department of State, Passport Division, Washington, D. C." A passport should always be carried upon the person—never in a trunk or valise.

PATENTS.

1. **Definition.**—As here used the word Patent is defined to mean the granting by the United States to inventors for a limited time the use of their own inventions. The instrument by which this privilege is confirmed to the inventor is called the "Letters Patent" and is issued in the name of the United States

of America under the seal of the Patent office and is signed by the Secretary of the Interior, and countersigned by the Commissioner of Patents.

2. For What Granted.—Patents are granted for any new and useful machine, manufacture, or composition of matter, or any new and useful improvement thereon not known and used by others in this country and not patented or described in any printed publication in this or any foreign country before its invention and discovery here, and not in public use or on sale for more than two years prior to the application for a patent. Every civilized country in the world has taken out patents in the United States.

3. Foreign Patent Not a Bar.—A person is not debarred from receiving a patent for his inventions or discoveries by reason of its first having been patented in a foreign country unless the same has been introduced into public use in the United States for more than two years prior to the application therein.

4. Duration of Patent.—A patent is good for seventeen years, but now cannot be extended except by act of Congress. Inventions previously patented in a foreign country must expire at the same time that the foreign patent expires, but in no case shall they be extended more than seventeen years.

5. How Secured.—The method of securing patents is by petition, which must be in writing addressed to the Commissioner of Patents, and must state the name and residence of the petitioner requesting the granting of a patent, designating by title the invention sought to be patented, and contain a reference to the specifications for a full disclosure of such invention and must be signed by the applicant and attested by two witnesses. An alien may obtain a patent on the same terms as a citizen.

6. Specifications.—The specifications above referred to are a written description of the invention or discovery, and the manner of making, constructing, composing, and using the same, and they are required to be in such full, clear, concise and exact terms as to enable any person skilled in the art or science to which the invention or discovery appertains to make, construct, compose and use the same.

The specifications and claims should be absolutely written

on but one side of the paper. All interlineations and erasures should be avoided.

7. **The Oath.**—The applicant for a patent must make oath or affirmation that he verily believes himself to be the first and original discoverer of the art, machine, manufacture, composition, or improvement for which he solicits a patent; that he does not know and does not believe that the same was ever before known and used and shall state of what country he is a citizen and where he resides.

The oath should be sworn to before a notary public or some other officer authorized to administer oaths having an official seal.

8. **Drawings.**—The applicant for patent is required also to furnish drawings for his invention whenever the nature of the case admits. The drawing must be signed by the inventor and must be attested by two witnesses; it must show every feature of the invention covered by the claims. When the invention is an improvement on some old machine the drawing must exhibit in one or more views the invention itself disconnected from the old structure and also in another view so much of the old structure as will suffice to show the connection of the invention therewith.

9. **Material.**—Drawings must be made upon pure white, calendered, smooth, bristol board paper, of three sheet thickness. India ink alone must be used, sheets must be exactly ten by fifteen inches in size. Drawings must be made with pen only, and must be absolutely black. Drawings must be made with the fewest lines possible consistent with clearness.

The scale to which a drawing is made must be large enough to show the mechanism without crowding.

10. **Signature** of the inventor should be placed at the lower right hand corner of each sheet of drawing and two attesting witnesses should sign at the lower left hand corner. Drawings should be rolled for transmission to the patent office.

11. **Model.**—A model must be furnished when required by the commissioner.

12. **Specimens** must be furnished when required by t commissioner.

13. **Attorneys.**—The practice of the patent office allows

the applicant to retain an attorney and when the petition is prosecuted by an attorney a power of attorney should be included in the petition. In ordinary cases it is always best to retain some experienced patent attorney to prosecute the application.

14. **Caveats.**—A caveat, under the patent law, is a notice given to the Patent Office of the caveator's claim as inventor, in order to prevent the grant of a patent to another person for the same alleged invention upon an application filed during the life of the caveat without notice to the caveator.

15. **Object.**—A caveat sets forth the object and the distinguishing characteristics of the invention, and prays protection of the inventor's right until he shall have matured his invention. Such caveats are filed in the confidential archives of the office and preserved in secrecy, and are operative for the term of one year from the filing thereof.

16. **To Whom Granted.**—A caveat is granted to any citizen of the United States or any alien, if he has resided in the United States one year next preceding the filing of his caveat, and has made oath of his intention to become a citizen.

17. **Renewal.**—The caveat may be renewed, on request in writing, by the payment of a second caveat fee of $10, and it will continue in force for one year from the date of the payment of such second fee. Subsequent renewals may be made with like effect.

18. **Fees.**—The schedule of fees and prices of publications can be had on application to the Commissioner of Patents, Washington, D. C. The fee for filing applications ranges from $10 to $30; for filing each caveat $10. For any other information concerning patents address the commissioner as above.

19. **Preliminary Examinations.**—Applicant for patent can save considerable expense oftentimes by having a preliminary examination of the patents allowed by the patent office made to determine whether or not the invention has been patented by somebody else. This examination cannot be made by the commissioner or any one of his office, but patent attorneys will make the examination for a small fee.

20. **Assignments.**—Patents may be assigned in whole or in part, and the right to manufacture, sell and use the patent

in any county, State, township or other district may be granted by the holder of the patent. All such assignments or transfers should be in writing, and are void unless recorded in the Patent Office within three months from their date.

PENSIONS.

Amount paid to pensioners, 1790 to 1920, inclusive:

War of the Revolution........................$	70,000,000.00
War of 1812..............................	46,070,413.18
Indian Wars	18,452,059.38
War with Mexico............................	53,582,977.63
Civil War	5,502,445,815.43
War with Spain and Philippine Insurrection....	69,835,764.39
Regular Establishment	53,846,229.59
World War	74,010.03
Unclassified	16,508,447.41
Total ....$	5,830,815,717.04

WAR RISK INSURANCE.

War Risk Insurance, or Soldiers' and Sailors' Insurance, is a form of life and disability insurance offered by the U. S. Government for the benefit of all persons in the military service. The insurance is offered in accordance with Act of Congress approved October 6, 1917, and was designed to do away with the wasteful and expensive pension system.

Who May Be Insured.—Any member of the military forces of the United States when employed in active service may, upon application and without medical examination, take out government term insurance against death or total disability, not less than $1,000 nor more than $10,000.

The rate is based on the American Experience Table of Mortality and interest at 3½%, the government bearing all expense of administration and excess mortality cost due to the hazards of war. Consequently, War Risk Insurance is the lowest in the world.

The insurance must be converted within five years after the termination of the war into any standard form of insurance without medical examination.

According to the original enactment, in case of death or permanent total disability, the policy was payable in monthly installments only. A recent amendment, however, permits the payment in a lump sum.

The term rates are as follows for $1,000 of insurance:

Age	Per Year	Per Month
20	$ 7.68	$ 0.64
30	8.28	.69
40	9.72	.81
50	13.68	1.14

The converted insurance rates are correspondingly low.

Compensation and Vocational Education.—Disabled service men may also receive government compensation and free tuition at educational institutions by presenting satisfactory medical evidence to the Board of Vocational Education. American Legion Posts throughout the country will supply necessary information.

LICENSE.

Definition.—License is a right or permission given by competent authority which without such authority would be illegal.

Licenses are of almost infinite variety and are issued by the National Government to distillers, brewers, liquor dealers of all kind, cigar manufacturers and dealers in many other articles. They are also issued by States, by counties, and also by cities, towns and villages to peddlers, hawkers, hackmen, draymen, bus drivers, cabmen, porters, expressmen, and itinerant merchants. They are also issued to saloons and druggists.

License from the National Government to a saloon keeper does not, however, authorize him to sell liquors in violation of any city or State statute, and constitutes no protection for so doing.

Licenses of the character hereinbefore named are issued usually under what is called the police power of the State, and are governed by rules peculiar to that power.

Licenses to liquor dealers and cigar manufacturers are issued by the Government upon application to the local internal revenue collector.

The following is a form of license commonly in use in cities, towns and villages for peddlers, hackmen, cab drivers, and other individuals requiring license from such authorities:

BY AUTHORITY OF THE CITY OF CHICAGO

Permission is hereby given to John Henry to keep for use or hire two Hacks or Carriages in the City of Chicago, State of Illinois, from July 1, 1901, to June 30, 1902, under the ordinances in such case made and provided, subject, nevertheless, to revocation or suspension by the mayor or City Council.

Witness the hand of ——— ———, Mayor of said City, and the Corporate Seal thereof, this 1st day of July, 1901.

(Corporate Seal.) .... Mayor.

ATTEST:

..............City Clerk.

A LIST OF FOURTEEN OF OUR LARGEST TRUSTS.

	Capital Stock.
American Can Co., New York	$ 88,000,000.00
American Tobacco Co., Jersey City	180,000,000.00
Amalgamated Copper Co., New York	155,000,000.00
American Woolen Co., Boston	60,000,000.00
American Sugar Refining Co., Jersey City	90,000,000.00
American Smelting & Refining Co., New York	115,000,000.00
Corn Product Co., New York	80,000,000.00
Central Leather Co., New York	80,000,000.00
International Harvester Co., Chicago	140,000,000.00
National Lead Co., New York	50,000,000.00
Standard Oil Co., New York	100,000,000.00
U. S. Rubber Co., New York	65,000,000.00
U. S. Steel Corporation, New York	950,000,000.00
U. S. Smelting, Refining & Mining Co., Boston	75,000,000.00
Total Capital Stock Common and Preferred	$2,228,000,000.00

The capitalization of these trusts has been increased from year to year so that the combined capital stock of these fourteen trusts has been more than doubled in ten years. It is true that according to a decision of the U. S. Supreme Court in 1911 the Standard Oil Co., the American Tobacco Co. and the U. S. Steel Co., the three greatest and most dangèrous trusts, were dissolved, but without any apparent effect on their power. They have raised prices and watered stock since this decision just as they did before.

Insurance.

Definition.—A contract whereby, for an agreed premium, one party undertakes to indemnify the other against loss on a specified subject by specified perils. The party agreeing to make the indemnity is called the insurer, or underwriter, the other the insured or assured. The agreed consideration is called the premium. The written contract is called the policy. The subject, right or interest to be protected is called the insurable interest.

2. **Forms.**—The most usual forms of insurance are Fire, Life, Marine and Accident insurance.

3. **Insurable Interest.**—The insurer must always have an insurable interest in the subject matter of the insurance. Such an interest has been defined to be any interest in property or relation thereto or liability in respect thereof of such a nature that a contemplated peril might directly damnify the insured.

4. **Corporations.**—All kinds of insurance are carried on by large corporations. These corporations in this country are usually organized under general laws and are conducted under the supervision and control of the State authorities. There are, however, scattered through the country a large number of mutual companies. These companies also are organized under special statutes governing the same and the stockholders are also in general the insured. In most of the States an insurance department has been established and the management and supervision of insurance both life and fire is under the control of this department, which is generally managed by an officer called either a superintendent or commissioner of insurance.

5. **Foreign Insurance Companies** are generally required to deposit a certain amount of funds in this department in each State as a security for the payment of losses on all insurances carried by them in said State. Companies doing business in any State are required to make annual reports to the insurance department of their business and of the character and quality of their assets.

6. **Authority.**—The insurance department also has authority to examine into the business of any company and in case

of weakness require that any losses and failure of assets be made good, and in case of insolvency they have authority to take possession of this company and wind up the business.

7. **Suits.**—All foreign insurance companies are also required to designate some individual living within the State upon whom legal process can be served. Suits against insurance companies by statute in most of the States can be commenced in any county where the party having claims against such company resides and service of summons can be had on the proper agent in any county of the State.

8. **Fire Insurance is Furnishing Indemnity Against Loss by Fire.**—It is now generally conducted by large private corporations or by mutual companies.

9. **Mutual Companies.**—These mutual companies are generally established by statute and provide for the payment of losses by a pro rata assessment upon the policy holders, who constitute the stockholders and who manage the affairs of the company. Some of these mutual companies require a small premium paid in advance. Others simply require a small fee to pay for the expense of making the survey and issuing the policy. All of them, however, in case of a loss make an assessment pro rata upon the policy holders to pay the same. Such companies are not very common in cities, but are quite general throughout the rural districts.

10. **Old Line Companies.**—The insurance business of private corporations generally called Line Companies is carried on through the country by means of agents established in nearly every town and city of any size throughout the country. Many of the States have adopted a standard form of fire policy and nearly all reputable companies have adopted forms which are similar in their terms and conditions.

11. **Kind of Risks.**—The fire insurance policies are usually divided into commercial, dwelling house and farm risks. The time for which commercial risks are usually written is for a year, although on the very best class of buildings a three-year risk is permitted. Risks on stocks of goods and machinery are always limited to one year. The rate for the three-year term is two and one-half times the annual rate.

Dwelling house and farm risks are usually written for one,

three and five years, the three-year term being 2½ times the annual rate and the five-year term four times the annual rate.

12. Boards.—The old line insurance companies of the country are nearly all united into a National Underwriters' Association which has general charge of the fire insurance business of the country. Under this national board the old line companies doing business in each State have an underwriters' association which has charge of the insurance business in the State. In nearly every town or city of any size the agents of the respective companies are also organized into local boards. The agencies of the different companies are all required by an iron-bound contract to maintain the rates of insurance fixed by the State board of underwriters, and violations of the provisions of this contract are punished by heavy fines. By these agreements agents of the different companies are prohibited from cutting rates or offering inducements to secure insurances and they are limited to a fixed rate of the premium as their commission. Nearly every town of any size in the respective States is rated, that is the rates of insurance upon all the commercial buildings and the stocks contained therein are fixed and a rate sheet issued to the agents of all companies doing business in the town. This rating is not done by the local agents of the company living in the town or city, but is done by agents appointed by the State board of underwriters and sent there for the purpose.

13. Assignment of Policy.—The policy of insurance cannot be assigned except with the consent of the insurance company. Notice of all change in the title to property covered by insurance, whether personal or real, should immediately be given to the local agent of the company carrying the insurance and the consent of such agent to the assignment secured.

14. Mortgage Clause.—In case of mortgage on real property the loss should be made payable to the mortgagee as his interest may appear by mortgage clause, which is usually printed on a separate sheet of paper and attached to the policy.

15. Loss.—In case of loss under an insurance policy notice should be immediately given to the company or its agent and a request made for a form of proof of loss. These forms are usually furnished by the company gratis, and the provisions of the policy in regard to making proof of loss should be strictly followed. Always get a removal permit before moving goods covered by insurance.

16. Lightning Clauses.—An ordinary policy of insurance does not usually insure against lightning, but lightning clauses without extra expense will be attached to nearly all policies if requested at the time of issue.

17. Life Insurance.—Life insurance is now usually carried on by large corporations and benevolent orders having insurance departments connected therewith. The forms of policies are almost infinite. They differ from fire insurance in that they extend for life or for a definite period of years. The premium is required to be paid either annually or semi-annually.

18. Applications.—Nearly all life insurance companies require applications therefor to be in writing and they are usually accompanied by a medical examination made by the Local Medical Examiner of the company. These applications are forwarded to the home office, and if the same pass the head Medical Examiner the policy is issued to the insured and the application is made a part of the policy Any false statement contained therein will vitiate the policy and applicants for insurance should be careful to see that all questions are fully and truthfully answered. Most life insurance policies provide that the insurance shall not be in force until the first premium is paid, and most policies are now incontestable after the payment of two or three premiums. By the laws of all of the States in case default is made in the payment of premium after three full premiums have been paid, the policy holder may have the option of securing a paid up policy for a certain portion of the original risk, and all good companies now insert an option of this character into their policies. Sometimes the policies provide that after the payments cease the applicants shall be entitled to three or four years' paid-up insurance.

The usual clauses contained in life insurance policies are these: That the insurance ceases unless the premiums are promptly paid; that the company shall be exempt if the insured commits suicide whether sane or insane, or if death shall come by the hands of justice for a violation of law; that agents are not authorized to alter or discharge any part of the contract; that assignments of the policy shall not take effect until notice thereof shall be given to the company at its home office; that after two years the policy will be incontestable except for fraud or non-payment of premium.

19. Marine Insurance.—Marine insurance is governed largely by the same rules that control fire insurance. This form of insurance may include all casualties resulting from the unusual or violent actions of the elements, foundering at sea, grounding, collision, fire, perils of war, rests and restraints, jettison, and any other perils, losses, or misfortunes of the sea.

20. Accident Insurance is now over fifty years old and there are a great many companies which insure against all kinds of accidents. Upon payment of small premiums, policies may be had insuring against accident from one day to ten years, for any reasonable amount. The rates depend upon the occupation of the insured.

21. Other Kinds of Insurance include employers' liability, public liability, tornado, explosion, automobile, burglary, fraud, insolvency and loss through bad debts. Almost every kind of risk imaginable may now be covered by insurance.

FORMULA FOR 100 PER CENT PROOF OF LOSS IN CASE OF FIRE.

Inventory (as of certain date) plus Incoming Invoices (for goods bought subsequent to inventory) plus Freight and Dray Bills on same plus Credit Memorandums (for merchandise returned) plus Production Department Payrolls (is manufacturing business) plus Appreciation (increase in value of goods since purchased).	MINUS	Outgoing Charges (representing goods sold since Inventory extended at present cost) minus Depreciation (decrease in value of merchandise) minus Salvage (market value of goods not destroyed).	EQUALS	Value of goods or Proof of Loss.

ASSOCIATIONS FOR TRANSACTING BUSINESS.

PARTNERSHIPS, HOW FORMED AND LAWS GOVERNING THEM.

1. Partnership is a voluntary contract between two or more persons, to place their property, labor or credit, or some or all of them, in some lawful business, to share the gains and losses in certain proportions.

2. Where no time is specified, any partner may dissolve a partnership at will.

3. The death of any partner dissolves the whole firm.

4. Each partner has full authority to act for the firm.

5. A silent partner is one who is actually a partner by participation of profit, but is not known to be such.

6. A nominal partner is one who holds himself out to the world as such, but is not so in fact. He becomes liable to creditors of the firm because he justifies them in trusting the firm on his credit.

7. Partners may agree to share the profits in whatever proportion they choose. They may also agree as to any way of dividing the losses. Such agreement is valid between themselves, but it will not protect those partners who were to sustain no loss from responsibility to third parties.

8. Not only the common property, but also all the private property of each partner may be taken, to satisfy the debts of the firm.

9. Upon the dissolution the old partners are responsible to third persons for even new debts, unless such persons have had notice of the dissolution.

10. One partner may discharge himself from liability by giving express notice to any customer or other person not to trust one or more of his co-partners.

11. A partner cannot make the firm responsible for his separate or private debt, nor bind the firm by entering into engagements unconnected with, or foreign to, the partnership.

12. The authority of a partner extends to the making or indorsing negotiable paper, and to all transactions fairly connected with that business.

13. A person who after due care lends money to one of a partnership firm for the firm, can hold the firm liable, although the money is fraudulently appropriated by the partner to his own use.

14. If a partner borrows money to increase the capital of the firm, the firm cannot be held liable for the payment of such sum.

15. The contract of co-partnership may be made verbally or in writing. It is a serious engagement and easier to get into than to get out of. Every person should use great care in involving his property and business interests in a co-partnership, and where those interests are extensive, articles of co-partnership drawn by the best qualified lawyer available are the safest expedient, and will in all cases be a good investment.

Articles of Co-partnership.

ARTICLES OF AGREEMENT, made December 3d, 1901, between John H. Wagner and Gregory Ross:

The said parties hereby agree to become co-partners, under the firm name of Wagner & Ross, and as such partners to carry on together the business of buying and selling all sorts of dry goods, at No. 547 Fulton street, in the city of Brooklyn.

The said John H. Wagner agrees to contribute two thousand dollars ($2,000) to the capital of said firm; and the said Gregory Ross agrees to contribute one thousand dollars ($1,000) to the same; the sum of $2,500 of said capital to be expended in the purchase of a stock in trade.

The said Wagner shall have exclusive charge of all the buying for the firm.

All the net profits arising out of the business shall be divided in the following proportions, two-thirds to the said Wagner and one-third to the said Ross.

Each partner shall devote all his time, attention, and efforts to the said business.

Neither partner shall, without the consent of the other, sign any bond, bill or note as surety, or otherwise become obligated as security for any other person.

Witness the hands and seals of the parties hereto, this 1st day of January, A. D. 1902.

.... (Seal.)

.... (Seal.)

Agreement to Dissolve Partnership.

We, the undersigned, do mutually agree that the within mentioned partnership be, and the same is, hereby dissolved, except for the purpose of final liquidation and settlement of the business thereof, and upon such settlement wholly to cease and determine.

Witness our hands and seals, this twenty-ninth day of May, nineteen hundred and one.

Signed, Sealed and Delivered in Presence of
Harvey C. Chester.
Porter L. Fields.

JOHN H. WAGNER. (SEAL.)
REUBEN H. HOWARD. (SEAL.)

CORPORATIONS AND STOCK INVESTMENTS.

1. **An Incorporated Company** is an association authorized by law to transact business. It is a fictitious person that can sue or be sued.

2. **Stocks** are divided into parts called shares, and the owners of the shares are called stockholders.

3. **Certificates of Stock** are written statements specifying the number and value of the shares to which their holders are entitled. They are often called scrip.

4. **Par Value** of the stock is the sum named on the face of the certificate, and is thence called its nominal value; the market value is the sum for which it sells. When shares sell for their nominal value, they are at par; when they sell for more they are above par, or at a premium; when they sell for less, they are below par, or at a discount.

5. **Gross Earnings** of a company are its entire receipts; the net earnings are the sums left after deducting all expenses.

6. **Installments** are portions of the capital paid by the stockholders from time to time. Dividends are portions of the earnings distributed among the stockholders. They are usually paid at stated periods; as annually, etc.

7. **Kinds.**—Corporations may be divided into corporations for pecuniary profit, as banks, insurance companies, loan associations and railroad companies; corporations not for pecuniary profit, as religious organizations.

8. **Public Corporations** are those formed for the public interest, as towns counties, cities, etc. A municipal corporation, for example, makes laws for the government of the city and for improvements in general.

9. **Private Corporations** are generally formed for the benefit and pecuniary profit of the members; as banks, railroad companies, mining companies, electric lighting, trolley companies, etc.

10. **Close Corporations** are those whose members fill by appointment all vacancies occurring in their membership.

11. **Open Corporations** are those in which vacancies are filled by other individuals or bodies; for example, a college whose trustees are elected by the different legislative bodies of a church.

12. **State Laws.**—In most of the States general acts of incorporation have been passed under which companies may or-

ganize, without the necessity of special legislation in each case. Since the adoption of the present constitution in 1870, all corporations in Illinois have been organized under general statutes.

13. **Limited Companies.**—In some States, notably in New York and Pennsylvania "Limited" companies may be formed. Where this law prevails, "Limited" signifies that each shareholder is individually liable for the stock that he holds. In case of suit action can be taken against him only to the extent of shares held. Limited companies are also formed in Canada, but in many states the law makes no provision for such companies.

14. **How Laws Differ.**—Private corporations organized under the laws of one State are usually permitted to do business in another. This suggests the reason why many of the large stock companies of New York and Philadelphia are organized under the laws of the State of New Jersey, where laws are more favorable to the companies. It is said that a large majority of the merchants and large business enterprises of Boston are organized into stock companies under the laws of Maine, because Massachusetts requires a large part of the capital to be paid up when the company is organized, while Maine permits the organization of a company for $100,000, not a single stockholder being a resident of the State, and requiring a paid up capital of only twenty-five dollars.

15. **Methods of Organization.**—The methods of organization vary in the different States as to details, but in general are the same. In Illinois any number of persons not less than three, nor more than seven, may form a corporation by filing with the Secretary of State a statement giving name of corporation, object, amount of capital stock, number of shares, location of office, and duration of corporation. This statement must be signed and acknowledged as deeds are acknowledged. A license is then issued to open subscription books. As soon as the stock is subscribed for, a meeting is held and directors, not less than three or more than eleven, are elected.

16. **Elections.**—Each stockholder is entitled to as many votes as he has shares of stock, multiplied by the number of directors to be elected. This is in accordance with the cumulative system in vogue in general elections in Illinois.

17. **Charter.**—Upon receipt of information giving names of directors, etc., the Secretary of State issues the Charter, which must be recorded in the county office.

18. **Fees.**—In Illinois the fees charged are as follows, and must be paid when the first papers are filed with the Secretary of State: For a capital of $2,500, $30; over $2,500, and not over $5,000, $50; and one dollar per thousand for every thousand above $5,000.

19. **Corporations and Partnerships.**—A corporation differs from a partnership in two particulars: First, it cannot exist except by authority of State and National Legislature. Second, the private property of the stockholders cannot be taken for the debts of the corporation, unless the statutes of the State so declared when the charter was granted.

20. **Advantages.**—The advantages of corporations over partnerships have made a great change in all lines of business. Every business of any magnitude is at once formed into a stock company. There are very few partnerships existing today, because the laws are more favorable to corporations. Some of these advantages are: (1) Security of the private property of stockholders; (2) facilities for borrowing money are increased; (3) a retiring stockholder is no longer responsible for debts of the company; (4) change of stockholders exceedingly more simple than change of partners; (5) limited power of stockholders—a partner may do what a stockholder has no power to do.

21. **A Question.—For large enterprises corporation laws have** been a great benefit, but when the stock company finds adoption by all kinds of enterprises, with capital ranging from $1,000 upward, we may properly inquire into the motives of such organization. It is hardly just to plead an advantage to business for a small mercantile enterprise with $2,000 capital. There are in such cases usually some personal reasons.

22. **Preferred Stock.**—This kind of stock takes preference of the ordinary stock of a corporation, and the holders are entitled to a stated per cent. annually out of the net earning before a dividend can be declared on the common stock. Preferred stocks are generally the result of reorganization, although sometimes issued in payment of floating or unsecured debts.

Certificate of Stock.

No.__________ __________Shares.

JOLIET ELECTRIC LIGHT AND POWER COMPANY

Capital, $50,000. **Shares, $100 Each.**

This Certifies, *that . . . M. Sunderman . . . is entitled to*
. . . . Fifty . . . . Shares of the Capital Stock of the

JOLIET ELECTRIC LIGHT AND POWER COMPANY,

Transferable only on the books of the Company, in person or by Attorney, on the surrender of this Certificate.

In Witness Whereof, *the Corporate Seal of said Company, attested*
(SEAL.) *by the signatures of its President and Treasurer is hereby affixed.*

L. L. Orth, Treasurer. *W. J. Miller, President*

Joliet, Ills., May 10, 1918.

DISCOUNT AND COMMISSION.

Discount is a sum deducted or allowed for prompt payment of an account, or a deduction made at a certain rate of interest.

Commission is a discount allowed by certain business houses for selling their products.

Brokerage is the fee or commission charged for buying and selling certain commodities.

Examples:

A. buys a bill of goods from B. amounting to $750.00, terms 5% 10 days, 30 days net.

$750.00 x $0.05 = $37.50

$750.00 = list price.
37.50 = discount.

$712.50 = amount paid.

A wholesale Jeweler allows the Retailer discounts of 40, 25, and 10. This is known as a discount series.

	$80.00 Catalog Price
$80.00 x $0.40 =	32.00 = 40%
	$48.00
$48.00 x .25 =	12.00 = 25%
	$36.00
$36.00 x .10 =	3.60 = 10%
	$32.40 = Net Price to Retailer.

A salesman working on a 40% commission sells
20 Raincoats @ $9.75 each = $195.00
$195.00 x $0.40 = profit = 78.00 = 40%

COST PRICE = $ 97.00

A Real Estate Agent sells an Illinois Farm for $40,000.00 on a 2% commission.

$40,000.00 x $0.02 = $800.00 = Commission

Stock Brokers have adopted standard Brokerage Charges for buying and selling Stocks and Bonds according to the number and value of the shares.

BOARDS OF TRADE AND STOCK EXCHANGES.

Boards of Trade and Stock Exchanges were originally organized to facilitate trade in the various commercial interests of the country; they are great factors in financial circles. There is no reason why these institutions should not prove very beneficial to the financial interests of our nation.

Gambling.—Unfortunately, however, the business of nearly all stock exchanges is not confined to the legitimate; instead of blessing and benefiting mankind they have become gigantic engines of robbery and oppression. The confidence of the public has been shaken, and they are generally looked upon as gambling institutions.

Members are elected by ballot, the admission fee varying greatly in different organizations. In New York, where the membership is about 1,100, a vacant seat brings from $20,000 to $50,000. In London the membership is not limited.

Number.—There are many exchange institutions in the country. Besides those in large cities, in other trade centers are found produce exchanges, cotton exchanges, mining exchanges, etc.

Dealing in Futures.—This is simply a "high-toned" form of gambling, or, in other words, a system of "market guess ing" in which the best guesser wins. The game, like all other popular gambling games, is exceedingly simple. You simply bet on the market; if it goes up or down, you win or lose just as you have staked your money.

Margins are sums of money put up as a forfeit to secure the winner. When the margin is exhausted so that further loss is not guaranteed, it is the custom to close the trade and the winner "rakes in the pot," using the gambler's way of putting it.

Option Trading.—"Seller's option" gives the person selling the privilege of making delivery at any time before the expiration of the contract by giving one day's notice. "Buyer's option" gives the purchaser a claim for delivery at any time before the maturity of the contract.

Corners.—Thousands of bushels of grains are bought and sold for every bushel brought to the elevators. Chicago Board of Trade sells every day as much wheat as the State of Illinois harvests in a year. It can then be easily seen how "commerce" can be forced. In a Board of Trade each buyer buys upon the supposition that each seller is selling what he has not got, and the buyer is buying what he does not want. Now it is easy for a set of men with an unlimited amount of money to combine and "corner" any article in the market. It simply consists of buying more than can be delivered, and then making the sellers deliver or forfeit their margins.

Bull and Bear.—A "bull" is one who operates to raise the market—so called from the nature of the bull to toss with his horns. A "bear" is one who tries to lower the market, so called from the nature of the bear to tear down with his claws.

Lame Duck.—In stock-broker's slang, a "lame duck" is a member unable to fill his contracts, and he is therefore expelled.

Bucket Shops.—These are Boards of Trade and Stock Exchanges for the boys and poor clerks, generally kept by a broken down broker who lost all his self-respect with his fortune. Here the poorest can try his luck in betting upon the markets. These shops are not reliable; they doctor the markets with false figures and deceive and take in whoever falls into their power. They are demoralizing gambling dens and in no way can they be safely trusted. There are thousands of these counterfeit concerns throughout the country.

A Syndicate is a party of capitalists who unite their resources to make successful some financial enterprise where large capital is required.

TRUSTS.

1. **Trusts** are combinations formed for the purpose of restricting competition and controlling trade.

2. **Object.**—The object is to secure to a limited number of persons engaged in the manufacture or handling of a certain article absolute control of the market for that article, so that the organization is able to name prices and profits as well.

3. **Supply Too Great.**—If the supply is too large, certain of the mills or factories or refineries in the association are closed, and the owners can make no objections, because they are partners in the scheme, and are sure of their dividends on two or three times the capital they had invested in their former business. Reducing the production only makes their dividends more certain.

4. **Result.**—The results are that the consumer pays the increased profits of the bogus capital of the corporation, and the producer has to accept for his products just what the managers of the "trust" choose to pay.

5. **Robbery.**—It is organized robbery, and nothing else, and should be treated by our courts the same way as any other stealing.

6. **Laws Enacted.**—Laws have been enacted by Congress and by some of the States against trusts, and stringent punishment has been decreed against combinations to control prices. Strange as it may seem, these laws are ineffective and in no way check the accumulation of wealth by existing combines, or the formation of new organizations of the kind.

7. **Court Decisions.**—The courts have also declared the existence of trust combinations to be unlawful, but in the face of these decisions they continue to exist and multiply in numbers.

8. **New Jersey.**—Many of these combinations have been formed under the laws of the State of New Jersey, though little or none of the business is done in that State. New Jersey laws are peculiarly lax with regard to corporations, granting them unlimited license in conspiring against the public welfare.

COMMERCIAL AGENCIES.

1. **The Credit System.**—One of the greatest hindrances to successful business interests is the credit system. From the small country grocery to the largest wholesale house, one of the most perplexing questions is whom to trust. Merchants would gladly sell goods on credit if there were always a certainty that the goods would be paid for. Many large business houses have been compelled to go into bankruptcy because they extended credit to unworthy men.

2. **Early Efforts.**—As early as 1837 a mercantile agency was organized in New York, whereby the mercantile interests of the nation might be protected from great losses brought about through the credit system.

3. **First Agency.**—The efforts of this first agency were bent on collecting information concerning the financial standing of business men in New York and vicinity, that the largest merchants might have at least an estimate of the character and responsibility of those with whom they dealt.

4. **Increasing Trade.**—With the rapid increase of trade there was a corresponding increase in applications for credit. Laws for the collection of debts were then, as now, on the statute books, but were of little benefit to creditors.

5. **First Reference Book.**—The first reference book, giving information concerning the financial standing of merchants, was published about 1840, and although small was reliable.

6. **Competition.**—The success of the first agency soon brought competing agencies into the field, and while the information extended over a much greater territory, it lacked in reliability.

7. **Present Status.**—The two noted agencies today that aim to give information covering our whole nation are Dun & Co. and Bradstreet, both of New York.

8. **Object.**—The object of the commercial agency as it exists today is to give reliable information concerning business men throughout the country.

9. **Methods.**—This information is obtained from local correspondents and is published four times a year. Although subscribers to these reports pay a good, round sum for them, they are, nevertheless, good investments, for through them merchants generally know at once whom to trust.

10. **Aim.**—The reports from these agencies aim to give the nature of the Business, Locality, Capital, Assets and Liabilities, Character, Experience, Economy, Honesty, Ability, Industry, Punctuality, Amount of Business, etc., of each merchant.

11. **Difficulties.**—Some of the difficulties with which these agencies must contend in obtaining reliable reports are, incompetency of correspondents, carelessness and indifference, personal favoritism or prejudice. As local reporters get little or no pay the time is not given to it that it should have.

12. **Efficiency.**—There are over 1,000,000 business firms in the United States, and these agencies give information concerning them all.

13. **Value.**—While commercial agencies are the outgrowth of the credit system, they have been the means of greatly extending credit, so that at present credit is given very liberally in our country. The commercial agency alone has made this possible.

BUILDING AND LOAN ASSOCIATIONS.

These associations are formed by a number of persons joining together in the investment and loaning of money, for their mutual benefit. In these associations are found the Investor and the Borrower. The Investor simply invests his money in installments, and receives it back with the profits when the stock matures. The Borrower is also a member of the association, and must subscribe for stock at least equal to the amount of his loan. He pays for his stock and repays his loan in monthly installments. Thus a man owning a lot can obtain the money to build a house, and repay it in installments costing him a trifle more than ordinary rent. When his stock matures his house is paid for and belongs to him.

These associations are a blessing to many who have by economy secured homes of their own.

Although the State laws are stringent, yet many of these associations through bad management have failed.

The best associations are those that do a local business. The so-called "nationals" are frequently fraudulent schemes.

Any member can withdraw at any time, but the stock that matures makes the greatest percentage of profit.

A BIPLANE
Popular Type of a Modern Air Ship

TRANSPORTATION.

With the development and increase of trade and the settlement of the vast areas of our western plains there has been a corresponding increase in facilities for transporting mail, money, and merchandise, as well as the conveying of passengers from one point to another. The slow ox-cart, the tow-boat on the canal, and even the more speedy horse and wagon have yielded to the modern, rapid and convenient powers of steam and electricity. Although the speed of transportation has been greatly increased, the expense has been reduced.

1. **Improved Methods.**—With improved methods of transportation, distance is no longer an impediment to the exchange and transportation of fruits, vegetables and other perishable goods. The fruit and vegetable grower of Michigan can now successfully compete with the gardener residing just outside of the largest city, because of rapid yet cheap transportation.

2. **Government Control.**—On December 27, 1917, the principal railroads of the U. S. were placed under government control with the Secretary of the Treasury in charge as General Director. The elimination of expensive competition and greater efficiency in the operation of the roads is the result of government control.

MERCHANDISE.

1. **Common Carriers** are all those that carry goods for hire indiscriminately for all persons. These include all stage coach proprietors, railroad companies, truckmen, wagoners, teamsters, carmen, porters and express companies who hold themselves out to carry goods from one portion of the country to another, from one town to another, and from one place in the same town to another for all persons who desire to employ them.

2. **Responsibility.**—Common Carriers are responsible for all loss and damage caused by transportation from whatever cause, except the act of God and public enemy, and they are bound to carry all goods which are offered them, and if they refuse without just excuse they are liable to an action.

3. **Act of God** is held to extend only to such inevitable accidents as occur without the intervention of man's agency. The carrier is not responsible for losses occurring from natural causes, such as frosts, fermentation or natural decay of perishable articles, or the necessary and natural wear in the course of transportation, provided he exercises all reasonable care to have the loss or deterioration as little as practical.

4. **Loss by Fire.**—The carrier is liable for any and all loss occasioned by accidental fire.

5. **Perishable Goods.**—Carriers are not responsible for loss to fruits that decay in their possession or goods shipped in defective boxes, such as glassware not properly packed and other articles that are easily broken. Goods must be properly packed in order to make the carrier responsible.

6. **Bill of Lading.**—Bill of lading is the receipt given by the Common Carrier to the owner of the goods desiring to have the same shipped and should contain a description of the quantity, the marks on the merchandise, the name of the shipper, or the person sending the goods, and the consignee, the name of the person to whom the goods are shipped, place of departure and place of discharge of the goods and the price of freight, and also weight of the separate packages and the number of the car in which the same were shipped.

7. **Equal Liability.**—Railroad companies and other carriers who allow express companies to carry parcels and packages on their cars or other vehicles are liable as the Common

Carriers for all damages which occur, without regard to the contract between them and such express company.

8. **Baggage.**—In the transportation of the baggage of passengers the liability of the carrier for loss to the same is the same as in case of transportation of goods for hire, and in case of loss the carrier must make it good.

9. **When Liability Begins and Ends.**—The responsibility of the Common Carrier begins upon the delivery of the goods for immediate transportation. A delivery at the usual place of receiving freight or to the employes of the company in the usual course of business is sufficient. The responsibility of the carrier terminates after the arrival of the goods at their destination and sufficient time has elapsed thereafter for the owner to have received them during business hours. After the expiration of such time the responsibility of the carrier is simply that of a warehouse man and he is only required to keep the goods with ordinary care.

10. **Different Lines.**—Where goods are shipped to points beyond the line of the carrier to whom they are first delivered, such carrier is not responsible beyond his own portion of the route unless he gives bills of lading for the entire route and the contract contemplates the transportation and delivery of the goods at their destination.

11. **Demurrage** is the penalty exacted by transportation companies for not unloading goods from their cars within the time fixed by the rules of the companies. The rules of a large number of railroad companies require that the car be unloaded within twenty-four hours after its arrival at the destination and a fixed rate of demurrage for each twenty-four hours of delay after the expiration of the usual time for unloading is imposed on the persons to whom goods are shipped. In practice companies are not very strict in enforcing this penalty, unless they are unable to meet the demand for cars.

12. **American Railway Express Company.**—On July 1, 1918, the government took over the control of the principal express companies. These companies are now run as the American Railway Express Company with a president appointed by the government in charge of operations. While there has been some increase in rates, yet the safe and rapid transit of goods often makes it desirable to ship by express

rather than by freight. Express companies carry much of the money from one point to another. The special care of valuable parcels makes this method as safe as it can be.

TRANSPORTATION BY WATER.

Common Carriers.—Those engaged in the transportation of goods and passengers in ships are Common Carriers. The same rules and principles apply to Common Carriers. by water as apply to those on land, with one or two exceptions Common Carriers of goods are practically insurers of the safe delivery of goods at their destination.

DAMAGES RECOVERABLE FOR UNREASONABLE DELAY IN FORWARDING BAGGAGE.

The measure of damages recoverable for a Common Carrier's unreasonable delay in forwarding a passenger's baggage is the value of the use of the property to owner during the delay in delivering it. As to what that value is, the opinion of persons familiar with the facts, together with the facts and conditions, will be considered. It would be difficult in such cases to determine the value of use by a mere statement of the facts. And the opinion of persons having a knowledge of the facts. though some evidence, is not an absolute guide, but an assistance, which is available in the absence of more reliable proof. Gulf C. & S. F. Ry. Co. v. Vancil; C. Civil Appeals, 21 S. W. Rep. 303.

LIABILITY OF COMMON CARRIERS FOR LOSS OR INJURY TO FREIGHT.

A Common Carrier must pay the market value, at the point of destination, of all property intrusted to it for transportation, which, through its fault, is lost or destroyed, and is not delivered. The law, also, is that if a carrier receives property for transportation, and delivers it at the end of its route, but through its fault it is damaged, and it fails to deliver it in the same condition as when received, it must pay the difference between the value of the property in its damaged condition, at the point of destination, and what the value of the property would have been at that place if delivered in the same condition as when it was received for transportation. New York, L. E. & W. R. Co. v. Estill; 13 Sup. Ct. Rep. 444.

HOW TO SEND MONEY.

Bank Drafts.—A draft on some reliable bank is by far the best and most business-like way to send large amounts of money. It is safe, convenient, and cheap.

Better, however, have the draft issued in your favor (to your own order), and then indorse it, and make it payable to the party to whom you intend to send it.

Post Office Orders.—By Post Office Order is also a safe and reliable way to send money. It costs a little more than to remit by draft, but is equally as secure, and many times more convenient, because the Post Office is accessible at all hours of the day.

Registered Letters.—Registered Letters are reasonably safe since the Government exercises special care in their transmission and in case of loss indemnifies the owner up to Twenty-five Dollars. Formerly the Post Office Department could not be held responsible for the loss of a registered letter, but in the second session of the Fifty-fourth Congress a bill was passed making the department responsible to an amount not greater than Ten Dollars. This law was later amended and the extent of liability increased to Fifty Dollars, and that law is now in force.

Express Orders.—The Express Order, as to security, has all the advantage of the Bank Draft or Post Office Order. Unlike the Post Office Orders, they are paid through the Clearing Houses of the principal cities, being current as exchange thereon; moreover, they are good, practically, everywhere, payment not being confined to any one place, but, on identification, are available everywhere. A receipt is always given the remitter, and loss of money is practically impossible.

Personal Checks.—Never send money by your personal check, unless you are rated in commercial agencies. It may cause much delay in having it certified. There is also generally expense connected with the cashing of the check. This may be charged to your account. To avoid these annoyances, pay only your local bills with personal checks.

Telegraph.—It is sometimes necessary to send money by telegraph. Although this is more expensive it is sometimes convenient. The rate is one per cent. of the amount of the order, plus double the tolls on a single message of fifteen words between the transfer places.

TRANSPORTATION OF MAIL.

Post Office.—The name Post Office originated in the posts placed at intervals along the roads of the Roman Empire where couriers were kept ready to bear dispatches and intelligence.

Early Times.—The first letter post was established in the 13th century. In early times both public and private letters were sent by messengers. Before 1639 postal facilities in the colonies were simply those afforded by personal accommodation.

Monthly Mail.—In 1672, the government of New York established a monthly mail to Boston; later this, as well as mails to other points, were carried weekly.

First Post Master General.—Benjamin Franklin was appointed First American Postmaster General, July 26th, 1775.

Cost.—The entire cost of the Post Office Department from 1783 to 1833 was $34,700,000; revenue $36,400,000; up to 1851 the department was self-sustaining; since then there has been an annual deficit, except one year during the Civil war and in 1911 there was a surplus of $219,118.12. Annual expenditure now exceeds $237,000,000.

Postal Union.—Under the regulation of the universal Postal Union a letter may now be carried to almost any place in the civilized world for five cents. Every five years representatives of the different nations meet in the "Universal Postal Congress," and discuss and agree upon improvements in the system.

TRANSPORTATION OF PASSENGERS.

It is stated that in 1797, when the first extra session of Congress was called, one member from the west did not arrive in Philadelphia—then the Nation's capital—until after Congress had adjourned. Comparing the modes of travel of colonial days with the great speed of the elegantly furnished palace car of today, there can be no denial that we are a fast people.

Rates.—The usual local passenger rates are 2 and 3 cents a mile. Through tickets to principal terminal points are lower. Mileage books good for 1,000 miles are sold for two cents a mile. These can legally be used only by the purchaser, but deception is often practiced whereby different persons use the same ticket. In most of our large cities ticket scalpers are found who buy and sell tickets at reduced rates. Some states have laws prohibiting these scalpers from doing business.

THE BUSINESS MAN'S DIGEST OF LAWS.

PRESUMPTIONS OF LAW PERTAINING TO BUSINESS PAPERS.

1. **Law Takes Things for Granted.**—The law takes certain things for granted in connection with negotiable paper, and these things are accepted as true, unless proper evidence proves them to be false.

2. **A Valuable Consideration.**—Paper is always considered as having been given for a valuable consideration, unless the contrary can be shown.

3. **The Holder of the Paper is Considered the Owner.**—The holder of paper is regarded as the owner so long as no suspicious facts are shown in connection with his ownership.

4. **Received Before Maturity.**—It is presumed that the holder received the paper before maturity until it is proven to have been transferred after it was due.

5. **Possession in the Course of Business.**—The holder is regarded as having come into possession of the paper in the course of his business, and for value, unless good evidence disproves these presumptions.

6. **Indorsements Before Maturity.**—Indorsements are supposed to have been made before maturity, unless it clearly appears otherwise.

7. **Maker and Indorser's Liability.**—The maker of a note is considered as the first debtor, and the indorsers are looked upon as conditionally liable.

8. **Acceptor of a Draft the First Debtor.**—The acceptor of a draft is presumed to be the first debtor, and the drawer and indorsers to be only liable in the event of his failure to meet the obligation.

9. **Negotiable Paper Means Just What It Says.**—The law presumes that negotiable paper means just what it says, and evidence is not permitted to prove that it does not.

10. **Mistake in the Amount.**—If a mistake is made in stating the amount, evidence is allowed to correct it.

11. **Time.**—The time of negotiable paper, however, cannot be changed by outside evidence.

THE LAW GOVERNING FORGED PAPER.

1. **Forgery.**—Any material alteration made on commercial paper with intent to defraud is forgery.

2. **A Forged Instrument.**—A forged instrument is not commercial paper, for it represents neither a contract nor property, and no rights whatever are gained by its possession or transfer. The paper is worthless except as evidence against the forger.

3. **No Responsibility.**—The person whose name is forged cannot be made responsible. The act is not his, and one certainly should not be held responsible for another's acts which are entirely unauthorized and without notice.

4. **The Purchaser of Forged Paper.**—It makes no difference how careful or honest one is who takes forged paper; no matter what the consideration may be, the paper itself is worthless, and one who sells it to another in reality sells nothing. The one who buys forged paper, however, may recover what he paid for it from the one from whom he bought it, because it was money paid under mistake. The person who took the paper from the forger must always bear the loss, unless he can recover the money from the person who committed the forgery.

5. **Raising the Amount.**—The maker of a check must use due diligence in protecting it against alteration. Otherwise his carelessness renders him responsible for the fraudulent amount. The bank is responsible only for the genuineness of the signature and ordinary care in paying the check. Example: If a check is raised from $5 to $50 because of carelessness by the maker, and is cashed by the bank, the maker is responsible for the $50 unless he has used means easily obtainable to protect his check from alteration.

6. **Caution.**—Never buy a paper from a stranger, unless he can show evidence of legitimate business transaction with the person or persons whose papers he desires to transfer.

LAW ON OPENING LETTERS.

A person who opens letters belonging to another which have been in the possession of the post-office authorities, before they reach the possession of the person to whom directed, the letters being opened for the purpose of abstracting their contents, or of obtaining information concerning the affairs of another, is liable to a fine of $500 and imprisonment for one year. **It makes no difference as to relationship.**

"THE WAY OF THE TRANSGRESSOR IS HARD."

TERMS AND FACTS OF CRIMINAL LAW.

1. **The Rule,** "Every man's house is his castle" applies only to civil cases. Any locked door of the house may be forced open to arrest a criminal.

2. **Every Man** is compelled by law to obey the call of a sheriff for assistance in making an arrest.

3. **Embezzlement** is a fraudulent appropriation to one's own use of what is intrusted to one's care, and can only be charged against a clerk, servant, or agent.

4. **The Offense of Stealing** cannot be lawfully settled by receiving back stolen property.

5. **Bigamy** cannot be proved in law if one party to the marriage has been absent and not been heard from in five years.

6. **Petit Larceny** is where the value of the property stolen is less than $15. Grand larceny is when the value of the property stolen exceeds $15.

7. **Arson** is the burning of an inhabited building by night.

8. **Drunkenness** is not a legal excuse for crime.

9. **Assault and Battery** is where a person has inflicted physical injury; an assault, however, is only an offer or attempt to inflict physical injury.

10. **Mayhem** applies to any injury done to a limb. It formerly applied to the injury of the face, lip, tongue, eye, or ear.

11. **Felony** is a crime punishable by imprisonment in a State prison.

12. **An Accident** is not a crime unless criminal carelessness can be proved.

13. **Burglary** is the entering of a house at night or at twilight or in darkness where it is difficult to distinguish a man's face.

14. **Perjury** is false swearing willfully done. A witness should always qualify his statements as "to the best of my belief" or "as I am informed."

15. **Murder** in the first degree must be premeditated and malicious, or committed while the murderer is engaged in some felonious act.

16. **Duels.**—Killing a man in a duel is murder, and any person giving or accepting a challenge is guilty of a misdemeanor.

17. **A Police Officer** cannot arrest a person without a warrant, unless he has personal knowledge of the offense.

LAW ON LOST PROPERTY.

In point of law, the finder of lost property is entitled to keep it until the owner is found. To attempt to keep it when the owner is known, or where there are means of discovering him, is construed as larceny.

While walking along the road, A finds by the roadside a pocketbook containing a sum of money. He picks it up, examines its contents and puts it into his pocket, but it happens that there is a hole in the pocket, and it falls out. He does not discover the disappearance till he reaches home. He then retraces his steps, and near where he found the pocketbook he sees a young man who has it in his hands. The young man had picked it up when it fell from the pocket of the first finder. Which has the best right to the pocketbook and its contents? The young man has a right to it as against the other. A not uncommon maxim is, "The last finder is the best owner."

EMPLOYER AND EMPLOYE.

1. **Service.**—Where one individual renders personal service to another by request, compensation, if not agreed upon, is implied.

2. **Duties of Employer.**—It is the duty of the employer to furnish proper tools and machinery. He must never expose the employe to danger without informing him of the danger. Neglect of the employer in this respect makes him liable for damages in case of injury.

3. **Liability of Employer.**—The employer is liable for the wrongful acts of his employe producing injury to others, provided the acts are done in the course of the ordinary employment. Thus a railroad company is liable to passengers for negligence of conductors and engineers while running trains on the road.

4. **Duties of Employe.**—The employe should faithfully perform the services for which he contracted for the entire term or period of service. If he leaves before expiration of time, he can claim no pay for the work done. This is the general rule and law, but some able judges have decided that even in this case the employe is entitled to pay for work done, less what the employer lost by necessity of paying higher wages, or what he lost by the employe's failing to perform his contract.

5. **Wages.**—If no agreement has been made before, the employe can claim the price usually paid for such service. If the employe leaves because of insufficient food, ill-treatment or disabling sickness, he is entitled to pay for the time he worked.

6. **Discharge.**—If the employe is discharged for dishonesty, incapacity, or misconduct, some courts hold that the employer is under no obligation to pay him, but in all such cases a mutual agreement and settlement are far better in every way than resorting to law.

7. **Law of Kindness.**—A kind and pleasant treatment on the part of the employer, even an expression of appreciation of work well done, goes far, very far, in making the employe worthy and competent. Harsh means and manners have often discouraged those who would by kind treatment have become efficient and competent in their work.

ARGUING THE CASE OF A LOST NOTE.

THE LAW GOVERNING LOST NOTES OR BILLS.

1. The Old Law.—Formerly no action could be brought on a negotiable note or bill which was lost, if at the time it was lost it was transferable by delivery only, or had been endorsed and transferred before or after maturity.

2. Bond.—If a party should refuse to pay a note or bill which has been lost, he may be sued and compelled to pay it, but the party collecting it may be required to give a bond, so that the note in question may never appear for payment.

3. Proved.—Of course it is necessary to establish by sufficient proof that the note for a certain amount by a certain party or parties had been given and up to date not paid. The maker of the note can compel the holder of the note to give evidence of the unsatisfied debt covered by the lost note.

4. Payable to Bearer.—If payment of a lost note or bill is made without notice of loss to the finder, the paper being due and payable to the bearer, the payment is good. And if it comes into the hands of an innocent purchaser, before due, he may collect the full amount of note, and the loser of the note cannot recover it.

5. **A Part of a Bill or Note.**—Where part of the bill or note has been torn off and lost by accident, that fact can be shown by presenting the remaining part as evidence of the debt and showing loss or destruction of the balance.

6. **Caution.**—If a note or due-bill has been lost, it is best to take disinterested parties and interview the maker and secure his open acknowledgment of the amount of said note or bill before letting him know the bill or note has been lost or burned, for it may often be difficult to secure a sufficient amount of evidence to establish the debt.

LEGAL GIFTS.

1. **Who Can Make Gifts?**—Any person legally competent to transact business may give whatever he or she owns to any other person. A gift by a minor, a married woman, an insane person, or a person under guardianship, or under duress, would be void, or voidable, according to the circumstances.

2. **Delivery of Gift Necessary.**—A gift must be consummated—that is, the thing given must be delivered before any legal right rests in the grantee. A promise to give is not binding, as it is supported by no consideration. Delivery may be actual or constructive.

3. **Cannot be Revoked by Donor.**—A gift made perfect by delivery cannot be revoked by the donor; but if it prejudices the rights of existing creditors, it is void as to them. It is not, however, void as to future creditors, unless made under actual or expective insolvency, or with a fraudulent purpose.

4. **Gifts Because of Expected Death Revocable.**—Gifts because of expected death are revocable by the donor if life is continued; even after delivery and acceptance. Such gifts are held to have been made because death was supposed to be at hand; and if it does not ensue, the gift is defeated, as the death, such was the cause of the gift, has not taken place.

THE LAW OF TRADING—OFFER AND ACCEPTANCE.

1. **Jesting.**—An offer made in a jest, though accepted is not binding. The law presumes that an offer must be made with good intention.

2. **An Unconditional Acceptance.**—If an offer has been made, the acceptance must be without any conditions attached. Any acceptance upon terms varying in the slightest degree from those proposed is not binding until all the conditions are accepted.

3. **A Good Acceptance.**—An acceptance, to be good, must be such as to conclude a contract between the parties; and to do this it must, in every respect, meet and correspond with the offer, neither falling within nor going beyond the terms proposed, but exactly meeting them at all points and closing them just as they stand.

4. **An Offer.**—An offer may be withdrawn any time before it is accepted, but if no time is specified, then by the expiration of a reasonable length of time for acceptance the offer thereafter cannot be legally accepted. A limitation of time for which an offer is to run is an equivalent to the withdrawal of the offer at the end of the time named. Where parties are so situated that it is necessary to communicate by letter or telegram, the contract is complete the moment the acceptance is dispatched or the letter put into the post-office, provided this is done within a reasonable length of time, or before notice of withdrawal of the offer is received. Anyone receiving an offer by mail or telegraph is entitled to a reasonable time in which to accept or reject it.

5. **A Notice of Reward for Information.**—The offer by way of advertisement of a reward for information leading to the restoration of property or the conviction of a criminal, addressed to the public at large, becomes obligatory, if not previously reckoned, as soon as an individual, with a view to the reward, renders the specified service, but not before. To entitle one to the reward, he must have had notice of the offer at the time he rendered the service; for no one can assent to that which he has not heard of.

WHEN TO SIGN YOUR NAME IN FULL.

When you sign deeds, mortgages, wills, contracts involving land or other instruments of a permanent character, always write your name in full. Never use your ordinary business initials for signatures of this kind. In affixing your signature to a note or receipt, it is always better to write your first name out in full. There are sometimes several individuals in a community with the same initials and name, but when the first name is written out in full the names are different and consequently in mail matters, as well as in other things, much confusion is avoided. Therefore, in order to avoid possible errors in public records and confusion of titles, it is always better to sign your name in full. For instance, instead of writing H. A. Smith, write Henry A. Smith.

HOW A MARRIED WOMAN SHOULD SIGN HER NAME.

A married woman doing business for herself and handling her own individual money, would better use her own name instead of her husband's. For example, Mrs. Clark should sign Lucy A. Clark and not Mrs. Henry Clark.

A married woman is always at a disadvantage if she signs at one time her own name and then at another her husband's name, and it always results in more or less confusion. If she prefers to use her own name, she should always write it that way and not write L. A. Clark, Lucy Clark, or Mrs. Henry Clark, but always write it Lucy A. Clark.

A married woman in writing a letter to a stranger should always prefix "Mrs." to her name.

HOW TO SECURE THE SIGNATURE OF A PERSON WHO CANNOT WRITE.

1. The signature of a person who cannot write should always be witnessed. Have the person who witnesses the signature sign his name at the left.

2. Use the following form:

his
Frederick x Miller.
mark

Witness, Clarence Ranck.

This signature will apply to all forms of business papers, such as notes, receipts, deeds, leases, etc.:

In these days the uneducated man or woman is laboring under a great disadvantage. Parents, you owe your children an education. Do not miss an opportunity to buy a good book. An educated man lives longer and takes in more in a month than the same man uneducated would in a year. But education should be mixed with labor and common sense.

"Whom Shall I Marry?"

MARRIAGE LAWS AND CONTRACTS.

1. **Marriage** is a civil contract. While marriage licenses are now required by all the states, many restrictions have been thrown around the issuing of such licenses within recent years. Marriages between whites and negroes, between whites and Indians, between whites and Chinese, are respectively forbidden in various states.

2. **Contract to Marry in the Future.**—Mutual promise by a man and a woman to marry at some future day constitutes a valid contract.

3. **A Marriage Contract.**—A marriage is a civil contract, and is entered into by the mere consent of the parties. If the man says to a woman, "Will you marry me?" or words to that effect, and she says "Yes," or words that imply an affirmative answer, it is by law an agreement or promise of marriage, and both parties are legally held to carry out in good faith the promise thus made.

4. **Breach of Promise.**—If either party refuses to carry out the contract, he or she is guilty of breach of promise, and may recover damages of the other party. It is not very often, however, that the man sues the woman, though he has the right to do so if she fails to make good her promise.

5. **Necessary Proof.**—Generally in case of a lawsuit for breach of promise, there are no direct witnesses, as people generally become engaged without the presence of a third party, but the engagement may be implied by the conduct of the party sued.

6. **Implied Evidence.**—The promise of marriage is implied from circumstances, such as constant visits, presents, or open declaration of the parties, the reception of parents or friends, as an engaged couple, without any objections from the party accused. There are many ways of expressing serious intentions without an open declaration of words. Conduct speaks louder than words.

7. **Excuses for Breaking the Promises.**—A refusal may be justified on the ground of the bad character or conduct of the other party; poor health of either party is sometimes a good excuse, but not generally. If the woman were a widow or divorced, and concealed this fact from the man, this justifies a refusal to marry on his part.

8. **Time of Marriage.**—When a man promises to marry a woman without stating any special time, the law holds him guilty of breach of promise, unless he is ready to fulfill his engagement within a reasonable time; five years was held by law as being an unreasonable time.

9. **When a Promise Is Not Binding.**—If either party is under twenty-one years of age, he or she is not bound by promise to marry, and the law will excuse them any time from making good the promise; but, if the man is over twenty-one years of age, he can be held, and must make his promise good or pay the damages.

10. **Seduction.**—Seduction of a woman of lawful age under promise of marriage, and subsequent refusal to marry on his part, while not a crime, subjects the person so doing to heavy damages in a civil action for a breach of promise to marry, the seduction being used in aggravation of the ordinary damages allowed in actions for breach of promise to marry.

11. **A Cowardly Act.**—A young man who makes promises of marriage to a young lady, or gives her reason to believe that he is sincere in his visits and intentions, and then without excuse or cause devotes his attentions to another, commits a cowardly act. No honorable young man will do it.

No young man has a right to demand a young lady's exclusive company, without some definite understanding, and a young lady is very injudicious, if not foolish, if she receives the attentions of a young man, who claims her entire society, without some understanding or promise of sincerity. When the promise of marriage has once been made, it should be kept in good faith, unless both parties mutually agree to dissolve. The law always requires the promises of marriage to be met in good faith.

THE RIGHT OF MARRIED WOMEN TO OWN PROPERTY.

One of the marked evidences of the growth of true civilization in the United States is the legislative provisions enacted during the past fifty years for the benefit of married women. These legal enactments differ greatly in the different States, and there are frequent changes in some States, but all tend toward the releasing of woman from her former condition of absolute dependence upon her husband. By the old common law a married woman had few rights. She was subject to the authority of her husband, and he could rule over her, but the States have changed the common law and the rights of married women are now recognized by every court.

1. All property owned by the wife before marriage, or received after marriage and held as her separate property, can be sold and transferred without the consent of her husband.

2. If a husband fails to make proper provision for the support of his wife, the law will compel him to furnish her proper support if he has sufficient property.

3 The wife must support her husband out of her separate property when he has no separate property and is without help or means of self-support.

4. The earnings of the wife are not liable for the debts of the husband.

5. The separate property of the wife is not liable for the debts of her husband.

6. The property owned by the husband before marriage, or acquired after marriage by gift or inheritance, is his separate property; but his wife, however, has a dower interest in the real estate.

7. The wife who deserts her husband cannot hold him for her support, unless she was justified in leaving, or offers to return.

8. The earnings of the wife and her minor children after living separate from her husband are the property of the wife.

9. If husband or wife transfer real estate of any kind both must sign the deed, mortgage or contract.

AUTHORITY OF WIFE LIVING APART FROM HUSBAND TO BIND HIM.

Whether or not the person who supplies a wife with necessaries has knowledge at the time of her husband's provision for her support, the presumption of a wife's authority to pledge her husband's credit is negatived by the fact of their living apart, and the tradesman who supplies her under such circumstances upon the credit of her husband, and without his express sanction or approval, does so at his own peril, and in order to charge her husband with supplies furnished her he must show that they were not only of the kind usually denominated "necessaries," because their need is common to all persons, but that in consequence of the inadequacy of the husband's provision, they were actually required for the wife's proper support, commensurate with his means. her wonted living as his spouse. and her station in the community. Bloomingdale vs. Brinckerhoff. C. Common Pleas, N. Y. City and County. 20 N. Y. Sup. 858.

GETTING A DIVORCE.

DIVORCE AND DIVORCE LAWS.

Causes.—Martin Luther, speaking of his wife, said: "I would not exchange my poverty with her, for all the riches of Croesus without her. The utmost blessing that God can confer on a man is the possession of a good and pious wife with whom he may live in peace and tranquillity." It is the lack of this spirit that brings about so many divorces. Some persons are disappointed in marriage because they expect too much from it; but many more because they do not bring into the copartnership their fair share of cheerfulness, kindness, forbearance, and common sense.

Danger.—The family is the nucleus of the State and the very foundation of all that is good. Its relations are too vital to the happiness of the individual and the good of the public generally to be lightly destroyed. Easy divorces are deplorable. They are threatening evils.

Increase.—It is safe to say that divorce has been doubled in proportion to marriages or population in most of the northern States within forty years. The number is still increasing as present figures indicate. President Woolsey says that there can be no question that in our country the ratio of divorces to marriages or to population exceeds that of any country in the Christian world. Even some heathen nations set us examples that we might profitably follow.

Laws of States.—South Carolina is the only State where marriage knots cannot be untied. The violation of the marriage vow is cause for absolute divorce in all other States. The divorce laws of the different States vary greatly. Some of the principal causes for divorce are impotency, willful desertion, cruel and abusive treatment, habitual drunkenness, imprisonment for felony, failure by husband to provide, duress, insanity or idiocy, ungovernable temper, grossly immoral before marriage, but unknown to wife, fugitive from justice. There are at present more than 1,000,000 divorced persons in the United States. This tide of evil ought to be stayed.

THE LEGAL RELATION OF PARENT AND CHILD.

If the marriage and family relations were what they should be, then the legal relation of parent and child would not be so prominent and important. It is the unhappy marriages and the unfortunate family relations that call into question the authority of the parent and the rights of the child. In our country alone 25,000 children were deserted by their parents in 1896, and no less than 100,000 were homeless. Look at these figures, and then think of the many legal questions that are involved by the action of one or the other of the parents, or of the child itself. Let the home be what it should be, let parents make home, however humble, a place of comfort and cheerfulness, and legal relations will be unheard of. The conditions of society are, however, such that in almost every community it is essential that the legal relations of parents and children be clearly and definitely understood.

1. **Ancient Authority.**—In past ages the father was by custom considered as absolute monarch of the home. In the oriental countries of to-day, the same custom still prevails; modern progress and modern ideas, however, have changed old customs, and the authority of the parent in civilized countries has been considerably limited by law.

2. **Rights of Parents.**—The parent has control of his minor child, and has all reasonable authority to enforce obedience. As long as the parent treats his child properly, no one has a right to interfere with his authority, or take the child away and retain him against the wishes of the parent.

3. **A Runaway Child.**—A child has no right to leave home without permission of the parent, and should a child run away he can be brought back by force. If relatives or other parties keep him and refuse to give him up, the parent by legal process can obtain possession of his child, unless it can be shown that the father is brutal, or is not capable, on account of drunkenness or other causes, to take proper care of his child.

4. **Adoption.**—Any child, whether its parents are living or not, may be adopted. In that case the parent is no longer entitled to the custody, but the adopting person is. The child cannot be adopted without the consent of its parents, if they are living, but the consent having once been given cannot be revoked. If the child is over fourteen years of age, it must also consent to the adoption. Under any circumstances the court has the right to refuse to permit the adoption if it considers that the person petitioning is not a proper person to have the custody.

5. **Method of Adoption.**—Application must be made at the county court, and the judge will consider the application and will pass judgment.

6. **Punishment of Children.**—A parent has a right to punish his minor child, providing he is not guilty of cruelty. Brutality is a crime, punished by severe legal penalties. The parent must be reasonable in his punishment, leave no bruises or in any way injure the health of the child.

7. **Rights to Earnings.**—A parent is entitled to all the earnings of his minor child. If the child should refuse to turn over his earnings to the parent, the employer of the child may be notified, and be compelled to pay the parent only.

8. **Special Rights.**—The parent may, however, make free his child from all obligations to himself and allow the child to collect his own wages and do for himself. When a parent thus makes public such a declaration, he cannot thereafter collect the child's wages.

9. **The Property of the Child.**—A parent may control the

earnings of the child, yet he has no control of the property belonging to the child, either acquired by gift, legacy or any other way. If a parent should appropriate his child's property, it would be just as criminal in the eyes of the law as stealing any one else's property.

10. **Parent's Obligation to Support.**—Parents are legally held for the support of their minor children. If a child has property, it does not relieve the parent from the support of his child; he, however, can apply to court and get permission to use a part, or all, of the income of the property for the child's support.

11. **Illegitimate Children.**—It is a parent's duty to support even an illegitimate child. Such a child has legally no father, but his putative father, as he is called, may be compelled by the overseers of the poor to furnish the child with reasonable support, so that it shall not become a "burden on the parish." All children born in wedlock are legitimate, unless it is proved that the husband could not possibly be the father. The adultery of the wife cannot affect the legitimacy of the child. He is conclusively presumed to be the child of the husband. It makes no difference how soon after the marriage the child is born. A child born the same day as the marriage, if subsequent to the ceremony, is legitimate, provided there is good reason for believing that the husband is the father.

12. **Effect of Illegitimacy.**—The only legal effect of illegitimacy of any consequence is that the child cannot inherit property from his father; nor from his mother, if she has any legitimate children. He may, of course, take a legacy given to him by his putative father's will, but if there is no will he cannot inherit.

13. **Children's Obligations.**—Where the parents are unable to support themselves, the child is legally held for their support and care, but it must be first shown that the parent, or parents, are unable to support themselves.

14. **Crimes.**—The parent cannot be held for crimes committed by his minor child. If a child commits a premeditated crime, he is personally liable.

15. **Guardian.**—If a child has no parents living, a guardian may be appointed, or he may appoint his own guardian, who will in a legal sense exercise the prerogative of a parent.

THE LAWS GOVERNING OUR COMMON AND PUBLIC SCHOOLS. FACTS WHICH EVERY TEACHER AND PARENT SHOULD KNOW.

1. **Teachers.**—It will be found that in all the States the authority to employ teachers is conferred upon officers known as directors, trustees, or committees.

2. The contract made by school officers with a person to teach for a period extending beyond the trustees' term of office is valid and binding on successors in office.

3. A person under age possessing the requisite qualifications may with the consent of his parent or guardian contract to teach school.

4. At common law married women were disabled from making such contracts, but most of the States have removed this disability and they can now contract the same as unmarried women.

5. **Certificates.**—Every teacher must have a certificate of mental and moral qualifications properly signed by the examining officer.

If, however, the teacher has obtained a certificate without fraud, although the certificate was issued without any examination having been made, still it is held that the certificate is good and that the teacher can hold the directors responsible for his salary.

6. Should a person be employed to teach school without a proper certificate he cannot be restrained by the superintendent, but any citizen or resident of the district can make a complaint and secure the removal of such a teacher.

CONDITIONS OF SCHOOL CONTRACTS.

1. It is always best to have a written contract properly signed between teacher and officers.

2. A person hired to perform the duties of a teacher cannot substitute a proxy, no matter how competent, without the consent of the trustees or directors.

3. The trustees of any school district have no right to dismiss any teacher holding a proper certificate, without good and sufficient cause. If the teacher is not faithful, or incompetent, or cannot properly govern the school, these or any one of these deficiencies shall be a sufficient cause for dismissal.

4. If a teacher is dismissed without sufficient cause, full compensation for the time hired can be collected. The teacher must present himself and show willingness to go on with the school in order to show sufficient evidence that he is ready to faithfully perform his part of the contract.

If directors wantonly obstruct him in the discharge of his duties, or dispossess him of the school-house, they will be individually liable for damages.

5. **Sweeping the School-House.**—A contract to teach school does not imply that the teacher is to sweep, build fires, or perform other janitorial work. He is not compelled to do so unless it is specified in the contract or agreement.

6. **A Calendar Month.**—The word month has various meanings. There are calendar months, solar months, and several kinds of lunar months.

In law the word month means either a calendar or lunar month. The calendar months are the months as adjusted in the Gregorian calendar, and known as January, February, March, etc.

A lunar month is the period of one synodical revolution of the moon, and its length is 29 days, 12 hours, 44 minutes and 2.87 seconds, but in common usage four weeks are called a lunar month.

In making a contract it is always best to specify the kind of month to be taught. If there is no mention of the term month in the contract, then the teacher will be compelled to teach calendar months.

7. Closing School.—If the district officers close the school on account of the prevalence of scarlet fever, small-pox, or on account of any other contagious disease, and the teacher continues ready to perform his contract, he is entitled to full wages during such a period.

OLD TIME SCHOOL.

CORPORAL PUNISHMENT.

1. Let it be remembered by parents that children well governed at home, rarely, if ever, have any difficulty with teachers in the school-room. The sacred duty to be performed by every parent is to teach his child to be respectful to his teacher and obedient to the rules of school.

2. There would be no success in the management of a school if the teacher were not armed with some coercive power, and the law universally recognizes the fact that the school-teacher stands in the place of the parent, in relation to the pupils committed to his charge, while they are under his care. He therefore can enforce obedience to his commands, lawfully given in his capacity as a schoolmaster, and he may enforce them by a moderate correction.

3. A good school means good order and the authority to keep it so, therefore the teacher has undoubtedly the right to chastise his pupils for any conduct which interferes with the order and discipline of the school.

4. If the teacher in punishing a child administers more than reasonable punishment, he becomes criminally liable.

5. A teacher must punish a child without any ill-will, vindictive feeling, hatred or malice. The punishment must be done when necessary, and in the proper spirit.

6. The teacher must exercise a reasonable degree of discretion, and must temper the punishment according to the nature of the offense, at the same time taking into consideration age, size, and apparent powers of endurance of the child, and the teacher must always remember that the jury must say whether the punishment is excessive and unjust.

7. Malice on the part of the teacher may be proved or may be presumed from the circumstances under which the punishment took place.

8. A teacher in order to conduct a successful school must command obedience, and control stubbornness in order to quicken diligence and reform bad habits. In order to enable the teacher to exercise this salutary sway, he must be armed with a power to administer moderate correction when he shall believe it to be just and necessary.

9. The teacher is a substitute of the parent and he is responsible for the successful management of the school for which he is hired to teach, and the law has therefore not undertaken to prescribe punishments for particular offenses, but has contented itself with the general grant of power of moderate correction, and has confided the graduation of punishments to the discretion and judgment of the teacher.

10. Any punishment, therefore, which may seriously endan-

ger life, limbs or health, or disfigure the child, or cause any permanent injury, may be pronounced immoderate, and the teacher will be liable for criminal prosecution; but any correction, however severe, which produces temporary pain only and no permanent ill, cannot be pronounced immoderate punishment. The law therefore is that the teacher exceeds the limits of his authority when he causes lasting mischief, though he acts within the limits of his authority.

11. Many severe cases of discipline may better be referred to the board of school directors, but teachers are often compelled to act promptly in order to maintain order.

12. It is always best before expelling a pupil from school to consult the board and place the facts plainly before them and allow them to act for the teacher. An incorrigible child at school can work great mischief, and where parents are in sympathy with a disobedient child the best thing that can be done is to dismiss such a pupil from school.

13. How many men and women are there today who have made life a failure; who owe their present condition in life to the fact that their parents always took their part in every matter of disobedience when they were attending school. The writer personally knows of several young men who have spent several years between the stone walls and behind iron bars of penitentiaries, and who owe their condition in life to the fact that they were not properly governed at home, and were not allowed to be governed properly at school.

14. Parents, have the respect and obedience of your children at home, and their school life will not only be pleasant but it will prepare them for a life of usefulness and success.

15. When it is known by the child that the teacher is supported by the parent and that the government of the school is upheld in the home, there is very little occasion for corporal punishment. Our public schools have greatly improved in this respect. The rod has given way to methods that tend to inspire confidence, respect, and an eagerness to acquire knowledge.

16. It is wise for a teacher to have a private interview with the disobedient student, and often results in a most pleasing and lasting friendship. Misunderstanding is the cause of a great deal of trouble.

EXEMPTION LAWS.

The Amount of Property That Cannot be Taken for Debts in Different States.

1. Exemption Laws are for the purpose of protecting those who are unable to pay their debts without causing distress to themselves and their families.

2. Property covered by mortgage cannot be held.

3. A safe estimate of the property of the person desiring credit should be made before the credit is given.

States.	Value of Personal Property. Married.	Value of Personal Property. Single.	Value of Homestead. Married.	Exceptions and Explanations
Alabama........	$1,000	$1,000	$2,000	or 160 acres of land.
Alaska Territory (a)	....	175	....	160 acres value not to exceed $2,500.
Arizona (a).......	....	....	4,000	Earnings for 30 days prior to levy.
Arkansas	500	200	2,500	160 acres of land.
California (c).....	1,000	....	5,000	Must be designated as such in writing and recorded.
Colorado (a)......	300	....	2,000	Word "Homestead" must be written on record of deed.
Connecticut (c)....	....	....	1,000	....
Delaware (b)......	200	....	none	....
Dist. of Columbia (c)	300	....	none	....
Florida	1,000	....	....	160 acres of land in country, ½ acre in city.
Georgia...........	1,600*	....	....	
Idaho (c).........	....	....	5,000	Single, $1,000. (e) Homestead must be designated by a writing executed and recorded like a deed.
Illinois...........	400	100	1,000	....
Indiana...........	600†	....	....	....
Iowa (c)	200	....	....	40 acres in country, ½ acre in city. No limit as to value.
Kansas (c)........	400	400	....	160 acres in country, 1 acre in city.
Kentucky (c)......	....	....	1,000	....
Louisiana (a)......	....	....	....	160 acres of land. Written declaration must be recorded in New Orleans.
Maine (c).........	....	....	500	....
Maryland (c)......	100	100	none	....
Massachusetts (c)	....	....	800	....
Michigan (c)......	....	....	1,500	40 acres in country, $1,500 in city.

States.	Value of Personal Property. Married.	Single.	Value of Homestead. Married.	Exceptions and Explanations.
Minnesota (c)......	$ 500	$	$	80 acres in country, ½ to 1 acre in city, varying with size of city.
Mississippi (c)......	250	....	3,000	160 acres of land.
Missouri (c)......	00	....	....	From $1,500 to $3,000, according to size of city. 160 acres of land.
Montana (c)........	....	....	2,500	And not to exceed 160 acres of farm land or ¼ acre in city.
Nebraska (f)........	500	....	2,000	....
Nevada (d)........	1,000	....	5,000	Written declaration must be recorded.
New Hampshire (c)	....	....	500	Also $500 homestead for single man (e).
New Jersey	200	....	1,000	....
New Mexico (c)....	500	....	1,000	....
New York (a)......	250	....	1,000	....
North Carolina	500	....	1,000	....
North Dakota (c)..	1,500	....	5,000	160 acres in country, or 2 acres in city not exceeding $5,000 in value.
Ohio (c)	100	....	1,000	....
Oklahoma (c)	....	....	5,000	160 acres in country, 1 acre in city.
Oregon (c)	....	....	1,500	160 acres in country, 1 block in city.
Pennsylvania	‡ 300	....	....	....
Rhode Island (c)...	300	....	....	....
South Carolina	500	....	1,000	....
South Dakota	750	300	....	160 acres in country, 1 acre in town, limit $5,000.
Tennessee (c)	....	....	1,000	....
Texas (c)	....	....	....	200 acres in country, $5,000 in city.
Utah (c)	....	....	2,000	$1,000 for debtor, $500 for wife, $250 all members of family.
Vermont (c)	200	....	500	....
Virginia (c)........	....	....	2,000	....
Washington	500	....	2,000	Varies from $500 to $2,000 according to trade or profession.
West Virginia (w)..	200	....	1,000	....
Wisconsin (c)......	200	....	....	40 acres in country, ¼ acre in city, not exceeding $5,000.
Wyoming	500	....	1,500	Over 60 years of age, $2,500.

(a) Articles of specific property too numerous to mention, no value fixed. (b) Exemptions vary in different counties. (*) In either personalty, realty or both. (†) In personalty or realty. (c) Articles of specific property too numerous to mention, varying in amount in different trades and professions. (d) Articles of specific property, ranging in value from $100 to $500. (‡) Real or personal. (e) A single man can claim homestead only in Idaho and New Hampshire. (f) If no homestead is taken, $500 in personalty is exempt, and the exemption laws in New Mexico are the same as in Nebraska. (w) Homestead must be so designated and recorded before debt is contracted.

* THE HOMESTEAD LAW.

Any person who is the head of a family, or who is 21 years old and is a citizen of the United States or has filed his declaration of intention to become such, and who is not the proprietor of more than 160 acres of land in any state or territory, is entitled to enter one-quarter section (160 acres) or less quantity of unappropriated public land under the homestead laws. The applicant must make affidavit that he is entitled to the privileges of the homestead act and that the entry is made for his exclusive use and for actual settlement and cultivation, and must pay the legal fee and that part of the commission required, as follows: Fee for more than eighty acres, $10.00; for eighty acres or less, $5.00; commission, $1 for each forty-acre tract entered outside the limits of a railroad grant and $2.00 for each forty-acre tract entered within such limits. Within six months from the date of entry the settler must take up his residence upon the land unless an extension of time is granted, and cultivate the same for three years. He may absent himself each year for one or two periods of not exceeding five months in the aggregate, but notice must be given. During the second year not less than one-sixteenth of the area entered must be actually cultivated, and during the third year and until final proof cultivation of not less than one-eighth is required. There must be actual breaking of the soil followed by planting, sowing of seed and tillage for a crop other than native grasses. Summer fallowing or grazing of cattle cannot be accepted. The homestead entryman must have a habitable house upon the land entered at the time of submitting proof. Other improvements should be of such character and amount as are sufficient to show good faith.

Either final or commutation proof may be made at any time when it can be shown that residence and cultivation have been maintained in good faith for the required length of time and to the required extent. Proof under the act of June 6, 1912,

*What is said under this head applies to homesteads under United States statutes. It has no application to homesteads under state laws.

must be submitted within five years after the date of the entry, while proof submitted under the law in force before that date must be made within seven years after the date of the entry. Failure to submit proof within the proper period is ground for cancellation of the entry unless good reason for the delay appears.

ENLARGED HOMESTEADS.

The acts of February 19, 1909, June 17, 1910, and June 13, 1912 (37 Stat., 101), provide for the making of homestead entries for areas of not exceeding 320 acres of public lands in the states of Arizona, California, Colorado, Idaho, Montana, Nevada, New Mexico, North Dakota, Oregon, Utah, Washington, and Wyoming designated by the secretary of the interior as non-mineral, non-timbered, non-irrigable.

A homestead entry of 640 acres can be made under the Act of December 29, 1916 (Public No. 290, 64th Cong.), which provides that the Secretary of the Interior may designate unappropriated, unreserved public lands as "stock-raising lands," where the surface thereof is, in his opinion, chiefly valuable for grazing and raising forage crops, provided they do not contain merchantable timber, are not susceptible of irrigation from any known source of water supply, are of such character that 640 acres are reasonably required for the support of a family, and contain no water holes or other bodies of water needed or used by the public for watering purposes.

STATUTES OF LIMITATIONS OR THE TIME IN WHICH DEBTS ARE OUTLAWED IN THE DIFFERENT STATES AND BRITISH PROVINCES.

1. All of our States have statutes of limitation providing different periods of time, varying from one to twenty years, within which actions specified in the statutes must be brought.

"THE MAN WHO IS IN DEBT CARRIES A WORLD OF TROUBLE."—BURKE.

2. In accounts it generally begins from the purchase of the last item, and is renewed by every partial payment.

3. In case the debtor makes a written acknowledgment in a note, or papers of that character, the claim is renewed.

STATES AND TERRITORIES.	Contracts in Writing.	Sealed Instruments.	Judgments.	Open Accounts.	STATES AND TERRITORIES.	Contracts in Writing.	Sealed Instruments.	Judgments.	Open Accounts.
	Yrs.	Yrs.	Yrs.	Yrs.		Yrs.	Yrs.	Yrs.	Yrs.
Alabama	6	10	10	3	Nevada	6	6	6	4
Alaska	6	10	10	6	New Hampshire	6	20	20	6
Arkansas	5	5	10	3	New Jersey	6	16	20	6
Arizona	4	4	5	3	New Mexico	6	6	7	4
California	4	4	5	4	New York	6	20	20	6
Colorado	6	6	6	6	North Carolina	3	10	10	3
Connecticut	6	17	15	3	North Dakota	6	6	10	6
Delaware	6	20	10	3	Ohio	15	15	20	6
Dist. of Columbia	3	12	12	3	Oklahoma	5	5'	5	3
Florida	5	20	20	4	Oregon	6	10	10	6
Georgia	6	20	7	4	Pennsylvania	6	20	20	6
Idaho	5	5	6	4	Rhode Island	6	20	20	6
Illinois	10	10	20	5	South Carolina	6	20	10	6
Indiana	10	20	20	6	South Dakota	6	20	20	6
Iowa	10	10	20	5	Tennessee	6	10	10	6
Kansas	5	5	5	3	Texas	4	4	10	2
*Kentucky	15	15	15	5	Utah	6	6	8	4
Louisiana	5	10	10	3	Vermont	6	8	8	6
Maine	6	20	20	6	Virginia	5	10	20	3
Maryland	3	12	12	3	Washington	6	6	5	3
Massachusetts	6	20	20	6	W. Virginia	10	10	10	5
Michigan	6	10	10	6	Wisconsin	6	20	20	6
Minnesota	6	6	10	6	Wyoming	5	5	5	8*
Mississippi	6	6	7	3	Hawaii Isl.	6		20	6
Missouri	10	10	10	5	Canada	6	20	20	6
Montana	8	8	10	3	New Brunswick	6	20	20	6
Nebraska	5	5	5	4	Nova Scotia	6	20	20	6

* Except as to foreign claims, then 2 years.

*Store accounts 2 years.

TAXES AND DUTIES.

Definition.—Taxes are assessments of money on persons or property, for public purposes and the public good. Duties are taxes on imported goods.

A Direct Tax is levied upon the person who it is intended should pay it. The expenses of towns, cities, counties and States are paid by a direct tax upon the property or polls.

An Indirect Tax is one demanded of the merchant or manufacturer, but really paid by the consumer. Such are duties and customs collected upon imported goods.

Poll Tax.—In some States a tax is levied upon all able-bodied men over twenty-one years of age, or, in some States, upon all voters. This is called a Poll Tax.

A Property Tax is an amount assessed upon all property within the limits of the State, County or Town.

An Assessor is a person elected annually by the people. He is required to make a careful and true valuation of all the property in the town or township.

How a Tax is Levied.—Having obtained a valuation of all taxable property in a district, the amount of the tax to be raised is divided by this, giving the rate of taxation. Property is liable to be taxed for each of several purposes, one amount being assessed for State tax, another for county, the town and the school. In each case the rate may be different, because in each case the amount to be raised is different. Poll tax, if any, must first be deducted from the whole amount to be raised before the rate of taxation can be found.

Equalization Boards.—The work of these boards is to make such changes in the valuation of the property as the case demands. Any one believing his property to be assessed for too great a sum has the privilege of appealing to a board for correction of assessment. This must be done within a specified time. The State Board of Equalization adjusts the rate of taxation among the counties of the State. This is done by raising or lowering the valuation of property of different counties.

Special Assessments are assessments against property benefited, for public improvements, such as widening, opening or paving of streets, water pipes, sewers, etc. These are usually made by the town or city authorities upon the petition of property owners interested. Frequently a vote is taken by the town before the assessment is made by the authorities.

Great Care should be taken in buying real estate near cities or growing towns. Through the manipulations of real estate boomers special assessments are often made that are far ahead of the actual needs and very expensive to all property holders.

Internal Revenue and Duties on Imports.—The expenses of the United States Government are paid by internal revenue and taxes on imports. By internal revenue is meant the tax on tobacco, cigars, distilled spirits, fermented liquors, etc. Duties on imports are charged for the support of the Government and for the protection of home industries.

Collection Districts.—The waters and shores of the United States are divided into collection districts and a collector placed in charge of each of them.

Ad Valorem Duty is a tax assessed at certain per cent. upon the value of the goods in the country from which they were exported.

Specific Duty is a tax assessed at a certain sum per ton, pound, foot, gallon, or other measure without respect to value.

Bonded Warehouses.—These are places for the storage of goods on which the duties or taxes have not yet been paid. If an importer does not wish to place his goods upon the market at once, he may have them stored in bonded warehouse by giving his bond for the payment of the duties and making the entry in the proper form.

BREACH OF TRUST.

Breach in law signifies a breaking or a violation of a right or of an obligation or engagement legally binding.

If you give a person money, jewels, or valuables to be used by him, for you, for any specific purpose, such as paying a debt for you, or buying some article for you, or delivering them to some one else, and if that person applies the money, etc., to his own use, he is guilty only of a breach of trust. You have no recourse except to sue him for the value of the money or property, provided, however, that he undertook the service without pay. If you pay, or agree to pay, him anything, no matter what the amount, for his services, and he then applies the money or valuables to his own use, he is guilty of embezzlement, which is a criminal offense.

HOW TO SECURE AN APPOINTMENT UNDER THE CIVIL SERVICE LAW.

OFFICE SEEKERS WELCOMING A NEWLY ELECTED MEMBER OF CONGRESS ON HIS ARRIVAL AT WASHINGTON.

1. In 1883 Congress passed a law for the improvement of the civil service in the United States. This law provides for three commissioners appointed by the President. They have general charge of filling the vacancies in the various subordinate departments at Washington, and in all custom-houses and postoffices having as many as fifty officeholders.

2. There are over 120,000 clerks in the government employ by whom the business of each administration is carried on. About 5,000 of these are directly appointed by the President; about 15,000 are under what is known as the "Civil Service Rules." Thus it is seen that a great body of officeholders are appointed by the heads of departments.

3. In order to have better service and secure men according to their fitness rather than party affiliation, a system of competitive examinations has been organized, and the competitors are required to be examined on the following subjects: 1. Orthography, penmanship and copying. 2. Arithmetic—fundamental rules, fractions and percentage. 3. Interest, discount and the elements of book-keeping and accounts. 4. Elements of the English language, letter writing, and the proper construction of sentences. 5. Elements of the geography, history and government of the United States.

4. A standing of 65 per cent. in the first three branches is necessary in order to qualify an applicant for an appointment.

Where special qualifications are necessary, special examinations are given.

5. Every applicant must furnish proof that he is of good moral character and in good health.

6. There is a board of examiners in each of the principal cities of the United States, and several examinations are held each year. Several of our States have adopted the principles of the general government, and are employing clerks under their own civil service rules.

7. If you desire to enter an examination, address, "Civil Service Commissioner," Washington, D. C., and you will secure a full set of papers, and complete information as to time and place where the examinations are held, and full instructions for entering same.

DOMESTIC POSTAGE.

To all parts of the United States:

1. **First-Class.**—Letters, 2 cents per ounce or fraction thereof; postal cards, 1 cent each.

2. **Second-Class.**—Newspapers and periodicals, 1 cent for each 4 ounces or fractional part thereof; special rates for publishers and news agents.

3. **Third-Class.**—For books, circulars, etc., 1 cent for each 2 ounces or fraction thereof. Parcel Post rate over 8 ounces.

4. **Fourth-Class.**—Merchandise and samples, 1 cent for each ounce or fraction thereof. Parcel Post rate over 4 ounces.

5. **Registry Fee.**—Ten cents additional to regular postage of first-class matter.

6. Immediate Delivery.—Ten cents additional to regular postage.

7. Postal Money Orders.—For orders not exceeding $2.50, 3 cents; $2.50 to $5, 5 cents; $5 to $10, 8 cents; $10 to $20, 10 cents; $20 to $30, 12 cents; $30 to $40, 15 cents; $40 to $50, 18 cents; $50 to $60, 20 cents; $60 to $75, 25 cents; $75 to $100, 30 cents.

FOREIGN POSTAGE.

1. **On Letters.**—Five cents for each ounce or fraction thereof to all foreign countries except:

Canada, England, Rep. Panama, Bahamas, British Guiana, Mexico, New Zealand, Canal Zone, Barbadoes, British Honduras, Dutch W. Indies, Leeward Islands, and Newfoundland, where the rate is 2 cents per ounce.

2. **On Books,** newspapers, pamphlets, photographs, engravings and similar printed matter, 1 cent for each 2 ounces or fraction.

3. **Limits of Size.**—Samples of merchandise to all postal union countries are admissible to 12 inches in length, 8 inches in width, and 4 inches in depth. If they are in the form of a roll, 12 inches in length and 6 inches in diameter.

4. **Limit of Weight.**—The general limit of weight is 8¾ ounces; but by special agreement between the United States and Great Britain, France, Belgium, Switzerland, Argentine Republic, Italy, Austria, Egypt, and the British colonies, except India, Canada and Australia, samples of merchandise are admissible in the mails up to 12 ounces in weight.

5. **Parcels Posts.**—Unsealed packages of mailable merchandise may be sent by parcels post to Jamaica, Barbadoes, the Bahamas, British Honduras, Mexico, Leeward Islands, Costa Rica, Colombia, Salvador, British Guiana, Danish West Indies, Windward Islands and Newfoundland at the following rate: For every pound or additional fraction thereof, 12 cents. The maximum weight is 11 pounds.

6. **Prepaid Postage.**—Foreign postage should always be prepaid in stamps of the country from which matter is sent. If not prepaid it is chargeable with double the amount.

PARCEL POST AND EXPRESS TABLE

COMPARATIVE RATES

Weight in Pounds	Local Parcel Post Rate	Zone 1 Up to 50 Miles Parcel Post	Zone 1 Up to 50 Miles Express	Zone 2 50-150 Parcel Post	Zone 2 50-150 Express	Zone 3 150-300 Parcel Post	Zone 3 150-300 Express
1	$0.05	$0.05	$0.28	$0.05	$0.29	$0.06	$0.30
2	.06	.06	.29	.06	.31	.08	.31
3	.06	.07	.29	.07	.32	.10	.33
4	.07	.08	.30	.08	.33	.12	.35
5	.07	.09	.30	.09	.34	.14	.36
6	.08	.10	.31	.10	.36	.16	.38
7	.08	.11	.31	.11	.37	.18	.41
8	.09	.12	.32	.12	.38	.20	.43
9	.09	.13	.32	.13	.41	.22	.44
10	.10	.14	.33	.14	.42	.24	.46
11	.10	.15	.33	.15	.43	.26	.48
12	.11	.16	.34	.16	.45	.28	.49
13	.11	.17	.34	.17	.46	.30	.52
14	.12	.18	.35	.18	.47	.32	.54
15	.12	.19	.35	.19	.48	.34	.55
16	.13	.20	.36	.20	.51	.36	.57
17	.13	.21	.36	.21	.52	.38	.59
18	.14	.22	.37	.22	.53	.40	.62
19	.14	.23	.37	.23	.55	.42	.63
20	.15	.24	.38	.24	.56	.44	.65
21	.15	.25	.38	.25	.57	.46	.67
22	.16	.26	.40	.26	.58	.48	.68
23	.16	.27	.40	.27	.60	.50	.70
24	.17	.28	.41	.28	.62	.52	.73
25	.17	.29	.41	.29	.63	.54	.74
26	.18	.30	.42	.30	.65	.56	.76
27	.18	.31	.42	.31	.66	.58	.78
28	.19	.32	.43	.32	.67	.60	.80
29	.19	.33	.43	.33	.69	.62	.81
30	.20	.34	.44	.34	.70	.64	.84
31	.20	.35	.44	.35	.71	.66	.86
32	.21	.36	.45	.36	.74	.68	.87
33	.21	.37	.45	.37	.75	.70	.89
34	.22	.38	.46	.38	.76	.72	.91
35	.22	.39	.46	.39	.77	.74	.92
36	.23	.40	.47	.40	.79	.76	.95
37	.23	.41	.47	.41	.80	.78	.97
38	.24	.42	.48	.42	.81	.80	.99
39	.24	.43	.48	.43	.84	.82	1.00
40	.25	.44	.49	.44	.85	.84	1.02
41	.25	.45	.49	.45	.86	.86	1.04
42	.26	.46	.51	.46	.88	.88	1.06
43	.26	.47	.51	.47	.89	.90	1.08
44	.27	.48	.52	.48	.90	.92	1.10
45	.27	.49	.52	.49	.91	.94	1.11
46	.28	.50	.53	.50	.93	.96	1.13
47	.28	.51	.53	.51	.95	.98	1.15
48	.29	.52	.54	.52	.96	1.00	1.18
49	.29	.53	.54	.53	.98	1.02	1.19
50	.30	.54	.55	.54	.99	1.04	1.21
51	.30	.55	.55	.55	1.00	1.06	1.23
52	.31	.56	.56	.56	1.02	1.08	1.24
53	.31	.57	.56	.57	1.03	1.10	1.26
54	.32	.58	.57	.58	1.04	1.12	1.29
55	.32	.59	.57	.59	1.06	1.14	1.30
56	.33	.60	.58	.60	1.08	1.16	1.32
57	.33	.61	.58	.61	1.09	1.18	1.34
58	.34	.62	.59	.62	1.10	1.20	1.36
59	.34	.63	.59	.63	1.12	1.22	1.37
60	.35	.64	.60	.64	1.13	1.24	1.40
61	.35	.65	.60	.65	1.14	1.26	1.42
62	.33	.66	.62	.66	1.17	1.28	1.43
63	.36	.67	.62	.67	1.18	1.30	1.45
64	.37	.68	.63	.68	1.19	1.32	1.47
65	.37	.69	.63	.69	1.20	1.34	1.48
66	.38	.70	.64	.70	1.22	1.36	1.51
67	.38	.71	.64	.71	1.23	1.38	1.53
68	.39	.72	.65	.72	1.24	1.40	1.55
69	.39	.73	.65	.73	1.26	1.42	1.56
70	.40	.74	.66	.74	1.28	1.44	1.58
Freight, per 100 pounds or less.............			$0.40		$0.60		$0.80

EXCLUDING WAR TAX

Weight in Pounds	Zone 4 300-600 Parcel Post	Zone 4 Express	Zone 5 600-1,000 Parcel Post	Zone 5 Express	Zone 6 1,000-1,400 Parcel Post	Zone 6 Express	Zone 7 1,400-1,800 Parcel Post	Zone 7 Express
1	$0.07	$0.30	$0.08	$0.31	$0.09	$0.33	$0.11	$0.36
2	.11	.32	.14	.34	.17	.37	.21	.46
3	.15	.35	.20	.38	.25	.43	.31	.55
4	.19	.37	.26	.42	.33	.48	.41	.65
5	.23	.40	.32	.45	.41	.53	.51	.74
6	.27	.42	.38	.48	.49	.58	.61	.84
7	.31	.44	.44	.52	.57	.64	.71	.92
8	.35	.47	.50	.56	.65	.69	.81	1.02
9	.39	.49	.56	.59	.73	.74	.91	1.11
10	.43	.52	.62	.63	.81	.79	1.01	1.21
11	.47	.54	.68	.66	.89	.85	1.11	1.30
12	.51	.56	.74	.69	.97	.89	1.21	1.40
13	.55	.59	.80	.74	1.05	.95	1.31	1.48
14	.59	.62	.86	.77	1.13	1.00	1.41	1.58
15	.63	.64	.92	.80	1.21	1.04	1.51	1.67
16	.67	.66	.98	.84	1.29	1.10	1.61	1.77
17	.71	.68	1.04	.87	1.37	1.15	1.71	1.86
18	.75	.71	1.10	.91	1.45	1.21	1.81	1.96
19	.79	.74	1.16	.95	1.53	1.25	1.91	2.05
20	.83	.76	1.22	.98	1.61	1.31	2.01	2.14
21	.87	.78	1.28	1.01	1.69	1.36	2.11	2.23
22	.91	.80	1.34	1.04	1.77	1.41	2.21	2.33
23	.95	.84	1.40	1.09	1.85	1.46	2.31	2.42
24	.99	.86	1.46	1.12	1.93	1.52	2.41	2.52
25	1.03	.88	1.52	1.15	2.01	1.56	2.51	2.61
26	1.07	.90	1.58	1.19	2.09	1.62	2.61	2.71
27	1.11	92	1.64	1.22	2.17	1.67	2.71	2,79
28	1.15	.96	1.70	1.26	2.25	1.73	2.81	2.89
29	1.19	.98	1.76	1.30	2.33	1.77	2.91	2.98
30	1.23	1.00	1.82	1.33	2.41	1.83	3.01	3.08
31	1.27	1.02	1.88	1.36	2.49	1.88	3.11	3.17
32	1.31	1.04	1.94	1.40	2.57	1.92	3.21	3.27
33	1.35	1.08	2.00	1.44	2.65	1.98	3.31	3.35
34	1.39	1.10	2.06	1.47	2.73	2.03	3.41	3.45
35	1.43	1.12	2.12	1.51	2.81	2.08	3.51	3.54
36	1.47	1.14	2.18	1.54	2.89	2.13	3.61	3.64
37	1.51	1.17	2.24	1.57	2.97	2.19	3.71	3.73
38	1.55	1.20	2.30	1.62	3.05	2.24	3.81	3.83
39	1.59	1.22	2.36	1.65	3.13	2.29	3.91	3.92
40	1.63	1.24	2.42	1.68	3.21	2.34	4.01	4.01
41	1.67	1.26	2.48	1.72	3.29	2.40	4.11	4.10
42	1.71	1.29	2.54	1.75	3.37	2.44	4.21	4.20
43	1.75	1.32	2.60	1.79	3.45	2.50	4.31	4.29
44	1.79	1.34	2.66	1.83	3.53	2.55	4.41	4.39
45	1.83	1.36	2.72	1.86	3.61	2.60	4.51	4.48
46	1.87	1.39	2.78	1.89	3.69	2.65	4.61	4.58
47	1.91	1.41	2.84	1.92	3.77	2.71	4.71	4.66
48	1.95	1.44	2.90	1.97	3.85	2.76	4.81	4.76
49	1.99	1.46	2.96	2.00	3.93	2.80	4.91	4.85
50	2.03	1.48	3.02	2.03	4.01	2.86	5.01	4.95
Freight per 100 lbs. or less	$1.00		$1.50		$3.00		$4.00	

PARCEL POST.—Packages weighing up to 70 lbs., with combined length and girth not exceeding 84 inches, may be sent by parcel post. To find the measurements quickly, add the extreme length to the distance once around the largest part of the package. The total must not exceed 84 inches. Valuable parcels may be insured for a small fee.

EXPRESS AND FREIGHT.—Rates shown are approximate and may vary slightly. Paper wrapped express packages must not exceed 25 lbs. in weight. Heavier shipments must be made in standard cartons, boxes, barrels, crates, sacks, bales or trunks.

WAR TAX.—The following war tax must be added to the above figures: On freight shipments, a tax of 3%; on parcel post shipments 1c tax for every 25c postage; on express shipments 1c tax on each 20c charge or fraction thereof.

WORKING ON HOLIDAYS.

There is no law which says a farm hand or any other laborer shall not work on holidays. Generally the laborer should work on such days if required to do so, or forfeit his right to pay. In many localities it is customary not to work on some of the principal days, such as Christmas, Thanksgiving Day in the East, and the Fourth of July, and still to pay the men their regular wages. If this custom is common and well known in any place, it will probably govern, so that pay can be collected although the work is not done. Of course, ordinary farm chores should be done, as on Sundays, at least.

THE FIRST PRINTING PRESS.

THE LAW OF NEWSPAPER SUBSCRIPTIONS.

1. There is no postal law regulating the transactions between publishers and subscribers. The ordinary rules of contract govern all relations between the parties concerned, and the postoffice has no part except to deliver the article, or return it when ordered to do so.

2. If the publisher of any paper or periodical sends his paper or magazine, the postmaster must deliver it, if the person to whom it is sent will take it. If he will not take it, the postmaster must notify the publisher.

3. The publisher must collect his subscription the same as any other debt.

4. If a man subscribes for a paper or periodical for one year, he cannot stop his paper at any time during that year, but at the end of the year he can stop his paper, whether he has paid for it or not.

5. If at the end of the year the publisher continues to send his paper and the subscriber to receive it, the sending is the offer of another year's subscription at the same price, and the taking of the paper out of the postoffice is an acceptance.

6. If a subscriber has by express or implied agreement become liable for another year's subscription, he cannot during and before the expiration of that year stop his paper, even by paying up all he owes to the publisher.

7. If the publisher advertises terms of subscription, all parties taking the paper under these conditions will be held according to the conditions.

RESPONSIBILITY IN RUNAWAY HORSES AND TEAMS.

1. If a horse naturally quiet to ride and drive is frightened by a railroad train, steam thrasher, or other causes, not under the control of the rider or driver, does any damage, or injures any person or persons, the owner is not responsible.

2. If horses are known to be vicious, or sustain a runaway reputation, break loose or run away with their driver, or injure any person or persons, the owner is responsible, unless it can be shown that the horses were frightened by some obstacle which would naturally frighten a gentle or ordinarily quiet horse.

3. A person owning or driving a team must always use proper caution and ordinary diligence, in order to escape any damages that may be done in case his team should break loose and run away.

4. If a person enters the barn or pasture of another, and is injured by a vicious horse or bull, it must be shown that the owner used all reasonable means in the care of his animals for the safety of his help and neighbors.

5. If a person enters upon the land of another, and is injured, he must show good cause for entering upon said land, and also prove ordinary caution, in going where cattle and horses were kept.

TRESPASSING ANIMALS.

If cattle, or horses, or sheep, or hogs, or chickens, or dogs, or any other animals trespass upon the land of a neighbor, they cannot be injured or killed by the owner of the land upon which the trespass is committed, no matter how often repeated. The law regulates these matters by damages, and every innocent person is protected, and generally fully compensated for all damages caused by trespassing animals.

Many States and local authorities have laws by which trespassing animals can be taken up, and either held by the party upon whose land the trespassing is committed or placed in a public corral or pound. They are kept there at the expense of the owner, and damages or fines or both must be paid before the animals can be taken or removed by the owner.

FENCE LAWS.

1. Fence laws are generally regulated by State statutes or local authorities.

2. A few general laws are commonly held in all the States.

3. **Legal Fence.**—First find out from the state statute or local law what constitutes a legal fence. A legal fence is generally a four foot fence with sufficient boards or wire, or both, to turn cattle and sheep.

4. If cattle or horses break through fences in any way defective or neglected, the owner of the cattle or horses doing the damage is not responsible, if it was not his fence, or the injury brought about through his neglect.

5. Every man is compelled to look after his own part of the fence and keep it .. good repair, and look out and restrain his own animals in trespassing upon the lands of another.

6. Owners of adjoining cultivated lands are required to make division fences in common.

7. In erecting a division fence according to law, half of it may be placed upon the adjoining land. No man has a right to build a fence on another man's land, unless there is a law that will permit him to do so.

8. Fences are fixtures that pass with the sale of land. Posts or boards that have been used as fences on a farm, though when the farm is sold are piled up, and not used at the time for fencing purposes, cannot be removed as personal property.

LAWS OF THE PUBLIC ROAD.

1. **Public Roads** are those which are laid out and supported by officers entrusted with that power. Their care and control are regulated by the statutes of the different States, and in detail will not be referred to here, as they can be easily looked up by those who desire information so entirely local.

2. **Ownership.**—The soil and the land remains in the owner, who may put the land to any use, and derive from it any profit, not inconsistent with the rights of the public. If the road is at any time discontinued, the land reverts back to the owner.

3. **Liability.**—The repairing of highways is usually imposed upon towns, and they are made liable by statute for all damages, against persons or estates, from injuries received or happening in consequence of a neglect of duty on the part of the officers having the same in charge.

4. **Laws of the Road.**—Persons traveling with carriages or vehicles of transportation, meeting on any public way, are required to turn their carriages or wagons to the right of the center of the road, so far as to permit such carriages or wagons to pass without interruption.

5. **Runaways.**—The owner of a runaway horse or horses if negligent, or not exercising due care, is responsible for all damages that may occur.

6. Any unreasonable occupation of the public way, whether arising out of a refusal to turn out and allow a more rapid vehicle to pass, or from an unjustifiable occupancy of such a part of the road as to prevent others from passing, will render the party so trespassing liable for damages to any suffering injuries therefrom. A loaded vehicle must turn out, and allow those to pass who may reasonably and lawfully travel faster.

Petition for Laying Out a Road.

To the Commissioners of the Town of Lisle,
County of Du Page, and State of Indiana.

Your petitioners of the town of Lisle would respectfully represent that the public convenience and wants require that a road and highway should be laid and constructed, beginning at the Northwest corner of J. D. Wild's farm, in the town of Lisle, and leading in a direct line South to the town of Bennington.

Your petitioners would therefore ask that your honors would view the premises, and locate and construct said road and highway, according to the laws in such cases made and provided, as shown by the Statutes of the State.

(Signatures.) **(Signatures.)**

THE RESPONSIBILITY OF OWNING A DOG.

1. Dogs must be kept upon the owner's premises, unless accompanied by the owner or some member of the family.

2. If a dog annoys travelers upon the public highway by scaring horses and frightening children, the owner is responsible for damages.

3. The owner of a dog is responsible for damages caused by his dog trespassing upon the public highway in running after teams or doing other damages.

4. If a dog not accompanied by its owner annoys travelers upon the public highway, he may be killed, without any claim of damages on the part of the owner of the dog. When a dog becomes a nuisance he may be killed anywhere except on the owner's premises.

5. If a dog kills sheep or destroys or injures any other domestic animals, the owner is responsible for damages.

6. Every owner of a savage and dangerous dog must keep him properly chained or otherwise secured that no injury may be done to others.

7. If a person on a social or business errand is bitten or otherwise injured by a savage dog on the premises of the owner, the owner is responsible. Dangerous animals are not permitted to run at large, even on the owner's own premises, unless he has sufficient safeguards to protect his neighbor against injury.

EARLY CALIFORNIA MINING

LAW GOVERNING MINES AND MINERS

1. The General Rule.—**Laws differ in different States and Territories, but there are some general principles and general laws which apply to all States and Territories.** The first thing a prospector should do is to find under which laws the Territory or State is governed, and then by inquiry determine the steps necessary in order to legally locate the claim. But the following principles will apply to all unless recent changes have taken place:

2. How to Stake Off a Claim.—If there is evidence of mineral in paying quantity, and the property is not owned by a private party, the miner is entitled to stake off the land, and is entitled to it according to the law of the State or Territory in which the ore is found. Caution must be taken to stake off the claim and give correct boundaries, or an application for a patent will be refused. The claim must be located according to law, and publication made by inserting the notice in some weekly newspaper for ten consecutive weeks, and a notice must be posted on a conspicuous part of the claim staked out.

3. **An Adverse Claim.**—An adverse claim, to be effective, must be made out in proper form and filed in a proper legal office during the period of publication of the application for the patent. The adverse claimant must commence suit in proper form within the required time, and runs a risk if he trusts the uncertainty of the United States Mail. He must set forth in detail the facts on which he bases his adverse claim.

4. **A Foreigner.**—A foreigner may make a mining location and dispose of it if he becomes a citizen before disposing of the mine.

5. **A Prospector.**—A prospector with a discovery claim is allowed sixty days to sink a discovery shaft to the distance of ten feet. At the place of discovery it is customary to post a notice.

Notice of Location.

Notice is hereby given, That the undersigned having complied with the requirements of Section 2324 of the Revised Statutes of the United States, and the local laws, customs and regulations of this district, have located fifteen hundred feet in length by six hundred feet in width, on this, the California lode, vein or deposit, bearing gold, silver and other precious metals, situated in Levan Mining District, Juab County, Utah, the location being described and marked on the ground as follows, to-wit:

Commencing at this monument and running 300 feet easterly, thence 1,000 feet southerly, thence 600 feet westerly, thence 1,500 feet northerly, thence 600 feet easterly, thence 500 feet southerly, thence 300 feet westerly to point of beginning; point of discovery and corners being designated by monument, stakes or blazed trees. The above mine is located about four miles up Levan Canyon on the left hand side and about six miles west of the town of Levan.

The Mining Claim above described shall be known as the California Mine.

Located this 17th day of September, 1901.

NAMES OF LOCATORS:

Richard Roe. John Doe.

6. **Lawful Survey Made.**—After sinking the shaft ten feet the miner will, if possible, have a competent and lawful survey made. But without a survey a claim will be defined sufficiently to enable a record to be made if it is marked off by stakes driven into the ground or supported by a pile of stone around each. The next step is to have a record made in the recorder's office of that county.

7. **The Term.**—The term of a mining tunnel, ditch or mining company cannot exceed twenty years. No miner has a right to undermine the improvements of another unless by legal permission. A copy of mining laws in each district will be found at the county clerk's office in the district where the mine is located.

8. **Right of Way.**—Miners have the right of way across any claim when hauling quartz. Water may be brought across any claim, road or ditch, or other mining improvement, provided it is so guarded that it does not interfere with the prior rights of another.

9. **In Locating a Placer.**—In locating a placer (that is surface or loose dirt) claim, the amount of land is limited to 20 acres to one person. An association of eight persons may locate 160 acres.

10. **Citizens of the United States.**—To secure claims from the government the miner must be a citizen of the United States, or have legally declared his intention to become such.

11. **Destroy or Remove Location Stakes.**—Any person who shall destroy or remove location stakes, except on abandoned property, shall be liable to a fine of $1,000 and one year's imprisonment.

12. **Jumping a Claim.**—The person jumping a claim owned by another and gaining the same by threats or violence shall be liable to a fine of $250 and imprisonment in the county jail for six months.

13. **United States Law.**—The United States law allows five acres to be taken as a claim for a mill site, but the site must not be upon known mineral lands. Sometimes the district regulations restrict the amount to much less dimensions.

14. **Change the True Value.**—Any person engaged in milling, sampling, reducing, shipping or producing ores, who shall knowingly change the true value of the same, whereby the owner of such ore shall not obtain its true value, shall be liable to a fine of $1,000 and one year's imprisonment.

15. **"Salting."**—"Salting" a claim, that is, taking ore from another mine and placing it in the one that is to be sold, thereby deceiving the purchaser, is punishable by a fine of $1,000 and confinement in the State prison fourteen years.

16. **Liable to a Fine.**—The superintendent, manager or owner of a quartz mill, mill furnace or cupel, engaged in extracting ore, who shall neglect or refuse to account for and pay the owner of the quartz or mineral all sums which shall be due, except such as may be retained for services, shall be liable to a fine of $1,000 and imprisonment not exceeding one year.

HOW TO LOCATE A MINE.

1. **Who May Locate a Mine.**—Any person of lawful age who is a citizen of the United States or shall have legally declared his intention to become such may locate a mine.

2. **Must Be Actually Discovered.**—A mineral bearing ledge, lode or vein must be actually discovered on the claim it is proposed to locate.

3. **The Ground Entitled to.**—Unless the width is modified by the laws of a local mining district, the ground entitled to with a mining claim is 1,500 feet along the ledge by 300 feet each side of the ledge, or 600 feet wide.

4. **Point of Discovery.**—The point of discovery may be within any part of the 1,500 feet.

5. **Boundary Description.**—In the boundary description of a mine use the terms easterly and westerly, northerly and southerly instead of the more positive terms east, west, etc.

6. **General Description.**—Make the general description as short as possible, and mention adjacent or neighboring mines, distance and direction, well-known natural objects, or permanent monuments.

7. **Location Notice.**—The location notice must be posted at the point of discovery. The corners of claims must be marked by blazed trees, stakes or monuments.

About five days are allowed to post up location notice, and from ten to thirty days to have the same recorded. Record with the district recorder, or if an unorganized mining district, record with the county recorder. If not in actual personal possession of the proposed location, post location notice and have it recorded as soon as possible.

8. **Assessment Work.**—To hold a mine $100 worth of assessment work in labor or improvement must be done on it annually, and the calendar year in which to commence the assessment work begins with the January following the fractional year in which the location is made.

9. **Two or More Locators.**—Two or more locators on the same ledge may consolidate and do the amount of their combined assessment work on one claim of the group.

10. **How to Obtain a Patent.**—The affidavits of assessment work by two credible witnesses should annually be filed

with the district or county recorder. When $500 worth of assessment work has been done on a mine a patent to it may be obtained from the Government.

MONEY.

Definition.—Any material that by agreement serves as a medium of exchange and measure of value in trade. The earliest money of our country was wampum, beads, pieces of cloth, corn, cattle, etc.

Gold and Silver.—Gold and silver have, from the earliest times, been used by all commercial nations as either customary or legalized money.

Functions of Money.—It is a commodity—having a value of its own. It is a common measure of values. It has general exchangeability, and hence is a general medium of exchange.

Bullion—Gold or silver in bars, or ingots, uncoined.

Kinds of Money in Use.—Gold coins of $20, $10, $5 and $2½; silver coins of $1, 50 cents, 25 cents and 10 cents; nickel 5 cent coins; cents; United States notes ("greenbacks"). Treasury notes; United States gold certificates, issued upon deposits of gold coin; United States silver certificates, issued upon deposits of silver dollars; United States currency certificates, issued on deposits of United States notes, to National banks only (issue now suspended); National bank notes issued by National Banks; Federal Reserve notes.

Subsidiary Coin.—Silver coin of 50 cents, 25 cents and 10 cents.

Minor Coin.—Nickel 5 cent pieces and cents.

Legal Tender.—Lawful money; money which may be offered in payment of debts. Gold is the only absolute legal tender in the United States. Silver dollars, greenbacks and Treasury notes, and fractional silver coins in amounts of $10 and less, are a legal tender, except where otherwise stipulated in the contract. Gold certificates, silver certificates, currency certificates and National bank notes are not a legal tender, but are receivable for public dues, except the latter, which are not receivable for custom. Foreign coins are not legal tender in e United States.

Sound Money.—Standard money; no depreciated dollars.

Fiat Money.—The doctrine that the Government can make

paper, leather or any other material into money by simply putting its stamp upon it, without reference to its redemption in coin.

Amount in Circulation.—From a report of the Secretary of the Treasury, the following interesting items are taken: The amount of money in circulation in our country in 1860 was $435,407,252; in 1880 it had reached $973,382,228; in 1890, $1,429,251,270; 1909, $3,113,058,601; and in 1914, $3,419,168,368. In 1860 the circulation per capita was $13.85; in 1880, $19.41; in 1890, $22.82; in 1909, $35.01; in 1914, $34.53 and in 1917, $46.57.

The Monetary Question.—The question of what should be the medium of exchange has in the last few years grown into a problem of such magnitude that it has resulted in the formation of what is practically a political party.

MINTS.

Definition.—A mint is a place where the coin of a country is manufactured, and from which it is issued by sovereign or public authority.

First Mints.—The first United States mint was established at Philadelphia by the coinage act of April 2, 1792. The first coinage of the United States was silver half-dimes and copper cents. The first building erected in the United States for public use, under the authority of the Federal Government, was a structure for the United States mint. This was a plain brick building and was occupied for forty years.

Branches.—Branches of the Philadelphia mint were organized at New Orleans, Dahlonega, Ga., and Charlotte, N. C., in 1835; San Francisco, Cal., in 1854, and at Carson City, Nev., in 1870. Those at Dahlonega and Charlotte have been given up.

Mint Marks.—These are letters or marks on the coin designating the mint at which it was struck, as "S" for San Francisco; "C. C." for Carson City; "O" for New Orleans. The coins struck at the parent mint in Philadelphia bear no mint mark.

Assay Offices.—These are places where coins are examined to determine their economic value. Assay offices are located at Boise City, Idaho, Charlotte, N. C., Helena, Mont., New York and St. Louis. An assayer in charge is appointed over each of these offices.

PARLIAMENTARY RULES.

A Complete Set of Parliamentary Rules and Usages for Public Meetings, Political Gatherings and Debating Societies.

CONDUCTING PUBLIC MEETINGS.

In every community it is necessary to hold public meetings from time to time, and in order to expedite the proceedings of such meetings, as well as to settle matters of dispute, it is necessary that rules of proceedings be adopted. In order to be able to take an intelligent interest and part in such meeting, it is essential that young and old be informed on the most important points of parliamentary rules.

Ladies.—This does not include men only, for we are living in a time when women are called upon to carry on a public meeting as well as men. Then, again, women are taking a much more active part in public affairs than formerly.

The following suggestions, together with the three hundred points of order, if carefully followed, will be very helpful in conducting any public meeting.

The chairman selected should be a man of maturity and one held in general respect and confidence.

Any person of standing may call the meeting to order, and put the motion for the election of chairman.

Upon taking the chair, a few remarks by the chairman are generally expected.

The chairman should have a clear voice, positiveness of manner and self possession.

When a motion is presented to the meeting and seconded, it should be stated or read by the secretary or chairman, and remarks called for.

After debate, the motion should be put to the meeting, the chairman announcing the result.

No speaker should be interrupted unless his remarks are out of order, when he should be called to order by the chair. If the chairman fails to call him to order any member may do so.

Any violation of rules must be recognized and checked by the presiding officer, or demoralization must result.

When a member is called to order by the president, he should take his seat, unless he is permitted to explain.

It is the privilege of any member to call for the yeas and nays and thus put on record the vote of every member.

OVER THREE HUNDRED POINTS OF ORDER.

Trace up each reference at the right, and then look up the corresponding numbers on opposite page, which will give the full information desired.

Forms in which questions may be put	28, 29, 30, 31, 32
Questions of precedence of questions	19, 20, 21, 22, 23, 24, 25
Motion to withdraw a motion	1, 5, 7, 9, 13, 14, 16
To take up a question out of its proper order	1, 5, 7, 9, 12, 14, 16
Motion to take from the table	1, 5, 7, 11, 12, 14, 16
Motion to suspend the rules	3, 5, 8, 10, 13, 14, 16
To substitute in the nature of an amendment	3, 5, 8, 9, 13, 14, 16
Motion to make subject a special order	3, 5, 8, 9, 12, 14, 16
Question whether subject shall be discussed	1, 5, 7, 9, 12, 15, 17
Motion that committee do not rise	1, 5, 7, 10, 13, 14, 16
Motion to refer a question	3, 6, 8, 10, 13, 14, 16
Motion to reconsider an undebatable question	1, 5, 7, 10, 13, 14, 18
Motion to reconsider a debatable question	3, 6, 7, 10, 13, 14, 16
Reading papers	1, 5, 7, 9, 13, 14, 16
Questions of privilege	3, 5, 8, 9, 13, 14, 16
Questions touching priority of business	1, 5, 8, 9, 13, 14, 16
Motion for previous question	1, 5, 7, 9, 13, 14, 16
Motion to postpone indefinitely	3, 6, 7, 9, 13, 14, 16
Motion to postpone to a definite time	4, 5, 8, 9, 13, 14, 16
Motion for the orders of the day	1, 5, 7, 9, 13, 15, 17
Objection to consideration of question	1, 5, 7, 9, 12, 15, 17
Motion to limit debate on question	1, 5, 8, 9, 12, 14, 16
Motion to lay on the table	1, 5, 7, 11, 13, 14, 16
Leave to continue speaking after indecorum	1, 5, 7, 9, 13, 14, 16
Motion to extend limits of debate on question	1, 5, 8, 9, 13, 14, 16
Motion to commit	3, 6, 8, 9, 13, 14, 16
Motion to close debate on question	1, 5, 8, 9, 12, 14, 16
Call to order	1, 5, 7, 9, 13, 15, 17
Motion to appeal from Speaker's decision generally	3, 5, 7, 9, 13, 14, 17
Motion to appeal from Speaker's decision *re* indecorum	1, 5, 8, 9, 13, 14, 17
Motion to amend the rules	3, 5, 8, 9, 12, 14, 16
Motion to amend an amendment	3, 5, 7, 9, 13, 14, 16
Motion to amend	3, 5, 8, 9, 13, 14, 16
Motion to determine time to which to adjourn	2, 5, 8, 9, 13, 14, 16
Motion to adjourn	1, 5, 7, 10, 13, 14, 16

1. Question undebatable; sometimes remarks tacitly allowed.
2. Undebatable if another question is before the assembly.
3. Debatable question.
4. Limited debate only on propriety of postponement.
5. Does not allow reference to main question.
6. Opens the main question to debate.
7. Cannot be amended.
8. May be amended.

9. Can be reconsidered.
10. Cannot be reconsidered.
11. An affirmative vote on this question cannot be reconsidered.
12. Requires two-thirds vote, unless special rules have been enacted.
13. Simple majority suffices to determine the question.
14. Motion must be seconded.
15. Does not require to be seconded.
16. Not in order when another has the floor.
17. Always in order though another may have the floor.
18. May be moved and entered on the record when another has the floor, but the business then before the assembly may not be put aside. The motion must be made by one who voted with the prevailing side, and on the same day the original vote was taken.
19. Fixing the time to which an adjournment may be made; ranks first.
20. To adjourn without limitation; second.
21. Motion for the Orders of the Day; third.
22. Motion to lay on the table; fourth.
23. Motion for the previous question; fifth.
24. Motion to postpone definitely; sixth.
25. Motion to commit; seventh.
26. Motion to amend; eighth.
27. Motion to postpone indefinitely; ninth.
28. On motion to strike out words, "Shall the words stand part of the motion?" unless a majority sustains the words they are struck out.
29. On motion for previous question the form to be observed is: "Shall the main question be now put?" This, if carried, ends debate.
30. On an appeal from the chair's decision, "Shall the decision be sustained as the ruling of the house?" The chair is generally sustained.
31. On motion for Orders of the Day. "Will the house now proceed to the Orders of the Day?" This, if carried, supersedes intervening motions.
32. When an objection is raised to considering question, "Shall the question be considered?" objection may be made by any member before debate has commenced, but not subsequently.

POINTS WORTH REMEMBERING.

Except in vote by ballot, the chairman can vote only when the meeting is equally divided, or when his vote given to the minority would make the division equal.

That speaker is listened to with attention who speaks only when he has something to say.

Speak on the question before the meeting. Make your point and stop when you have made it.

Any ruling by the chairman may be appealed from and decided by a vote of the house.

When several persons rise and claim the chairman's attention at the same time, preference should be given to the one who first caught the chairman's eye.

The chairman is the servant and not the master of the house. When a point of order is raised the person speaking should cease and wait the decision of the chair.

To get rid of an undesirable chairman the house may refuse to do any business or may adjourn.

COUNTERFEITING, GAMBLING, BETTING AND SWINDLING.

COUNTERFEITING.

A Counterfeit is a fac-simile of the genuine, or made as nearly like it as possible. A spurious note is different in design from the genuine and is calculated to pass where the genuine is not known. An altered note is one altered from a lower to a higher denomination. Piecing is done by making ten notes or bills out of nine by cutting a counterfeit note into ten pieces.

Counterfeiting has its good and bad seasons. During the war the high price of metals prohibited the manufacture of spurious coins. High wages in war time industries lessened the incentive. Now, as we are returning to normal conditions there has appeared what is known as a "normal circulation."

Raised Bills, however, have increased in the largest proportion. Federal Reserve Notes in $1.00, $2.00, $5.00 and $10.00 denominations are easily altered but they also carry on their face an extremely simple means of detection. Washington's picture appears on a $1.00, Jefferson's on a $2.00, Lincoln on the $5.00 and Cleveland on the $10.00 note. It is easy to remember that no Federal Reserve Bill bearing the portrait of Washington or Jefferson is worth more than $2.00.

HOW TO DETECT COUNTERFEIT MONEY.

1. There are two silk threads through the bill lengthwise, one near the top, and one near the bottom. By holding it up to the light you can easily see the threads in each bill. This is one of the best tests of a genuine bill, because no counterfeiter can put in the silk threads and imitate the genuine bill in that respect.

2. See that the portraits are good, and notice that the pupil and the white of the eye show distinctly. Then see that the sky and water are clearly transparent. In counterfeit notes the pictures are always poor and the sky, water, etc., look scratchy and irregular.

3. The ink used in genuine notes is very difficult to imitate. It gives a clear, glossy expression, while counterfeiter's ink looks dull, smutty and muddy.

4. The paper of a counterfeit is always of an inferior quality, while the government has the best and most perfect system of manufacturing the highest grade of paper.

5. Examine the medallion rulings and circular ornaments around the figures with a microscope, and see if they are regular and in all parts mathematically exact. This is done by a machine that costs from $75,000 to $150,000, and consequently is beyond the reach of counterfeiters. Engravings by hand can never imitate this work. These medallion lines or rulings can be traced by means of a line through the figures, never breaking or losing itself in another line. In counterfeit it is always broken and irregular.

6. Notes are altered by raising the denomination by taking out the genuine with acid and printing in a higher denomination with a counterfeit die. They can be easily detected by the stain which the acid produces with which the figures are taken out.

7. Bank notes that have been altered by what is called the "pasting process" can be detected by holding them to the light. The parts pasted on will then be easily discovered. If any alteration has been made by substituting letters or figures for others that have been erased, the denomination in the center of the note, if carefully examined, letter by letter, will be found to be blurred and improperly formed, and the parallel lines irregular and imperfect.

RULES FOR DETECTING COUNTERFEIT COINS.

1. A counterfeit coin may sometimes be detected by its dull sound when thrown upon a counter. Some fake coins ring true but are so brittle that they are easily broken.

2. Size and weight are additional tests.

3. All counterfeit coins feel greasy.

4. The acid test consists in using a strong solution of nitric acid (6½ parts) muriatic acid (¼ part) and water (5 parts). When applied to a scratch on the edge of a spurious coin the color will instantly change. If the acid has no effect the coin is genuine.

5. The edges of counterfeit coins are usually imperfect.

6. **Sweating, Plugging and Filling** are methods used to debase coins, and the simplest tests are peculiarities in size, weight and appearance. SWEATING is done by means of abrasion, filing, or an acid bath. PLUGGING is accomplished by boring out a hole in the coin and filling in with a base metal, plating over with gold. In the FILLING process the coin is split in two thin pieces, removing the interior and filling in with a base metal. The outside parts are then joined and the edges plated and remilled.

FIFTY-FOUR VARIETIES OF BANK NOTES.

It is doubtful if many people realize that in all there are fifty-four different designs of various denominations in our paper currency.

Denomination	Kinds
$ 1.00	5
2.00	5
5.00	6
10.00	7
20.00	7
50.00	6
100.00	6
500.00	4
1,000.00	5
5,000.00	1
10,000.00	2

Naturally this makes counterfeiting easy and treasury officials should reduce the variety. All notes of the same denomination should be printed the same color with a distinct color for each denomination. There would then be no possibility of raising a note of low denomination to a higher one.

SWINDLING SCHEMES.

Six Practical Rules to Remember.

1. **Beware of the Swindler.**—He is everywhere and in all kinds of business.

2. Never sign a paper of any kind for a stranger. Make every man unknown to you, who desires to do business with you, prove to you, beyond a doubt, that his business is legitimate and that he acts within the limits of his authority.

3. Never try to beat a man at his own game. The sharpers at every fair and circus and other places where people in large numbers congregate will always offer you great inducements with cards, dice, wheels of fortune, etc. They will urge you to bet on a certain card or number and show you how one dollar could have won $20.00 or $100.00; but when you bet your money, you never win.

4. Never bet or gamble. In trying to get something for nothing, we too often find ourselves the victims of confidence and swindling schemes. Honesty is the best policy, always has been and always will be.

5. Never try to get the best of a sharper by buying a box, watch-case, or anything else in which you have seen him put a $10 or $20 bill.

6. Deal with responsible parties, or see that the article is worth the price before paying for it, and you will never suffer the mortification of being swindled.

THE CARD SWINDLER'S TRICKS.

How People Lose Their Hard-Earned Money.

1. **The Three-Card Monte Trick.**—The three-card monte game is, of course, the old one and the best one known to get the greenhorn's money.

2. The successful three-card monte player generally appears in the disguise of a farmer or cattle man, he speaks in the farmer's tone and acts in the farmer's manner and is dressed in the farmer's style. He appears ignorant and manifests more or less intoxication. Generally has his pockets full of rolls of money.

3. **The Game.**—The cards are three in number and are made especially stiff so that they will hold a corner when turned.

4. **The Capper.**—Every monte player has a capper. A capper is a green, ignorant looking man, who always plays the game and wins a great deal of money. This is done to induce others to play the game. The capper and gamblers are generally in partnership.

5. The first turn the capper wins. Then he turns the corner of a card when the player is not looking, and his friend thinking he has a sure thing bets on the card. In manipulating them the player flattens that card, with some sleight-of-hand movement, and turns the corner of another. The betting man of course picks up the wrong card and loses his money.

5. The capper sometimes marks the card by putting a wet spot on it, and the man who bets on that card finds that the spot

from the right card has been wiped off and the spot put on another card by the same sort of sleight-of-hand performance.

7. There are some three-card monte players that are such experts at the game that the capper will tear off the corner of a card, and the innocent farmer betting on the card thus marked finds it has been turned under the corner of another card and the corner of the right card is covered up with the corner of another card.

8. **Beware.**—The man who is fooling with cards and offering to bet is not fooling away his money. You will never win anything in that way. Do not try to get something for nothing and think you have a snap; for if you play the game with some one else you will soon become a wiser but a poorer man.

THE PATENT FENCE SWINDLE.

It is an old but true maxim, that "experience is an expensive teacher," but many will learn in no other way. The wire and picket fence combination is a good article for fencing gardens, etc., too expensive, however, for general use.

An agent, very nicely dressed, meets you in your garden or field, and shows you extensive engravings of the patent combination fence. He warrants the fence to be just as represented, 44 pickets to the rod, well painted, firmly fastened by six galvanized steel wires, etc. All of this he agrees to furnish at the low price of 20 cents per rod.

After convincing you of the cheapness of the fence, which is easily done, he offers you a special discount to take the agency for your township, for which you are to advance your credit to the amount of $128. After securing your note he sends you a sample of the fence. But you soon find that the fence cannot be made for any such price per rod, and you are out of the amount of credit advanced. The note has been sold, and after passing into the hands of an innocent party it can be collected.

1. **Caution.**—The fence is a Patent Right Fraud. Any man who asks you to sign a note to secure an agency is a swindler, or is acting the part of a rascal for some one else.

2. If the fence was not a fraud, our hardware merchants would long ago have investigated it, and if a good thing, would

have it in stock. It must be a poor concern that necessitates such an unbusinesslike introduction.

3. Whoever deals with an agent deals with him at his own risk, for an agency can be revoked at any time.

4. Most of those swindling contracts are for no specified time and consequently the agency can be terminated at the pleasure of the swindler.

5. Never sign a paper for an agent without satisfactory knowledge of his character, or of his business.

THE FARM-MACHINERY SWINDLE.

The latest scheme for fleecing unwary farmers is as follows: A plausible, well-dressed fellow drives up to the farmer's house with two or three different kinds of farm-machinery, and asks permission to store his machines in the farmer's barn, and the accommodating farmer usually gives permission.

After the machines are stored away, the sharper remarks that they are the last of a large lot that he has been selling through the country, and that he is anxious to close out the consignment, and if the farmer will sell two or more of the machines while they are stored in the barn, he shall have 50 per cent. commission on the sale. The offer is a tempting one, and the farmer usually accepts. He is then requested, merely as a business form, to affix his signature to a document, specifying the terms on which the machines are stored on the premises. The farmer signs a lengthy printed document without reading it, or perhaps if read without understanding it. At the expiration of thirty days he is astounded by finding himself called upon by another stranger to pay an exorbitant price for the machines stored in his barn. When the farmer objects, he is shown his signature attached to an agreement, which agreement, his lawyer tells him, is drawn in good legal form.

The victims of this game usually lose from $200 to $500.

ALWAYS READ BEFORE SIGNING.

Among the pithy sayings of a well-known German philosopher and reader occurs the following: "Sign no paper without reading it." In these days of education, enlightenment and progress, such a caution would hardly seem necessary to any person in the full possession of his faculties; yet it is astonishing how many people there are, including good business men, who attach their signatures to papers or documents whose contents may have a serious bearing upon themselves or their affairs, with scarcely a glance at their contents. Carelessness in failing to acquaint themselves with the contents of a paper before signing it has worked incalculable harm to thousands of well intentioned people. It is a good thing, therefore, to bear in mind continuously the above quotation, particularly with respect to such papers as express or imply anything in the nature of a contract or a legal obligation.

THE ENVELOPE SWINDLE.

1. The envelopes filling an ordinary box each have slips inclosed marked with numbers corresponding with numbers in a show case. There are generally numerous cappers around a game of this kind who play and win large prizes.

2. Many of the envelopes contain a double ticket and the man who plays the game generally opens the envelopes himself when there is nothing at stake and shows you the winning number, but when you draw it he will show you the other slip that contains the other number and you are the loser.

3. Many of these players give a lot of brass or silver washed prizes that are worth about two or three cents apiece.

4. If you desire to make money, remember that the man who plays games does not go around the country giving away money, but they are generally the sharpest and shrewdest of gamblers, and if you desire to be safe have nothing to do with them, and remember, "*that an honest man never gambles.*"

A SWINDLING NOTE

Naperville, Ills., Oct. 20, 1918.

One year after date, I promise to pay Fred. J. Davis or bearer Ten Dollars, when I sell by order Four Hundred and Seventy-five Dollars ($475.00) worth of Patent Fanning Mills for value received, at ten per cent. per annum. . . . . Said ten dollars when due is payable at Naperville, Illinois.

C. E. Selby, Agent for Fred. J. Davis.

Witness: M. J. Moyer.

---

1. Although the above scheme of the confidence man has been exposed time and time again, yet it still continues to add yearly to its list of victims. A paper is drawn up wherein a farmer agrees to pay ten or twenty dollars when he has sold goods to a given amount. By tearing off the right hand end of this paper, what is apparently an agreement for a small amount becomes a promissory note for a considerable sum. This note is sold at a bank, thereby becoming the property of a third and innocent party, and the signer of the agreement is called upon to pay the note.

2. Never sign a paper without carefully reading and examining the same. It is dangerous to sign a paper for an unidentified stranger.

COUNTERFEIT MONEY SWINDLE.

This scheme has long been practiced in different parts of the country, yet the victims are numerous, hundreds being added annually to the list.

It is simply a shrewd system of black-mailing, and worked as follows: The swindlers or black-mailers (as they can more properly be called) get together, make up plausible circulars, and secure advertisements in local newspapers in the territory which they intend to work up. The "gang" has a number of schemes, but the favorite one is to send some person, who has answered their circulars, a genuine new bill, and to get him on pretense to see if it is good. As the bill is genuine there is no difficulty in passing it. The dupe is then informed that he will be supplied with any amount of similar good money at a trifling cost.

If the man bites the tempting bait placed before him, he is made to sign a document which he is told admits him to membership in a secret society known as the Y. F. A. R., and the money is to come in a few days. Instead, however, a man makes his appearance who represents himself as a United States officer; he shows up the document signed by the poor fellow, which practically proves to be a confession of circulating counterfeit money, and calls attention to the bill which he passed.

The victim is told that he must go to Washington and be tried by a United States Court, and the penalty for making and passing counterfeit money is also read. He is cleverly told the long delay at heavy cost and the sure penalty.

When the victim is sufficiently wrought up, the officer offers to compromise for all the way from $200 to $2,000. The money is paid or secured, the document torn up and the dupe released.

Note.—A man who is caught in a swindling scheme of this kind is utterly helpless and at the mercy of his captors. He can not go to officers and make complaint against the rascals without exposing himself, because he never would have been caught in the trap had he not shown a willingness to handle and pass counterfeit money, and consequently is as guilty as the swindler in the eyes of the law.

A SWINDLER SECURING THE SIGNATURE OF HIS VICTIM.

THE BARB-WIRE SWINDLE.

The "Wire Fence Man" is a new swindler working the farmers. The scheme is a shrewd one and is executed as follows: A nicely dressed man, very pleasant in his manner, meets the farmer in his field or at his home, and desires the privilege of exhibiting his wire fence stretcher machine, for which privilege he will build the farmer thirty or forty rods of good fence for exhibition. All the agent asks is board while he is at work on the fence, with the understanding that the farmer is to go after the machine at the nearest depot and pay the charges, not to exceed $3 for the fence, all set up where he wants it. In order to have everything understood, and as a warrant of the farmer's good intentions, he requires him to sign a written order on a postal card, which he mails (as he says) to his partner, which proves to be a written contract for the machine, price $200 (worth less than $25). After the machine comes, a new man turns up with the postal order for the machine, and requires the payment of $200 as per agreement on the card. He claims to be an attorney for the company and threatens to sue in the highest courts until he secures the payment of the order.

When will people begin to study the "Safe Methods of Business" and learn that it is not safe to sign a paper for a stranger?

THE LIGHTNING-ROD SWINDLE.

Contract.

A good lightning rod properly applied is the cheapest and best insurance known.

Naperville, July 8, 1918.

Mr. F. J. Bechtold, **please erect at your earliest convenience your lightning rods on my *House* according to your rules, of which said *House* I am the owner, for which I agree to pay you .... cents per foot and $3.00 for each point, $4.00 each for vanes, $5.00 each for arrows, $1.50 each for balls, and $2.00 for braces, cash, when completed, or a note due on the first day of *January* next, *1919.***

F. Hauswirth.

---

1. In the blank for cents......, the canvasser or agent puts in some single figure, say 7, that being understood to be the regular price per foot, but after the contract is signed, the agent at his leisure quietly inserts a 6 before the 7, or some other figure, making the amount 67 cents per foot instead of 7 cents, as signed and agreed upon.

2. A swindling note is generally obtained, and the contract is kept in the background; but when the collector comes along and presents the note backed by the contract in plain figures, the farmer sees that he himself has been struck by lightning while trying to protect his house.

3. The note is generally in the hands of an innocent party, and according to law may be collected.

4. The agent canvassing the victim generally promises that the rodding of the house shall not cost over $28.00 or $35.00. But that man, however, never appears on the scene again.

5. Never deal with irresponsible persons. If you desire rods, employ your hardware merchants; or if you desire anything in the machinery line, patronize honest and trusted dealers, and take no chances of "being taken in."

DON'T TRY TO GET SOMETHING FOR NOTHING.

THE CHEAP JEWELRY SWINDLE.

Experience has proven again and again that there is nothing gained BY TRYING TO BEAT A MAN AT HIS OWN GAME and succeed in getting something for nothing.

The auctioneer starts out, after getting a crowd about him, by giving back to the purchasers more money than they paid for the article, but this does not generally last long. Higher priced articles are soon put up, such as watches, etc., and the price raised from 50 cts., or $1.00 to $10.00 or $20.00. The purchaser sees the seller stick a $20.00 bill or a $50.00 bill into the watch and close it up, and so sure are the spectators that they saw the money go into the watch that there is no lack of purchasers. But when the watch is purchased and opened it contains a $1.00 bill instead of a $20.00, and the purchaser is a wiser, but not a richer man.

Bookkeeping.

HOW TO LEARN BOOKKEEPING.

1. **Mathematics.**—Bookkeeping is purely a branch of mathematics, and every one should be familiar with the rules and principles of common arithmetic.

2. **Ignorance.**—It is lamentably true that people do business all their lives, settle accounts and transact various kinds of business, and never know anything about the first principles of bookkeeping. They settle all their accounts according to somebody else's bookkeeping. There is no excuse for the younger generation to be ignorant of the principles of bookkeeping. It is easily acquired and may be self-taught if a young man or woman has any degree of perseverance.

3. **How to Learn.**—If you cannot get book-keeping in the common or public school, secure some primary work on bookkeeping and devote your evenings to study, and you will be surprised at your progress. You can easily, if necessary, secure the assistance of some one that is familiar with the subject. But this will be scarcely needed, as the subject of bookkeeping is simple as well as interesting.

4. **Necessity for Bookkeeping.**—The particular necessity for bookkeeping is to preserve a record of such exchanges as would otherwise be trusted to memory; although its ultimate purpose embraces other important results. Bookkeeping is nothing more nor less than a history of business; a record of business transactions.

5. **A Successful Man.**—A man who is successful in business invariably keeps a correct record of his transactions. He does not depend upon the merchant or lumberman with whom he deals, but he has all his own records correctly kept and by that means proves every account of those with whom he deals. Keep your own accounts; do your own figuring and never trust to the accounts or figures of others. It is the only sure road to success.

RULES FOR BOOK-KEEPING.

1. **The Law of Debit and Credit.**—The first thing that a student must learn in book-keeping is the law of Debit and Credit. Debit and Credit are terms used to express the relation which exists between persons or commodities that enter into any business transaction. The simplest meaning of debit is to charge, and of credit to trust.

2. **Cash.**—Cash is a title used to designate money. We include under it currency, bank checks, sight drafts, postal orders, etc.

3. **Merchandise.**—Merchandise includes all goods and wares dealt in by the concern as a business, and which are in store or stock.

4. **Bills Payable.**—Bills payable are our notes or written obligations which others hold, for which we are to pay a certain amount when due. If you give your note it is a Bill Payable.

5. **Bills Receivable.**—Bills receivable are other persons' notes or written obligations, which we hold, for which we are to receive a specified sum when due.

6. **Debit and Credit Side.**—When anything is received or bought, it is always placed on the left hand or debtor side; when money is paid or anything sold, the amount is always placed on the right hand or credit side of the account. If a man buys goods on credit, you charge him, and he then is a debtor. When he pays the amount, he then is credited in the books.

7. **The Day Book.**—The Day Book affords a regular daily history of the business. The Day Book simply states what has been done and is called in law the Original Book of Entry. The form of the Day Book is simple and direct, first giving the name of the person to be debited or credited with the fact of "Dr." or "Cr.," and next, the detail of the purchase, sale or payment, with the final extension of the amount in the proper column.

8. **The Ledger.**—The Ledger is simply a classification of accounts. It places all the accounts together that belong under the same heading. (See Ledger.)

9. **Posting.**—The student will first copy the Day Book with much care, then post the items to the Ledger—indicating

in the margin of the Day Book the page or number of the account in the Ledger, as shown in the written-up set—next construct a Day Book and Ledger of your own from material thus selected, and you will soon master the subject of bookkeeping.

SYSTEMS.

There are two systems of bookkeeping. Single Entry and Double Entry.

In Single Entry, accounts are opened only with individuals, the books used being the Day Book and the Ledger.

In Double Entry, business transactions are recorded so that each entry has a debit and a credit of equal amounts. Here accounts are kept with both persons and things.

MODERN BOOKKEEPING.

With the increase of business and the resulting increase of labor in keeping books the tendency in recent times is to simplify and to make practical the methods of keeping accounts. Whatever tends to save labor and at the same time gives the business man an insight into his financial standing is accepted in preference to the old methods. What concerns the business man most is what he owes others, what others owe him, and what he possesses. Modern bookkeeping varies greatly from the old systems. The immense business of the department stores of our large cities has tended greatly to simplify the keeping of accounts. Since every line of business has its own peculiar features, it is more important that the young man learn the underlying principles of good bookkeeping, and then these can be adapted to any line of business. There should constantly be an effort to use labor-saving methods, at the same time facilitating the ascertaining of gains and losses and of taking balances.

LEGAL POINTS ON BOOKKEEPING.

Practical Suggestions for Business Men.

1. The Day Book, or other books of original entries, is evidence of sale and delivery of goods, and work done.

2. The time to make an entry against the purchaser is when the goods are ready for delivery.

3. Entries, to be admissible as evidence, should be made by the proper person, and made without erasure, alterations or interlineations.

4. Mistakes should be corrected by marking the wrong entry void, and then making a correct entry, or if there is sufficient room, make a brief explanation.

5. All accounts must be itemized, and no general charge can be considered as evidence without giving the items.

6. If A. guarantees that he will see that B. will pay a certain bill of goods, then the goods must be charged to A. and not to B., but if A. guarantees the account of B., if the account is for some date of the past, then such a guarantee must be in writing.

7. To collect a debt on the evidence of book account, from a person in a distant place, a copy of the account should be made out, and accompanied with an affidavit, setting forth that the above account is correctly taken from the book of original entries, and that the charges were made at or about the time of their respective dates, that the goods were sold and delivered at or about the time the charges were made, and the charges are correct, and accounts just, and that the person named is not entitled to any credits not mentioned in the account. This affidavit should be sworn to before a magistrate, commissioner or notary public, and it will save the trouble of producing or sending books.

HOW TO DETECT ERRORS IN A TRIAL BALANCE.

No rule or set of rules can be given for the certain detection of all errors in a Trial Balance, save a careful review of the entire work. If the errors are few the following rules may be of service:

If the error be exactly $1, $100, $1,000, etc., the mistake is very likely to be found in the additions either in the Ledger accounts or in the Trial Balance.

2. If the error is a large amount, see that all the amounts have been entered in the Trial Balance.

3. If an amount has been omitted in posting, the Trial Balance will be out just that amount. Look for the amount in Journal or other books.

4. The Cash Balance can never be on the credit side. The balance of Bills Receivable should never be on the credit side, nor the balance of Bills Payable on the debit side of the account.

5. If the amount has been posted on the wrong side of the Ledger the Trial Balance will be just twice that amount out of balance. Look for half that amount through the books.

6. If the error is divisible by 9, it is very likely that the mistake was made by a transposition of figures as, 345 posted 453 makes an error of 108, which is divisible by 9, again 753 posted 735 makes an error of 18, also divisible by 9. Errors of transposition are the most difficult to find.

7. If the error is in the dollar column or cents column only, the columns on the left need not be re-added.

8. If the above rules fail, only a careful review of the entire work, checking each entry, will determine where the mistake has been made.

TRANSACTIONS.

This Set Is Written Up in the Following Pages.

July 1.—Commenced business with the following resources: Cash, $1,000; Merchandise, $500.—Total investment, $1,500.

June 2.—Sold A. C. Knox, on %, 5 bbls. Flour @ $5.—Sold Frank Fisher 25 lbs. Coffee, @ 20c; 15 lbs. Oolong Tea, @ 80c. Received cash on % $10.—Paid for drayage on merchandise $5.

July 3.—Bought of David Spencer, on %, 50 bushels Apples, @ 50c; 100 bushels Potatoes, @ $1.—Sold D. N. Brown, on %, 3 bbls. Flour, @ $5; 10 bushels Apples, @ 75c.—Sold A. C. Knox, on %, 2 bbls. Flour, @ $5; 25 bushels Potatoes, @ $1.25. Received cash on % $30.—Paid for postage stamps, $10.

July 5.—Sold G. W. Williams, on %, 25 bushels Potatoes, @ $1.25; 20 bushels Apples, @ 75c.

July 5.—Paid David Spencer on % $50.—Received of A. C. Knox on % $10.

July 6.—Bought of G. N. Hudson, on %, 10 bbls. Mess Pork, @ $15.—Paid David Spencer on % $20.

July 8.—Sold to A. N. Peters, on %, 5 bbls. Mess Pork, @ $18.—Sold H. C. Stockbridge, on %, 10 lbs. Oolong Tea, @ 80c; 10 bushels Apples, @ 75c.—Received cash of G. W. Williams in full of %, $46.25. Paid for help around the store $12.

July 9.—Sold Chas. E. Henker, 5 bbls. Mess Pork, @ $17.—Received cash on same $50.—Paid David Spencer on % $20.

July 10.—Sold A. N. Peters, 20 bushels Potatoes, @ $1.20, on %.—Received of H. C. Stockbridge, cash on %, $10.

July 11.—Sold D. N. Brown, on %, 10 bushels Apples @ 70c. Sold Frank Fisher on %, 5 bushels Potatoes @ $1.20.

July 12.—Received of A. N. Peters, cash on %, $100. Received of D. N. Brown, cash on %, $25.

July 13.—Paid G. N. Hudson, cash in full of %, $1.50.—Received of D. N. Brown on % $5.00.

July 15.—Inventory: Merchandise on hand, $625.

DAY BOOK.

	July 1.			
	Commenced business with the following resources:			
	Cash	*$1000.*		
	Merchandise	*500.*		
		$1500.		
	2			
(1)	*A. C. Knox, Dr.*		25	
	To 5 bbls. Flour, @ $5.00,			
	"			
(2)	*Frank Fisher, Dr.*			
	To 25 lbs. Coffee, @ 20c,	*$ 5.00*		
	" 15 " Oolong Tea, @ 80c,	*12.00*	17	
	Cr.			
(2)	*By Cash on account*		10	
	3			
(3)	*David Spencer, Cr.*			
	By 50 bu. Apples, @ 50c,	*$ 25.00*		
	" 100 " Potatoes, @ $1.00	*100.00*	125	
	"			
(4)	*D. N. Brown, Dr.*			
	To 3 bbls. Flour, @ $5.00,	*$15.00*		
	" 10 bush. Apples, @ 75c,	*7.50*	22	50
(1)	*A. C. Knox, Dr.*			
	To 2 bbls. Flour, @ $5.00	*$10.00*		
	" 25 bush. Potatoes, @ $1.25,	*31.25*	41	25
	Cr.			
(1)	*By cash on account*		30	
	5			
(5)	*G. W. Williams, Dr.*			
	To 25 bu. Potatoes, @ $1.25,	*$31.25*		
	" 20 " Apples, @ 75c,	*15.00*	46	25
	"			
(3)	*David Spencer, Dr.*			
	To Cash paid him on account		50	
	"			
(1)	*A. C. Knox, Cr.*			
	By Cash on account		10	
	6			
(6)	*G. N. Hudson, Cr.*			
	By 10 bbls. Mess Pork, @ $15.00.		150	

DAY BOOK.

	July 6.			
(3)	*David Spencer, Dr.* *To Cash paid on account*		20	
	8			
(7)	*A. N. Peters, Dr.* *To 5 bbls. Mess Pork, @ $18.00,*		90	
	"			
(8)	*H. C. Stockbridge, Dr.* *To 10 lbs. Oolong Tea, @ 80c,* *" 10 bush. Apples, @ 75c,*	*$8.00* *7.50*	15	50
	"			
(5)	*G. W. Williams, Cr.* *By Cash in full of account*		46	25
	9			
(9)	*Chas. E. Henker, Dr.* *To 5 bbls. Mess Pork, @ $17.00,*		85	
	Cr.			
(9)	*By Cash on above*		50	
	"			
(3)	*David Spencer, Dr.* *To Cash paid on account*		20	
	10			
(7)	*A. N. Peters, Dr.* *To 20 bush. Potatoes, @ $1.20,*		24	
	"			
(8)	*H. C. Stockbridge, Cr.* *By Cash on account*		10	
	11			
(4)	*D. N. Brown, Dr.* *To 10 bush. Apples, @ 70c,*		7	
	"			
(2)	*Frank Fisher, Dr.* *To 5 bush. Potatoes, @ $1.20,*		6	
	12			
(7)	*A. N. Peters, Cr.* *By Cash on account*		100	
	"			
(4)	*D. N. Brown, Cr.* *By Cash on account*		25	
	13			
(6)	*G. N. Hudson, Dr.* *To Cash in full of account*		150	
	"			
(4)	*D. N. Brown, Cr.* *By Cash on account*		5	

CASH BOOK.

			Received.		Paid.	
July	1	Amount on hand	1000			
"	2	Received on account from Frank Fisher	10			
"	"	Paid for drayage on Mdse.			5	
"	3	Received on account from A. C. Knox	30			
"	"	Paid for Postage Stamps			10	
"	5	Paid David Spencer on account			50	
"	"	Received of A. C. Knox on account	10			
"	6	Paid David Spencer on account			20	
"	8	Rec'd of G. W. Williams in full of account	48	25		
"	"	Paid for help around the store			12	
"	9	Received from Chas. E. Henker on account	50			
"	"	Paid David Spencer on account			20	
"	10	Rec'd from H. C. Stockbridge on account	10			
"	12	Received from A. N. Peters on account	100			
"	"	Received from D. N. Brown on account	25			
"	13	Paid G. N. Hudson in full of account			150	
"	"	Received of D. N. Brown on account	5			
"	14	Balance on hand			1019	[illegible]
			1286	25	1286	25

LEDGER.

1. A. C. Knox.

Dr. | Cr.

July	2	To 5 bbls. Flour	25		July	3	By Cash	30	
"	3	" Mdse.	41	25	"	5	" "	10	
					"	15	" Balance	26	25
			66	25				66	25

2. Frank Fisher.

July	2	To Mdse.	17		July	2	By Cash	10	
"	21	" 5 bu. Potatoes	6		"	15	" Balance	13	
			23					23	

3. *David Spencer.*

Dr.							Cr.	
July	5	To Cash	50		July	8	By Mdse.	125
"	6	" "	20					
"	9	" "	20					
"	15	" Balance	35					
			125					125

4. *D. N. Brown.*

July	8	To Mdse.	22	50	July	12	By Cash	25
"	11	" 10 bu. Apples	7		"	13	" "	5
"	15	" Balance		50				
			30	00				30

5. *G. W. Williams.*

July	5	To Mdse.	46	25	July	8	By Cash	46	25

6. *G. N. Hudson.*

July	13	To Cash	150		July	6	By 10 bbls. [Mess Pork	150

7. *A. N. Peters.*

Dr.							Cr.	
July	8	To 5 bbls. Mess [Pork	90		July	12	By Cash	100
"	10	" 20 bushels [Potatoes	24		"	15	" Balance	14
			114					114

8. H. C. Stockbridge.

July	8	To Mdse.	15	50	July	10	By Cash	10	
					"	15	" Balance	5	50
			15	50				15	50

9. Chas. E. Henker.

July	9	To 5 bbls. Mess Pork	85		July	9	By Cash	50	
					"	15	" Balance	35	
			85					85	

STATEMENT.

Resources or Property.				
1. *From Ledger Accounts—Balances due from persons:—*				
A. C. Knox	26	25		
Frank Fisher	13			
A. N. Peters	14			
H. C. Stockbridge	5	50		
Chas. E. Henker	35			
2. *From Cash Book:—Balance of Cash on hand*	1019	25		
3. *Inventory:—Merchandise on hand*	625			
			1738	
Liabilities or Debts.				
From Ledger Accounts—Balances due other parties:—				
David Spencer	35			
D. N. Brown		50		
			35	50
Worth at close			1702	50
Investment			1500	
Net Gain			202	50

HOW TO KEEP FARM ACCOUNTS.

Rules for Keeping Accounts.

The following are suggested as simple forms for keeping accounts for the use of those whose business or taste does not require a more elaborate form of bookkeeping:

Always charge or "debit" a person for what he may get, and "credit" him for what you receive from him. The word "To," prefixed to an entry, indicates a debit, and the word "By," a credit.

The books necessary are two, called a Day Book and Ledger. In the Day Book should be entered, in diary form, every transaction as it occurs, using as simple and concise wording as possible to express all the facts.

Accounts may be opened with "Cash," "Stock," "Merchandise," "Bills Payable," "Bills Receivable," "Interest," "Profit and Loss," "Expense," etc.; and the farmer may open accounts with each field of his farm, as "Field No. 1," "Field No. 2," "Orchard," "Meadow," etc., charging each field with the amount of labor and material expended upon it, and crediting it with its products. He may also keep an account with his cows, pigs, fowls, etc., and thus at any time tell at a glance the profits or losses of each department of his business.

Cash Book.

			Cash Rec'd.		*Cash Paid.*	
May	2	Received for 500 bush. Corn	$200	00	$	
"	5	Paid Hired Man			20	00
"	6	Paid Interest			150	40
"	10	Received for 22 Hogs	208	90		
"	12	Paid for Groceries			11	90
"	15	Received for 20 doz. Eggs	2	00		
"	19	Received for One Cow	20	00		
"	23	Paid for Coal			16	00
"	27	Paid for Lumber			102	65
June	1	Received for Butter	9	25		
"	2	Received One Load of Hay	6	30		
"	10	Balance Cash on Hand			145	50
		NOTE—To find the balance in cash add up the amount received and subtract from that the amount paid out and the result will always equal the cash on hand.	$446	45	$446	45

Corn Field.

			Dr.		Cr.	
April	4	To 7 days' Plowing @ $2.50	$17	50	$	
"	8	" 2 days' Furrowing @ $2.40	4	80		
"	"	" 2 bushel seed @ $2.50	5			
"	"	" 8 days' Planting @ $1.50	12			
May	1	" 3 days' Hoeing @ $1.25	3	75		
"	8	" 8 days' Cultivating @ $2.00	16			
"	"	" 12 days' Hoeing @ $1.25	15			
Aug.	14	" 9 days' Cutting Corn @ $1.25	11	25		
"	28	By 12 bushels Corn @ 75c			9	
Oct.	22	" 74 bushels Corn @ 42c; Cornstalks, $50			81	60
"	24	To 40 days' Husking @ $1.25	50			
"	"	" 5 days' work with team @ $2.50	12	50		
"	"	By 20 bushels Corn @ $40c			8	
Nov.	3	" 12 bushels Corn @ 40c			4	80
"	17	" Cash for 300 bushels Corn @ 75c			225	
"	25	" Cash for 80 bushels @ 75c			60	
"	31	To Marketing 380 bushels Corn @ 4c	15	20		
"	"	" Interest	35			
		Total Gain	189	88		
			$387	88	$387	88

Family Expense Account.

			Dr.		Cr.	
Jan...	5	To 2 prs. Boots @ $6.00	$12		$	
" ...	15	" 1 pr. Ladies' Boots	2	50		
" ...	19	" M. Cohn, Cutting Pants and Vest	3			
" ...	26	" 1 lb. Tea	1			
March	15	" 3 yds. Cassimere @ $2.00; Sundries $4.75	10	75		
May ..	29	" 1 pr. Boots $2.50; Repairing Shoes 50c	3			
June .	20	" 1 pr. Pants	8			
Sept...	24	" 1 pr. Shoes $1.75; 1 pr. Boots $4.00	5	75		
" ..	24	" 1 Umbrella $2.00; Sundries $2.75	4	75		
Nov...	3	" 1 pr. Boots	8			
Dec...	18	" M. Cohn Cutting Pants	1	50		
" ...	18	" 1 pr. Boots	5			
		Total Expense			65	25
			$ 65	25	$ 65	25

Convenient Form of Entries in Ledger for Farmers.

CHARLES WADSWORTH.

Jan. 5....	To 1 Ton Hay	$14 00	$
" 30....	" 2 Bbls. Potatoes, at $1.75	3 50	
March 4....	By Cash on account		10 00
" 20..	To 1 Cord Wood	4 25	
April 7....	By 1 Plow		17 50
May 3.....	To 10 Bush. Oats, at 40 cents	4 00	
June 10....	" 3 Bbls. Potatoes, at $2	6 00	
July 1.....	By balance charged below		4 25
		$31 75	$31 75
July 1.....	To balance	$4 25	

INTEREST.

LEGAL HINTS AND HELPS CONCERNING INTEREST.

1. **Interest** is money paid for the use of money. All civilized countries regulate the rate of interest by law. That which the law allows is called legal interest.

2. **Usury** is charging or taking more than the legal rate. Efforts to change the statutes so that parties may make any bargain for the use of money which suits them have succeeded in a number of States. Usurers resort to many devices to conceal their usury.

3. **Time.**—It is the general practice of the courts in this country to award interest computed at the legal rate, from the time when payment should have been made. Interest upon a judgment dates from the time the judgment is rendered.

4. **A Creditor** may charge interest on an account from the expiration of the time of credit. When no time is specified, interest may be charged from the time payment is demanded, or when the statement of account has been rendered.

5. **A Debt** for board and lodging, where there was no fixed price or time of payment fixed, will not draw interest until it is reduced to judgment, or until its amount is otherwise determined. Interest may not be charged upon the items of a running account until the balance is struck, and the statement rendered.

6. **Compound Interest** cannot be collected by law. When Interest has already accrued and become payable, an agreement that it shall be added to the principal thus formed will genarally be deemed legal. When such interest would not be recoverable upon an ordinary contract in which its payment was agreed upon, yet if it has actually been paid, it cannot be recovered.

7. **Guardians, Executors, Administrators and Trustees** of every kind may be charged interest upon all trust funds in their hands after their failure to invest them within a reasonable time.

8. **Custom.**—Where it is a uniform practice of the seller to charge interest and this is known to the customer or purchaser at the time when the transaction takes place, interest may be charged on book accounts.

9. **Partners.**—If a partner withdraws money from the partnership funds belonging to the firm, for private use or for the purpose of speculation, he will be liable for interest on the money so withdrawn.

10. **Insurance Policy.**—When loss occurs under a policy of insurance, it bears interest from the time it is due according to the terms of the policy.

11. **Banks** by their method of discounting notes get more than legal interest. The interest is always deducted from the face of the note. Take an extreme case: a bank discounting a note for $500 at six per cent., for fifteen years, would deduct the interest, $450, and the borrower would receive $50, and at the end of fifteen years he would pay the bank $500. This would practically be paying $450 for the use of $50 for fifteen years. The legal interest of $50 for the same time would be but $45. But this method is established by usage and sanctioned by law.

THE CELEBRATED LIGHTNING METHOD FOR CALCULATING INTEREST.

Where the Time Is for Days Only.

Rule.—To find the interest on any given sum for any number of days, multiply the principal by the number of days, then point off two places and divide as follows:

At 5 per cent. divide by 72
At 6 per cent. divide by 60
At 7 per cent. divide by 52
At 8 per cent. divide by 45
At 9 per cent. divide by 40
At 10 per cent. divide by 36
At 12 per cent. divide by 30

Example: What is the interest on $900.00 for 8 days at 6 per cent.?

Solution: 900 × 8 ÷ 60 = $1.20 interest.

When the Time Consists of Years, Months, and Days.

1. Rule.—Reduce years to months, adding the number of months, then place ⅓ of the number of days to the right of the months with a decimal point between.

2. Then remove the decimal point two places to the left in the principal, and divide by 2, and the result will equal the interest for one month at 6 per cent.

3. Multiply the interest for one month by the number of months, and the product is the interest at 6 per cent. for the given time.

Then add $\frac{1}{6}$ of itself for 7 per cent.
Then add $\frac{1}{3}$ of itself for 8 per cent
Then add $\frac{1}{2}$ of itself for 9 per cent
Then add $\frac{2}{3}$ of itself for 10 per cent.
Subtract $\frac{1}{6}$ of itself for 5 per cent.
Subtract $\frac{1}{3}$ of itself for 4 per cent.

Example: Find the interest on $150, at 9 per cent. for 1 year, 4 months, and 12 days:

Solution: $1.50 ÷ 2 = .75 interest for 1 month, 1 year, 4 months and 12 days — 16.4 months.

.75 × 16.4 = $12.30, interest at 6 per cent.
12.30 + 6.15 = $18.45, interest at 9 per cent.

N. B.—The $6.15 is one-half of $12.30.

HOW MONEY GROWS AT INTEREST.

If one dollar be invested and the interest added to the principal annually, at the rates named, we shall have the following result as the accumulation of one hundred years.

One dollar, 100 years at 1 per cent, $2¾; 2 per cent	$7¼
One dollar, 100 years at 3 per cent, $19¼; 4 per cent	50½
One dollar, 100 years at 5 per cent................	131½
One dollar, 100 years at 6 per cent................	340
One dollar, 100 years at 7 per cent................	868
One dollar, 100 years at 8 per cent................	2,203
One dollar, 100 years at 9 per cent................	5,513
One dollar, 100 years at 10 per cent................	13,809
One dollar, 100 years at 12 per cent................	84,675
One dollar, 100 years at 15 per cent................	1,174,405
One dollar, 100 years at 18 per cent................	15,145,000
One dollar, 100 years at 24 per cent................	2,551,799,404

BANKERS' METHOD OF CALCULATING INTEREST.

In banking nearly all the business is transacted on the basis of 30, 60, and 90 days.

Rule.—To find the interest on any amount at 60 days, remove the decimal point two places to the left, and you have the interest at 6 per cent.
Increase or diminish according as the time is increased or diminished.

For 90 days add ½ of itself; for 30 days divide by 2; for 15 days divide by 4; for 120 days multiply by 2.

Example: What is the interest on $240 for 90 days at 6 per cent?

2.40 interest for 60 days.
1.20 interest for ½ of 60 days, or 30 days.

3.60 interest for 90 days.

BANKERS' TIME TABLE.

Showing the number of days from any day in one month to the same day in any other.

From / To	Jan.	Feb.	March.	April.	May.	June.	July.	Aug.	Sep.	Oct.	Nov.	Dec.
Jan.	365	31	59	90	120	151	181	212	243	273	304	334
Feb.	334	365	28	59	89	120	150	181	212	242	273	303
March	306	337	365	31	61	92	122	153	184	214	245	275
April	275	306	334	365	30	61	91	122	153	183	214	244
May	245	276	304	335	365	31	61	92	123	153	184	214
June	214	245	273	304	334	365	30	61	92	122	153	183
July	184	215	243	274	304	335	365	31	62	92	123	153
Aug.	153	184	212	243	273	304	334	365	31	61	92	122
Sep.	122	153	181	212	242	273	303	334	365	30	61	91
Oct.	92	123	151	182	212	243	273	304	335	365	31	61
Nov.	61	92	120	151	181	212	242	273	304	334	365	30
Dec.	31	62	90	121	151	182	212	243	274	304	335	365

NOTE.—Find in the left-hand column the month from any day of which you wish to compute the number of days to the same day in any other month; then follow the line along until under the desired month, and you have the required number of days.

Example: How many days from May 17 to Nov. 17? 184 days. Ans.

TIME AT WHICH MONEY DOUBLES AT INTEREST.

RATE PER CENT.	SIMPLE INTEREST.	COMPOUND INTEREST.
2	50 years.	35 years 1 day.
2½	40 years.	28 years 26 days.
3	33 years 4 months.	23 years 164 days.
3½	28 years 208 days.	20 years 54 days.
4	25 years.	17 years 246 days.
4½	22 years 81 days.	15 years 273 days.
5	20 years.	15 years 75 days.
6	16 years 8 months.	12 years 327 days.
7	14 years 104 days.	10 years 89 days.
8	12½ years.	9 years 2 days.
9	11 years 40 days.	8 years 16 days.
10	10 years.	7 years 100 days.

HOW TO USE THE INTEREST TABLES.

1. The interest on any sum of money, and for any length of time, may be obtained, by adding to or doubling any certain sum, or length of time in the tables, viz.: If the interest on a certain sum of money at 8 per cent. for a given time should be $28, one-half of $28 or $14 would equal the interest at 4 per cent., etc.

2. If the interest at 6 per cent. should amount to $26 on a certain sum of money for a given time, twice that amount or $52 would equal the interest at 12 per cent., and half that amount would equal the interest at 3 per cent.

3. The tables are computed on the principle of 360 days in a year, the rule adopted by bankers and merchants throughout the entire country.

4. When the fraction of interest is a half cent or more, a whole cent is taken, but when less than a half cent, nothing is charged.

EXAMPLE: Find the interest on $1,108 for one year, three months and twenty-nine days, at 7%.

Interest on	$1,000,	for 1 year,	at 7	per cent.,	$70.00
" "	100,	" 1 "	" 7	"	7.00
" "	8,	" 1 "	" 7	"	56
" "	1,000,	" 3 mos.,	" 7	"	17.50
" "	100,	" 3 "	" 7	"	1.75
" "	8,	" 3 "	" 7	"	14
" "	1,000,	" 29 days	" 7	"	5.64
" "	100,	" 29 "	" 7	"	56
" "	8,	" 29 "	" 7	"	05
Interest on amount................					$103.20

EXAMPLE: Find the interest on $1,024 for 1 year, 7 months, 19 days, at 4½ per cent.

From table interest on	$1,000,	for 1 year,	at 9	per cent.,	$ 90.00
" "	20,	" " "	" 9	"	1.80
" "	4,	" " "	" 9	"	.36
Interest on	$1.000,	for 7 mos.,	at 9	per cent.,	52.50
" "	20,	" " "	" 9	"	1.05
" "	4,	" " "	" 9	"	.21
Interest on	$1,000,	for 19 days,	at 9	per cent.,	4.75
" "	20,	" " "	" 9	"	.10
" "	4,	" " "	" 9	"	.02
Interest at 9 per cent..................					$150.79

Interest at 4½ per cent.=$75.40 Ans.

INTEREST AT FIVE PER CENT.

TIME.	$1	$2	$3	$4	$5	$6	$7	$8	$9	$10	$100	$1000
1 Day.	.00	.00	.00	.00	.00	.00	.00	.00	.00	$.00	$ .01	$ .14
2 "	.00	.00	.00	.00	.00	.00	.00	.00	.00	.00	.03	.28
3 "	.00	.00	.00	.00	.00	.00	.00	.00	.00	.00	.04	.42
4 "	.00	.00	.00	.00	.00	.00	.00	.00	.01	.01	.06	.56
5 "	.00	.00	.00	.00	.00	.00	.01	.01	.01	.01	.07	.69
6 "	.00	.00	.00	.00	.00	.01	.01	.01	.01	.01	.08	.83
7 "	.00	.00	.00	.00	.00	.01	.01	.01	.01	.01	.10	.97
8 "	.00	.00	.00	.00	.01	.01	.01	.01	.01	.01	.11	1.11
9 "	.00	.00	.00	.01	.01	.01	.01	.01	.01	.01	.13	1.25
10 "	.00	.00	.00	.01	.01	.01	.01	.01	.01	.01	.14	1.39
11 "	.00	.00	.00	.01	.01	.01	.01	.01	.01	.02	.15	1.53
12 "	.00	.00	.01	.01	.01	.01	.01	.01	.01	.02	.17	1.67
13 "	.00	.00	.01	.01	.01	.01	.01	.01	.02	.02	.18	1.81
14 "	.00	.00	.01	.01	.01	.01	.01	.02	.02	.02	.19	1.94
15 "	.00	.00	.01	.01	.01	.01	.01	.02	.02	.02	.21	2.08
16 "	.00	.00	.01	.01	.01	.01	.02	.02	.02	.02	.22	2.22
17 "	.00	.00	.01	.01	.01	.01	.02	.02	.02	.02	.24	2.36
18 "	.00	.01	.01	.01	.01	.02	.02	.02	.02	.03	.25	2.50
19 "	.00	.01	.01	.01	.01	.02	.02	.02	.02	.03	.26	2.64
20 "	.00	.01	.01	.01	.01	.02	.02	.02	.03	.03	.28	2.78
21 "	.00	.01	.01	.01	.01	.02	.02	.02	.03	.03	.29	2.92
22 "	.00	.01	.01	.01	.01	.02	.02	.02	.03	.03	.31	3.06
23 "	.00	.01	.01	.01	.02	.02	.02	.03	.03	.03	.32	3.19
24 "	.00	.01	.01	.01	.02	.02	.02	.03	.03	.03	.33	3.33
25 "	.00	.01	.01	.01	.02	.02	.02	.03	.03	.03	.35	3.47
26 "	.00	.01	.01	.01	.02	.02	.03	.03	.03	.04	.36	3.61
27 "	.00	.01	.01	.02	.02	.02	.03	.03	.03	.04	.38	3.75
28 "	.00	.01	.01	.02	.02	.02	.03	.03	.04	.04	.39	3.80
29 "	.00	.01	.01	.02	.02	.02	.03	.03	.04	.04	.40	4.03
1 Month.	.00	.01	.01	.02	.02	.03	.03	.03	.04	.04	.42	4.17
2 "	.01	.02	.03	.03	.04	.05	.06	.07	.08	.08	.83	8.33
3 "	.01	.03	.04	.05	.06	.08	.09	.10	.11	.13	1.25	12.50
4 "	.02	.03	.05	.07	.08	.10	.12	.13	.15	.17	1.67	16.67
5 "	.02	.04	.06	.08	.10	.13	.15	.17	.19	.21	2.08	20.83
6 "	.03	.05	.08	.10	.13	.15	.18	.20	.23	.25	2.50	25.00
7 "	.03	.06	.09	.12	.15	.18	.20	.23	.26	.29	2.92	29.17
8 "	.03	.07	.10	.13	.17	.20	23	.27	.30	.33	3.33	33.33
9 "	.04	.08	.11	.15	.19	.23	.26	.30	.34	.38	3.75	37.50
10 "	.04	.08	.13	.17	.21	.25	.29	.33	.38	.42	4.17	41.67
11 "	.05	.09	.14	.18	.23	.28	.32	.37	.41	.46	4.58	45.83
1 Year.	.05	.10	.15	.20	.25	.30	.35	.40	.45	.50	5.00	50.00

INTEREST AT SIX PER CENT.

TIME.	$1	$2	$3	$4	$5	$6	$7	$8	$9	$10	$100	$1000
1 Day.	.00	.00	.00	.00	.00	.00	.00	.00	.00	$.00	$ .02	$ .17
2 "	.00	.00	.00	.00	.00	.00	.00	.00	.00	.00	.03	.33
3 "	.00	.00	.00	.00	.00	.00	.00	.00	.00	.01	.05	.50
4 "	.00	.00	.00	.00	.00	.00	.01	.01	.01	.01	.07	.67
5 "	.00	.00	.00	.00	.00	.01	.01	.01	.01	.01	.08	.83
6 "	.00	.00	.00	.00	.01	.01	.01	.01	.01	.01	.10	1.00
7 "	.00	.00	.00	.00	.01	.01	.01	.01	.01	.01	.12	1.17
8 "	.00	.00	.00	.01	.01	.01	.01	.01	.01	.01	.13	1.33
9 "	.00	.00	.00	.01	.01	.01	.01	.01	.01	.02	.15	1.50
10 "	.00	.00	.01	.01	.01	.01	.01	.01	.02	.02	.17	1.67
11 "	.00	.00	.01	.01	.01	.01	.01	.01	.02	.02	.18	1.83
12 "	.00	.00	.01	.01	.01	.01	.01	.02	.02	.02	.20	2.00
13 "	.00	.00	.01	.01	.01	.01	.02	.02	.02	.02	.22	2.17
14 "	.00	.00	.01	.01	.01	.01	.02	.02	.02	.02	.23	2.33
15 "	.00	.01	.01	.01	.01	.02	.02	.02	.02	.03	.25	2.50
16 "	.00	.01	.01	.01	.01	.02	.02	.02	.02	.03	.27	2.67
17 "	.00	.01	.01	.01	.01	.02	.02	.02	.03	.03	.28	2.83
18 "	.00	.01	.01	.01	.02	.02	.02	.02	.03	.03	.30	3.00
19 "	.00	.01	.01	.01	.02	.02	.02	.03	.03	.03	.32	3.17
20 "	.00	.01	.01	.01	.02	.02	.02	.03	.03	.03	.33	3.33
21 "	.00	.01	.01	.01	.02	.02	.02	.03	.03	.04	.35	3.50
22 "	.00	.01	.01	.01	.02	.02	.03	.03	.03	.04	.37	3.67
23 "	.00	.01	.01	.02	.02	.02	.03	.03	.03	.04	.38	3.83
24 "	.00	.01	.01	.02	.02	.02	.03	.03	.04	.04	.40	4.00
25 "	.00	.01	.01	.02	.02	.03	.03	.03	.04	.04	.42	4.17
26 "	.00	.01	.01	.02	.02	.03	.03	.03	.04	.04	.43	4.33
27 "	.00	.01	.01	.02	.02	.03	.03	.04	.04	.05	.45	4.50
28 "	.00	.01	.01	.02	.02	.03	.03	.04	.04	.05	.47	4.67
29 "	.00	.01	.01	.02	.02	.03	.03	.04	.04	.05	.48	4.83
1 Month.	.01	.01	.02	.02	.03	.03	.04	.04	.05	.05	.50	5.00
2 "	.01	.02	.03	.04	.05	.06	.07	.08	.09	.10	1.00	10.00
3 "	.02	.03	.05	.06	.08	.09	.11	.12	.14	.15	1.50	15.00
4 "	.02	.04	.06	.08	.10	.12	.14	.16	.18	.20	2.00	20.00
5 "	.03	.05	.08	.10	.13	.15	.18	.20	.23	.25	2.50	25.00
6 "	.03	.06	.09	.12	.15	.18	.21	.24	.27	.30	3.00	30.00
7 "	.04	.07	.11	.14	.18	.21	.25	.28	.32	.35	3.50	35.00
8 "	.04	.08	.12	.16	.20	.24	28	.32	.36	.40	4.00	40.00
9 "	.05	.09	.14	.18	.23	.27	.32	.36	.41	.45	4.50	45.00
10 "	.05	.10	.15	.20	.25	.30	.35	.40	.45	.50	5.00	50.00
11 "	.06	.11	.17	.22	.28	.33	.39	.44	.50	.55	5.50	55.00
1 Year.	.06	.12	.18	.24	.30	.36	.42	.48	.54	.60	6.00	60.00

INTEREST AT SEVEN PER CENT.

TIME.	$1	$2	$3	$4	$5	$6	$7	$8	$9	$10	$100	$1000
1 Day.	.00	.00	.00	.00	.00	.00	.00	.00	.00	$.00	$ .02	$ .19
2 "	.00	.00	.00	.00	.00	.00	.00	.00	.00	.00	.04	.39
3 "	.00	.00	.00	.00	.00	.00	.00	.00	.01	.01	.06	.58
4 "	.00	.00	.00	.00	.00	.00	.01	.01	.01	.01	.08	.78
5 "	.00	.00	.00	.00	.00	.01	.01	.01	.01	.01	.10	.97
6 "	.00	.00	.00	.00	.01	.01	.01	.01	.01	.01	.12	1.17
7 "	.00	.00	.00	.01	.01	.01	.01	.01	.01	.01	.14	1.36
8 "	.00	.00	.00	.01	.01	.01	.01	.01	.01	.02	.16	1.56
9 "	.00	.00	.01	.01	.01	.01	.01	.01	.02	.02	.18	1.75
10 "	.00	.00	.01	.01	.01	.01	.01	.02	.02	.02	.19	1.94
11 "	.00	.00	.01	.01	.01	.01	.01	.02	.02	.02	.21	2.14
12 "	.00	.00	.01	.01	.01	.01	.02	.02	.02	.02	.23	2.33
13 "	.00	.01	.01	.01	.01	.02	.02	.02	.02	.03	.25	2.53
14 "	.00	.01	.01	.01	.01	.02	.02	.02	.02	.03	.27	2.72
15 "	.00	.01	.01	.01	.01	.02	.02	.02	.03	.03	.29	2.92
16 "	.00	.01	.01	.01	.02	.02	.02	.02	.03	.03	.31	3.11
17 "	.00	.01	.01	.01	.02	.02	.02	.03	.03	.03	.33	3.31
18 "	.00	.01	.01	.01	.02	.02	.02	.03	.03	.04	.35	3.50
19 "	.00	.01	.01	.01	.02	.02	.03	.03	.03	.04	.37	3.69
20 "	.00	.01	.01	.02	.02	.02	.03	.03	.04	.04	.39	3.89
21 "	.00	.01	.01	.02	.02	.02	.03	.03	.04	.04	.41	4.08
22 "	.00	.01	.01	.02	.02	.03	.03	.03	.04	.04	.43	4.28
23 "	.00	.01	.01	.02	.02	.03	.03	.04	.04	.04	.45	4.47
24 "	.00	.01	.01	.02	.02	.03	.03	.04	.04	.05	.47	4.67
25 "	.00	.01	.01	.02	.02	.03	.03	.04	.04	.05	.49	4.86
26 "	.01	.01	.02	.02	.03	.03	.04	.04	.05	.05	.51	5.06
27 "	.01	.01	.02	.02	.03	.03	.04	.04	.05	.05	.53	5.25
28 "	.01	.01	.02	.02	.03	.03	.04	.04	.05	.05	.54	5.44
29 "	.01	.01	.02	.02	.03	.03	.04	.05	.05	.05	.56	5.64
1 Month.	.01	.01	.02	.02	.03	.04	.04	.05	.05	.06	.58	5.83
2 "	.01	.02	.04	.05	.06	.07	.08	.09	.11	.12	1.17	11.67
3 "	.02	.04	.05	.07	.09	.11	.12	.14	.16	.18	1.75	17.50
4 "	.02	.05	.07	.09	.12	.14	.16	.19	.21	.23	2.33	23.33
5 "	.03	.06	.09	.12	.15	.18	.20	.23	.26	.29	2.92	29.17
6 "	.04	.07	.11	.14	.18	.21	.25	.28	.32	.35	3.50	35.00
7 "	.04	.08	.12	.16	.20	.25	.29	.33	.37	.41	4.08	40.83
8 "	.05	.09	.14	.19	.23	.28	33	.37	.42	.47	4.67	46.67
9 "	.05	.11	.16	.21	.26	.32	.37	.42	.47	.53	5.25	52.50
10 "	.06	.12	.18	.23	.29	.35	.41	.47	.53	.58	5.83	58.33
11 "	.06	.13	.19	.26	.32	.39	.45	.51	.58	.64	6.42	64.17
1 Year.	.07	.14	.21	.28	.35	.42	.49	.56	.63	.70	7.00	70.00

INTEREST AT EIGHT PER CENT.

TIME.	$1	$2	$3	$4	$5	$6	$7	$8	$9	$10	$100	$1000
1 Day.	.00	.00	.00	.00	.00	.00	.00	.00	.00	$.00	$ .02	$ .22
2 "	.00	.00	.00	.00	.00	.00	.00	.00	.00	.00	.04	.44
3 "	.00	.00	.00	.00	.00	.00	.00	.01	.01	.01	.07	.67
4 "	.00	.00	.00	.00	.00	.01	.01	.01	.01	.01	.09	.89
5 "	.00	.00	.00	.00	.01	.01	.01	.01	.01	.01	.11	1.11
6 "	.00	.00	.00	.01	.01	.01	.01	.01	.01	.01	.13	1.33
7 "	.00	.00	.00	.01	.01	.01	.01	.01	.01	.02	.16	1.56
8 "	.00	.00	.01	.01	.01	.01	.01	.01	.02	.02	.18	1.78
9 "	.00	.00	.01	.01	.01	.01	.01	.02	.02	.02	.20	2.00
10 "	.00	.00	.01	.01	.01	.01	.02	.02	.02	.02	.22	2.22
11 "	.00	.00	.01	.01	.01	.01	.02	.02	.02	.02	.24	2.44
12 "	.00	.01	.01	.01	.01	.02	.02	.02	.02	.03	.27	2.67
13 "	.00	.01	.01	.01	.01	.02	.02	.02	.03	.03	.29	2.89
14 "	.00	.01	.01	.01	.02	.02	.02	.02	.03	.03	.31	3.11
15 "	.00	.01	.01	.01	.02	.02	.02	.03	.03	.03	.33	3.33
16 "	.00	.01	.01	.01	.02	.02	.02	.03	.03	.04	.36	3.56
17 "	.00	.01	.01	.02	.02	.02	.03	.03	.03	.04	.38	3.78
18 "	.00	.01	.01	.02	.02	.02	.03	.03	.04	.04	.40	4.00
19 "	.00	.01	.01	.02	.02	.03	.03	.03	.04	.04	.42	4.22
20 "	.00	.01	.01	.02	.02	.03	.03	.04	.04	.04	.44	4.44
21 "	.00	.01	.01	.02	.02	.03	.03	.04	.04	.05	.47	4.67
22 "	.00	.01	.01	.02	.02	.03	.03	.04	.04	.05	.49	4.89
23 "	.01	.01	.02	.02	.03	.03	.04	.04	.05	.05	.51	5.11
24 "	.01	.01	.02	.02	.03	.03	.04	.04	.05	.05	.53	5.33
25 "	.01	.01	.02	.02	.03	.03	.04	.04	.05	.06	.56	5.56
26 "	.01	.01	.02	.02	.03	.03	.04	.05	.05	.06	.58	5.78
27 "	.01	.01	.02	.02	.03	.04	.04	.05	.05	.06	.60	6.00
28 "	.01	.01	.02	.02	.03	.04	.04	.05	.06	.06	.62	6.22
29 "	.01	.01	.02	.03	.03	.04	.05	.05	.06	.06	.64	6.44
1 Month.	.01	.01	.02	.03	.03	.04	.05	.05	.06	.07	.67	6.67
2 "	.01	.03	.04	.05	.07	.08	.09	.11	.12	.13	1.33	13.33
3 "	.02	.04	.06	.08	.10	.12	.14	.16	.18	.20	2.00	20.00
4 "	.03	.05	.08	.11	.13	.16	.19	.21	.24	.27	2.67	26.67
5 "	.03	.07	.10	.13	.17	.20	.23	.27	.30	.33	3.33	33.33
6 "	.04	.08	.12	.16	.20	.24	.28	.32	.36	.40	4.00	40.00
7 "	.05	.09	.14	.19	.23	.28	.33	.37	.42	.47	4.67	46.67
8 "	.05	.11	.16	.21	.27	.32	37	.43	.48	.53	5.33	53.33
9 "	.06	.12	.18	.24	.30	.36	.42	.48	.54	.60	6.00	60.00
10 "	.07	.13	.20	.27	.33	.40	.47	.53	.60	.67	6.67	66.67
11 "	.07	.15	.22	.29	.37	.44	.51	.59	.66	.73	7.33	73.33
1 Year.	.08	.16	.24	.32	.40	.48	.56	.64	.72	.80	8.00	80.00

INTEREST AT NINE PER CENT.

TIME.	$1	$2	$3	$4	$5	$6	$7	$8	$9	$10	$100	$1000
1 Day.	.00	.00	.00	.00	.00	.00	.00	.00	.00	$.00	$ .02	$ .25
2 "	.00	.00	.00	.00	.00	.00	.00	.00	.00	.00	05	.50
3 "	.00	.00	.00	.00	.00	.00	.00	.01	.01	.01	.08	.75
4 "	.00	.00	.00	.00	.00	.01	.01	.01	.01	.01	.10	1.00
5 "	.00	.00	.00	.00	.01	.01	.01	.01	.01	.01	.12	1.25
6 "	.00	.00	.00	.01	.01	.01	.01	.01	.01	.02	.15	1.50
7 "	.00	.00	.00	.01	.01	.01	.01	.01	.02	.02	.17	1.75
8 "	.00	.00	.01	.01	.01	.01	.01	.02	.02	.02	.20	2.00
9 "	.00	.00	.01	.01	.01	.01	.02	.02	.02	.02	.23	2.25
10 "	.00	.00	.01	.01	.01	.02	.02	.02	.02	.02	.25	2.50
11 "	.00	.00	.01	.01	.01	.02	.02	.02	.02	.03	.27	2.75
12 "	.00	.01	.01	.01	.02	.02	.02	.02	.03	.03	.30	3.00
13 "	.00	.01	.01	.01	.02	.02	.02	.03	.03	.03	.32	3.25
14 "	.00	.01	.01	.01	.02	.02	.02	.03	.03	.03	.35	3.50
15 "	.00	.01	.01	.02	.02	.02	.03	.03	.03	.04	.38	3.75
16 "	.00	.01	.01	.02	.02	.02	.03	.03	.04	.04	.40	4.00
17 "	.00	.01	.01	.02	.02	.03	.03	.03	.04	.04	.42	4.25
18 "	.00	.01	.01	.02	.02	.03	.03	.04	.04	.05	.45	4.50
19 "	.00	.01	.01	.02	.02	.03	.03	.04	.04	.05	.47	4.75
20 "	.00	.01	.01	.02	.02	.03	.03	.04	.05	.05	.50	5.00
21 "	.00	.01	.01	.02	.03	.03	.04	.04	.05	.05	.53	5.25
22 "	.00	.01	.01	.02	.03	.03	.04	.04	.05	.05	.55	5.50
23 "	.00	.01	.02	.02	.03	.03	.04	.05	.05	.06	.57	5 75
24 "	.01	.01	.02	.02	.03	.03	.04	.05	.05	.06	.60	6.00
25 "	.01	.01	.02	.02	.03	.04	.04	.05	.06	.06	.62	6.25
26 "	.01	.01	.02	.03	.03	.04	.05	.05	.06	.06	.65	6.50
27 "	.01	.01	.02	.03	.03	.04	.05	.05	.06	.07	.68	6.75
28 "	.01	.01	.02	.03	.03	.04	.05	.06	.06	.07	.70	7.00
29 "	.01	.01	.02	.03	.03	.04	.05	.06	.06	.07	.72	7.25
1 Month.	.01	.02	.02	.03	.04	.05	.05	.06	.07	.08	.75	7.50
2 "	.02	.03	.05	.06	.08	.09	.11	.12	.14	.15	1.50	15.00
3 "	.02	.05	.07	.09	.11	.14	.16	.18	.20	.23	2.25	22.50
4 "	.03	.06	.09	.12	.15	.18	.21	.24	.27	.30	3.00	30.00
5 "	.04	.08	.11	.15	.19	.23	.26	.30	.34	.38	3.75	37.50
6 "	.05	.09	.14	.18	.23	.27	.32	.36	.41	.45	4.50	45.00
7 "	.05	.11	.16	.21	.26	.32	.37	.42	.47	.53	5.25	52.50
8 "	.06	.12	.18	.24	.30	.36	42	.48	.54	.60	6.00	60.00
9 "	.06	.14	.20	.27	.33	.41	.47	.54	.60	.68	6.75	67.50
10 "	.08	.15	.23	.30	.38	.45	.53	.60	.68	.75	7.50	75.00
11 "	.08	.17	.24	.33	.41	.50	.57	.66	.74	.83	8.25	82.50
1 Year.	.09	.18	.27	.36	.45	.54	.63	.72	.81	.90	9.00	90.0[illegible]

INTEREST AT TEN PER CENT.

TIME.	$1	$2	$3	$4	$5	$6	$7	$8	$9	$10	$100	$1000
1 Day.	.00	.00	.00	.00	.00	.00	.00	.00	.00	$.00	$ .03	$ .28
2 "	.00	.00	.00	.00	.00	.00	.00	.00	.01	.01	.06	.56
3 "	.00	.00	.00	.00	.01	.01	.01	.01	.01	.01	.08	.83
4 "	.00	.00	.00	.00	.01	.01	.01	.01	.01	.01	.11	1.11
5 "	.00	.00	.00	.01	.01	.01	.01	.01	.01	.01	.14	1.39
6 "	.00	.00	.01	.01	.01	.01	.01	.01	.02	.02	.17	1.67
7 "	.00	.00	.01	.01	.01	.01	.01	.02	.02	.02	.19	1.94
8 "	.00	.00	.01	.01	.01	.01	.02	.02	.02	.02	.22	2.22
9 "	.00	.01	.01	.01	.01	.02	.02	.02	.02	.03	.25	2.50
10 "	.00	.01	.01	.01	.01	.02	.02	.02	.03	.03	.28	2.78
11 "	.00	.01	.01	.01	.02	.02	.02	.02	.03	.03	.31	3.06
12 "	.00	.01	.01	.01	.02	.02	.02	.03	.03	.03	.33	3.33
13 "	.00	.01	.01	.01	.02	.02	.03	.03	.03	.04	.36	3.61
14 "	.00	.01	.01	.02	.02	.02	.03	.03	.04	.04	.39	3.89
15 "	.00	.01	.01	.02	.02	.03	.03	.03	.04	.04	.42	4.17
16 "	.00	.01	.01	.02	.02	.03	.03	.04	.04	.04	.44	4.44
17 "	.00	.01	.01	.02	.02	.03	.03	.04	.04	.05	.47	4.72
18 "	.01	.01	.02	.02	.03	.03	.04	.04	.05	.05	.50	5.00
19 "	.01	.01	.02	.02	.03	.03	.04	.04	.05	.05	.53	5.28
20 "	.01	.01	.02	.02	.03	.03	.04	.04	.05	.06	.56	5.56
21 "	.01	.01	.02	.02	.03	.04	.04	.05	.05	.06	.58	5.83
22 "	.01	.01	.02	.02	.03	.04	.04	.05	.06	.06	.61	6.11
23 "	.01	.01	.02	.03	.03	.04	.04	.05	.06	.06	.64	6.39
24 "	.01	.01	.02	.03	.03	.04	.05	.05	.06	.07	.67	6.67
25 "	.01	.01	.02	.03	.03	.04	.05	.06	.06	.07	.69	6.94
26 "	.01	.01	.02	.03	.04	.04	.05	.06	.07	.07	.72	7.22
27 "	.01	.02	.02	.03	.04	.05	.05	.06	.07	.08	.75	7.50
28 "	.01	.02	.02	.03	.04	.05	.05	.06	.07	.08	.78	7.78
29 "	.01	.02	.02	.03	.04	.05	.06	.06	.07	.08	.81	8.06
1 Month.	.01	.02	.03	.03	.04	.05	.06	.07	.08	.08	.83	8.33
2 "	.02	.03	.05	.07	.08	.10	.12	.13	.15	.17	1.67	16.67
3 "	.03	.05	.08	.10	.13	.15	.18	.20	.23	.25	2.50	25.00
4 "	.03	.07	.10	.13	.17	.20	.23	.27	.30	.33	3.33	33.33
5 "	.04	.08	.13	.17	.21	.25	.29	.33	.38	.42	4.17	41.67
6 "	.05	.10	.15	.20	.25	.30	.35	.40	.45	.50	5.00	50.00
7 "	.06	.12	.18	.23	.29	.35	.41	.47	.53	.58	5.83	58.33
8 "	.07	.13	.20	.27	.33	.40	47	.53	.60	.67	6.67	66.67
9 "	.08	.15	.23	.30	.38	.45	.53	.60	.68	.75	7.50	75.00
10 "	.08	.17	.25	.33	.42	.50	.58	.67	.75	.83	8.33	3.33
11 "	.09	.18	.28	.37	.46	.55	.64	.73	.83	.92	9.17	91.67
1 Year.	.10	.20	.30	.40	.50	.60	.70	.80	.90	1.00	10.00	100.00

POSSIBILITIES OF COMPOUND INTEREST.

An Idaho correspondent sends the New York Tribune a photograph of an old Idaho mortgage, which shows in a startling way the amazing possibilities of compound interest. The mortgage was executed in 1861, on a piece of land in Boise City, "to secure the sum of $340, if paid in legal tender, with interest, at the rate of 10 per cent. per month. But if the said note shall not be paid......then the sum of $170, with interest, at 10 per cent. per month, and if said interest is not paid at the time of maturity of this note, said interest to be added to the principal, and said principal and interest together shall draw interest per month as above stated." These conditions were evidently not fulfilled, for a note is appended to the document as follows: "The above mortgage is not satisfied, according to the records of Ada County. With interest on $170, at 10 per cent. per month, compounded every six months, the debt would now amount to $45,972,003,182,826.50." There are a great many millionaires in the country, but there is probably only one man in the world who is indebted in the sum of nearly forty-six trillions of dollars.

THE APPLICATION OF COMPOUND INTEREST.

Direct compound interest is illegal in all the States. But every man that loans his money and keeps it out at a legal rate of interest receives and makes a compound rate of interest. He annually collects his interest, and that in turn loaned out again makes an accumulation equal to a regular compound rate of interest.

EXAMPLE:—If Captain Newport, at his first landing at Jamestown, Virginia, in 1607, had loaned out $100 at compound interest, it would now equal a sum greater than the entire wealth of the United States.

COMPOUND INTEREST TABLE.

Showing the amount of $1 from 1 to 15 years at compound interest, interest added semi-annually, at different rates. This table will be found valuable in computing interest on Savings Bank deposits, &c.

YEARS.	3 Per Cent.	4 Per Cent.	5 Per Cent.	6 Per Cent.	7 Per Cent.	8 Per Cent.	10 Per Cent.
½	1.015000	1.020000	1.025000	1.030000	1.035000	1.040000	1.050000
1	1.030225	1.040400	1.050625	1.060900	1.071225	1.081600	1.102500
1½	1.045678	1.061208	1.076890	1.092727	1.108718	1.124864	1.157625
2	1.061363	1.082432	1.103813	1.125509	1.147523	1.169858	1.215506
2½	1.077284	1.104081	1.131408	1.159274	1.187686	1.216653	1.276281
3	1.093443	1.126162	1.159693	1.194052	1.229255	1.265319	1.340095
3½	1.109845	1.148685	1.188685	1.229874	1.272279	1.315931	1.407100
4	1.126492	1.171659	1.218403	1.226770	1.316809	1.368569	1.477455
4½	1.143390	1.195092	1.248863	1.304773	1.363897	1.423312	1.551328
5	1.160541	1.218994	1.280084	1.343916	1.410598	1.480244	1,628894
5½	1.177949	1.243374	1.312086	1.384234	1.459969	1.539454	1.710339
6	1.195618	1.268241	1.344888	1.425761	1.511068	1.601032	1.795856
6½	1.213552	1.293606	1.378511	1.468533	1.563956	1.665073	1.885649
7	1.231755	1.319478	1.412973	1.512589	1.618694	1.731676	1.979931
7½	1.250232	1.345868	1.448298	1.557967	1.675349	1.800943	2.078928
8	1.268985	1.372785	1.484505	1.604706	1.733986	1.872981	2.182874
8½	1.288020	1.400241	1.521618	1.652847	1.794675	1.947900	2.292019
9	1.307340	1.428246	1.559658	1.702433	1.857489	2.025816	2.406619
9½	1.326950	1.456811	1.598650	1.753506	1.922501	2.106849	2.526950
10	1.346855	1.485947	1.638616	1.806111	1.989789	2.191123	2.653297
10½	1.367058	1.515666	1.679581	1.860294	2.059431	2.278768	2.785962
11	1.387563	1.545980	1.721571	1,916103	2.131511	2.369919	2.925260
11½	1.408377	1.576899	1.764610	1.973586	2.206114	2.464715	3.071523
12	1.429503	1.608437	1.808726	2.032794	2.283328	2.563304	3.225100
12½	1.450945	1.640606	1.853944	2.093778	2.363245	2.665836	3.386355
13	1.472709	1.673418	1.900292	2.156591	2.445959	2.772470	3.555672
13½	1.494800	1.706886	1.947800	2.221289	2.531567	2.883368	3.733456
14	1.517222	1.741024	1.996595	2.287927	2.620172	2.998703	3.920129
14½	1.539980	1.775845	2.046407	2.356565	2.711878	3.118651	4.116135
15	1.563080	1.811361	2.097567	2.427262	2.806793	3.243397	4.321940

EXAMPLE.—What will $400 amount to in 8 years and 6 months at 4 per cent compound interest, interest added semi-annually? Referring to table. it is found $1 in 8 years and 6 months at 4 per cent will amount to $1.400241. The amount of $400 will be 400 times this or $560.0964.

NOTE.—If the interest only be wanted, deduct the principal, $400, from $560.0964.

INTEREST LAWS OF THE UNITED STATES

Showing days of grace in the various States.

States and Territories	Penalty of Usury	Rate	Special
Alabama	Forfeiture of all interest (a)	8	8 per ct.
Alaska	Forfeiture of debt (a)	8	12 per ct.
Arizona	Forfeiture of all interest (b)	6	10 per ct.
Arkansas	Forfeiture of principal and interest (a)	6	10 per ct.
California	None (b)	7	No limit.
Colorado	None (b)	8	No limit.
Connecticut	Criminal offence (b)	6	12 per ct.
Delaware	Forfeiture of interest and principal (b)	6	6 per ct.
District of Col.	Forfeiture of entire interest (b)	6	10 per ct.
Florida	Forfeiture of interest (b)	8	10 per ct.
Georgia	Forfeiture of excess of interest	7	8 per ct.
Idaho	(c) (b)	7	12 per ct.
Illinois	Forfeiture of entire interest (b)	5	7 per ct.
Indiana	Forfeiture of excess of interest (b)	6	8 per ct.
Iowa	Forfeiture of interest and costs (e) (b)	8	6 per ct.
Kansas	Forfeiture of excess of interest (b)	6	10 per ct.
Kentucky	Forfeiture of excess of interest (b)	6	6 per ct.
Louisiana	Forfeiture of interest (b)	5	8 per ct.
Maine	None (a) (f)	6	No limit.
Maryland	Forfeiture of all excess interest (b)	6	6 per ct.
Massachusetts	None (a) (f)	6	No limit.
Michigan	Forfeiture of interest (b)	5	7 per ct.
Minnesota	Forfeiture of all interest with costs (b)	6	10 per ct.
Mississippi	Forfeiture of interest (a)	6	8 per ct.
Missouri	Forfeiture of interest to common school fund	6	8 per ct.
Montana	None (b)	8	No limit.
Nebraska	Forfeiture of interest and costs (b)	7	10 per ct.
Nevada	None (b)	7	12 per ct.
New Hampshire	Forfeiture of three times the excess interest (b) (f)	6	6 per ct.
New Jersey	Forfeiture of entire interest and costs (b)	6	6 per ct.
New Mexico	Misdemeanor or contract for more (a)	6	12 per ct.
New York	Neither principal or interest can be collected (d) (b)	6	6 per ct.
North Carolina	Forfeiture of interest (a) (f)	6	6 per ct.
North Dakota	None (b)	6	10 per ct.
Ohio	None (b)	6	8 per ct.
Oklahoma	Forfeiture of interest (a)	6	10 per ct.
Oregon	Forfeiture of principal and interest to school funds (a)	6	10 per ct.
Pennsylvania	Forfeiture of excess interest (b)	6	6 per ct.
Rhode Island	None (a) (f)	6	No limit.
South Carolina	Forfeiture of double the interest (a) (f)	7	8 per ct.
South Dakota	Forfeiture of all interest (a)	7	12 per ct.
Tennessee	None (b)	6	6 per ct.
Texas	Forfeiture of entire interest (a) (f)	6	10 per ct.
Utah	Forfeiture of both principal and interest (b)	8	12 per ct.
Vermont	Forfeiture of excess of interest (b)	6	6 per ct.
Virginia	Forfeiture of excess over 6 per cent (b)	6	6 per ct.
Washington	(g)	6	12 per ct.
West Virginia	Forfeiture of excess of interest (b)	6	6 per ct.
Wisconsin	Forfeiture of entire interest (b)	6	10 per ct.
Wyoming	Forfeiture of entire interest (a)	8	12 per ct.

(a) Grace. (b) No grace. (c) Loss of interest by lender; 10 per cent from borrower for school fund. (d) Contract void; punishable as misdemeanor. (e) Defendant also forfeits 10 per cent. a year to school fund.

18 per cent on less than $1,000. Corporations only 7 per cent.

(f) Days of grace. Sight, yes. Demand, no.

(g) Judgment recoverable for the principal less twice the amount of interest and once the amount of interest due at rate contracted for.

SHORT METHODS OF COMPUTATION AND BUSINESS RECKONING TABLES.

SHORT RULES OF ARITHMETIC.

In these short rules, which we have developed and compiled, our aim has been to make them superior to anything that has ever been published. We have endeavored to teach the how, and not the why. Our object is brevity and completeness. Business demands brief and practical rules. To every farmer, teacher, mechanic, merchant, lawyer and laborer, these rules will prove available and valuable knowledge.

AN EASY WAY TO ADD.

This is a very simple and easy method, and will be a great help to those who find difficulty in adding long columns of figures correctly:

4'	EXAMPLE:
7	*Process.*—Begin at 9 to add as near 20 as you can, thus:
6	$9+2+4+3=18$, reject the tens and place the 8 to
8•	the right of the 3, as in example; begin at 6 and
4	add $6+8+4=18$, reject the tens, as before, and
9	place 8 to the right of 4, as in example; begin at
4'	$6+7+4=17$, reject tens, place 7 to the right of
7	4, as in example; then $9+4+3=16$, reject tens,
6	place 6 to the right of 3; then $6+7+4=17$, reject
4•	tens and place 7 to the right, as before, having
8	arrived at the top of the column, add the figures
6	in the new column, thus: $8+8+7+6+7=36$,
3•	or 3 tens and 6 units; place the 6 units as the
4	unit's figure of the sum, having 3 tens to carry to
2	5 tens, the number of integers or catch figures already
9	rejected. $3+5=8$ tens, which prefixed with the 6,
86	makes 86 the sum.

N. B.—Two or more columns may be added in the same way by using a lead pencil, and then erasing the figures used after the addition is completed.

The Civil Service Method of Addition.

This method may be new to some, but it should be understood by all.

$2492.27	24
9636.85	24
3254.36	25
8927.05	27
1622.31	34
400.10	32
4321.70	$35697.64
5043.00	

Commence at the right and add each column of figures by itself, as for instance the first column equals 24; put down the 24; the next column equals 24; put it down as above; the next column equals 25, the next 27, and so on, and then add the results as shown in the above form.

The advantage of this method is that a person's attention may be called to other things, while he is in the midst of his results, and not lose any time or suffer any disadvantage. In the counting-house or places of business where there is a great deal of talking and many other things call the clerk, when he left off he is never at a loss to resume his work.

ADDING AND SUBTRACTING FRACTIONS.

To find the sum of two fractions with ones for numerators, add the denominators for the numerator of the answer and multiply them for the denominator. To subtract them, subtract the denominators for the numerator of the answer and multiply them for the denominator.

Thus, $\frac{1}{4}+\frac{1}{5}=\frac{9}{20}$ $\frac{1}{7}-\frac{1}{10}=\frac{3}{70}$.

This rule is well worth remembering.

ADDITION.

Lightning Method

```
7 8 5 7 6 8 9
5 4 3 1 0 7 4
4 5 6 8 9 2 5
4 8 3 2 6 5 0
3 7 5 5 5 4 2
5 2 0 3 7 5 9
-------------
        6 3 9
```

"Lightning addition" lies in the ability to see and take in the result of two or more figures without stopping to add each figure separately, i. e., to read results in figures as in reading a book, the meaning of the word or sentence is known without spelling out each syllable or word.

Process.—Commence at the bottom at the right and add thus in the above example: 11, 20, 29; then carry the 2 tens to the second column; then add, 7, 16, 25, 33; carry the 3 hundreds to the third column and add the same way; 10, 21, 30, 36, etc., etc.

Never allow yourself to add up a column in this manner: 9 and 2 are 11 and 5 are 16 and 4 are 20 and 9 are 29. It is just as easy to name the results of two or more figures at once, and five times as rapid.

Make combinations of 10 or of other numbers and add them as simple numbers. Thus in adding

$$8+\overline{6+4}+9+\overline{3+7}+\overline{4+5+1}+4+2$$

say 8, 18, 27, 37, 47, 53, taking each group at a glance as a single figure. Group figures as conveniently as possible. After a little practice the mind readily grasps the groups of figures and results are quickly reached. You will be astonished at the result after practicing a half hour daily for a month.

THE NEW MULTIPLICATION TABLE

THIS TABLE shows that the large **1** figures in front of each double row are intended to multiply the small head figures in said row; for instance the large 9 is followed by 2, 3, 4, 5, 6, 7, 8, 9, beneath which stands the increase of each, multiplied by 9, namely, 9 times 2 are eighteen 9 times 3 are 27, 9 times 4 are 36, etc., 9 times 9 are 81, as will be seen at the end of the row; and in the last row, 25 times 2 are 50, etc., and at the end 25 times 25 are 625.

2	2																							
	4																							
3	2	3																						
	6	9																						
4	2	3	4																					
	8	12	16																					
5	2	3	4	5																				
	10	15	20	25																				
6	2	3	4	5	6																			
	12	18	24	30	36																			
7	2	3	4	5	6	7																		
	14	21	28	35	42	49																		
8	2	3	4	5	6	7	8																	
	16	24	32	40	48	56	64																	
9	2	3	4	5	6	7	8	9																
	18	27	36	45	54	63	72	81																
10	2	3	4	5	6	7	8	9	10															
	20	30	40	50	60	70	80	90	100															
11	2	3	4	5	6	7	8	9	10	11														
	22	33	44	55	66	77	88	99	110	121														
12	2	3	4	5	6	7	8	9	10	11	12													
	24	36	48	60	72	84	96	108	120	132	144													
13	2	3	4	5	6	7	8	9	10	11	12	13												
	26	89	52	65	78	91	104	117	130	143	156	169												
14	2	3	4	5	6	7	8	9	10	11	12	13	14											
	28	42	56	70	84	98	112	126	140	154	168	182	196											
15	2	3	4	5	6	7	8	9	10	11	12	13	14	15										
	30	45	60	75	90	105	120	135	150	165	180	195	210	225										
16	2	3	4	5	6	7	8	9	10	11	12	13	14	15	16									
	32	48	64	80	96	112	128	144	160	176	192	208	224	240	256									
17	2	3	4	5	6	7	8	9	10	11	12	13	14	15	16	17								
	34	51	68	85	102	119	136	153	170	187	204	221	238	255	272	289								
18	2	3	4	5	6	7	8	9	10	11	12	13	14	15	16	17	18							
	36	54	72	90	108	126	144	162	180	198	216	234	252	270	288	306	324							
19	2	3	4	5	6	7	8	9	10	11	12	13	14	15	16	17	18	19						
	38	57	76	95	114	133	152	171	190	209	228	247	266	285	304	323	342	361						
20	2	3	4	5	6	7	8	9	10	11	12	13	14	15	16	17	18	19	20					
	40	60	80	100	120	140	160	180	200	220	240	260	280	300	320	340	360	380	400					
21	2	3	4	5	6	7	8	9	10	11	12	13	14	15	16	17	18	19	20	21				
	42	63	84	105	126	147	168	189	210	231	252	273	294	315	336	357	378	399	420	441				
22	2	3	4	5	6	7	8	9	10	11	12	13	14	15	16	17	18	19	20	21	22			
	44	66	88	110	132	154	176	198	220	242	264	286	308	330	352	374	396	418	440	462	484			
23	2	3	4	5	6	7	8	9	10	11	12	13	14	15	16	17	18	19	20	21	22	23		
	46	69	92	115	138	161	184	207	230	253	276	299	322	345	368	391	414	437	460	483	506	529		
24	2	3	4	5	6	7	8	9	10	11	12	13	14	15	16	17	18	19	20	21	22	23	24	
	48	72	96	120	144	168	192	216	240	264	288	312	336	360	384	408	432	456	480	504	528	552	576	
25	2	3	4	5	6	7	8	9	10	11	12	13	14	15	16	17	18	19	20	21	22	23	24	25
	50	75	100	125	150	175	200	225	250	275	300	325	350	375	400	425	450	475	500	525	550	575	600	625

LIGHTNING METHOD OF MULTIPLICATION AND DIVISION.

To multiply by 125, divide by 8, and call it thousands, because 125 is ⅛ of a thousand.

To multiply by 12½, divide by 8; call it hundreds.

To multiply by 1¼, divide by 8; call it tens.

To multiply by 62½, divide by 16, and call it thousands.

To multiply by 6¼, divide by 16, and call it hundreds.

To multiply by 31¼, divide by 32, and call it thousands.

To multiply by 333 1-3, divide by 3, and call it thousands.

To multiply by 33 1-3, divide by 3, and call it hundreds.

To multiply by 3 1-3, divide by 3, and call it tens.

To multiply by 50, divide by 2, and call it hundreds.

To multiply by 66 2-3, divide by 15, and call it thousands.

To multiply by 833 1-3, divide by 15, and call it ten thousands, by annexing four ciphers.

To multiply by 83 1-3, divide by 12, and call it thousands.

To multiply by 8 1-3, divide by 12, and call it hundreds, because 8 1-3 is 1-12 of a hundred. The reason is similar in each case.

To multiply by 166 2-3, divide by 6, and call it thousands.

To multiply by 16 2-3, divide by 6, and call it hundreds.

To multiply by 1 2-3, divide by 6, and call it tens.

To multiply by 37½, take ⅜ of the number, and call it hundreds; 87½, ⅞ of the number, and call it hundreds, etc.

We simply reverse these methods to divide. To divide by 10,100, 1,000, etc., we remove the point one, two and three places to the left.

To divide by 25, remove the decimal point two places to the left, and multiply by 4.

Removing the point two places divides by one hundred; hence the quotient is four times too small; hence we remove the point two places, and multiply by 4.

To divide by 2½, remove the point one place to the left, and multiply by 4.

To divide by 125, remove the point three places to the left, and multiply by 8.

To divide by 12½, remove the point two places to the left, and multiply by 8.

To divide by 1¼, remove the point one point to the left, and multiply by 8. There are about 1¼ cubic feet in one bushel. Hence dividing the number of cubic feet by 1¼ gives the number of bushels nearly.

To divide by 133⅓, remove the point three places to the left, then multiply by 3 and divide by 4.

To divide by 8⅓, remove the point two places to the left, and and multiply by 12.

SHORT METHODS OF MULTIPLICATION.

How to Multiply Any Small Number Ending with 5.

Example: 25×85. To the product of 2 and 8 add one-half their sum, and to this result annex 25.

Solution: 25 / 85 / 2125 — $5\times5=25$; $2\times8=16$, $16+\frac{1}{2}(2+8)=21$.

This rule is very simple and useful; practice it, it never fails.

The Complement Rule.

98–2
91–9
8918

The complement of a number added to the number makes it 10, or 100, or 1000, etc. The complement of 98 is 2, of 91 is 9. To find the product of these two numbers multiply the complements together; and for the other two figures subtract across, either the two from the 91, or the 9 from the 98.

How to Multiply Any Number by 21, 22, 23, 24, etc.

2102
23
48346

Multiply each figure in the multiplicand by the units figure in the multiplier, increasing each separate product by double the figure to the right of the one multiplied; double the last figure.

Solution: 3×2=6, 3×0=0, and double the right hand figure, 2, =4. 3×1=3, and double the right-hand figure, 0, =3. 3×2=6, double the 1, =8. Double the last figure.

How to Multiply Any Number by 21, 31, 41, etc.

230412
460824
4838652

To multiply any number of two figures when the last is 1, or of three figures when the last two are 01.

Example: Multiply 230412 by 21. Instead of the ordinary long process, simply multiply by 2, placing the product one figure to the left, and then add. This rule is as practical as it is simple; try it, using 31, 51, 201, etc.

How to Multiply Any Two Numbers Whose Right-Hand Figures Add to Ten, and the Left-Hand Figures Are the Same.

87
83
7221

Example: Three times 7 are 21. Put down both figures, add one to the second figure, and then say 9 times 8 are 72. Put down both figures, and you have the correct result. This rule is practical, and the application of it is simple.

Try it with, 21/29, 32/38, 43/47, 54/56, 65/65, 76/74, 87/83, 98/92.

To Multiply by 9's.

To multiply by 9, 99, or any number of 9's annex as many ciphers to the multiplicand as there are 9's in the multiplier, and from the result subtract the muliplicand.

Example: Multiply 2,736 by 999=2,736,000
2,736
2,733,264 Ans.

To Multiply by 11.

To multiply any two figures by 11, add two figures together and place their sum between the two figures of that number.

Example: 43×11=473, or 4, (4+3,) and 3. If the sum of the two figures exceeds 9, the left-hand figure must be increased by 1. Thus 48×11=528.

To Multiply by 75.

Find cost of 428 yards at 75 cents. Take ¼ of the number of yards, 107, subtract this from the number, 428-107=321 and call the remainder dollars. This is a very convenient and practical rule.

HOW TO DETERMINE RESULTS BY CANCELLATION.

1. Cancellation is the method of shortening operations by rejecting equal factors from numbers used as a divisor and the numbers used as a dividend.

2. Cancellation shortens the process of multiplication and division and is very practical in the following examples:

ILLUSTRATION: Multiply 18 x 16 x 28 and divide the result by 12 x 7 x 14, and it will equal $6\frac{6}{7}$.

SOLUTION:

$$\frac{\overset{3}{\cancel{18}}\times 16\times \overset{2}{\cancel{28}}}{\underset{2}{\cancel{12}}\times \cancel{7}\times \cancel{14}}=\frac{3\times16}{7}=6\tfrac{6}{7},\ \textit{Ans.}$$

Or,

2 ~~12~~	~~18~~ 3
7	16
~~14~~	~~28~~ 2
7	48 = $6\frac{6}{7}$, *Ans.*

HOW TO ESTIMATE ALL KINDS OF PRODUCE, AND FIGURE UP WHEAT, OATS, POTATOES, ETC., SOLD BY THE BUSHEL.

Cancellation Method.

EXAMPLE: What will 1660 pounds of wheat cost at 80 cents a bushel?

SOLUTION:

3 ~~60~~	1660
	~~.80~~ .4
3	66.40 = $\$22.13\frac{1}{3}$, *Ans.*

Explanation: It will be seen at a glance that the number of pounds and the price are to be multiplied together and the result divided by 60; so place 1660 and 80 on one side of the line and 60 on the other and determine the result by cancellation, as shown in the above. This principle will apply to any commodity, and is one of the best and most rapid methods in solving practical examples.

Example: What will 2849 pounds of corn cost at 36 cents per bushel.

Solution:

~~70~~	284~~9~~
	.36
7	102.24 = $14.60\frac{4}{7}$, *Ans.*

HOW TO FIGURE LUMBER BY CANCELLATION.

Rule.—Lumber is measured by the running foot. A foot square and one inch thick is the unit of measurement. It is easily seen that the number of pieces of lumber, multiplied by the length, and that result multiplied by the cost, and the total result divided by 12, will determine the cost of any quantity of lumber that may be desired.

Example: How many feet in a stick of lumber 6x8 and 18 feet long?

Solution:

	~~6~~
~~12~~	8
~~2~~	~~18~~ 9
	72 feet, *Ans.*

Example: What will be the cost of 10 planks 14 inches wide, 2 inches thick, 14 feet long, at $20 per thousand?

Solution:

	~~14~~ 7
3	~~2~~
~~6~~	14
~~12~~	10
	20
3	196.00 = $6.53⅓, *Ans.*

Example: What will be the cost of 20 pieces 2x4, 18 feet long, at $12 per thousand.

Solution:

	2
	~~4~~
~~12~~	18
	20
	~~12~~
	$2.880, *Ans.*

HOW TO FIGURE UP THE PLASTERING OF A ROOM BY CANCELLATION.

Rule.—Multiply the distance around the room in feet by the height of the room in feet, and this result by the price per square yard, and divide the product by 9, because there are 9 square feet in a square yard. For the ceiling, multiply the length of the room by the width of the room in feet, and this by the price per square yard, and divide the product by 9. Add the two results, and you have the cost of plastering the room.

EXAMPLE: What would it cost to plaster a room 18 feet wido, 22 feet long, and 9 feet high, at 20 cents per square yard?

SOLUTION:

~~9~~	80	~~18~~ 2
	~~9~~ ~~9~~	22
	20	20

$16.00 + $8.80=$24.80, *Ans.*

RAPID METHODS IN BUSINESS CALCULATIONS.

To Multiply Any Two Numbers Together, Each Having the Same Fractions.

Rule.—1. Multiply the whole numbers together.

2. Add the two numbers together and multiply this sum by either one of the fractions.

3. Multiply the two fractions together.

4. Add the results together.

EXAMPLE:

12¾
8¾
96
15
$\frac{9}{16}$
111$\frac{9}{16}$ Ans.

How to Multiply Any Mixed Numbers.

EXAMPLE.—MULTIPLY 16⅔ BY 9¾.

	16⅔
	9¾
Rule.—1. Multiply the whole numbers together	144
2. Multiply the upper whole number by the lower fraction	12
3. Multiply the lower whole number by the upper fraction	6
4. Multiply the fractions together	½
5. Add the four products together	162½ Ans.

N. B.—The middle parts should be added mentally without writing them out.

Business Methods for Multiplying All Kinds of Mixed Numbers.

Rule.—Multiply the whole numbers together, then multiply each whole number by the fraction in the other number to its nearest unit and add the products.

NOTE.—In business it is the custom to reject fractions less than ½ in each sum and count one for each fraction over ½.

How much will 34¾ yards of cloth cost at 22½ cents per yard.

Solution:	34 x 22=	$7.48
	34 x ½=	.17
Nearest unit,	22 x ¾=	.16½
	¾ x ½=	⅜
		$7.81⅞=7.82 Ans.

What is the cost of 17 dozen and 9 eggs at 12½ cents per dozen?

Solution:	17 x 12=	$2.04	
	17 x ½=	9	(Make the ½ a unit.)
9 eggs=¾ dozen,	12 x ¾=	9	
		$2.22 Ans.	

The Curious Figure 9.

Multiply 9 by any figure you like, and the sum of the digits of the product will be 9. Thus, 4 × 9=36; add the digits, 3 + 6=9. So it goes up to 11 times 9=99; add these, 9 + 9=18, add again 8 + 1=9. You will never be able to get away from the figure nine. 9 × 454=4086, add the digits and the result is 18, and 8 and 1=9.

Again:	Take a row of figures.	487,632
	Reverse the order of the figures.	236,784
	Subtract,	250,848

Add the digits and the result is 27, and 2 + 7=9.

How to Find the Number of Yards of Carpet to Cover a Floor.

Ingrain carpet is 1 yard wide, Brussels and velvet carpets are ¾ yard wide.

Rule.—Divide the width of the carpet into the width of the room and the result will be the number of strips; multiply the number of strips by the length of the room and the result will equal the number of yards of carpeting to cover the floor.

If there is a fraction in the division add one to the number of strips. In that case it will be necessary to turn under the carpet at one side.

Example: A room is 12 feet, 9 inches by 14 feet, 6 inches. How much ingrain carpet is required to cover the floor?

12¾ ft., width of room ÷ 3 width of ingrain carpet = 4 and a fraction. 5 strips are therefore required. 14½ ft. length of room × 5 = 72½ ft ÷ 3 = 24⅙ yards.

It is sometimes more desirable or economical to run the strips crosswise. In that case divide the *length* of the room by the width of the carpet, and multiply this, the number of strips, by the width of the room.

Example above: 14½ ft., length of room, ÷ 3 = 4 and a fraction. It, therefore, takes 5 strips. 12¾ ft., width of room. × 5 = 63¾ ft. ÷ 3 = 21¼ yds.

The difference in the results arises from the fact that more must be turned under when the strips run lengthwise.

For Brussels carpet reduce the width or length to inches and divide by 27, width of Brussels in inches. The result will be the number of strips, then proceed as above.

How to Find the Amount of Paper Required to Paper a Room.

Measure the distance around the room; deduct the width of each window and door; take ⅔ of the result and it will equal the number of strips required. Divide the result thus found by the number of strips that can be cut from one roll, and it will equal the number of rolls required to paper the room.

Each roll is 1½ feet wide, 24 feet long and contains 36 square feet or 4 square yards.

If the room has but few doors and windows, no allowance is made for them, as there is always a waste in cutting the paper. Paper will stick better on new walls, if they are brushed over with a sizing of weak glue. If you have no glue, brush paste over the wall, as well as over the paper.

How to Find the Contents of a Watering-Trough.

Rule.—Multiply the height in feet by the length in feet, and the product by the width in feet, and divide the result by 4, and you will have the contents in barrels of 31½ gallons each.

Example: What are the contents of a watering trough 8 feet long, 4 feet wide, and 3 feet deep?
Solution: 3×4×8 ÷ 4=24 barrels.

NOTE.—For exact results multiply the length in inches by the height in inches, by the width in inches, and divide the result by 231, and you will have the contents in gallons.

How to Find the Contents of a Round Tank.

Multiply the square of the diameter in feet by the depth in feet, and multiply this result by 6, and you have the approximate contents of the tank in gallons. (For exact results multiply the product by 5⅞ instead of 6.)

Example: How many gallons will a tank hold 6 feet in diameter and 8 feet deep?

Solution: 6×6×8=288.
288×6=1728 gallons. Ans.

NOTE.—If the tank is larger at the bottom than at the top, find the average diameter by measuring the middle part of the tank, half way between the top and bottom.

FOR MORE EXACT RESULTS.

Rule.—Multiply the square of the diameter in feet by the depth in feet, and multiply this result by 47, and divide the product by 8, and you will have the number of gallons.

NOTE.—In calculating the capacity of tanks, 31½ gallons are estimated to one barrel, and 63 gallons to one hogshead.

A TABLE FOR CIRCULAR TANKS ONE FOOT IN DEPTH.

Five feet in diameter holds........	4½	barrels.
Six feet in diameter holds..........	6¾	"
Seven feet in diameter holds........	9	"
Eight feet in diameter holds.......	12	"
Nine feet in diameter holds........	15	"
Ten feet in diameter holds.........	19½	"

N. B.—To find the contents of a tank by the table, multiply the contents of one foot in depth by the number of feet deep.

Table for Square Tanks One Foot in Depth.

A Tank	Five feet by five feet holds........	6	barrels.
"	Six feet by six feet holds...........	8½	"
"	Seven feet by seven feet holds......	11½	"
"	Eight feet by eight feet holds......	15¼	"
"	Nine feet by nine feet holds........	19½	"
"	Ten feet by ten feet holds..........	23¾	"

To find the contents of a trough, measure its depth in feet and multiply it by the contents of one foot in depth.

Shorter Forms of How to Find the Contents of Cylindrical Cisterns, Tanks, Etc.

If you cut the largest possible square from a circle drawn on paper, the square will be a little more than ¾ of the whole circle. Therefore, to find the area of a circle, take ¾ of the square of the diameter (or for exactness .78) and the result will be the area of the circle.

Rule.—Multiply the square of the diameter of the cistern in feet, by the height in feet, and divide this result by 5, and it will equal the number of barrels the cistern will hold (approximately). (*Or for exact results, instead of dividing by 5, take* $\frac{4}{25}$ *of the product.*)

Example: A cistern is 5 feet in diameter, and 8 feet deep. How many barrels will it hold?

Solution: 5×5×8=200.

200÷5=40 barrels. Ans.

To find the number of gallons, multiply by 31½.

FINDING THE CONTENTS OF A BARREL.

BARRELS

In measuring cisterns, reservoirs, vats, etc., the barrel is estimated at 31½ gallons, and the hogshead at 63 gallons.

A gallon of water weighs nearly 8⅓ pounds, avoirdupois.

A pint is generally estimated as a pound.

How to Find the Contents of Barrels and Casks.

Rule.—Add together the diameters of the bung and head in inches, and divide the sum by 2, and its result will equal the average diameter. Then multiply the square of the average diameter by the length in inches and multiply this result by 34 and cut off the four right hand figures, and you will have the number of gallons.

Example: How many gallons in a barrel whose bung diameter is 22 inches, head diameter 18 inches, and length 30 inches?

Solution: $22+18\div2=20$, average diameter. $20\times20\times30\times34=40.8000$, or 40⅘ gallons

To Find the Number of Barrels in a Square Cistern.

Multiply the height, width and depth together, and divide the product obtained by 4 (or for exactness, by 4.2), and the result will equal the number of barrels of 31½ gals. each the cistern will hold.

Example: $4\times8\times5=160$.
$160\div4=40$ barrels.

STONE-WORK.

A cord of stone, three bushels of lime and a cubic yard of sand will make 100 cubic feet of wall.

One cubic foot of stone-work weighs from 130 to 175 pounds.

Short Method of Estimating Stone-work.

Rule.—Multiply the length in feet by the height in feet, and that by the thickness in feet, and divide this result by 27½ and the quotient will be the number of perches of stone in the wall.

Example: A wall is $4 \times 15 \times 2 = 120$ the solid contents, $120 \div 27\frac{1}{2} = 4\frac{4}{11}$ perches.

N. B.—A perch of stone is a variable measure of about 25 cubic feet. Usually 24¾ cubic feet are allowed, to which 2¾ cubic feet are added for the mortar and filling, making 27½ cubic feet of wall for every perch of stone.

How to Find the Number of Cords of Stone to Build Cellar and Barn Walls.

RULE.—Multiply the length, height and thickness together in feet and divide the result by 156.

N. B.—There are 128 cubic feet in a cord, but the mortar and sand make it necessary to use but 100 cubic feet of stone.

FACTS FOR BUILDERS.

A cubic yard of sand is called a load.

Five hundred bricks make a load.

A bricklayer's hod will hold 20 bricks; the ordinary load, however, is 16 walling, or 12 facing bricks. A bricklayer can lay about 1,500 bricks in a day of 10 hours, where the joints are left rough; about 1,000 when both faces are to be worked fair, and not more than 500 when carefully joined and faced with picked bricks of a uniform color.

To every barrel of lime estimate about ⅝ of a cubic yard of good sand for plastering and brickwork.

One-third of a barrel of stucco will hard-finish 100 square yards of plastering.

One and one-quarter barrels cement and ¾ yards sand will lay 100 feet rubble stone.

One and one-eighth barrels of lime and ⅝ yards of sand will lay 1,000 bricks.

HOW TO FIND THE NUMBER OF COMMON BRICKS IN A WALL OR BUILDING.

A BRICK is 8 inches long, 4 inches wide and 2 inches thick, and contains 64 cubic inches. Twenty-seven bricks make one cubic foot of wall without mortar, and it takes from 20 to 22 bricks according to the amount of mortar used to make a cubic foot of wall with mortar.

Rule.—Multiply the length of the wall in feet by the height in feet, and that by its thickness in feet, and then multiply that result by 20, and the product will be the number of bricks in the wall.

Example: How many bricks in a wall 30 feet long, 20 feet high, and 18 inches thick?

Solution: 30 length × 20 height × 1½ thick = 900 × 20 = 18,000. Ans.

N. B.—For a wall 8 inches thick, multiply the length in feet by the height in feet, and that result by 14, and the product will equal the number of bricks.

When doors and windows occur in the wall, multiply their height, width and thickness together, and deduct the amount from the solid contents of the wall before multiplying by 20 or 14, as the case may be.

BRICK-WORK.

Five courses of bricks will make one foot in height on a chimney.

One cubic foot of brick-work with common mortar weighs from 100 to 110 pounds.

A cask of lime will make mortar sufficient for 1,000 bricks.

FOR PLASTERING.

Six bushels of lime, 40 cubic feet* of sand, and 1½ bushels of hair will plaster 100 square yards with two coats of mortar.

In plastering no deductions are made for openings, because the extra work in finishing around them balances the material saved.

***N. B.—There are about 1¼ cubic feet in a bushel.**

CEMENT AND HOW TO USE IT.

The word "Concrete" itself is of Latin origin, meaning "grown together" and implies a body formed by separate particles of different materials combined into a solid mass.

Kinds of Cement.—There are two general kinds, Natural and Portland Cement. The raw material from which natural cement is made is found in a natural state and is made by calcining (burning) cement rock, but the temperature required is considerably lower than that needed for making Portland Cement.

Portland Cement, however, is the kind used almost exclusively in this country and is manufactured in about 25 different states. The raw materials used by different plants vary greatly, nor is the chemical composition the same, so that it cannot be reduced to a formula.

What Portland Cement is.—So far, then, as it is possible to give an accurate definition, Portland cement may be defined as any cement which, on being tested, will manifest the characteristic properties that engineers have agreed to associate with the name "Portland" and which will meet the requirements that have been accepted as standard.

Raw Materials.—As a matter of fact, however, the raw materials are limestone (also chalk and marl, which are really forms of limestone), clay, shale and slate as is also blast-furnace slag. These in proper proportion are heated to a temperature at which melting begins (2000° to 4000°F). The resulting cement clinker is then ground to an impalpable powder to which a very small percentage of gypsum is added.

How to Use Cement.—In using cement for concrete work it is necessary to mix it with water and aggregates—these aggregates consist of sand, crushed stone or gravel. That is to say, you must use either cement, sand and gravel or cement, sand and crushed stone, or any material that can take the place of gravel or crushed stone. These must be thoroughly mixed and the proper amount of water added.

The Proportions required for different kinds of cement or concrete construction are shown in the following TABLE. For example for a rich mixture 1:2:4 means one part cement, 2 parts sand and 4 parts gravel or crushed stone.

By Consistency is meant the relative wetness of the mixture. VERY WET is mushy enough to run readily off the shovel. MEDIUM WET is wet enough to make it jelly-like. DRY MIXTURE is about like damp earth used generally for foundations, etc.

APPROXIMATE MIXTURES ADAPTABLE TO VARIOUS CLASSES OF WORK.

Rich, 1:2:4; Medium, 1:2½:5; Ordinary, 1:3:6; Lean, 1:4:8.

Kind of Work	Mixture	Consistency
Abutments	Rich to Ordinary	Medium
Arches	Rich to Medium	Medium
Backing for Masonry....	Lean	Medium to Dry
Beams, Reinforced	Rich to Medium	Very Wet
Beams, Plain	Rich to Medium	Very Wet to Medium
Building Blocks	Rich to Medium	Very Wet to Medium
Cisterns	Rich to Medium	Very Wet to Medium
Columns, Reinforced.....	Rich	Very Wet
Conduits, Water.........	Rich	Very Wet
Coping	Rich to Medium	Medium
Culverts, Reinforced	Medium to Ordinary	Medium
Culverts, Plain	Medium to Ordinary	Medium
Driveways	Same as Sidewalks	
Fence Posts	Rich	Very Wet to Medium
Floors, Reinforced	Rich to Ordinary	Very Wet to Medium
Floors, Ordinary Ground,	Medium to Ordinary	Medium
Footings	Ordinary to Lean	Medium
Foundations, Heavy Vibrating Machinery......	Rich	Very Wet to Medium
Foundations, Ordinary Machinery	Medium	Medium
Foundations, Thin Walls	Rich to Medium	Very Wet to Medium
Foundations, Thick Walls	Medium to Lean	Medium to Dry
Girders, Reinforced	Rich to Medium	Very Wet
Girders, Plain	Same as Beans	
Gutters	Same as Sidewalks	
Pavements	Same as Sidewalks	
Piers	Rich to Ordinary	Medium
Reservoirs	Rich to Medium	Very Wet to Medium
Roof Slabs	Medium to Ordinary	Medium
Sewers, Reinforced	Rich to Medium	Medium
Sewers, Plain	Medium	Medium
Sidewalks (Base)	Medium to Ordinary	Medium to Dry
Sidewalks (Sub-Base) ..	Ordinary to Lean	Medium to Dry
Silos	Rich to Medium	Very Wet to Medium
Tanks	Rich to Medium	Very Wet to Medium
Walls, Dwelling Houses..	Rich to Medium	Very Wet to Medium
Walls, Large Buildings.. (Compression and Tension)	Rich to Medium	Very Wet to Medium
Walls, Large Buildings.. (Compression Only)	Medium to Ordinary	Medium
Walls, Massive	Medium to Ordinary	Medium
Walls, Retaining	Medium to Ordinary	Medium
Walls, Thin Foundations.	Rich to Medium	Very Wet to Medium
Walls, Tunnel	Medium to Ordinary	Medium

NOTE.—The above facts and table are used by permission of W. A. Radford, editor-in-chief of the "Cement World," etc.

A TILE FACTORY.

HOW TO FIND THE CARRYING CAPACITY OF TILE.

Gallons Per Minute.

	FALL PER 100 FEET.						
SIZE OF TILE.	1 in.	3 in.	6 in.	9 in.	12 in.	24 in.	36 in.
3-inch..................	13	23	32	40	46	64	79
4-inch..................	27	47	66	81	93	131	163
6-inch..................	75	129	183	224	258	364	450
8-inch..................	153	265	375	460	529	750	923
9-inch..................	205	355	593	617	711	1006	1240
10-inch.................	267	463	655	803	926	1310	1613
12-inch.................	422	730	1033	1273	1468	2076	2551

A large tile will carry more water according to its size than a small one. This is because there is less surface on the inside of the large tile compared with the size of stream, and therefore less friction. More water will flow through a straight tile than a crooked one having the same diameter.

EXAMPLE: A nine-inch tile at 6 inches fall to the 100 feet will flow 593 gals. per minute.

AREA AND WEIGHT OF TILE.

The following table shows the area and the weight of the different sized tile:

SIZE.	WEIGHT.	AREA.	SIZE.	WEIGHT.	AREA.
3 inch	5 lbs. ea.	8½ sq. in.	7 inch.........	15 lbs. ea.	41 sq. in.
3½ "	6 "	9½ "	8 "	18 "	58⅓ "
4 "	7 "	14 "	9 "	21 "	67 "
5 "	10 "	21⅓ "	10 "	24 "	80⅜ "
6 "	12 "	30⅓ "	12 "	28 "	113 "

A COMPLETE SET OF CARPENTER'S RULES.

Plain, Simple and Practical.

THE GABLE is a space the form of a triangle on the end of a building, with a common double roof.

QUARTER PITCH.—Is a roof that is one-fourth as high as the width of the building.

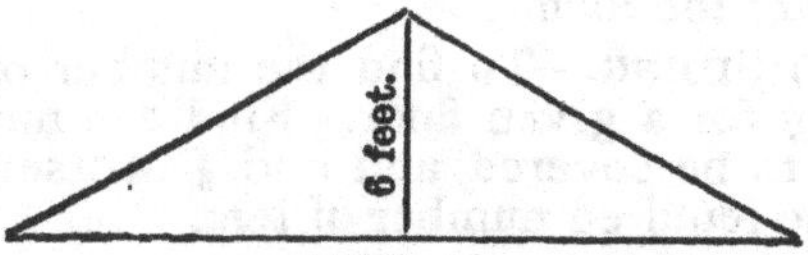

Rule.—To find the area of the gable end, multiply the width of the building by the height of the roof, and take one-half of the result. Or, if the roof is "quarter pitch," find the area by multiplying width of the roof by ⅛ of itself.

To find the number of feet of stock boards to cover a house or barn.

Rule.—Multiply the distance around the barn by the height of the post, and to this result add the area of the two gable ends. (If there are many openings, allowance should be made for them).

How to Find the Number of Shingles Required for a Roof.

Rule.—Multiply the length of the ridge pole by twice the length of one rafter, and, if the shingles are to be exposed 4½ inches to the weather, multiply by 9, and if exposed 5 inches to the weather, multiply by 8, and you have the number of shingles.

NOTE.—Shingles are 16 inches long, and average about 4 inches wide. They are put up in bundles of 250 each.

Rule.—900 *shingles, laid* 4 *inches to the weather, will cover* 100 *square feet, and* 800 *shingles laid* 4½ *inches to the weather will cover* 100 *square feet.*

How to Find the Number of Laths for a Room.

Laths are 4 feet long and 1½ inches wide, and 16 laths are generally estimated to the square yard. There are 50 in a bunch.

RULE.—Find the number of square yards in the room, and multiply by 16, and the result will equal the number of laths necessary to cover the room.

FLOORS AND SIDING.—To find the number of feet of 6-inch *matched flooring* for a given floor. Find the number of square feet of surface to be covered, and add ⅕ of itself to it, and the result will be the required number of feet.

FOR THREE-INCH FLOORING.—Find the number of square feet to be covered, to which add ½ of itself.

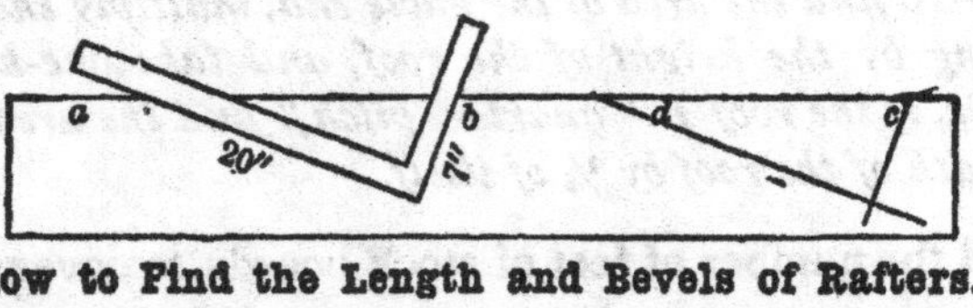

How to Find the Length and Bevels of Rafters.

1. Place your steel square on a board (say the building is 40 feet long), 20 inches from the corner one way, and 7 inches the other, and mark it as shown in the above figure. Now the angle at *c* will be the bevel of the upper end, and the angle at *d* the bevel at the lower end of the rafter.

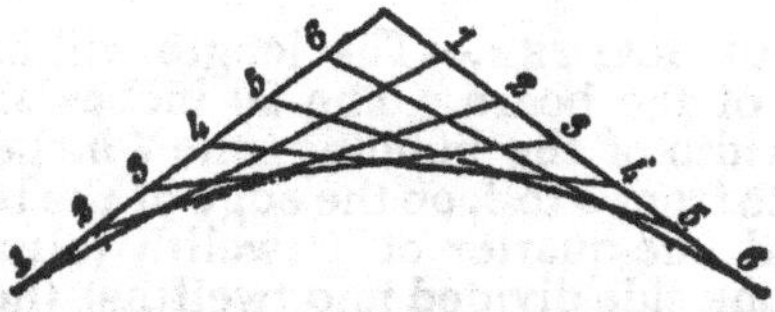

How to Make the Curves for Brick and Stone Arches.

Measure the width, and draw the figure as above. If the points in 1, 2, 3, 4, etc., are equal on both sides, the curve will be an exact part of a circle.

DEFINITIONS FOR MECHANICS.

An angle is the opening between two lines that have a different direction.

When two straight lines cross each other so as to form four equal angles, each angle is called a right angle.

An acute angle is less than a right angle. An obtuse angle is greater than a right angle.

A triangle is a figure having three sides.

A surface having four straight lines and four right angles is called a rectangle.

A rectangle whose sides are equal is called a square.

The perimeter of a figure is the distance around it.

An arc is any part of the circumference of a circle.

A chord is a line drawn through the circle and ending on the circumference.

A quadrant is a quarter circle.

A tangent is a line that touches a circle but does not cut it.

A polygon is a figure bounded by straight lines.

The following figures show the principal polygons used with numbers of sides of each:

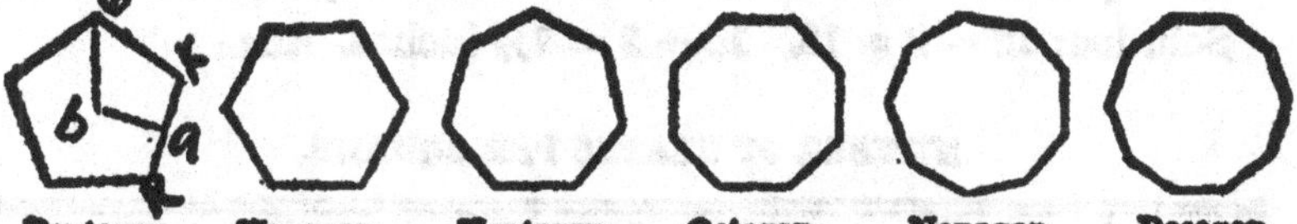

Pentagon. Hexagon. Heptagon. Octagon. Nonagon. Decagon.

Concentric circles are circles that have the same center and the space included between their circumference is called a ring.

POINTERS FOR MECHANICS.

A good stain for floors is made by boiling shellac and borax in water.

Marble mantels require very careful handling.

Gas fixtures should be carefully stored away in some dry place, for they may often be in service, and can easily be renovated if tarnished or soiled.

2. Length of Rafter.—The length will be from *a* to *b* on the outer edge of the board. The 20 inches shows the 20 feet, or half of the width of the building; the 7 inches the 7 foot rise. Now the distance from *a* to *b*, on the edge of the board, is 21 inches, two-twelfths and one-quarter of a twelfth (always use a square with inches on one side divided into twelfths), therefore this rafter will be 21 feet and 2¼ inches long.

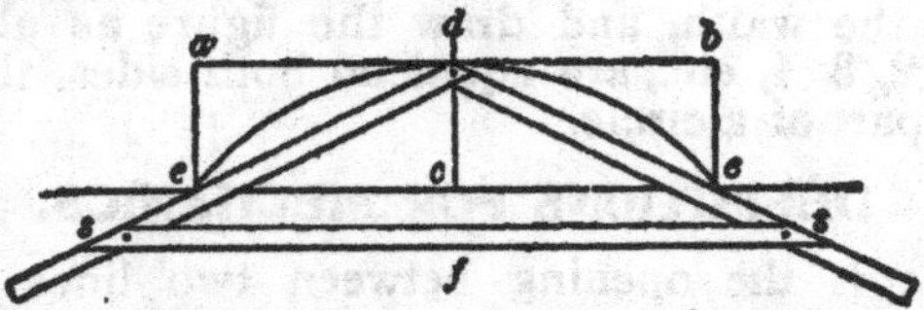

How to Make a Curve with a Set Triangle.

1. In the above figure let *a*, *b* represent the length, and *c*, *d* the height of the curve. Drive two awls at *e* and *e*; then take two strips, marked *s s*, and nail them together at the point *d*, and spread out the sides to the awls at *e* and *e*; then tack on the brace *f*, hold a pencil at the point *d*, then move the point toward the point *e* both ways. Be sure and keep the strips *s s* hard against the awls at *e* and *e*, and the pencil will mark out the exact curve.

SLATE TABLES.

Slates are sold by the square, which covers 100 square feet, weighs about 600 pounds and costs from $3.00 to $10.00: average about $5.00. They are laid with three inches under-lap, and to find how much to lay each size to the weather subtract three inches from the length of the slate and divide the remainder by two.

Example: How much will an 18 inch slate lay to the weather?

Solution: 18 − 3 = 15. 15 ÷ 2 = 7½ inches. Ans.

NUMBER OF SLATES PER SQUARE.

Sizes	Number	Sizes	Number	Sizes	Number	Sizes	Number
6x10	685	8x14	328	10x18	192	13x22	116
7x10	588	9x14	291	11x18	175	14x22	108
8x10	515	10x14	262	12x18	160	12x24	115
6x12	534	12x14	219	10x20	170	13x24	105
7x12	458	8x16	277	11x20	154	14x24	98
8x12	400	9x16	247	12x20	142	16x24	86
9x12	356	10x16	222	14x20	121	18x24	77
10x12	320	12x16	185	11x22	138	14x26	90
7x14	374	9x18	214	12x22	127	14x28	83

Furnace registers should never be placed near a mantel if it is desired to utilize the heat.

A monthly rubbing of floors with oil is much better than painting. This will also make them look as good as new.

Locks, hinges, keys and other hardware should have special care, every piece represents money, and if not well cared for will result in waste.

Porch floors should be made of narrow stuff! it is well to lay the joints in white lead.

Shingles or any other light wood work can be made fire proof by using lime water.

Poor work testifies to the fact that the lowest priced builder is not always the cheapest.

Use oak instead of maple for basement flooring, because it will stand dampness better.

Tools should be kept in a handy place and in good condition.

There is nothing like having an exact place for every tool and keeping it there when not in use.

Keeping tools in good order is as essential as keeping them in the proper place.

No man should use a dull tool. If there is time to use it there ought to be time to keep it in good order.

Old material should never be destroyed because it is old.

Do not use one chimney flue for two stove-pipes; one draught may counteract the other.

It is well to have a ventilating flue from the kitchen into the chimney; this will do away with atmospheric meals.

Don't grumble if you do not get as good results from the use of old material as from new.

Fasten stops to doors and windows with round-headed screws; they can be easily removed.

Moths and insects will not be found in closets finished with red cedar shelves and drawers.

All fixtures, such as grates, hearth-stones, bath-tubs, desks, heating appliances, should be moved with care; they may frequently be used for inferior fixings and thus much money saved.

Furnaces should be located with care. It is easier to force warm air through a furnace flue 50 feet away from the prevalent wind than 10 feet in the opposite direction.

Hot air flues should not be carried for any distance through cold cellars or basements, as they will become chilled, and will not draw, unless they are inclosed in some non-conducting material.

Hot water heating has a number of advantages in its favor. For mild climates it answers very well; there are, however, objections to its use in northern latitudes.

Hot water will cool down and freeze much quicker than ordinary water, under the same circumstances.

In soldering, see that the surface to be soldered is clean; if not, make it so by filing or scraping.

There is no surer way of gaining knowledge than by a careful and understanding watchfulness of others in the same line of business as yourself.

Don't tell all you know, or else others will know one valuable thing that you don't know, and that is that you don't know as much as you pretend to know.

USEFUL AND PRACTICAL RULES FOR MECHANICS.

To Find the Diagonal of a Square.

Multiply the side of the square by 1.41421.

To Find the Circumference of a Circle.

Multiply the diameter by 3$\frac{1}{7}$ or multiply the area by 12.566 and extract the square root of the product.

To Find the Area of a Circle.

Multiply the square of the radius by 3$\frac{1}{7}$.
The radius is one-half the diameter.

To Find the Diameter of a Circle.

Divide the circumference by 3$\frac{1}{7}$.

To Draw a Circle Through Three Points.

Let the three points be A, B and C. Join A and B and B and C by straight lines. At the middle points of these lines draw lines perpendicular to them. This can easily be done by using a square. Produce these lines and let them meet at O. O is the center of the circle. With O as center and OA as radius construct the circle.

To Find the Area of any Polygon.

Find the center of the figure and multiply distance around the figure (perimeter) by one-half of the diameter and the result will equal the area.

Inscribed and Circumscribed Squares.

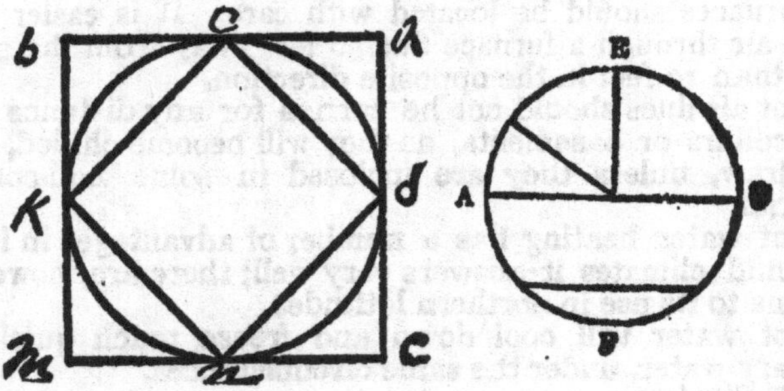

The square described within the circle is exactly half as large as the square described outside of the circle, that is the described one is one half the area of the circumscribed square.

The square *c d n k* contains exactly one-half the area of the square *a c m b.*

It is thus easily seen that the area of the circumscribed square—(that is the square *a c m b*) is equal to the square of the diameter of the circle.

How to Lay Off Small Lots of Land.

Farmers and gardners often find it necessary to lay off small portions of land for the purpose of experimenting with different crops, fertilisers, etc. To such the following rules will be helpful:

One acre contains 160 sq. rods, or 4,840 sq. yards, or 43,560 sq. feet.

One acre it will take 208$\frac{7}{10}$ feet each way.
One-half acre it will take 147½ feet each way.
One-third acre it will take 120½ feet each way.
One-fourth acre it will take 104⅜ feet each way.
One-eighth acre it will take 73¾ feet each way.

How to Make an Ice Chest.

Take two dry goods boxes, one enough smaller than the other to leave a space of three or four inches all around when placed inside the larger box. Pack this space between the two boxes closely with sawdust and make a heavy cover to fit neatly inside the top of the larger box. A small pipe inserted in the bottom of the chest will carry off the waste water. For family use and all ordinary purposes it will be as serviceable as refrigerators costing twenty-five times as much.

THE LIGHTNING METHOD FOR MEASURING LUMBER.

1. A FOOT OF LUMBER is one foot long, one foot wide and one inch thick. This is called a Board Foot.
2. PIECE STUFF OR DIMENSION STUFF is lumber that is two or more inches thick and of uniform width and length.
3. SCANTLING is usually from three to four inches wide and from two to four inches thick.
4. JOIST is two-inch lumber of any width.
5. PLANK is two inches in thickness and wider than a scantling.

Rule for 12-foot Boards: Find the width of the boards in inches and add together, and the sum obtained will be equal to the number of feet in the pile. (Each inch in width equals one foot of lumber.)

Note: Use no fractions. If a board is between 9 and 10 inches wide, but nearer 9 than 10, call it 9; if nearer 10 than 9, call it 10. If it is 9½, call it either 9 or 10.

For 14-foot boards add the width of the boards in inches, and to the sum add $\frac{1}{6}$ of itself, and the result will equal the number of feet in the pile.

For 16-foot lumber, add the width of the boards in inches and to that sum add $\frac{1}{3}$ of itself, and you will have the number of feet in the pile.

Example: How many feet of lumber in ten boards, 9 inches wide and 16 feet long?

Solution, 10×9=90.
⅓ of 90=30.
30+90=120, the number of feet.

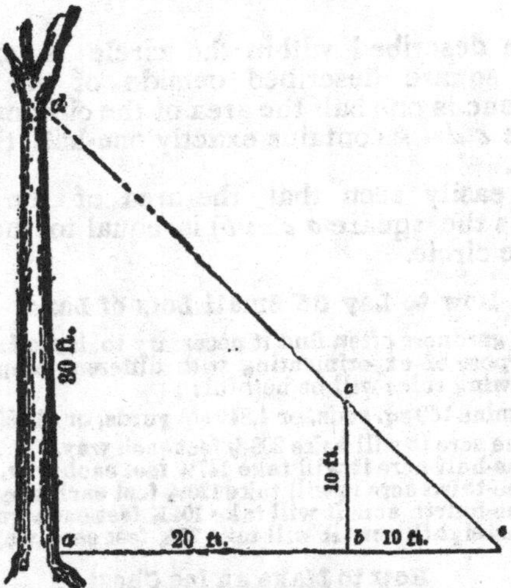

How to Find the Height of a Tree.

Suppose you desire a log 30 feet long—measure off from the base of the tree 30 feet—(allow for the height of the stump), then measure 10 feet back, and put your 10-foot pole at *b*; let some one hold it the height of the stump from the ground, then put your eye at *e*, looking over the top of the pole at *c*, and where the eye strikes the tree at *d*, will be 30 feet from *a*.

N. B.—This rule will apply to any tree, or any height. The principle hold true in any case.

How to Find the Height by Measuring the Shadow.

Rule: Measure a pole, and hold it perpendicular in the sun, and measure its shadow, then measure the shadow of the tree whose height is desired. Then multiply the length of the pole by the length of the tree's shadow, and divide the product by the length of the shadow of the pole, and the result will be the height of the tree.

Example:—If a pole 3 feet long casts a shadow 4½ feet long, what is the height of a tree whose shadow measures 180 feet?

Solution:—180x3÷4½=120 feet, the height of the tree.

How to Ascertain the Number of Feet (Board Measure) in a Log.

Rule: Subtract from the diameter of the log in inches, 4 inches (for slabs); one-fourth of this result squared and multiplied by the length in feet will give the correct amount of lumber made from any log.

Example:—How many feet of lumber can be made from a log which is 36 inches in diameter and 10 feet long?

Solution:—From 36 (diameter) subtract 4 (for slabs) =32. Take ¼ of 32 =8, which multiplied by itself equals 64. Then multiply 64 by 10 (length) =640. Ans.

Ropp's Rule: Square the diameter in inches and subtract 60 from the result, then multiply this result by the length and divide by 2, and cut off the right hand figure.

EASTERN LOG TABLE.

(For larger logs see table on page 354.)

Ft. long	Dia. 6	Dia. 7	Dia. 8	Dia. 9	Dia. 10	Dia. 11	Dia. 12	Dia. 13	Dia. 14	Dia. 15	Dia. 16	Dia. 17	Dia. 18	Dia. 19	Dia. 20	Dia. 21	Dia. 22
10	15	20	25	30	35	40	49	61	72	89	99	116	133	150	175	190	209
11	16	22	27	33	38	44	54	67	79	98	109	127	147	165	192	209	230
12	18	24	30	36	42	48	59	73	86	107	119	139	160	180	210	228	251
13	19	26	32	39	45	52	64	79	93	116	129	150	173	195	227	247	272
14	21	28	35	42	49	56	69	85	100	125	139	162	187	210	245	266	292
15	22	30	37	45	52	60	74	91	107	134	149	173	200	225	262	285	313
16	24	32	40	48	56	64	79	97	114	142	159	185	213	240	280	304	334
17	25	34	42	51	59	68	84	103	122	151	168	196	227	255	297	323	355
18	27	36	45	54	63	72	88	109	129	160	178	208	240	270	315	349	376
19	28	38	47	57	66	76	93	116	136	169	188	219	253	285	332	361	397
20	30	40	50	60	70	80	98	122	143	178	198	232	267	300	350	380	418
21	31	42	52	63	73	84	103	128	150	187	208	243	280	315	368	399	439
22	33	44	55	66	77	88	108	134	157	196	218	255	293	330	385	418	460
23	34	46	57	69	80	92	113	140	164	205	228	266	307	345	403	437	480
24	36	48	60	72	84	96	118	146	172	214	238	278	320	360	420	456	501
25	37	50	62	75	87	100	123	152	179	223	248	289	333	375	438	475	522

CUBICAL CONTENTS OF ROUND TIMBER.

Ft. long	Dia. 6	Dia. 7	Dia. 8	Dia. 9	Dia. 10	Dia. 11	Dia. 12	Dia. 13	Dia. 14	Dia. 15	Dia. 16	Dia. 17	Dia. 18	Dia. 19	Dia. 20	Dia. 21
8	1.57	2.14	2.79	3.53	4	5	6	7	8	10	11	12	14	16	17	19
9	1.76	2.40	3.14	3.97	5	6	7	8	9	11	12	14	16	18	20	22
10	1.96	2.67	3.49	4.42	5	7	8	9	10	12	14	16	18	20	22	24
11	2.16	2.94	3.84	4.86	6	7	8	10	12	13	15	17	19	22	24	26
12	2.35	3.20	4.19	5.30	6	8	9	11	13	15	17	19	21	24	26	29
13	2.55	3.47	4.54	5.74	7	9	10	12	14	16	18	20	23	26	28	31
14	2.75	3.74	4.89	6.19	7	9	11	13	15	17	19	22	25	28	31	34
15	2.94	4.05	5.24	6.63	8	10	12	14	16	18	21	23	26	30	33	36
16	3.14	4.27	5.58	7.07	9	11	12	14	17	20	22	25	28	32	35	39
17	3.33	4.54	5.93	7.51	9	11	13	16	18	21	24	27	30	33	37	41
18	3.53	4.81	6.28	7.95	10	12	14	16	19	22	25	28	32	35	39	43
19	3.73	5.07	6.63	8.39	10	13	15	17	21	23	27	30	33	37	41	45
20	3.92	5.34	6.98	8.84	11	13	16	18	21	25	28	31	35	39	44	48

Ft. long	Dia. 22	Dia. 23	Dia. 24	Dia. 25	Dia. 26	Dia. 27	Dia. 28	Dia. 29	Dia. 30	Dia. 31	Dia. 32	Dia. 33	Dia. 34	Dia. 35	Dia. 36	Dia. 37	Dia. 38
8	21	23	25	27	29	32	34	37	39	42	45	48	50	53	57	60	63
9	24	26	28	31	33	36	38	41	44	47	50	53	57	60	64	67	70
10	26	29	31	34	37	40	43	46	49	52	56	59	63	67	71	75	79
11	29	32	35	37	41	43	47	50	53	57	61	65	69	73	77	82	86
12	32	34	38	41	44	47	51	55	58	62	67	71	76	80	85	90	94
13	34	37	41	44	48	51	56	60	63	68	72	77	82	87	92	97	103
14	37	40	44	48	52	55	60	64	68	73	78	83	88	94	99	105	110
15	40	43	47	51	55	59	64	69	73	78	84	89	95	100	106	112	118
16	42	46	50	55	59	63	68	73	78	83	89	95	101	107	113	119	126
17	45	49	53	58	63	68	73	78	83	89	95	101	107	114	121	127	135
18	48	52	57	61	66	72	77	82	88	94	100	106	114	120	128	134	142
19	50	55	60	65	70	75	81	87	93	99	106	112	120	127	135	142	151
20	53	58	63	68	74	79	85	91	98	105	112	118	126	134	142	149	159

If a log is longer than given in table, unite two numbers. Thus, if it is 38 feet, double the product of 19.

STATISTICS ON LUMBER.

Manufactures—Census of 1890.

	Establishments.	Capital.	Employes.	Wages.	Cost of Material.	Value of Products.
Mill Products from Logs	21,011	$496,339,968	286,197	$87,784,433	$231,555,618	$403,667,575
Planing Mill Products	3,670	120,271,440	86,888	48,970,080	104,926,834	183,681,552
Looking Glass and Picture Frames	1,290	8,554,995	9,664	5,257,553	7,069,115	16,376,173
Furniture	5,970	93,642,147	92,504	48,792,752	55,125,830	135,627,332

JOISTS, SCANTLING AND TIMBER MEASUREMENT.

Size in Inches.	Length in Feet. 12	14	16	18	20	22	24	26	28	30
2 x 4.........	8	9⅓	10⅔	12	13⅓	14⅔	16	17⅓	18⅔	20
2 x 6.........	12	14	16	18	20	22	24	26	28	30
2 x 8.........	16	18⅔	21⅓	24	26⅔	29⅓	32	34⅔	37⅓	40
2 x 10.........	20	23⅓	26⅔	30	33⅓	36⅔	40	43⅓	46⅔	50
2 x 12.........	24	28	32	36	40	44	48	52	56	60
3 x 4.........	12	14	16	18	20	22	24	26	28	30
3 x 6.........	18	21	24	27	30	33	36	39	42	45
3 x 8.........	24	28	32	36	40	44	48	52	56	60
3 x 10.........	30	35	40	45	50	55	60	65	70	75
3 x 12.........	36	42	48	54	60	66	72	78	84	90
4 x 4.........	16	18⅔	21⅓	24	26⅔	29⅓	32	34⅔	37⅓	40
4 x 6.........	24	28	32	36	40	44	48	52	5d	60
4 x 8.........	32	37⅓	42⅔	48	53⅓	58⅔	64	69⅓	74⅔	80
4 x 10.........	40	46⅔	53⅓	60	66⅔	73⅓	80	86⅔	93⅓	100
4 x 12.........	48	56	64	72	80	88	96	104	112	120
6 x 6.........	36	42	48	54	60	66	72	78	84	90
6 x 8.........	48	56	64	72	80	88	96	104	112	120
6 x 10.........	60	70	80	90	100	110	120	130	140	150
6 x 12.........	72	84	96	108	120	136	144	156	168	180
8 x 8.........	64	74⅔	85⅓	96	106⅔	117⅓	128	138⅔	149⅓	160
8 x 10.........	80	93⅓	106⅔	120	133⅓	146⅔	160	173⅓	186⅔	200
8 x 12.........	96	112	128	144	160	176	192	208	224	240
10 x 10.........	100	116⅔	133⅓	150.	166⅔	183⅓	200	216⅔	233⅓	250
10 x 12.........	120	140	160	180	200	220	240	260	280	300
12 x 12.........	144	168	192	216	240	264	288	312	336	360
12 x 14.........	168	196	224	252	280	308	336	364	392	420
14 x 14.........	196	228⅔	261⅓	294	226⅔	359⅓	392	424⅔	457⅓	490

Example: **A timber 12 by 14 inches, 18 feet long, contains 252 square feet.**

BOARD AND PLANK MEASUREMENT—AT SIGHT.

This table gives the sq. ft. and inches in boards from 6 to 25 in. wide, and from 8 to 36 ft. long. If a board be longer than 36 ft., unite two numbers. Thus, if a board is 40 ft. long and 16 in. wide, add 30 and 10 and you have 53 ft. 4 inches. For 2 in. plank double the product.

Ft. long	4 in. w. ft. in.	5 in. w. ft. in.	6 in. w. ft. in.	7 in. w. ft. in.	8 in. w. ft. in.	9 in. w. ft. in.	10 in. w. ft. in.	11 in. w. ft. in.	12 in. w. ft. in.	13 in. w. ft. in.	14 in. w. ft. in.	15 in. w. ft. in.
8	2 8	3 4	4 0	4 8	5 4	6 0	6 8	7 4	8 0	8 8	9 4	10 0
9	3 0	3 9	4 6	5 3	6 0	6 9	7 6	8 3	9 0	9 9	10 6	11 3
10	3 4	4 2	5 0	5 10	6 8	7 6	8 4	9 2	10 0	10 10	11 8	12 6
11	3 8	4 7	5 6	6 5	7 4	8 3	9 2	10 1	11 0	11 11	12 10	13 9
12	4 0	5 0	6 0	7 0	8 0	9 0	10 0	11 0	12 0	13 0	14 0	15 0
13	4 4	5 5	6 6	7 7	8 8	9 9	10 10	11 11	13 0	14 1	15 2	16 3
14	4 8	5 10	7 0	8 2	9 4	10 6	11 8	12 10	14 0	15 2	16 4	17 6
15	5 0	6 3	7 6	8 9	10 0	11 3	12 6	13 9	15 0	16 3	17 6	18 9
16	5 4	6 8	8 0	9 4	10 8	12 0	13 4	14 8	16 0	17 4	18 8	20 0
17	5 8	7 1	8 6	9 11	11 4	12 9	14 2	15 7	17 0	18 5	19 10	21 3
18	6 0	7 6	9 0	10 6	12 0	13 6	15 0	16 6	18 0	19 6	21 0	22 6
19	6 4	7 11	9 6	11 1	12 8	14 3	15 10	17 5	19 0	20 7	22 2	23 9
20	6 8	8 4	10 0	11 8	13 4	15 0	16 8	18 4	20 0	21 8	23 4	25 0
21	7 0	8 9	10 6	12 3	14 0	15 9	17 6	19 3	21 0	22 9	24 6	26 3
22	7 4	9 2	11 0	12 10	14 8	16 6	18 4	20 2	22 0	23 10	25 8	27 6
23	7 8	9 7	11 6	13 5	15 4	17 3	19 2	21 1	23 0	24 11	26 10	28 9
24	8 0	10 0	12 0	14 0	16 0	18 0	20 0	22 0	24 0	26 0	28 0	30 0
25	8 4	10 5	12 6	14 7	16 8	18 9	20 10	22 11	25 0	27 1	29 2	31 3
26	8 8	10 10	13 0	15 2	17 4	19 6	21 8	23 10	26 0	28 2	30 4	32 6
27	9 0	11 3	13 6	15 9	18 0	20 3	22 6	24 9	27 0	29 3	31 6	33 9
28	9 4	11 8	14 0	16 4	18 8	21 0	23 4	25 8	28 0	30 4	32 8	35 0
29	9 8	12 1	14 6	16 11	19 4	21 9	24 2	26 7	29 0	31 5	33 10	36 3
30	10 0	12 6	15 0	17 6	20 0	22 6	25 0	27 6	30 0	32 6	35 0	37 6
31	10 4	12 11	15 6	18 1	20 8	23 3	25 10	28 5	31 0	33 7	36 2	38 9
32	10 8	13 4	16 0	18 8	21 4	24 0	26 8	29 4	32 0	34 8	37 4	40 0
33	11 0	13 9	16 6	19 3	22 0	24 9	27 6	30 3	33 0	35 9	38 6	41 3
34	11 4	14 2	17 0	19 10	22 8	25 6	28 4	31 2	34 0	36 10	39 8	42 6
35	11 8	14 7	17 6	20 5	23 4	26 3	29 2	32 1	35 0	37 11	40 10	43 9
36	12 0	15 0	18 0	21 0	24 0	27 0	30 0	33 0	36 0	39 0	42 0	45 0

	16 in.	17 in.	18 in.	19 in.	20 in.	21 in.	22 in.	23 in.	24 in.	25 in.	26 in.	27 in.
8	10 8	11 4	12 0	12 8	13 4	14 0	14 8	15 4	16 0	16 8	17 4	18 0
9	12 0	12 9	13 6	14 3	15 0	15 9	16 6	17 3	18 0	18 9	19 6	20 3
10	13 4	14 2	15 0	15 10	16 8	17 6	18 4	19 2	20 0	20 10	21 8	22 6
11	14 8	15 7	16 6	17 5	18 4	19 3	20 2	21 1	22 0	22 11	23 10	24 9
12	16 0	17 0	18 0	19 0	20 0	21 0	22 0	23 0	24 0	25 0	26 0	27 0
13	17 4	18 5	19 6	20 7	21 8	22 9	23 10	24 11	26 0	27 1	28 2	29 3
14	18 8	19 10	21 0	22 2	23 4	24 6	25 8	26 10	28 0	29 2	30 4	31 6
15	20 0	21 3	22 6	23 9	25 0	26 3	27 6	28 9	30 0	31 3	32 6	33 9
16	21 4	22 8	24 0	25 4	26 8	28 0	29 4	30 8	32 0	33 4	34 8	36 0
17	22 8	24 1	25 6	26 11	28 4	29 9	31 2	32 7	34 0	35 5	36 10	38 3
18	24 0	25 .6	27 0	28 6	30 0	31 6	33 0	34 6	36 0	37 6	39 0	40 6
19	25 4	26 11	28 6	30 1	31 8	33 3	34 10	36 5	38 0	39 7	41 2	42 9
20	26 8	28 4	30 0	31 8	33 4	35 0	36 8	38 4	40 0	41 8	43 4	45 0
21	28 0	29 9	31 6	33 3	35 0	36 9	38 6	40 3	42 0	43 9	45 6	47 3
22	29 4	31 2	33 0	34 10	36 8	38 6	40 4	42 2	44 0	45 10	47 8	49 6
23	30 8	32 7	34 6	36 5	38 4	40 3	42 2	44 1	46 0	47 11	49 10	51 9
24	33 0	34 0	36 0	38 0	40 0	42 0	44 0	46 0	48 0	50 0	52 0	54 0
25	34 4	35 5	37 6	39 7	41 8	43 9	45 10	47 11	50 0	52 1	54 2	56 3
26	35 8	36 10	39 0	41 2	43 4	45 6	47 8	49 10	52 0	54 2	56 4	58 6
27	36 0	38 3	40 6	42 9	45 0	47 3	49 6	51 9	54 0	56 3	58 6	60 9
28	37	39 8	42 0	44 4	46 8	49 0	51 4	53 8	56 0	58 4	60 8	63 0
29	38 8	41 1	43 6	45 11	48 4	50 9	53 2	55 7	58 0	60 5	62 10	65 3
30	40 0	42 6	45 0	47 6	50 0	51 6	55 0	57 6	60 0	62 6	65 0	67 6

HOW TO REDUCE LOGS TO INCH BOARD MEASURE.

Ft. long.	Diam. 10.	Diam. 11.	Diam. 12.	Diam. 13.	Diam. 14.	Diam. 15.	Diam. 16.	Diam. 17.	Diam. 18.	Diam. 19.	Diam. 20.	Diam. 21.	Diam. 22.	Diam. 23.	Diam. 24.	Diam. 25.	Diam. 26.
10..	23	31	40	50	62	75	90	105	122	140	160	180	202	225	250	275	302
11..	25	34	44	55	69	83	99	116	135	154	176	198	223	248	275	302	333
12..	27	37	48	61	75	91	108	126	147	169	192	217	243	271	300	331	363
13..	29	40	52	66	81	98	117	137	159	183	208	235	263	298	325	358	393
14..	32	43	56	71	88	106	126	148	171	197	224	253	283	313	350	386	433
15..	34	46	60	76	94	113	135	158	184	211	240	271	303	336	375	413	453
16..	36	49	64	81	100	121	144	169	196	225	256	289	324	359	400	441	484
17..	38	52	68	86	106	128	153	179	208	239	272	307	344	383	425	468	514
18..	41	55	72	91	112	136	162	190	220	253	288	325	364	406	450	496	544
19..	43	58	76	96	119	143	171	201	232	267	304	343	384	429	475	523	574
20..	45	61	80	101	125	151	180	211	244	280	320	361	404	452	500	550	605
21..	47	64	84	106	131	158	189	222	257	295	336	379	425	473	525	579	635
22..	50	66	88	111	137	166	198	232	269	309	352	397	445	496	550	605	665
23..	52	70	92	116	144	174	207	243	281	323	368	415	465	519	575	632	695
24..	54	74	96	122	150	181	216	254	294	338	384	433	486	541	600	662	726
25..	56	77	100	127	156	189	225	264	308	351	400	451	506	562	625	689	756

Ft. long.	Diam. 27.	Diam. 28	Diam. 29.	Diam. 30.	Diam. 31.	Diam. 32.	Diam. 33.	Diam. 34.	Diam. 35.	Diam. 36.	Diam. 37.	Diam. 38.	Diam. 39.	Diam. 40.	Diam. 41.	Diam. 42.	Diam. 43.
10..	330	360	391	422	456	490	526	562	601	640	681	723	765	810	850	903	952
11..	363	396	430	465	502	539	578	619	661	704	749	795	842	891	942	994	1046
12..	397	432	469	507	547	588	631	675	721	768	817	867	910	972	1027	1083	1141
13..	430	468	508	549	592	637	684	731	781	832	884	939	996	1058	1113	1173	1237
14..	463	504	547	591	638	686	736	787	841	896	953	1011	1070	1134	1198	1264	1331
15..	496	540	586	633	683	735	789	844	901	960	1021	1083	1199	1215	1284	1354	1426
16..	530	576	625	676	729	784	842	900	961	1024	1089	1156	1225	1296	1369	1444	1521
17..	563	612	664	718	774	833	895	956	1021	1088	1157	1228	1302	1377	1455	1534	1616
18..	596	648	703	761	820	882	946	1012	1081	1152	1225	1300	1379	1458	1541	1525	1711
19..	620	684	742	803	865	931	999	1069	1141	1216	1293	1372	1455	1539	1626	1715	1806
20..	661	720	782	845	912	980	1052	1125	1202	1280	1361	1446	1530	1620	1712	1805	1902
21..	693	756	820	887	957	1029	1103	1181	1261	1344	1430	1518	1607	1701	1792	1896	1997
22..	726	792	860	930	1004	1078	1156	1238	1322	1408	1497	1590	1684	1782	1882	1986	2091
23..	760	828	898	972	1049	1127	1209	1295	1381	1472	1566	1662	1761	1863	1969	2077	2187
24..	794	864	938	1014	1094	1176	1262	1350	1442	1536	1634	1734	1838	1944	2055	2166	2282
25..	827	900	977	1056	1139	1225	1315	1406	1501	1600	1702	1806	1915	2025	2139	2256	2376

HOW TO USE THE LOG TABLE.

First find the average diameter of the log by adding together the two ends of the log, in inches; then divide by two, and the result will equal the average diameter, and then apply the above table.

Example.—How many feet of lumber are there in a log 15 inches at one end and 21 inches at the other, and 22 feet long?

Solution.—15+21=36; one-half of 36=18 inches, the average diameter.

Then refer to the column under 18 inches opposite to 22 and you will find the answer—269 feet.

HOW TO FIND THE DISTANCE TRAVELED IN PLOWING.

Showing the distance traveled by a horse in plowing an acre of land, and the quantity of land cultivated per day, computed at the rate of 16 and 18 miles per day of 9 hours:

Breadth of furrow slice in inches.	Miles traveled in plowing an acre.	Acres plowed per day.		Breadth of furrow slice in inches.	Miles traveled in plowing an acre.	Acres plowed per day.	
		18 Mi.	16 Mi.			18 Mi.	16 Mi.
7	14⅛	1¼	1⅛	14	7	2½	2¼
8	12⅜	1½	1⅓	15	6⅗	2¾	2⅜
9	11	1⅗	1½	16	6⅛	2 9/10	2⅝
10	9 9/10	1⅘	1⅗	17	5¾	3⅛	2¾
11	9	2	1¾	18	5½	3¼	2 9/10
12	8¼	2⅕	1 9/10	19	5¼	3⅜	3 1/10
13	7½	2⅜	2⅛	20	4 9/10	3⅝	3¼

HOW MUCH ADVANTAGE IS GIVEN IN CHANGING THE EVENER.

***Caution.**—In moving the center pin of an evener one inch toward one of the end pins it changes the draft twice as much as it does to move one of the end pins one inch toward the center pin. Or in other words, moving the center pin changes the draft twice as much as changing one of the end pins or clevises.*

An average evener is 42 inches in length.

Now if the center pin is moved one inch from the center to the right or left, the horse drawing on the short end will pull about $\frac{2}{40}$ more than the horse drawing on the opposite end.

If one of the end pins is moved one inch the difference will be about $\frac{1}{40}$.

Example: If a team of horses draw 2000 pounds, and the center pin is moved one inch from the center, what part of the whole load will each draw?

$2000 \times \frac{2}{40} = 100$ **pounds, the difference.**

$50 + 1000 = 1050$ **pounds.** $1000 - 50 = 950$ **pounds.**

Hence the horse at the short end of the evener draws 1050 lbs., and the other horse draws 950 lbs.

The draft on a 14 inch plow, plowing 4 inches deep, is about 1000 lbs.; 5 inches deep 1250 lbs.; 6 inches deep, 1500 lbs.

HOW TO MEASURE HAY IN THE MOW OR STACK.

*A ton of dry hay is variously estimated from 400 to 500 cubic feet to the ton.

To be on the safe side it is best to estimate about 500 cubic feet to the ton.

Hay in a Mow.

Rule.—Multiply the length in feet by the height in feet, and this by the breadth in feet, and divide the result by 500 and you have the number of tons.

Example: How many tons of hay in a mow 20 feet long, 10 feet high, and 15 feet wide?

Solution: $20 \times 10 \times 15 \div 500 = 6$. Ans.

How to Estimate the Number of Tons in a Stack.

Rule.—Multiply the length in feet by the width in feet, and this by one-half the height, and divide the product by 300.

Example: How many tons of hay in a stack 20 feet long, 12 feet high, and 15 feet wide?

Solution: $20 \times 6 \times 15 \div 300 = 6$ tons. Ans.

How to Estimate the Contents of a Round Stack.

Rule.—Multiply the square of the distance around the stack in yards by 4 times the height in yards, and point off two places from the right, and this will be the number of cubic yards in the stack, which divided by 20 will equal the number of tons.

Example: How many tons of hay in a stack, distance around the bulge, 25 yards, and height, 9 yards?

Solution: $25 \times 25 = 625$, then $625 \times 36 = 22{,}500$, pointing off two places makes 225, then $225 \div 20 = 11\frac{1}{4}$ tons. Ans.

***Some authorities allow only 350 cubic feet for a ton of timothy hay when thoroughly settled. Others allow 343 to 420. For millet allow only 216 cubic feet to a ton. The fact is, hay in stack or mow can only be approximately ascertained by measurement.**

NOTE.—No exact rule can be given for measuring hay in the bulk because of its settling more in one case than another, and the different kinds of hay vary greatly. While timothy hay requires from 400 to 500 cubic feet for a ton, common meadow hay requires from 800 to 1,000 cubic feet. The above estimates are as reliable as estimates can be made.

There were about 67,000,000 tons of hay harvested in the United States in 1890.

HOW TO FIND THE CONTENTS OF A WAGON BOX.

A common wagon box is a little more than 10 feet long and 3 feet wide, and will hold about 2 bushels for every inch in depth.

Rule.—Multiply the depth of the wagon box in inches by 2, and you have the number of bushels.

If the wagon box is 11 feet long, multiply the depth in inches by 2, and add one-tenth of the number of bushels to itself.

Example: How many bushels of grain will a wagon box hold, 22 inches deep and 10 feet long?

Solution: 22 × 2=44. Ans.

N. B.—A bushel to the inch is calculated for corn on the cob.

HOW TO FIND THE NUMBER OF BUSHELS OF GRAIN IN A BIN OR BOX.

Rule.—Multiply the length in feet by the height in feet, and then again by the breadth in feet, and then again by 8, and cut off the right hand figure. The last result will be the number of bushels.

Example: How many bushels in a bin 12 feet long, 10 feet wide, and 6 feet high?

Solution: 12 × 10 × 6 × 8=576.0. Ans.

NOTE.—For exact results multiply the length in inches by the height in inches, and that again by the width in inches, and divide the result by 2150.4, the number of cubic inches in a bushel.

SHRINKAGE OF GRAIN.

In deciding to keep their grain farmers should take into account the shrinkage. Wheat will shrink two quarts to the bushel in six months from the time it is threshed. Corn shrinks much more, the shrinkage being nearly one fifth of the whole amount. So that for corn forty cents from the field is as much as fifty cents in March. In the case of potatoes, the loss from October to May is about thirty-three per cent.

BUSHELS.

The dimensions of the bushel are 18½ inches inner diameter; 19½ inches outer diameter, and 8 inches deep; and when heaped the cone is not to be less than 6 inches high, which makes a heaped bushel equal to 1¼ struck ones.

HOW TO MEASURE EAR CORN IN THE CRIB.

Measuring corn in the crib is at best an estimate. Much depends upon the condition of the corn. A bushel of corn means either a bushel of shelled corn or ear corn enough to make a bushel of shelled corn.

Rule.—Multiply the length in feet by the height in feet and that again by the width in feet, multiply the result by 4 and cut off the right hand figure and you have the contents in bushels of shelled corn.

Example: How many bushels of shelled corn in a crib of corn in the ear, 20 feet long, 10 feet high and 8 feet wide?

Solution: 20×10×8×4=640.0 bushels. Ans.

This is the result when 2½ cubic feet or 4320 cubic inches are taken for a bushel.

Counting	4200 cubic inches in a bushel multiply by	411
"	4100 " " " " "	421
"	4000 " " " " "	432
"	3900 " " " " "	443
"	3800 " " " " "	455

In each of these cases cut off the three right hand figures after multiplying. The result will be the number of bushels. There is often a disagreement in measuring ear corn in the crib. As will be seen from the above, the differences result from taking a different number of cubic inches to the bushel.

Here is another very simple rule:

Multiply the cubic feet by 4 and divide the product by 9.

Example: A crib of corn is 15 feet long, 8 feet wide and 9 feet high. How many bushels of corn does it contain?

Solution: 15×8×9=1080×4=4320÷9=480 bushels.

This allows 2¼ cubic feet, or about 3900 cubic inches for a bushel.

This rule is not only very simple but is very frequently used. It will hold out in good dry corn.

When the crib is flared at the side multiply half the sum of the top and bottom widths in feet by the perpendicular height in feet, and then again by the length in feet. This gives the number of cubic feet. Then proceed as above.

HOW TO ESTIMATE THE CONTENTS OF A PILE OF GRAIN, POTATOES, ETC.

Rule.—Put the commodity in the form of a heap. Then multiply the diameter in feet by itself, and then again by the height in feet, and divide the result by 4, and you have the approximate contents in bushels.

Example: How many bushels in a heap of grain 6 feet in diameter and 3 feet high?

Solution: $6 \times 6 \times 3 \div 4 = 27$ bushels. Ans.

HOW TO FIGURE UP A LOAD OF GRAIN.

Rule.—Find the total number of pounds and divide that by the number of pounds in one bushel and it will equal the number of bushels.

Example: How many bushels in 2840 pounds of wheat, and what will it cost at 90 cents per bushel?

Solution: $2840 \div 60 = 47$ bushels and 20 pounds or $47\frac{1}{3}$ **bushels.**

$47\frac{1}{3} \times 90$c.=$42.60. Ans.

HOW TO USE THE GRAIN TABLE.

The heavy type column represents the weight of the load, and the number of bushels and pounds are at the right under the kind of grain.

Example: How many bushels of oats in 2490 pounds?

Answer: 77 bushels and 26 pounds.

HOW TO FIND THE NUMBER OF BUSHELS IN A LOAD OF GRAIN AT SIGHT.

Weig't.	Oats. 32 lbs.		Corn, rye. 56 lbs.		Barley. 48 lbs.		Wheat. 60 lbs.		Weig't.	Oats. 32 lbs.		Corn, rye. 56 lbs.		Barley. 48 lbs.		Wheat. 60 lbs.	
	Bus	Lbs	Bus	Lbs	Bus	Lbs	Bus	Lbs		Bus	Lbs	Bus	Lbs	Bus	Lbs	Bus	Lbs
1500	46	28	26	44	31	12	25	00	2010	62	26	35	50	41	42	33	30
1510	47	06	26	54	31	22	25	10	2020	63	04	36	04	42	04	33	40
1520	47	16	27	08	31	32	25	20	2030	63	14	36	14	42	14	33	50
1530	47	26	27	18	31	42	25	30	2040	63	24	36	24	42	24	34	00
1540	48	04	27	28	32	04	25	40	2050	64	02	36	34	42	34	34	10
1550	48	14	27	38	32	14	25	50	2060	64	12	36	44	42	44	34	20
1560	48	24	27	48	32	24	26	00	2070	64	22	36	54	43	06	34	30
1570	49	02	28	02	32	34	26	10	2080	65	00	37	08	43	16	34	40
1580	49	12	28	12	32	44	26	20	2090	65	10	37	18	43	26	34	50
1590	49	22	28	22	33	06	26	30	2100	65	20	37	28	43	36	35	00
1600	50	00	28	32	33	16	26	40	2110	65	30	37	38	43	46	35	10
1610	50	10	28	42	33	26	26	50	2120	66	08	37	48	44	08	35	20
1620	50	20	28	52	33	36	27	00	2130	66	18	38	02	44	18	35	30
1630	50	30	29	06	33	46	27	10	2140	66	28	38	12	44	28	35	40
1640	51	08	29	16	34	08	27	20	2150	67	06	38	22	44	38	35	50
1650	51	18	29	26	34	18	27	30	2160	67	16	38	32	45	00	36	00
1660	51	28	29	36	34	28	27	40	2170	67	26	38	42	45	10	36	10
1670	52	06	29	46	34	38	27	50	2180	68	04	38	52	45	20	36	20
1680	52	16	30	00	35	00	28	00	2190	68	14	39	06	45	30	36	30
1690	52	26	30	10	35	10	28	10	2200	68	24	39	16	45	40	36	40
1700	53	04	30	20	35	20	28	20	2210	69	02	39	26	46	02	36	50
1710	53	14	30	30	35	30	28	30	2220	69	12	39	36	46	12	37	00
1720	53	24	30	40	35	40	28	40	2230	69	22	39	46	46	22	37	10
1730	54	02	30	50	36	02	28	50	2240	70	00	40	00	46	32	37	20
1740	54	12	31	04	36	12	29	00	2250	70	10	40	10	46	42	37	30
1750	54	22	31	14	36	22	29	10	2260	70	20	40	20	47	04	37	40
1760	55	00	31	24	36	32	29	20	2270	70	30	40	30	47	14	37	50
1770	55	10	31	34	36	42	29	30	2280	71	08	40	40	47	24	38	00
1780	55	20	31	44	37	04	29	40	2290	71	18	40	50	47	34	38	10
1790	55	30	31	54	37	14	29	50	2300	71	28	41	04	47	44	38	20
1800	56	08	32	08	37	24	30	00	2310	72	06	41	14	48	06	38	30
1810	56	18	32	18	37	34	30	10	2320	72	16	41	24	48	16	38	40
1820	56	28	32	28	37	44	30	20	2330	72	26	41	34	48	26	38	50
1830	57	06	32	38	38	06	30	30	2340	73	04	41	44	48	36	39	00
1840	57	16	32	48	38	16	30	40	2350	73	14	41	54	48	46	39	10
1850	57	26	33	02	38	26	30	50	2360	73	24	42	08	49	08	39	20
1860	58	04	33	12	38	36	31	00	2370	74	02	42	18	49	18	39	30
1870	58	14	33	22	38	46	31	10	2380	74	12	42	28	49	28	39	40
1880	58	24	33	32	39	08	31	20	2390	74	22	42	38	49	38	39	50
1890	59	02	33	42	39	18	31	30	2400	75	00	42	48	50	00	40	00
1900	59	12	33	52	39	28	31	40	2410	75	10	43	02	50	10	40	10
1910	59	22	34	06	39	38	31	50	2420	75	20	43	12	50	20	40	20
1920	60	00	34	16	40	00	32	00	2430	75	30	43	22	50	30	40	30
1930	60	10	34	26	40	10	32	10	2440	76	08	43	32	50	40	40	40
1940	60	20	34	36	40	20	32	20	2450	76	18	43	42	51	02	40	50
1950	60	30	34	46	40	30	32	30	2460	76	28	43	52	51	12	41	00
1960	61	08	35	00	40	40	32	40	2470	77	06	44	06	51	22	41	10
1970	61	18	35	10	41	02	32	50	2480	77	16	44	16	51	32	41	20
1980	61	28	35	20	41	12	33	00	2490	77	26	44	26	51	42	41	30
1990	62	06	35	30	41	22	33	10	2500	78	04	44	36	52	04	41	40
2000	62	16	35	40	41	32	33	20	2510	78	14	44	46	52	14	41	50

HOW TO FIND THE NUMBER OF BUSHELS IN A LOAD OF GRAIN AT SIGHT.

Weig't.	Oats. 32 lbs.		Corn, rye. 56 lbs.		Barley. 48 lbs.		Wheat. 60 lbs.		Weig't.	Oats. 32 lbs.		Corn, rye. 56 lbs.		Barley. 48 lbs.		Wheat. 60 lbs.	
	Bus	Lbs	Bus	Lbs	Bus	Lbs	Bus	Lbs		Bus	Lbs	Bus	Lbs	Bus	Lbs	Bus	Lbs
2520	78	24	45	00	52	24	42	00	3020	94	12	53	52	62	44	50	20
2530	79	02	45	10	52	34	42	10	3030	94	22	54	06	63	06	50	30
2540	79	12	45	20	52	44	42	20	3040	95	00	54	16	63	16	50	40
2550	79	22	45	30	53	06	42	30	3050	95	10	54	26	63	26	50	50
2560	80	00	45	40	53	16	42	40	3060	95	20	54	36	63	36	51	00
2570	80	10	45	50	53	26	42	50	3070	95	30	54	46	63	46	51	10
2580	80	20	46	04	53	36	43	00	3080	96	08	55	00	64	08	51	20
2590	80	30	46	14	53	46	43	10	3090	96	18	55	10	64	18	51	30
2600	81	08	46	24	54	08	43	20	3100	96	28	55	20	64	28	51	40
2610	81	18	46	34	54	18	43	30	3110	97	06	55	30	64	38	51	50
2620	81	28	46	44	54	28	43	40	3120	97	16	55	40	65	00	52	00
2630	82	06	46	54	54	38	43	50	3130	97	26	55	50	65	10	52	10
2640	82	16	47	08	55	00	44	00	3140	98	04	56	04	65	20	52	20
2650	82	26	47	18	55	10	44	10	3150	98	14	56	14	65	30	52	30
2660	83	04	47	28	55	20	44	20	3160	98	24	56	24	65	40	52	40
2670	83	14	47	38	55	30	44	30	3170	99	02	56	34	66	02	52	50
2680	83	24	47	48	55	40	44	40	3180	99	12	56	44	66	12	53	00
2690	84	02	48	02	56	02	44	50	3190	99	22	56	54	66	22	53	10
2700	84	12	48	12	56	12	45	00	3200	100	00	57	08	66	32	53	20
2710	84	22	48	22	56	22	45	10	3210	100	10	57	18	66	42	53	30
2720	85	00	48	32	56	32	45	20	3220	100	20	57	28	67	04	53	40
2730	85	10	48	42	56	42	45	30	3230	100	30	57	38	67	14	53	50
2740	85	20	48	52	57	04	45	40	3240	101	08	57	48	67	24	54	00
2750	85	30	49	06	57	14	45	50	3250	101	18	58	02	67	34	54	10
2760	86	08	49	16	57	24	46	00	3260	101	28	58	12	67	44	54	20
2770	86	18	49	26	57	34	46	10	3270	102	06	58	22	68	06	54	30
2780	86	28	49	36	57	44	46	20	3280	102	16	58	32	68	16	54	40
2790	87	06	49	46	58	06	46	30	3290	102	26	58	42	68	26	54	50
2800	87	16	50	00	58	16	46	40	3300	103	04	58	52	68	36	55	00
2810	87	26	50	10	58	26	46	50	3310	103	14	59	06	68	46	55	10
2820	88	04	50	20	58	36	47	00	3320	103	24	59	16	69	08	55	20
2830	88	14	50	30	58	46	47	10	3330	104	02	59	26	69	18	55	30
2840	88	24	50	40	59	08	47	20	3340	104	12	59	36	69	28	55	40
2850	89	02	50	50	59	18	47	30	3350	104	22	59	46	69	38	55	50
2860	89	12	51	04	59	28	47	40	3360	105	00	60	00	70	00	56	00
2870	89	22	51	14	59	38	47	50	3370	105	10	60	10	70	10	56	10
2880	90	00	51	24	60	00	48	00	3380	105	20	60	20	70	20	56	20
2890	90	10	51	34	60	10	48	10	3390	105	30	60	30	70	30	56	30
2900	90	20	51	44	60	20	48	20	3400	106	08	60	40	70	40	56	40
2910	90	30	51	54	60	30	48	30	3410	106	18	60	50	71	02	56	50
2920	91	08	52	08	60	40	48	40	3420	106	28	61	04	71	12	57	00
2930	91	18	52	18	61	02	48	50	3430	107	06	61	14	71	22	57	10
2940	91	28	52	28	61	12	49	00	3440	107	16	61	24	71	32	57	20
2950	92	06	52	38	61	22	49	10	3450	107	26	61	34	71	42	57	30
2960	92	16	52	48	61	32	49	20	3460	108	04	61	44	72	04	57	40
2970	92	26	53	02	61	42	49	30	3470	108	14	61	54	72	14	57	50
2980	93	04	53	12	62	04	49	40	3480	108	24	62	08	72	24	58	00
2990	93	14	53	22	62	14	49	50	3490	109	02	62	18	72	34	58	10
3000	93	24	53	32	62	24	50	00	3500	109	12	62	28	72	44	58	20
3010	94	02	53	42	62	34	50	10									

NUMBER OF POUNDS TO THE BUSHEL, LEGAL WEIGHT, IN DIFFERENT STATES.

STATES.	Wheat.	Rye.	Oats.	Barley.	Buckwheat	Shelled Corn.	Corn on the Cob.	Corn Meal.	Potatoes.	Sweet Potatoes.	Onions.	Turnips.	Beans.	Peas.	Dried Apples.	Dried Peaches.	Flax Seed.	Timothy Seed.	Blue Grass Seed.	Clover Seed.	Anthracite Coal.	Millet.
Arkansas	60	56	32	48	52	....	70	50	60	50	57	....	60	60	24	33	56	45	14	60	80	50
California	60	54	32	50	40	52	....	....	....	....	....	....	....	....	....	....	....	....	....	....	....	....
Connecticut	60	56	32	48	48	56	....	50	60	....	50	50	60	60	....	....	....	....	....	....	....	....
Georgia	60	56	32	47	52	56	70	48	60	55	57	55	60	60	24	33	56	45	14	60	80	50
Illinois	60	56	32	48	52	56	70	48	60	50	57	55	60	....	24	33	56	45	14	60	80	50
Indiana	60	56	32	48	50	56	68	50	60	....	48	....	60	....	25	33	....	45	14	60	....	....
Iowa	60	56	32	48	52	56	70	....	60	46	57	....	60	....	24	33	56	45	14	60	80	48
Kansas	60	56	32	48	50	56	70	50	60	50	57	55	60	....	24	33	56	45	14	60	80	50
Kentucky	60	56	32	47	56	56	70	50	60	55	57	60	60	60	24	39	56	45	14	60	76	50
Louisiana	60	56	32	48	....	56	....	....	60	....	....	....	60	60	....	....	....	45	14	60	....	....
Maine	60	50	32	48	48	56	....	50	60	....	52	60	62	60	....	....	....	....	....	....	....	....
Massachusetts	60	56	32	48	48	56	....	50	60	54	52	....	....	....	....	....	....	....	....	....	....	....
Michigan	60	56	32	48	48	56	70	50	60	56	54	58	60	60	22	28	56	45	14	60	....	....
Minnesota	60	56	32	48	50	56	....	....	60	....	....	....	....	....	28	28	....	....	....	60	....	....
Missouri	60	56	32	48	52	56	....	....	60	....	57	....	60	....	24	33	56	45	14	60	....	....
Mississippi	60	56	30	....	....	56	....	....	60	....	....	....	60	60	....	....	....	45	14	60	80	....
Nebraska	60	56	32	48	52	56	70	50	60	50	57	55	60	60	24	33	56	45	14	60	80	50
New Hampshire	60	56	32	....	....	56	....	50	60	....	....	....	60	60	....	....	....	....	....	....	....	....
New Jersey	60	56	30	48	50	56	....	....	60	54	57	....	60	60	25	33	55	....	....	64	....	....
New York	60	56	32	48	48	58	....	....	60	....	....	....	62	60	....	....	55	44	....	60	....	....
North Carolina	60	56	30	48	50	54	....	46	....	....	....	....	....	50	....	....	....	....	....	64	....	....
North Dakota	60	56	32	48	42	56	....	....	60	....	57	....	....	60	....	....	56	45	....	60	....	....
Ohio	60	56	33	48	50	56	70	....	60	50	55	....	60	60	24	33	56	45	....	60	....	50
Oregon	60	56	36	45	42	56	....	....	60	....	50	50	60	60	28	28	....	40	....	60	....	....
Pennsylvania	60	56	32	47	48	56	....	....	60	....	....	....	....	....	....	....	....	....	....	62	....	....
Rhode Island	60	56	32	48	....	56	....	50	60	....	50	....	....	....	....	....	....	....	....	....	....	....
South Carolina	60	56	33	48	56	56	72	50	60	60	57	....	60	60	28	33	56	....	14	60	....	....
South Dakota	60	53	32	48	42	56	....	....	60	....	57	....	....	60	....	....	56	45	....	60	....	....
Tennessee	60	56	32	48	50	56	70	50	60	50	56	....	60	60	24	....	56	45	14	....	....	....
Vermont	60	56	32	48	48	56	....	....	60	....	52	60	60	60	....	....	....	45	....	60	....	....
Virginia	60	56	32	48	52	56	70	50	60	56	57	55	60	60	28	32	56	45	14	60	80	50
Washington	60	56	32	48	42	56	....	....	60	....	50	50	60	60	28	28	....	40	....	60	....	....
Wisconsin	60	56	32	48	48	56	70	....	60	....	57	42	60	....	25	28	56	45	....	60	....	55

Some States have no legal weights.

HOW TO FIND THE COST OF COAL, HAY, STRAW, ETC., AT SIGHT.

Cost per Pound or Ton.

No. Lbs.	$0.25	$0.50	$0.75	$1.00	$2.00	$3.00	$4.00	$5.00	$6.00	$7.00	$8.00	$9.00	$10.00	$20.00	$30.00	$40.00	$50.00
10	....	....	....	.01	.01	.02	.02	.03	03	.04	.04	.05	.05	.10	.15	.20	.25
20	....	.01	.01	.01	.02	.03	.04	.05	.06	.07	.08	.09	.10	.20	.30	.40	.50
30	....	.01	.01	.02	.03	.05	.06	.08	.09	.11	.12	.14	.15	.30	.45	.60	.75
40	.01	.01	.02	.02	.04	.06	.08	.10	.12	.14	.16	.18	.20	.40	.60	.80	1.00
50	.01	.01	.02	.03	.05	.08	.10	.13	.15	.18	.20	.23	.25	.50	.75	1.00	1.25
60	.01	.02	.02	.03	.06	.09	.12	.15	.18	.21	.24	.27	.30	.60	.90	1.20	1.50
70	.01	.02	.03	.04	.07	.11	.14	.18	.21	.25	.28	.32	.35	.70	1.05	1.40	1.75
80	.01	.02	.03	.04	.08	.12	.16	.20	.24	.28	.32	.36	.40	.80	1.20	1.60	2.00
90	.01	.02	.03	.05	.09	.14	.18	.23	.27	.32	.36	.41	.45	.90	1.35	1.80	2.25
100	.01	.03	.04	.05	.10	.15	.20	.25	.30	.35	.40	.45	.50	1.00	1.50	2.00	2.50
200	.03	.05	.08	.10	.20	.30	.40	.50	.60	.70	.80	.90	1.00	2.00	3.00	4.00	5.00
300	.04	.08	.11	.15	.30	.45	.60	.75	.90	1.05	1.20	1.35	1.50	3.00	4.50	6.00	7.50
400	.05	.10	.15	.20	.40	.60	.80	1.00	1.20	1.40	1.60	1.80	2.00	4.00	6.00	8.00	10.00
500	.06	.13	.19	.25	.50	.75	1.00	1.25	1.50	1.75	2.00	2.25	2.50	5.00	7.50	10.00	12.50
600	.08	.15	.23	.30	.60	.90	1.20	1.50	1.80	2.10	2.40	2.70	3.00	6.00	9.00	12.00	15.00
700	.09	.18	.26	.35	.70	1.05	1.40	1.75	2.10	2.45	2.80	3.15	3.50	7.00	10.50	14.00	17.50
800	.10	.20	.30	.40	.80	1.20	1.60	2.00	2.40	2.80	3.20	3.60	4.00	8.00	12.00	16.00	20.00
900	.11	.23	.34	.45	.90	1.35	1.80	2.25	2.70	3.15	3.60	4.05	4.50	9.00	13.50	18.00	22.50
1000	.13	.25	.38	.50	1.00	1.50	2.00	2.50	3.00	3.50	4.00	4.50	5.00	10.00	15.00	20.00	25.00
1100	.14	.28	.41	.55	1.10	1.65	2.20	2.75	3.30	3.85	4.40	4.95	5.50	11.00	16.50	22.00	27.50
1200	.15	.30	.45	.60	1.20	1.80	2.40	3.00	3.60	4.20	4.80	5.40	6.00	12.00	18.00	24 00	30.00
1300	.16	.33	.49	.65	1.30	1.95	2.60	3.25	3.90	4.55	5.20	5.85	6.50	13.00	19.50	26.00	32.50
1400	.18	.35	.53	.70	1.40	2.10	2.80	3.50	4.20	4.90	5.60	6.30	7.00	14.00	21.00	28.00	35.00
1500	.19	.38	.56	.75	1.50	2.25	3.00	3.75	4.50	5.25	6.00	6.75	7.50	15.00	22.50	30.00	37.50
1600	.20	.40	.60	.80	1.60	2.40	3.20	4.00	4.80	5.60	6.40	7.20	8.00	16.00	24.00	32.00	40.00
1700	.21	.43	.64	.85	1.70	2.55	3.40	4.25	5.10	5.95	6.80	7.65	8.50	17.00	25.50	34.00	42.50
1800	.23	.45	.68	.90	1.80	2.70	3.60	4.50	5.40	6.30	7.20	8.10	9.00	18.00	27.00	36.00	45.00
1900	.24	.48	.71	.95	1.90	2.85	3.80	4.75	5.70	6.65	7.60	8.55	9.50	19.00	28.50	38.00	47.50
1 ton	.25	.50	.75	1.00	2.00	3.00	4.00	5.00	6.00	7.00	8.00	9.00	10.00	20.00	30.00	40.00	50.00
2 tons	.50	1.00	1.50	2.00	4.00	6.00	8.00	10.00	12.00	14.00	16.00	18.00	20.00	40.00	60.00	80.00	100.00
3 tons	.75	1.50	2.25	3.00	6.00	9.00	12.00	15.00	18.00	21.00	24.00	27.00	30.00	60.00	90.00	120.00	150.00
4 tons	1.00	2.00	3.00	4.00	8.00	12.00	16.00	20.00	24.00	28.00	32.00	36.00	40.00	80.00	120.00	160.00	200.00
5 tons	1.25	2.50	3.75	5.00	10.00	15.00	20.00	25.00	30.00	35.00	40.00	45.00	50.00	100.00	150.00	200.00	250.00

Example: What is the cost of 1300 lbs. of coal @ $4.50 per ton?

Solution: 1300 lbs. @ $4.00 $2.60
1300 lbs. @ .50 = .33

$2.93 *Ans.*

Example: What is the cost of 1750 lbs. hay @ $40.00 per ton?

Solution: 1700 lbs. @ $40.00 $34.00
50 lbs. @ 40.00 = 1.00

$35.00 *Ans.*

WAGES IN THE UNITED STATES FROM CENSUS

	Employes.	Wages.	Cost of Materials.	Value of Products.
Agricultural Implements.....	42.544	$ 21,811,761	$ 31,603,265	$ 81,271,651
Bicycles	2,231	1,267,411	786 180	2,970,035
Book Making..................	13,815	6,903,951	6,007,417	17,067,780
Boots and Shoes.............	184,275	92,919,349	146,801,968	280,215,185
Buttons	4,036	1,673,876	1,551,603	4,216,795
Carpets	31,213	12,438,631	29,582,188	49,996,373
Clothing	353,463	153,576,095	237,096,809	503,258,566
Iron and Steel..............	193,558	104,477,194	356,279,162	524,592,775
Jewelry	16,799	10,857,967	16,593,660	36,215,511
Liquors	41,525	31,678,166	80,230,532	189,775,639
Printing	166,093	105,569,181	69,426,553	276,911,949
Tobacco and Cigars.........	135,927	54,792,006	92,304,317	211,746,623

THE LABORER'S GREETING AT EVENING.

HOW TO USE THE WAGE TABLES.

EXAMPLES:

Find the amount due for 7 months, 19 days at $19.00 a month?

Solution:	For 7 months..................	$133.00
	For 19 days..................	13.88
		$146.88 *Ans.*

Find the wages for 3 months, 9 days at $95.00 per month?

Solution:	3 months at $90.00 per month..	$270.00
	9 days at $90.00 per month....	31.20
	3 months at $5.00 per month..	15.00
	9 days at $5.00 per month......	1.73
		$317.03 *Ans.*

MONTHLY WAGES TABLE.*

From $1.00 to $200.00 per Month Calculated at Sight.

$1	$2	$3	$4	$5	Time	$6	$7	$8	$9	$10
.04	.08	.12	.16	.19	1 Day	.24	.27	.32	.35	.38
.08	.16	.24	.32	.39	2	.48	.54	.64	.69	.77
.12	.24	.36	.48	.58	3	.72	.81	.96	1.04	1.15
.15	.30	.45	.60	.77	4	.90	1.08	1.20	1.38	1.54
.19	.38	.57	.76	.96	5	1.14	1.35	1.52	1.73	1.92
.23	.46	.69	.92	1.15	6	1.38	1.62	1.84	2.08	2.31
.27	.54	.81	1.08	1.34	7	1.62	1.88	2.16	2.42	2.69
.31	.62	.93	1.24	1.54	8	1.86	2.15	2.48	2.77	3.08
.35	.70	1.05	1.40	1.73	9	2.10	2.42	2.80	3.12	3.46
.38	.77	1.15	1.54	1.92	10	2.30	2.69	3.07	3.46	3.85
.42	.84	1.26	1.68	2.12	11	2.52	2.96	3.36	3.81	4.23
.46	.92	1.38	1.84	2.31	12	2.76	3.23	3.68	4.15	4.62
.50	1.00	1.50	2.00	2.50	13	3.00	3.50	4.00	4.50	5.00
.54	1.08	1.62	2.16	2.69	14	3.24	3.77	4.32	4.85	5.38
.58	1.16	1.73	2.32	2.89	15	3.46	4.04	4.64	5.19	5.77
.62	1.24	1.85	2.48	3.08	16	3.70	4.31	4.96	5.54	6.15
.65	1.30	1.96	2.60	3.27	17	3.92	4.58	5.20	5.88	6.54
.69	1.38	2.08	2.76	3.46	18	4.16	4.85	5.52	6.23	6.92
.73	1.46	2.19	2.92	3.65	19	4.38	5.12	5.84	6.58	7.31
.77	1.54	2.31	3.08	3.85	20	4.62	5.38	6.16	6.92	7.69
.81	1.62	2.42	3.24	4.04	21	4.84	5.65	6.48	7.27	8.08
.85	1.70	2.54	3.40	4.23	22	5.08	5.92	6.80	7.62	8.46
.88	1.76	2.65	3.52	4.42	23	5.30	6.19	7.04	7.96	8.85
.92	1.84	2.77	3.68	4.62	24	5.54	6.46	7.36	8.31	9.23
.96	1.92	2.88	3.84	4.81	25	5.76	6.73	7.68	8.65	9.62
1.00	2.00	3.00	4.00	5.00	1 Mo.	6.00	7.00	8.00	9.00	10.00
2.00	4.00	6.00	8.00	10.00	2	12.00	14.00	16.00	18.00	20.00
3.00	6.00	9.00	12.00	15.00	3	18.00	21.00	24.00	27.00	30.00
4.00	8.00	12.00	16.00	20.00	4	24.00	28.00	32.00	36.00	40.00
5.00	10.00	15.00	20.00	25.00	5	30.00	35.00	40.00	45.00	50.00
6.00	12.00	18.00	24.00	30.00	6	36.00	42.00	48.00	54.00	60.00
7.00	14.00	21.00	28.00	35.00	7	42.00	49.00	56.00	63.00	70.00
8.00	16.00	24.00	32.00	40.00	8	48.00	56.00	64.00	72.00	80.00
9.00	18.00	27.00	36.00	45.00	9	54.00	63.00	72.00	81.00	90.00
10.00	20.00	30.00	40.00	50.00	10	60.00	70.00	80.00	90.00	100.00
11.00	22.00	33.00	44.00	55.00	11	66.00	77.00	88.00	99.00	110.00
12.00	24.00	36.00	48.00	60.00	1 Yr.	72.00	84.00	96.00	108.00	120.00

* 26 working days in a month.

MONTHLY WAGES TABLE.*

From $1.00 to $200.00 per Month Calculated at Sight.

$20	$30	$40	$50	$60	Time	$70	$80	$90	$100	$200
.77	1.15	1.54	1.92	2.31	1 Day	2.69	3.08	3.46	3.85	7.70
1.54	2.31	3.08	3.85	4.62	2	5.38	6.16	6.92	7.70	15.40
2.31	3.46	4.62	5.77	6.92	3	8.07	9.24	10.38	11.54	23.10
3.08	4.62	6.15	7.69	9.23	4	10.77	12.31	13.84	15.39	30.80
3.85	5.77	7.69	9.62	11.54	5	13.46	15.39	17.30	19.23	38.50
4.62	6.92	9.23	11.54	13.85	6	16.15	18.47	20.77	23.08	46.20
5.38	8.08	10.77	13.46	16.15	7	18.84	21.54	24.23	26.93	53.80
6.15	9.23	12.31	15.38	18.46	8	21.54	24.62	27.69	30.77	61.50
6.92	10.38	13.84	17.31	20.77	9	24.23	27.70	31.15	34.62	69.20
7.69	11.44	15.38	19.53	23.08	10	26.92	30.77	34.61	38.46	76.90
8.46	12.69	16.92	21.15	25.38	11	29.61	33.85	38.07	42.31	84.60
9.23	13.85	18.46	23.08	27.69	12	32.31	36.93	41.54	46.15	92.30
10.00	15.00	20.00	25.00	30.00	13	35.00	40.00	45.00	50.00	100.00
10.77	16.15	21.54	26.92	32.31	14	37.69	43.08	48.46	53.84	107.00
11.54	17.31	23.08	28.85	34.62	15	40.38	46.16	51.92	57.69	115.40
12.31	18.46	24.62	30.77	36.92	16	43.08	49.23	55.38	61.53	107.70
13.08	19.62	26.15	32.69	39.23	17	45.77	52.31	58.84	65.38	123.10
13.85	20.77	27.69	34.62	41.54	18	48.46	55.39	62.31	69.22	130.80
14.62	21.92	29.23	36.54	43.85	19	51.15	58.46	65.77	73.07	138.50
15.38	23.08	30.77	38.46	46.15	20	53.85	61.54	69.23	76.91	146.20
16.15	24.23	32.31	40.38	48.46	21	56.54	64.62	72.69	80.76	153.80
16.92	25.38	33.85	42.31	50.77	22	59.23	67.69	76.15	84.60	161.50
17.69	26.54	35.38	44.23	53.08	23	61.92	70.77	79.61	88.45	169.20
18.46	27.69	36.92	46.15	55.38	24	64.62	73.85	83.08	92.30	184.60
19.23	28.85	38.46	48.08	57.69	25	67.31	76.92	86.54	96.15	192.20
20.00	30.00	40.00	50.00	60.00	1 Mo.	70.00	80.00	90.00	100.00	200.00
40.00	60.00	80.00	100.00	120.00	2	140.00	160.00	180.00	200.00	400.00
60.00	90.00	120.00	150.00	180.00	3	210.00	240.00	270.00	300.00	600.00
80.00	120.00	160.00	200.00	240.00	4	280.00	320.00	360.00	400.00	800.00
100.00	150.00	200.00	250.00	300.00	5	350.00	400.00	450.00	500.00	1000.00
120.00	180.00	240.00	300.00	360.00	6	420.00	480.00	540.00	600.00	1200.00
140.00	210.00	280.00	350.00	420.00	7	490.00	560.00	530.00	700.00	1400.00
160.00	240.00	320.00	400.00	480.00	8	560.00	640.00	720.00	800.00	1600.00
180.00	270.00	360.00	450.00	540.00	9	630.00	720.00	810.00	900.00	1800.00
200.00	300.00	400.00	500.00	600.00	10	700.00	800.00	900.00	1000.00	2000.00
220.00	330.00	440.00	550.00	660.00	11	770.00	880.00	990.00	1100.00	2200.00
240.00	360.00	480.00	600.00	720.00	1 Yr.	840.00	960.00	1080.00	1200.00	2400.00

* 26 working days in a month.

TABLE OF WAGES BY THE WEEK, GIVEN BY THE DAY AND HOUR.

	$1	$2	$3	$4	$5	$6	$7	$8	$9	$10	$11	$12	$13	$14	$15	$16	$17	$18
½ hr.		1⅔	2½	3⅓	4⅙	5	5⅚	6⅔	7½	8⅓	9⅙	10	10⅚	11⅔	12½	13⅓	14⅙	15
1 hr.	1⅔	3⅓	5	6⅔	8⅓	10	11⅔	13⅓	15	16⅔	18⅓	20	21⅔	23⅓	25	26⅔	28⅓	30
2 hrs.	3⅓	6⅔	10	13⅓	16⅔	20	23⅓	26⅔	30	33⅓	36⅔	40	43⅓	46⅔	50	53⅓	56⅔	60
3 hrs.	5	10	15	20	25	30	35	40	45	50	55	60	65	70	75	80	85	90
4 hrs.	6⅔	13⅓	20	26⅔	33⅓	40	46⅔	53⅓	60	66⅔	73⅓	80	86⅔	93⅓	1.00	1.06⅔	1.13⅓	1.20
5 hrs.	8⅓	16⅔	25	33⅓	41⅔	50	58⅓	66⅔	75	83⅓	91⅔	1.00	1.08⅓	1.16⅔	1.25	1.33⅓	1.41⅔	1.50
6 hrs.	10	20	30	40	50	60	70	80	90	1.00	1.10	1.20	1.30	1.40	1.50	1.60	1.70	1.80
7 hrs.	11⅔	23⅓	35	46⅔	58⅓	70	81⅔	93⅓	1.05	1.16⅔	1.28⅓	1.40	1.51⅔	1.63⅓	1.75	1.86⅔	1.98⅓	2.10
8 hrs.	13⅓	26⅔	40	53⅓	66⅔	80	93⅓	1.06⅔	1.20	1.33⅓	1.46⅔	1.60	1.73⅓	1.86⅔	2.00	2.13⅓	2.26⅔	2.40
9 hrs.	15	30	45	60	75	90	1.05	1.20	1.35	1.50	1.65	1.80	1.95	2.10	2.25	2.40	2.55	2.70
1 day.	16⅔	33⅓	50	66⅔	83⅓	1.00	1.16⅔	1.33⅓	1.50	1.66⅔	1.83⅓	2.00	2.16⅔	2.33⅓	2 50	2.66⅔	2.83⅓	3.00
2 ds.	33⅓	66⅔	1.00	1.33⅓	1.66⅔	2.00	2.33⅓	2.66⅔	3.00	3.33⅓	3.66⅔	4.00	4.33⅓	4.66⅔	5.00	5.33⅓	5.66⅔	6.00
3 ds.	50	1.00	1.50	2.00	2.50	3.00	3.50	4.00	4.50	5.00	5.50	6.00	6.50	7.00	7.50	8.00	8.50	9.00
4 ds.	66⅔	1.33⅓	2.00	2.66⅔	3.33⅓	4.00	4.66⅔	5.33⅓	6.00	6.66⅔	7.33⅓	8.00	8.66⅔	9.33⅓	10.00	10.66⅔	11.33⅓	12.00
5 ds.	83⅓	1.66⅔	2.50	3.33⅓	4.16⅔	5.00	5.83⅓	6.66⅔	7.50	8.33⅓	9 16⅔	10.00	10.83⅓	11.66⅔	12.50	13.33⅓	14.16⅔	15.00
6 ds.	1.00	2.00	3.00	4.00	5.00	6.00	7.00	8.00	9.00	10.00	11.00	12.00	13.00	14.00	15.00	16.00	17.00	18.00

EXAMPLE: What will the wages for 4 days and 7 hours amount to at $9.00 per week? Ans., $7.05.

The above table is based on 10 hours a day. To find the amount for any number of days, 8 or 9 hours a day, multiply the number opposite 8 hours or 9 hours, as the case may be, by the number of days.

Thus, 8 days and 6 hours at $11.00 a week, working 9 hours a day, will amount to $1.65×8=$13.20+$1.10, amount for 6 hours=$14.30.

Eight days and 6 hours at $11.00 a week, working 8 hours a day, will amount to $1.46⅔ × 8 = $11.73 + $1.10, amount for 6 hours = $12.83.

TABLE OF WAGES BY THE WEEK—GIVEN BY THE DAY AND HOUR.

Time	$19	$20	$21	$22	$23	$24	$25	$26	$27	$28	$29	$30	$31	$32	$33	$34	$35	$36
½ Hr.	.16	.17	.17	.18	.19	.20	.21	.21	.22	.23	.24	.25	.26	.27	.27	.28	.29	.30
1	.32	.33	.35	.37	.38	.40	.42	.43	.45	.47	.48	.50	.52	.53	.55	.57	.58	.60
2	.63	.67	.70	.73	.77	.80	.83	.87	.90	.93	.97	1.00	1.03	1.07	1.10	1.13	1.16	1.20
3	.95	1.00	1.05	1.10	1.15	1.20	1.25	1.30	1.35	1.40	1.45	1.50	1.55	1.60	1.65	1.70	1.75	1.80
4	1.27	1.33	1.40	1.47	1.53	1.60	1.67	1.73	1.80	1.87	1.93	2.00	2.07	2.13	2.20	2.27	2.33	2.40
5	1.58	1.67	1.75	1.83	1.92	2.00	2.08	2.17	2.25	2.33	2.42	2.50	2.58	2.67	2.75	2.83	2.92	3.00
6	1.90	2.00	2.10	2.20	2.30	2.40	2.50	2.60	2.70	2.80	2.90	3.00	3.10	3.20	3.30	3.40	3.50	3.60
7	2.22	2.33	2.45	2.57	2.68	2.80	2.92	3.03	3.15	3.27	3.38	3.50	3.62	3.73	3.85	3.97	4.08	4.20
8	2.53	3.67	2.80	2.93	3.07	3.20	3.33	3.47	3.60	3.73	3.87	4.00	4.13	4.27	4.40	4.53	4.67	4.80
9	2.85	3.00	3.15	3.30	3.45	3.60	3.75	3.90	4.05	4.20	4.35	4.50	4.65	4.80	4.95	5.10	5.25	5.40
1 Day	3.17	3.33	3.50	3.67	3.83	4.00	4.17	4.33	4.50	4.67	4.83	5.00	5.17	5.33	5.50	5.67	5.83	6.00
2	4.00	6.67	7.00	7.33	7.67	8.00	8.33	8.67	9.00	9.33	9.67	10.00	10.33	10.67	11.00	11.33	11.67	12.00
3	9.50	10.00	10.50	11.00	11.50	12.00	12.50	13.00	13.50	14.00	14.50	15.00	15.50	16.00	16.50	17.00	17.50	18.00
4	12.67	13.33	14.00	14.67	15.33	16.00	16.67	17.33	18.00	18.67	19.33	20.00	20.67	21.33	22.00	22.67	23.33	24.00
5	15.83	16.67	17.50	18.33	19.17	20.00	20.83	21.67	22.50	23.33	24.17	25.00	25.83	26.67	27.50	28.33	29.17	30.00
6	19.90	20.00	21.00	22.00	23.00	24.00	25.00	26.00	27.00	28.00	29.00	30.00	31.00	32.00	33.00	34.00	35.00	36.00

NOTE—*For explanation see bottom of page 367.*

How to Calculate the WEIGHT of Coal in a Bin or Box.

A solid cubic foot of anthracite coal weighs about 93 pounds. When broken for use it weighs about 54 pounds. Bituminous coal when broken up for use weighs about 50 pounds.

Rule.—Multiply the length in feet by the height in feet, and again by the breadth in feet, and this result by 54 for anthracite coal, or by 50 for bituminous coal, and the result will equal the number of pounds.

To find the number of tons, divide by 2,000.

Example: A coal bin is ten feet long, 8 feet wide, and 5 feet high. How many tons of anthracite coal will it hold?

Solution: 10×8×5×54=21,600. 21,600 ÷ 2,000=10 tons and 1,600 pounds.

Amount of Charcoal in a Bin.

Multiply length, breadth, and height (all in inches) together, and divide by 2571, the number of cubic inches in a bushel of charcoal.

How to Find the Number of Cords in a Pile of Wood.

A cord of wood is a pile 8 feet long, 4 feet wide and 4 feet high and contains 128 cubic feet.

Rule.—Multiply the length in feet by the width in feet and that result by the height in feet and divide the product by 128 and you have the number of cords.

Example: How many cords in a pile of wood 4 feet wide, 7 feet high, 24 feet long.

Solution; 4×7×24=672 cubic feet. 672÷128=5¼ cords. *Ans.*

A cord of wood contains 128 cubic feet when the wood is cut 4 feet long. It is an error to suppose that a cord should always contain 128 cubic feet, as, for instance, cooking stove wood is seldom over 20 inches in width when corded, but the width is counted the same as if it was four feet. As for instance in the following example:

Rule.—Multiply the length of the pile by the height, and divide by 32.

Example:—How many cords are contained in a pile of stove wood 17 feet long, 6 feet high and 19 inches in width?

Solution: 17 length × 6 height=102; 102÷32=3$\frac{3}{16}$ cords. —Ans.

HOW TO FIND THE WEIGHT OF CATTLE BY MEASUREMENT.

To find the approximate weight, measure as follows: 1. The girth behind the shoulders. 2. The length from the fore-part of the shoulder-blade along the back to the bone at the tail, in a vertical line with the buttocks. Then multiply the square of the girth in feet by five times the length in feet. Divide the product by 1.5 for average cattle (if cattle be very fat, by 1.425; if very lean, by 1.575) and the quotient will be the dressed weight of the quarters. Thus: The girth of a steer is 6.5 feet, and the length from the shoulder-blade to the tail bone is 5.25. The square of 6.5 is 42.25, and 5 times 5.25 is 26.25. Multiplying these together gives 1109.0625, which, when divided by 1.5, produces 739.375 lbs. the approximate net weight of the steer after being dressed.

THE SHORT METHOD.

Multiply the distance around the animal (back of the fore-shoulder) by itself, and then multiply that result by 17.5 and you have the weight of the animal (nearly.)

WEIGHT OF HOGS.

What will be the cost of 3345 pounds of live hogs, at $3.25 per hundred weight?—See table, next page.

3300 @ 3.25=107.25.
45 @ 3.25= 1.46.

108.71. Ans.

WEIGHT OF CATTLE.

What will 2255 lbs. of live cattle cost at $13.60 per hundred. (See table pp. 371-2.)

	2200 @ $10.00	
2200 lbs. @ $13.60=	2200 @ 3.00=	$220.00+$66.00+$13.20=$299.20
	2200 @ .60	
	55 @ $10.00	
55 lbs. @ 13.60=	55 @ 3.00=	5.50+ 1.65+ .33= 7.48
	55 @ .60	
Total		$306.68

HOG AND CATTLE TABLE.

The first column gives the number of pounds, and the top of each column the price per hundred weight.

WEIGHT.	5c.	10c.	15c.	20c.	30c.	40c.	50c.	60c.	70c.	80c.	90c.
3.....	.00	.00	.00	.01	.01	.01	.02	.02	.02	.02	.03
5.....	.00	.01	.01	.01	.02	.02	.03	.03	.04	.04	.05
10.....	.01	.01	.02	.02	.03	.04	.05	.06	.07	.08	.09
15.....	.01	.02	.02	.03	.05	.06	.08	.09	.11	.12	.14
20.....	.01	.02	.03	.04	.06	.08	.10	.12	.14	.16	.18
25.....	.01	.03	.04	.05	.08	.10	.13	.15	.18	.20	.23
30.....	.02	.03	.05	.06	.09	.12	.15	.18	.21	.24	.27
35.....	.02	.04	.05	.07	.11	.14	.18	.21	.25	.28	.32
40.....	.02	.04	.06	.08	.12	.16	.20	.24	.28	.32	.36
45.....	.02	.05	.07	.09	.14	.18	.23	.27	.32	.36	.41
50.....	.03	.05	.08	.10	.15	.20	.25	.30	.35	.40	.45
55.....	.03	.06	.08	.11	.17	.22	.28	.33	.39	.44	.50
60.....	.03	.06	.09	.12	.18	.24	.30	.36	.42	.48	.54
65.....	.03	.07	.10	.13	.20	.26	.33	.39	.46	.52	.59
70.....	.04	.07	.11	.14	.21	.28	.35	.42	.49	.56	.63
75.....	.04	.08	.11	.15	.23	.30	.38	.45	.53	.60	.68
80.....	.04	.08	.12	.16	.24	.32	.40	.48	.56	.64	.72
85.....	.04	.09	.13	.17	.26	.34	.43	.51	.60	.68	.77
90.....	.05	.09	.14	.18	.27	.36	.45	.54	.63	.72	.81
95.....	.05	.10	.14	.19	.29	.38	.48	.57	.67	.76	.86
100.....	.05	.10	.15	.20	.30	.40	.50	.60	.70	.80	.90
200.....	.10	.20	.30	.40	.60	.80	1.00	1.20	1.40	1.60	1.80
300.....	.15	.30	.45	.60	.90	1.20	1.50	1.80	2.10	2.40	2.70
400.....	.20	.40	.60	.80	1.20	1.60	2.00	2.40	2.80	3.20	3.60
500.....	.25	.50	.75	1.00	1.50	2.00	2.50	3.00	3.50	4.00	4.50
600.....	.30	.60	.90	1.20	1.80	2.40	3.00	3.60	4.20	4.80	5.40
700.....	.35	.70	1.05	1.40	2.10	2.80	3.50	4.20	4.90	5.60	6.30
800.....	.40	.80	1.20	1.60	2.40	3.20	4.00	4.80	5.60	6.40	7.20
900.....	.45	.90	1.35	1.80	2.70	3.60	4.50	5.40	6.30	7.20	8.10
1000.....	.50	1.00	1.50	2.00	3.00	4.00	5.00	6.00	7.00	8.00	9.00
1100.....	.55	1.10	1.65	2.20	3.30	4.40	5.50	6.60	7.70	8.80	9.90
1200.....	.60	1.20	1.80	2.40	3.60	4.80	6.00	7.20	8.40	9.60	10.80
1300.....	.65	1.30	1.95	2.60	3.90	5.20	6.50	7.80	9.10	10.40	11.70
1400.....	.70	1.40	2.10	2.80	4.20	5.60	7.00	8.40	9.80	11.20	12.60
1500.....	.75	1.50	2.25	3.00	4.50	6.00	7.50	9.00	10.50	12.00	13.50
1600.....	.80	1.60	2.40	3.20	4.80	6.40	8.00	9.60	11.20	12.80	14.40
1700.....	.85	1.70	2.55	3.40	5.10	6.80	8.50	10.20	11.90	13.60	15.30
1800.....	.90	1.80	2.70	3.60	5.40	7.20	9.00	10.80	12.60	14.40	16.20
1900.....	.95	1.90	2.85	3.80	5.70	7.60	9.50	11.40	13.30	15.20	17.10
2000.....	1.00	2.00	3.00	4.00	6.00	8.00	10.00	12.00	14.00	16.00	18.00
2100.....	1.05	2.10	3.15	4.20	6.30	8.40	10.50	12.60	14.70	16.80	18.90
2200.....	1.10	2.20	3.30	4.40	6.60	8.80	11.00	13.20	15.40	17.60	19.80
2300.....	1.15	2.30	3.45	4.60	6.90	9.20	11.50	13.80	16.10	18.40	20.70
2400.....	1.20	2.40	3.60	4.80	7.20	9.60	12.00	14.40	16.80	1[illegible] 20	21.60
2500.....	1.25	2.50	3.75	5.00	7.50	10.00	12.50	15.00	17.50	[illegible]	22.50
2600.....	1.30	[illegible]60	3.90	5.20	7.80	10.40	13.00	15.60	18.20	2[illegible].30	23.40
2700.....	1.35	2.[illegible]0	4.05	5.40	8.10	10.80	13 50	16.20	18.90	21.60	24.30
2800.....	1.40	2.80	4.20	5.60	8.40	11.20	14.00	16.80	19.60	22.40	25.20
2900.....	1.45	2.90	4.35	5.80	8.70	11.60	14.50	17.40	20.30	23.20	26.10
3000.....	1.50	3.00	4.50	6.00	9.00	12.00	15.00	18.00	21.00	24.00	27.00
3100.....	1.55	3.10	4.65	6.20	9.30	12.40	15.50	18.60	21.70	24.80	27.90
3200.....	1.60	3.20	4.80	6.40	9.60	12.80	16.00	19.20	22.40	25.60	28.80
3300.....	1.65	3.30	4.95	6.60	9.90	13.20	16.50	19.80	23.10	26.40	29.70
3400.....	1.70	3 40	5.10	6.80	10.20	13 60	17.00	20.40	23.80	27.20	30.60
3500.....	1.75	3.50	5.25	7.00	10.50	14.00	17.50	21.00	24.50	28.00	31.50
3600.....	1.80	3.60	5.40	7.20	10.80	14.40	18.00	21.60	25.20	28.80	32.40
3700.....	1.85	3.70	5.55	7.40	11.10	14.80	18.50	22.20	25.90	29.60	33.30
3800.....	1.90	3.80	5.70	7.60	11.40	15.20	19.00	22.80	26.60	30.40	34.20
3900.....	1.95	3.90	5.85	7.80	11.70	15.60	19.50	23.40	27.30	31.20	35.10
4000.....	2.00	4.00	6.00	8.00	12.00	16.00	20.00	24.00	28.00	32.00	36.00

HOG AND CATTLE TABLE.

The first column gives the number of pounds, and the top of each column the price per hundred weight.

Weight	$1.00	$2.00	$3.00	$4.00	$5.00	$6.00	$7.00	$8.00	$9.00	$10	$20
3...	.03	.06	.09	.12	.15	.18	.21	.24	.27	.30	.60
5...	.05	.10	.15	.20	.25	.30	.35	.40	.45	.50	1.00
10...	.10	.20	.30	.40	.50	.60	.70	.80	.90	1.00	2.00
15...	.15	.30	.45	.60	.75	.90	1.05	1.20	1.35	1.50	3.00
20...	.20	.40	.60	.80	1.00	1.20	1.40	1.60	1.80	2.00	4.00
25...	.25	.50	.75	1.00	1.25	1.50	1.75	2.00	2.25	2.50	5.00
30...	.30	.60	.90	1.20	1.50	1.80	2.10	2.40	2.70	3.00	6.00
35...	.35	.70	1.05	1.40	1.75	2.10	2.45	2.80	3.15	3.50	7.00
40...	.40	.80	1.20	1.60	2.00	2.40	2.80	3.20	3.60	4.00	8.00
45...	.45	.90	1.35	1.80	2.25	2.70	3.15	3.60	4.05	4.50	9.00
50...	.50	1.00	1.50	2.00	2.50	3.00	3.50	4.00	4.50	5.00	10.00
55...	.55	1.10	1.65	2.20	2.75	3.30	3.85	4.40	4.95	5.50	11.00
60...	.60	1.20	1.80	2.40	3.00	3.60	4.20	4.80	5.40	6.00	12.00
65...	.65	1.30	1.95	2.60	3.25	3.90	4.55	5.20	5.85	6.50	13.00
70...	.70	1.40	2.10	2.80	3.50	4.20	4.90	5.60	6.30	7.00	14.00
75...	.75	1.50	2.25	3.00	3.75	4.50	5.25	6.00	6.75	7.50	15.00
80...	.80	1.60	2.40	3.20	4.00	4.80	5.60	6.40	7.20	8.00	16.00
85...	.85	1.70	2.55	3.40	4.25	5.10	5.95	6.80	7.65	8.50	17.00
90...	.90	1.80	2.70	3.60	4.50	5.40	6.30	7.20	8.10	9.00	18.00
95...	.95	1.90	2.85	3.80	4.75	5.70	6.65	7.60	8.55	9.50	19.00
100...	1.00	2.00	3.00	4.00	5.00	6.00	7.00	8.00	9.00	10.00	20.00
200...	2.00	4.00	6.00	8.00	10.00	12.00	14.00	16.00	18.00	20.00	40.00
300...	3.00	6.00	9.00	12.00	15.00	18.00	21.00	24.00	27.00	30.00	60.00
400...	4.00	8.00	12.00	16.00	20.00	24.00	28.00	32.00	36.00	40.00	80.00
500...	5.00	10.00	15.00	20.00	25.00	30.00	35.00	40.00	45.00	50.00	100.00
600...	6.00	12.00	18.00	24.00	30.00	36.00	42.00	48.00	54.00	60.00	120.00
700...	7.00	14.00	21.00	28.00	35.00	42.00	49.00	56.00	63.00	70.00	140.00
800...	8.00	16.00	24.00	32.00	40.00	48.00	56.00	64.00	72.00	80.00	160.00
900...	9.00	18.00	27.00	36.00	45.00	54.00	63.00	72.00	81.00	90.00	180.00
1000...	10.00	20.00	30.00	40.00	50.00	60.00	70.00	80.00	90.00	100.00	200.00
1100...	11.00	22.00	33.00	44.00	55.00	66.00	77.00	88.00	99.00	110.00	220.00
1200...	12.00	24.00	36.00	48.00	60.00	72.00	84.00	96.00	108.00	120.00	240.00
1300...	13.00	26.00	39.00	52.00	65.00	78.00	91.00	104.00	117.00	130.00	260.00
1400...	14.00	28.00	42.00	56.00	70.00	84.00	98.00	112.00	126.00	140.00	280.00
1500...	15.00	30.00	45.00	60.00	75.00	90.00	105.00	120.00	135.00	150.00	300.00
1600...	16.00	32.00	48.00	64.00	80.00	96.00	112.00	128.00	144.00	160.00	320.00
1700...	17.00	34.00	51.00	68.00	85.00	102.00	119.00	136.00	153.00	170.00	340.00
1800...	18.00	36.00	54.00	72.00	90.00	108.00	126.00	144.00	162.00	180.00	360.00
1900...	19.00	38.00	57.00	76.00	95.00	114.00	133.00	152.00	171.00	190.00	380.00
2000...	20.00	40.00	60.00	80.00	100.00	120.00	140.00	160.00	180.00	200.00	400.00
2100...	21.00	42.00	63.00	84.00	105.00	126.00	147.00	168.00	189.00	210.00	420.00
2200...	22.00	44.00	66.00	88.00	110.00	132.00	154.00	176.00	198.00	220.00	440.00
2300...	23.00	46.00	69.00	92.00	115.00	138.00	161.00	184.00	207.00	230.00	460.00
2400...	24.00	48.00	72.00	96.00	120.00	144.00	168.00	192.00	216.00	240.00	480.00
2500...	25.00	50.00	75.00	100.00	125.00	150.00	175.00	200.00	225.00	250.00	500.00
2600...	26.00	52.00	78.00	104.00	130.00	156.00	182.00	208.00	234.00	260.00	520.00
2700...	27.00	54.00	81.00	108.00	135.00	162.00	189.00	216.00	243.00	270.00	540.00
2800...	28.00	56.00	84.00	112.00	140.00	168.00	196.00	224.00	252.00	280.00	560.00
2900...	29.00	58.00	87.00	116.00	145.00	174.00	203.00	232.00	261.00	290.00	580.00
3000...	30.00	60.00	90.00	120.00	150.00	180.00	210.00	240.00	270.00	300.00	600.00
3100...	31.00	62.00	93.00	124.00	155.00	186.00	217.00	248.00	279.00	310.00	620.00
3200...	32.00	64.00	96.00	128.00	160.00	192.00	224.00	256.00	288.00	320.00	640.00
3300...	33.00	66.00	99.00	132.00	165.00	198.00	231.00	264.00	297.00	330.00	660.00
3400...	34.00	68.00	102.00	136.00	170.00	204.00	238.00	272.00	306.00	340.00	680.00
3500...	35.00	70.00	105.00	140.00	175.00	210.00	245.00	280.00	315.00	350.00	700.00
3600...	36.00	72.00	108.00	144.00	180.00	216.00	252.00	288.00	324.00	360.00	720.00
3700...	37.00	74.00	111.00	148.00	185.00	222.00	259.00	296.00	333.00	370.00	740.00
3800...	38.00	76.00	114.00	152.00	190.00	228.00	266.00	304.00	342.00	380.00	760.00
3900...	39.00	78.00	117.00	156.00	195.00	234.00	273.00	312.00	351.00	390.00	780.00
4000...	40.00	80.00	120.00	160.00	200.00	240.00	280.00	320.00	360.00	400.00	800.00

READY RECKONER.

How to Find the Price of any Number of Pounds, Yards, Pieces or Bushels.

The first column gives the NUMBER—the top columns the PRICES.

Nos.	¼c.	½c.	¾c.	2c.	3c.	4c.	5c.	6c.	6¼c.	6⅔c.	7c.	8c.	8⅓c.	9c.	10c.	11c.
2	½	.01	.01½	.04	.06	.08	.10	.12	.12½	.13⅓	.14	.16	.16⅔	.18	.20	.22
3	¾	.01½	.02¼	.06	.09	.12	.15	.18	.18¾	.20	.21	.24	.25	.27	.30	.33
4	.01	.02	.03	.08	.12	.16	.20	.24	.25	.26⅔	.28	.32	.33⅓	.36	.40	.44
5	.01¼	.02½	.03¾	.10	.15	.20	.25	.30	.31¼	.33⅓	.35	.40	.41⅔	.45	.50	.55
6	.01½	.03	.04½	.12	.18	.24	.30	.36	.37½	.40	.42	.48	.50	.54	.60	.66
7	.01¾	.03½	.05¼	.14	.21	.28	.35	.42	.43¾	.46⅔	.49	.56	.58⅓	.63	.70	.77
8	.02	.04	.06	.16	.24	.32	.40	.48	.50	.53⅓	.56	.64	.66⅔	.72	.80	.88
9	.02¼	.04½	.06¾	.18	.27	.36	.45	.54	.56¼	.60	.63	.72	.75	.81	.90	.99
10	.02½	.05	.07½	.20	.30	.40	.50	.60	.62½	.66⅔	.70	.80	.83⅓	.90	1.00	1.10
11	.02¾	.05½	.08¼	.22	.33	.44	.55	.66	.68¾	.73⅓	.77	.88	.91⅔	.99	1.10	1.21
12	.03	.06	.09	.24	.36	.48	.60	.72	.75	.80	.84	.96	1.00	1.08	1.20	1.32
13	.03¼	.06½	.09¾	.26	.39	.52	.65	.78	.81¼	.86⅔	.91	1.04	1.08⅓	1.17	1.30	1.43
14	.03½	.07	.10½	.28	.42	.56	.70	.84	.87½	.93⅓	.98	1.12	1.16⅔	1.26	1.40	1.54
15	.03¾	.07½	.11¼	.30	.45	.60	.75	.90	.93¾	1.00	1.05	1.20	1.25	1.35	1.50	1.65
16	.04	.08	.12	.32	.48	.64	.80	.96	1.00	1.06⅔	1.12	1.28	1.33⅓	1.44	1.60	1.76
17	.04¼	.08½	.12¾	.34	.51	.68	.85	1.02	1.06¼	1.13⅓	1.19	1.36	1.41⅔	1.53	1.70	1.87
18	.04½	.09	.13½	.36	.54	.72	.90	1.08	1.12½	1.20	1.26	1.44	1.50	1.62	1.80	1.98
19	.04¾	.09½	.14¼	.38	.57	.76	.95	1.14	1.18¾	1.26⅔	1.33	1.52	1.58⅓	1.71	1.90	2.09
20	.05	.10	.15	.40	.60	.80	1.00	1.20	1.25	1.33⅓	1.40	1.60	1.66⅔	1.80	2.00	2.20
21	.05¼	.10½	.15¾	.42	.63	.84	1.05	1.26	1.31¼	1.40	1.47	1.68	1.75	1.89	2.10	2.31
22	.05½	.11	.16½	.44	.66	.88	1.10	1.32	1.37½	1.46⅔	1.54	1.76	1.83⅓	1.98	2.20	2.42
23	.05¾	.11½	.17¼	.46	.69	.92	1.15	1.38	1.43¾	1.53⅓	1.61	1.84	1.91⅔	2.07	2.30	2.53
24	.06	.12	.18	.48	.72	.96	1.20	1.41	1.50	1.60	1.68	1.92	2.00	2.16	2.40	2.64
25	.06¼	.12½	.18¾	.50	.75	1.00	1.25	1.50	1.56¼	1.66⅔	1.75	2.00	2.08⅓	2.25	2.50	2.75
26	.06½	.13	.19½	.52	.78	1.04	1.30	1.56	1.62½	1.73⅓	1.82	2.08	2.16⅔	2.34	2.60	2.86
27	.06¾	.13½	.20¼	.54	.81	1.08	1.35	1.62	1.68¾	1.80	1.89	2.16	2.25	2.43	2.70	2.97
28	.07	.14	.21	.56	.84	1.12	1.40	1.68	1.75	1.86⅔	1.96	2.24	2.33⅓	2.52	2.80	3.08
29	.07¼	.14½	.21¾	.58	.87	1.16	1.45	1.74	1.81¼	1.93⅓	2.03	2.32	2.41⅔	2.61	2.90	3.19
30	.07½	.15	.22½	.60	.90	1.20	1.50	1.80	1.87½	2.00	2.10	2.40	2.50	2.70	3.00	3.30
31	.07¾	.15½	.23¼	.62	.93	1.24	1.55	1.86	1.93¾	2.06⅔	2.17	2.48	2.58⅓	2.79	3.10	3.41
32	.08	.16	.24	.64	.96	1.28	1.60	1.92	2.00	2.13⅓	2.24	2.56	2.66⅔	2.88	3.20	3.52
33	.08¼	.16½	.24¾	.66	.99	1.32	1.65	1.98	2.06¼	2.20	2.31	2.64	2.75	2.97	3.30	3.63
34	.08½	.17	.25½	.68	1.02	1.36	1.70	2.04	2.12½	2.26⅔	2.38	2.72	2.83⅓	3.06	3.40	3.74
35	.08¾	.17½	.26¼	.70	1.05	1.40	1.75	2.10	2.18¾	2.33⅓	2.45	2.80	2.91⅔	3.15	3.50	3.85
36	.09	.18	.27	.72	1.08	1.44	1.80	2.16	2.25	2.40	2.52	2.88	3.00	3.24	3.60	3.96
37	.09¼	.18½	.27¾	.74	1.11	1.48	1.85	2.22	2.31¼	2.46⅔	2.59	2.96	3.08⅓	3.33	3.70	4.07
38	.09½	.19	.28½	.76	1.14	1.52	1.90	2.28	2.37½	2.53⅓	2.66	3.04	3.16⅔	3.42	3.80	4.18
39	.09¾	.19½	.29¼	.78	1.17	1.56	1.95	2.34	2.43¾	2.60	2.73	3.12	3.25	3.51	3.90	4.29
40	.10	.20	.30	.80	1.20	1.60	2.00	2.40	2.50	2.66⅔	2.80	3.20	3.33⅓	3.60	4.00	4.40
41	.10¼	.20½	.30¾	.82	1.23	1.64	2.05	2.46	2.56¼	2.73⅓	2.87	3.28	3.41⅔	3.69	4.10	4.51
42	.10½	.21	.31½	.84	1.26	1.68	2.10	2.52	2.62½	2.80	2.94	3.36	3.50	3.78	4.20	4.62
43	.10¾	.21½	.32¼	.86	1.29	1.72	2.15	2.58	2.68¾	2.86⅔	3.01	3.44	3.58⅓	3.87	4.30	4.73
44	.11	.22	.33	.88	1.32	1.76	2.20	2.64	2.75	2.93⅓	3.08	3.52	3.66⅔	3.96	4.40	4.84
45	.11¼	.22½	.33¾	.90	1.35	1.80	2.25	2.70	2.81¼	3.00	3.15	3.60	3.75	4.05	4.50	4.95
46	.11½	.23	.34½	.92	1.38	1.84	2.30	2.76	2.87½	3.06⅔	3.22	3.68	3.83⅓	4.14	4.60	5.06
47	.11¾	.23½	.35¼	.94	1.41	1.88	2.35	2.82	2.93¾	3.13⅓	3.29	3.76	3.91⅔	4.23	4.70	5.17
48	.12	.24	.36	.96	1.44	1.92	2.40	2.88	3.00	3.20	3.36	3.84	4.00	4.32	4.80	5.28
49	.12¼	.24½	.36¾	.98	1.47	1.96	2.45	2.94	3.06¼	3.26⅔	3.43	3.92	4.08⅓	4.41	4.90	5.39
50	.12½	.25	.37½	1.00	1.50	2.00	2.50	3.00	3.12½	3.33⅓	3.50	4.00	4.16⅔	4.50	5.00	5.50
60	.15	.30	.45	1.20	1.80	2.40	3.00	3.60	3.75	4.00	4.20	4.80	5.00	5.40	6.00	6.60
70	.17½	.35	.52½	1.40	2.10	2.80	3.50	4.20	4.37½	4.66⅔	4.90	5.60	5.83⅓	6.30	7.00	7.70
80	.20	.40	.60	1.60	2.40	3.20	4.00	4.80	5.00	5.33⅓	5.60	6.40	6.66⅔	7.20	8.00	8.80
90	.22½	.45	.67½	1.80	2.70	3.60	4.50	5.40	5.62½	6.00	6.30	7.20	7.50	8.10	9.00	9.90
100	.25	.50	.75	2.00	3.00	4.00	5.00	6.00	6.25	6.66⅔	7.00	8.00	8.33⅓	9.00	10.00	11.00

READY RECKONER—Continued.

The first column gives the NUMBER—the top columns the PRICES.

Nos.	12c.	12½c.	13c.	14c.	15c.	16c.	16⅔c.	17c.	18c.	18¾c.	19c.	20c.	21c.
2	.24	.25	.26	.28	.30	.32	.33⅓	.34	.36	.37½	.38	.40	.42
3	.36	.37½	.39	.42	.45	.48	.50	.51	.54	.56¼	.57	.60	.63
4	.48	.50	.52	.56	.60	.64	.66⅔	.68	.72	.75	.76	.80	.84
5	.60	.62½	.65	.70	.75	.80	.83⅓	.85	.90	.93¾	.95	1.00	1.05
6	.72	.75	.78	.84	.90	.96	1.00	1.02	1.08	1.12½	1.14	1.20	1.26
7	.84	.87½	.91	.98	1.05	1.12	1.16⅔	1.19	1.26	1.31¼	1.33	1.40	1.47
8	.96	1.00	1.04	1.12	1.20	1.28	1.33⅓	1.36	1.44	1.50	1.52	1.60	1.68
9	1.08	1.12½	1.17	1.26	1.35	1.44	1.50	1.53	1.62	1.68¾	1.71	1.80	1.89
10	1.20	1.25	1.30	1.40	1.50	1.60	1.66⅔	1.70	1.80	1.87½	1.90	2.00	2.10
11	1.32	1.37½	1.43	1.54	1.65	1.76	1.83⅓	1.87	1.98	2.06¼	2.09	2.20	2.31
12	1.44	1.50	1.56	1.68	1.80	1.92	2.00	2.04	2.16	2.25	2.28	2.40	2.52
13	1.56	1.62½	1.69	1.82	1.95	2.08	2.16⅔	2.21	2.34	2.43¾	2.47	2.60	2.73
14	1.68	1.75	1.82	1.96	2.10	2.24	2.33⅓	2.38	2.52	2.62½	2.66	2.80	2.94
15	1.80	1.87½	1.95	2.10	2.25	2.40	2.50	2.55	2.70	2.81¼	2.85	3.00	3.15
16	1.92	2.00	2.08	2.24	2.40	2.56	2.66⅔	2.72	2.88	3.00	3.04	3.20	3.36
17	2.04	2.12½	2.21	2.38	2.55	2.72	2.83⅓	2.89	3.06	3.18¾	3.23	3.40	3.57
18	2.16	2.25	2.34	2.52	2.70	2.88	3.00	3.06	3.24	3.37½	3.42	3.60	3.7
19	2.28	2.37½	2.47	2.66	2.85	3.04	3.16⅔	3.23	3.42	3.56¼	3.61	3.80	3.9
20	2.40	2.50	2.60	2.80	3.00	3.20	3.33⅓	3.40	3.60	3.75	3.80	4.00	4.20
21	2.52	2.62½	2.73	2.94	3.15	3.36	3.50	3.57	3.78	3.93¾	3.99	4.20	4.41
22	2.64	2.75	2.86	3.08	3.30	3.52	3.66⅔	3.74	3.96	4.12½	4.18	4.40	4.62
23	2.76	2.87½	2.99	3.22	3.45	3.68	3.83⅓	3.91	4.14	4.31¼	4.37	4.60	4.83
24	2.88	3.00	3.12	3.36	3.60	3.84	4.00	4.08	4.32	4.50	4.56	4.80	5.04
25	3.00	3.12½	3.25	3.50	3.75	4.00	4.16⅔	4.25	4.50	4.68¾	4.75	5.00	5.25
26	3.12	3.25	3.38	3.64	3.90	4.16	4.33⅓	4.42	4.68	4.87½	4.94	5.20	5.46
27	3.24	3.37½	3.51	3.78	4.05	4.32	4.50	4.59	4.86	5.06¼	5.13	5.40	5.67
28	3.36	3.50	3.64	3.92	4.20	4.48	4.66⅔	4.76	5.04	5.25	5.32	5.60	5.88
29	3.48	3.62½	3.77	4.06	4.35	4.64	4.83⅓	4.93	5.22	5.43¾	5.51	5.80	6.09
30	3.60	3.75	3.90	4.20	4.50	4.80	5.00	5.10	5.40	5.62½	5.70	6.00	6.30
31	3.72	3.87½	4.03	4.34	4.65	4.96	5.16⅔	5.27	5.58	5.81¼	5.89	6.20	6.51
32	3.84	4.00	4.16	4.48	4.80	5.12	5.33⅓	5.44	5.76	6.00	6.08	6.40	6.72
33	3.96	4.12½	4.29	4.62	4.95	5.28	5.50	5.61	5.94	6.18¾	6.27	6.60	6.93
34	.08	4.25	4.42	4.76	5.10	5.44	5.66⅔	5.78	6.12	6.37½	6.46	6.80	7.14
35	4.20	4.37½	4.55	4.90	5.25	5.60	5.83⅓	5.95	6.30	6.56¼	6.65	7.00	7.35
36	4.32	4.50	4.68	5.04	5.40	5.76	6.00	6.12	6.48	6.75	6.84	7.20	7.56
37	4.44	4.62½	4.81	5.18	5.55	5.92	6.16⅔	6.29	6.66	6.93¾	7.03	7.40	7.77
38	4.56	4.75	4.94	5.32	5.70	6.08	6.33⅓	6.46	6.84	7.12½	7.22	7.60	7.98
39	4.68	4.87½	5.07	5.46	5.85	6.24	6.50	6.58	7.02	7.31¼	7.41	7.80	8.19
40	4.80	5.00	5.20	5.60	6.00	6.40	6.66⅔	6.80	7.20	7.50	7.60	8.00	8.40
41	4.92	5.12½	5.33	5.74	6.15	6.56	6.83⅓	6.97	7.38	7.68¾	7.79	8.20	8.61
42	5.04	5.25	5.46	5.88	6.30	6.72	7.00	7.14	7.56	7.87½	7.98	8.40	8.82
43	5.16	5.37½	5.59	6.02	6.45	6.88	7.16⅔	7.31	7.74	8.06¼	8.17	8.60	9.03
44	5.28	5.50	5.72	6.16	6.60	7.04	7.33⅓	7.48	7.92	8.25	8.36	8.80	9.24
45	5.40	5.62½	5.85	6.30	6.75	7.20	7.50	7.65	8.10	8.43¾	8.55	9.00	9.45
46	5.52	5.75	5.98	6.44	6.90	7.36	7.66⅔	7.82	8.28	8.62½	8.74	9.20	9.66
47	5.64	5.87½	6.11	6.58	7.05	7.52	7.83⅓	7.99	8.46	8.81¼	8.93	9.40	9.87
48	5.76	6.00	6.24	6.72	7.20	7.68	8.00	8.16	8.64	9.00	9.12	9.60	10.08
49	5.88	6.12½	6.37	6.86	7.35	7.84	8.16⅔	8.33	8.82	9.18¾	9.31	9.80	10.29
50	6.00	6.25	6.50	7.00	7.50	8.00	8.33⅓	8.50	9.00	9.37½	9.50	10.00	10.50
60	7.20	7.50	7.80	8.40	9.00	9.60	10.00	10.20	10.80	11.25	11.40	12.00	12.60
70	8.40	8.75	9.10	9.80	10.50	11.20	11.66⅔	11.90	12.6	13.12½	13.30	14.00	14 70
80	9.60	10.00	10.40	11.20	12.00	12.80	13.33⅓	13.60	14. 0	15.00	15.20	16.00	16.80
90	10.80	11.25	11.70	12.60	13.50	14.40	15.00	15.30	16.20	16.87½	17.10	18.00	18.9
100	12.00	12.50	13.00	14.00	15.00	16.00	16.66⅔	17.00	18.00	18.7	19.00	20.00	21.00

READY RECKONER—Continued.

The first column gives the NUMBER—the top columns the PRICES.

Nos.	22c.	23c.	24c.	25c	26c.	27c.	28c.	29c.	30c.	31c.	32c.	33c.	33⅓c.	34c.
2	.44	.46	.48	.50	.52	.54	.56	.58	.60	.62	.64	.66	.66⅔	.68
3	.66	.69	.72	.75	.78	.81	.84	.87	.90	.93	.96	.99	1.00	1.02
4	.88	.92	.96	1.00	1.04	1.08	1.12	1.16	1.20	1.24	1.28	1.32	1.33⅓	1.36
5	1.10	1.15	1.20	1.25	1.30	1.35	1.40	1.45	1.50	1.55	1.60	1.65	1.66⅔	1.70
6	1.32	1.38	1.44	1.50	1.56	1.62	1.68	1.74	1.80	1.86	1.92	1.98	2.00	2.04
7	1.54	1.61	1.68	1.75	1.82	1.89	1.96	2.03	2.10	2.17	2.24	2.31	2.33⅓	2.38
8	1.76	1.84	1.92	2.00	2.08	2.16	2.24	2.32	2.40	2.48	2.56	2.64	2 66⅔	2.72
9	1.98	2.07	2.16	2.25	2.34	2.43	2.52	2.61	2.70	2.79	2.88	2.97	3.00	3.06
10	2.20	2.30	2.40	2.50	2.60	2.70	2.80	2.90	3.00	3.10	3.20	3.30	3.33⅓	3.40
11	2.42	2.53	2.64	2.75	2.86	2.97	3.08	3.19	3.30	3.41	3.52	3.63	3.66⅔	3.74
12	2.64	2.76	2.88	3.00	3.12	3.24	3.36	3.48	3.60	3.72	3.84	3.96	4.00	4.08
13	2.86	2.99	3.12	3.25	3.38	3.51	3.64	3.77	3.90	4.03	4.16	4.29	4.33⅓	4.42
14	3.08	3.22	3.36	3.50	3.64	3.78	3.92	4.06	4.20	4.34	4.48	4.62	4.66⅔	4.76
15	3.30	3.45	3.60	3.75	3.90	4.05	4.20	4.35	4.50	4.65	4.80	4.95	5.00	5.10
16	3.52	3.68	3.84	4.00	4.16	4.32	4.48	4.64	4.80	4.96	5.12	5.28	5.33⅓	5.44
17	3.74	3.91	4.08	4.25	4.42	4.59	4.76	4.93	5.10	5.27	5.44	5.61	5.66⅔	5.78
18	3.96	4.14	4.32	4.50	4.68	4.86	5.04	5.22	5.40	5.58	5.76	5.94	6.0	6.12
19	4.18	4.37	4.56	4.75	4.94	5.13	5.32	5.51	5.70	5.89	6.08	6.27	6.3[illegible]	6.46
20	4.40	4.60	4.80	5.00	5.20	5.40	5.60	5.80	6.00	6.20	6.40	6.60	6.66⅔	6.80
21	4.62	4.83	5.04	5.25	5.46	5.67	5.88	6.09	6.30	6.51	6.72	6.93	7.00	7.14
22	4.84	5.06	5.28	5.50	5.72	5.94	6.16	6.38	6.60	6.82	7.04	7.26	7.33⅓	7.48
23	5.06	5.29	5.52	5.75	5.98	6.21	6.44	6.67	6.90	7.13	7.36	7.59	7.66⅔	7.82
24	5.28	5.52	5.76	6.00	6.24	6.48	6.72	6.96	7.20	7.44	7.68	7.92	8.00	8.16
25	5.50	5.75	6.00	6.25	6.50	6.75	7.00	7.25	7.50	7.75	8.00	8.25	8.33⅓	8.50
26	5.72	5.98	6.24	6.50	6.76	7.02	7.28	7.54	7.80	8.06	8.32	8.58	8.66⅔	8.84
27	5.94	6.21	6.48	6.75	7.02	7.29	7.56	7.83	8.10	8.37	8.64	8.91	9.00	9.18
28	6.16	6.44	6.72	7.00	7 28	7.56	7.84	8.12	8.40	8.68	8.96	9.24	9.33⅓	9 52
29	6.38	6.67	6.96	7.25	7.54	7.83	8.12	8.41	8.70	8.99	9.28	9.57	9.66⅔	9.86
30	6.60	6.90	7.20	7.50	7.80	8.10	8.40	8.70	9.00	9.30	9.60	9.90	10.00	10.20
31	6.82	7.13	7.44	7.75	8.06	8.37	8.68	8.99	9.30	9.61	9.92	10.23	10.33⅓	10.54
32	7.04	7.36	7.68	8.00	8.32	8.64	8.96	9.28	9.60	9.92	10.24	10.56	10.66⅔	10.88
33	7.26	7.59	7.92	8.25	8.58	8.91	9.24	9.57	9.90	10.23	10.56	10.89	11.00	11.22
34	7.48	7.82	8.16	8.50	8.84	9.18	9.52	9.86	10.20	10.54	10.88	11 22	11.33⅓	11.56
35	7.70	8.05	8 40	8.75	9.10	9.45	9.80	10.15	10.50	10.85	11.20	11.55	11.66⅔	11.90
36	7.92	8.28	8.64	9.00	9.36	9.72	10.08	10.44	10.80	11.16	11.52	11.88	12.00	12.24
37	8.14	8.51	8.88	9.25	9.62	9.99	10.36	10.73	11.10	11.47	11.84	12.21	12.33⅓	12.58
38	8.36	8.74	9.12	9.50	9.88	10.26	10.64	11.02	11.40	11.78	12.16	12.54	12.66⅔	12.92
39	8.58	8.97	9.36	9.75	10.14	10.53	10.92	11.31	11.70	12.09	12.48	12.87	13.00	13.26
40	8.80	9.20	9.60	10.00	10.40	10.80	11.20	11.60	12.00	12.40	12.80	13.20	13.33⅓	13.60
41	9.02	9.43	9.84	10.25	10.66	11.07	11.48	11.89	12.30	12.71	13.12	13.53	13.66⅔	13.94
42	9.24	9.66	10.08	10.50	10.92	11.34	11.76	12.18	12.60	13.02	13.44	13.86	14.00	14.28
43	9.46	9.89	10.32	10.75	11.18	11.61	12.04	12.47	12.90	13.33	13.76	14.19	14.33⅓	14.62
44	9.68	10.12	10.56	11.00	11.44	11.88	12.32	12.76	13.20	13.64	14.08	14.52	14.66⅔	14.96
45	9.90	10.35	10.80	11.25	11.70	12.15	12.60	13.05	13.50	13.95	14.40	14.85	15.00	15.30
46	10.12	10.58	11.04	11.50	11.96	12.42	12.88	13.34	13.80	14.26	14.72	15.18	15.33⅓	15.64
47	10.34	10.81	11.28	11.75	12.22	12.69	13.16	13.63	14.10	14 57	15.04	15.51	15.66⅔	15.98
48	10.56	11.04	11.52	12.00	12.48	12.96	13.44	13.92	14.40	14.88	15.36	15.84	16.00	16.32
49	10.78	11.27	11.76	12.25	12.74	13.23	13.72	14.21	14.70	15.19	15.68	16.17	16.33⅓	16.66
50	11.00	11.50	12.00	12.50	13.00	13.50	14.00	14.50	15.00	15.50	16.00	16.50	16.66⅔	17.00
60	13.20	13.80	14.40	15.00	15.60	16.20	16.80	17.40	18.00	18.60	19.20	19.80	20.00	20.40
70	15.40	16.10	16.80	17.50	18.20	18.90	19.60	20.30	21.00	21.70	22.40	23.10	23.33⅓	23.80
80	17.60	18.40	19.20	20.00	20.80	21.60	22.40	23.20	24.00	24.80	25.60	26.40	26.66⅔	27.20
90	19.80	20.70	21.60	22.50	23.40	24.30	25.20	26.10	27.00	27.90	28.80	29.70	30.00	30.60
100	22.00	23.00	24.00	25.00	26.00	27.00	28.00	29.00	30.00	31.00	32.00	33.00	33.33⅓	34.0[illegible]

READY RECKONER—Continued.

The first column gives the NUMBER—the top columns the PRICES.

Nos.	35c.	36c.	37c.	37½c.	38c.	39c.	40c.	41c.	42c.	43c.	44c.	45c.	46c.	47c.
2	.70	.72	.74	.75	.76	.78	.80	.82	.84	.86	.88	.90	.92	.94
3	1,05	1,08	1.11	1.12½	1.14	1.17	1.20	1.23	1.26	1.29	1.32	1.35	1.38	1.41
4	1.40	1.44	1.48	1.50	1.52	1.56	1.60	1.64	1.68	1.72	1.76	1.80	1.84	1.88
5	1.75	1.80	1.85	1.87½	1.90	1.95	2.00	2.05	2.10	2.15	2.20	2.25	2.30	2.35
6	2.10	2.16	2.22	2.25	2.28	2.34	2.40	2.46	2.52	2.58	2 64	2.70	2.76	2.82
7	2.45	2.52	2.59	2.62½	2.66	2.73	2.80	2.87	2.94	3.01	3.08	3.15	3.22	3.29
8	2.80	2.88	2.96	3.00	3.04	3.12	3.20	3.28	3.36	3.44	3.52	3.60	3 68	3.76
9	3.15	3.24	3.33	3.37½	3.42	3.51	3.60	3.69	3.78	3.87	3.96	4.05	4.14	4.23
10	3.50	3.60	3.70	3.75	3.80	3.90	4.00	4.10	4.20	4.30	4.40	4.50	4.60	4.70
11	3.85	3.96	4.07	4.12½	4.18	4.29	4.40	4.51	4.62	4.73	4.84	4.95	5.06	5.17
12	4.20	4.32	4.44	4.50	4.56	4.68	4.80	4.92	5.04	5.16	5.28	5.40	5.52	5.64
13	4.55	4.68	4.81	4.87½	4.94	5.07	5.20	5.33	5.46	5.59	5.72	5.85	5.98	6.11
14	4.90	5.04	5.18	5.25	5.32	5.46	5.60	5.74	5.88	6.02	6.16	6.30	6.44	6.58
15	5.25	5.40	5.55	5.62½	5.70	5.85	6.00	6.15	6.30	6.45	6.60	6.75	6.90	7.05
16	5.60	5.76	5.92	6.00	6.08	6.24	6.40	6.56	6.72	6.88	7.04	7.20	7.36	7.52
17	5.95	6.12	6.29	6.37½	6.46	6.63	6.80	6.97	7.14	7.31	7.48	7.65	7.82	7.99
18	6.30	6.48	6.66	6.75	6.84	7.02	7.20	7.38	7.56	7.74	7.92	8.10	8.28	8 46
19	6.65	6.84	7.03	7.12½	7.22	7.41	7.60	7.79	7.98	8.17	8.36	8.55	8.74	8.93
20	7.00	7.20	7.40	7.50	7.60	7.80	8.00	8.20	8.40	8.60	8.80	9.00	9.20	9.40
21	7.35	7.56	7.77	7.87½	7.98	8.19	8.40	8.61	8.82	9.03	9.24	9.45	9.66	9.87
22	7.70	7.92	8.14	8.25	8.36	8.58	8.80	9.02	9.24	9.46	9.68	9.90	10.12	10.34
23	8.05	8.28	8.51	8.62½	8.74	8.97	9.20	9.43	9.66	9.89	10.12	10.35	10.58	10.81
24	8.40	8.64	8.88	9.00	9.12	9.36	9.60	9.84	10.08	10.32	10.56	10.80	11.04	11.28
25	8.75	9.00	9.25	9.37½	9.50	9.75	10.00	10.25	10.50	10.75	11.00	11.25	11.50	11.75
26	9.10	9.36	9.62	9.75	9.88	10.14	10.40	10.66	10.92	11.18	11.44	11.70	11.96	12.22
27	9.45	9.72	9.99	10.12½	10.26	10.53	10.80	11.07	11.34	11.61	11.88	12.15	12.42	12.69
28	9.80	10.08	10.36	10.50	10.64	10.92	11.20	11.48	11.76	12.04	12.32	12.60	12.88	13.16
29	10.15	10.44	10.73	10.87½	11.02	11.31	11.60	11.89	12.18	12.47	12.76	13.05	13.34	13.63
30	10.50	10.80	11.10	11.25	11.40	11.70	12.00	12.30	12.60	12.90	13.20	13.50	13.80	14.10
31	10.85	11.16	11.47	11.62½	11.78	12.09	12.40	12.71	13.02	13.33	13.64	13.95	14.26	14.57
32	11.20	11.52	11.84	12.00	12.16	12.48	12.80	13.12	13.44	13.76	14.08	14.40	14.72	15.04
33	11.55	11.88	12.21	12.37½	12.54	12.87	13.20	13.53	13.86	14.19	14.52	14.85	15.18	15.51
34	11.90	12.24	12.58	12.75	12.92	13.26	13.60	13.94	14.28	14.62	14.96	15.30	15.64	15.98
35	12.25	12.60	12.95	13.12½	13.30	13.65	14.00	14.35	14.70	15.05	15.40	15.75	16.10	16.45
36	12.60	12.96	13.32	13.50	13.68	14.04	14.40	14.76	15.12	15.48	15.84	16.20	16.56	16.92
37	12.95	13.32	13.69	13.87½	14.06	14.43	14.80	15.17	15.54	15.91	16.28	16.65	17.02	17.39
38	13.30	13.68	14.06	14.25	14.44	14.82	15.20	15.58	15.96	16.34	16.72	17.10	17.48	17.86
39	13.65	14.04	14.43	14.62½	14.82	15.21	15.60	15.99	16.38	16.77	17.16	17.55	17.94	18.33
40	14.00	14.40	14.80	15.00	15.20	15.60	16.00	16.40	16.80	17.20	17.60	18.00	18.40	18.80
41	14.35	14.76	15.17	15.37½	15.58	15.99	16.40	16.81	17.22	17.63	18.04	18.45	18.86	19.27
42	14.70	15.12	15.54	15.75	15 96	16.38	16.80	17.22	17.64	18.06	18.48	18.90	19.32	19.74
43	15.05	15.48	15.91	16.12½	16.34	16.77	17.20	17.63	18.06	18.49	18.92	19.35	19.78	20.21
44	15.40	15.84	16.28	16.50	16.72	17.16	17.60	18.04	18.48	18.92	19.36	19.80	20.24	20.68
45	15.75	16.20	16.65	16.87½	17.10	17.55	18.00	18.45	18.90	19.35	19.80	20.25	20.70	21.15
46	16.10	16.56	17.02	17.25	17.48	17.94	18.40	18.86	19.32	19.78	20.24	20.70	21.16	21.62
47	16.45	16.92	17.39	17.62½	17.86	18.33	18.80	19.27	19.74	20.21	20.68	21.15	21.62	22.09
48	16.80	17.28	17.76	18.00	18.24	18.72	19.20	19.68	20.16	20.64	21.12	21.60	22.08	22.56
49	17.15	17.64	18.13	18.37½	18.62	19.11	19.60	20.09	20.58	21.07	21.56	22.05	22.54	23.03
50	17.50	18.00	18.50	18.75	[illegible].00	19.50	20.00	20.50	21.00	21.50	22.00	22.50	23.00	23.50
60	21.00	21.60	22.20	22.50	22.80	23.40	24.00	24.60	25.20	25.80	26.40	27.00	27.60	28.20
70	24.50	25.20	25.90	26.25	26.60	27.30	28.00	28.70	29.40	30.10	30.80	31.50	32.20	32.90
80	28.00	28.80	29.60	30.00	30.40	31.20	32.00	32.80	33.60	34.40	35.20	36.00	36.80	37.60
90	31.50	32.40	33.30	33.75	34.20	35.10	36.00	36.90	37.80	38.70	39.60	40.50	41.40	42.30
100	35.00	36.00	37.00	37.50	38.00	39.00	40.00	41.00	42.00	43.00	44.00	45.00	46.00	47.00

READY RECKONER—Continued.

The first column gives the NUMBER—the top columns the PRICES.

Nos.	48c.	49c.	50c.	51c.	52c.	53c.	54c.	55c.	60c.	62½c.	65c.	66⅔c.	70c.	75c.
2	.96	.98	1.00	1.02	1.04	1.06	1.08	1.10	1.20	1.25	1.30	1.33⅓	1.40	1.50
3	1.44	1.47	1.50	1.53	1.56	1.59	1.62	1.65	1.80	1.87½	1.95	2.00	2.10	2.25
4	1.92	1.96	2.00	2.04	2.08	2.12	2.16	2.20	2.40	2.50	2.60	2.66⅔	2.80	3.00
5	2.40	2.45	2.50	2.55	2.60	2.65	2.70	2.75	3.00	3.12½	3.25	3.33⅓	3.50	3.75
6	2.88	2.94	3.00	3.06	3.12	3.18	3.24	3.30	3.60	3.75	3.90	4.00	4.20	4.50
7	3.36	3.43	3.50	3.57	3.64	3.71	3.78	3.85	4.20	4.37½	4.55	4.66⅔	4.90	5.25
8	3.84	3.92	4.00	4.08	4.16	4.24	4.32	4.40	4.80	5.00	5.20	5.33⅓	5.60	6.00
9	4.32	4.41	4.50	4.59	4.68	4.77	4.86	4.95	5.40	5.62½	5.85	6.00	6.30	6.75
10	4.80	4.90	5.00	5.10	5.20	5.30	5.40	5.50	6.00	6.25	6.50	6.66⅔	7.00	7.50
11	5.28	5.39	5.50	5.61	5.72	5.83	5.94	6.05	6.60	6.87½	7.15	7.33⅓	7.70	8.25
12	5.76	5.88	6.00	6.12	6.24	6.36	6.48	6.60	7.20	7.50	7.80	8.00	8.40	9.00
13	6.24	6.37	6.50	6.63	6.76	6.89	7.02	7.15	7.80	8.12½	8.45	8.66⅔	9.10	9.75
14	6.72	6.86	7.00	7.14	7.28	7.42	7.56	7.70	8.40	8.75	9.10	9.33⅓	9.80	10.50
15	7.20	7.35	7.50	7.65	7.80	7.95	8.10	8.25	9.00	9.37½	9.75	10.00	10.50	11.25
16	7.68	7.84	8.00	8.16	8.32	8.48	8.64	8.80	9.60	10.00	10.40	10.66⅔	11.20	12.00
17	8.16	8.33	8.50	8.67	8.84	9.01	9.18	9.35	10.20	10.62½	11.05	11.33⅓	11.90	12.75
18	8.64	8.82	9.00	9.18	9.36	9.54	9.72	9.90	10.80	11.25	11.70	12.00	12.60	13.50
19	9.12	9.31	9.50	9.69	9.88	10.07	10.26	10.45	11.40	11.87½	12.35	12.66⅔	13.30	14.25
20	9.60	9.80	10.00	10.20	10.40	10.60	10.80	11.00	12.00	12.50	13.00	13.33⅓	14.00	15.00
21	10.08	10.29	10.50	10.71	10.92	11.13	11.34	11.55	12.60	13.12½	13.65	14.00	14.70	15.75
22	10.56	10.78	11.00	11.22	11.44	11.66	11.88	12.10	13.20	13.75	14.30	14.66⅔	15.40	16.50
23	11.04	11.27	11.50	11.73	11.96	12.19	12.42	12.65	13.80	14.37½	14.95	15.33⅓	16.10	17.25
24	11.52	11.76	12.00	12.24	12.48	12.72	12.96	13.20	14.40	15.00	15.60	16.00	16.80	18.00
25	12.00	12.25	12.50	12.75	13.00	13.25	13.50	13.75	15.00	15.62½	16.25	16.66⅔	17.50	18.75
26	12.48	12.74	13.00	13.26	13.52	13.78	14.04	14.30	15.60	16.25	16.90	17.33⅓	18.20	19.50
27	12.96	13.23	13.50	13.77	14.04	14.31	14.58	14.85	16.20	16.87½	17.55	18.00	18.90	20.25
28	13.44	13.72	14.00	14.28	14.56	14.84	15.12	15.40	16.80	17.50	18.20	18.66⅔	19.60	21.00
29	13.92	14.21	14.50	14.79	15.08	15.37	15.66	15.95	17.40	18.12½	18.85	19.33⅓	20.30	21.75
30	14.40	14.70	15.00	15.30	15.60	15.90	16.20	16.50	18.00	18.75	19.50	20.00	21.00	22.50
31	14.88	15.19	15.50	15.81	16.12	16.43	16.74	17.05	18.60	19.37½	20.15	20.66⅔	21.70	23.25
32	15.36	15.68	16.00	16.32	16.64	16.96	17.28	17.60	19.20	20.00	20.80	21.33⅓	22.40	24.00
33	15.84	16.17	16.50	16.83	17.16	17.49	17.82	18.15	19.80	20.62½	21.45	22.00	23.10	24.75
34	16.32	16.66	17.00	17.34	17.68	18.02	18.36	18.70	20.40	21.25	22.10	22.66⅔	23.80	25.50
35	16.80	17.15	17.50	17.85	18.20	18.55	18.90	19.25	21.00	21.87½	22.75	23.33⅓	24.50	26.25
36	17.28	17.64	18.00	18.36	18.72	19.08	19.44	19.80	21.60	22.50	23.40	24.00	25.20	27.00
37	17.76	18.13	18.50	18.87	19.24	19.61	19.98	20.35	22.20	23.12½	24.05	24.66⅔	25.90	27.75
38	18.24	18.62	19.00	19.38	19.76	20.14	20.52	20.90	22.80	23.75	24.70	25.33⅓	26.60	28.50
39	18.72	19.11	19.50	19.89	20.28	20.67	21.06	21.45	23.40	24.37½	25.35	26.00	27.30	29.25
40	19.20	19.60	20.00	20.40	20.80	21.20	21.60	22.00	24.00	25.00	26.00	26.66⅔	28.00	30.00
41	19.68	20.09	20.50	20.91	21.32	21.73	22.14	22.55	24.60	25.62½	26.65	27.33⅓	28.70	30.75
42	20.16	20.58	21.00	21.42	21.84	22.26	22.68	23.10	25.20	26.25	27.30	28.00	29.40	31.50
43	20.64	21.07	21.50	21.93	22.36	22.79	23.22	23.65	25.80	26.87½	27.95	28.66⅔	30.10	32.25
44	21.12	21.56	22.00	22.44	22.88	23.32	23.76	24.20	26.40	27.50	28.60	29.33⅓	30.80	33.00
45	21.60	22.05	22.50	22.95	23.40	23.85	24.30	24.75	27.00	28.12½	29.25	30.00	31.50	33.75
46	22.08	22.54	23.00	23.46	23.92	24.38	24.84	25.30	27.60	28.75	29.90	30.66⅔	32.20	34.50
47	22.56	23.03	23.50	23.97	24.44	24.91	25.38	25.85	28.20	29.37½	30.55	31.33⅓	32.90	35.25
48	23.04	23.52	24.00	24.48	24.96	25.44	25.92	26.40	28.80	30.00	31.20	32.00	33.60	36.00
49	23.52	24.01	24.50	24.99	25.48	25.97	26.46	26.95	29.40	30.62½	31.85	32.66⅔	34.30	36.75
50	24.00	24.50	25.00	25.50	26.00	26.50	27.00	27.50	30.00	31.25	32.50	33.33⅓	35.00	37.50
60	28.80	29.40	30.00	30.60	31.20	31.80	32.40	33.00	36.00	37.50	39.00	40.00	42.00	45.00
70	33.60	34.30	35.00	35.70	36.40	37.10	37.80	38.50	42.00	43.75	45.50	46.66⅔	49.00	52.50
80	38.40	39.20	40.00	40.80	41.60	42.40	43.20	44.00	48.00	50.00	52.00	53.33⅓	56.00	60.00
90	43.20	44.10	45.00	45.90	46.80	47.70	48.60	49.50	54.00	56.25	58.50	60.00	63.00	67.50
100	48.00	49.00	50.00	51.00	52.00	53.00	54.00	55.00	60.00	62.50	65.00	66.66⅔	70.00	75.00

READY RECKONER—Continued.

The first column gives the NUMBER—the top columns the PRICES.

Nos.	80c.	85c.	87½c.	90c.	95c.	1.00	1.50	2.00	3.00	4.00	5.00	10.00
2	1.60	1.70	1.75	1.80	1.90	2.00	3.00	4.00	6.00	8.00	10.00	20.00
3	2.40	2.55	2.62½	2.70	2.85	3.00	4.50	6.00	9.00	12.00	15.00	30.00
4	3.20	3.40	3.50	3.60	3.80	4.00	6.00	8.00	12.00	16.00	20.00	40.00
5	4.00	4.25	4.37½	4.50	4.75	5.00	7.50	10.00	15.00	20.00	25.00	50.00
6	4.80	5.10	5.25	5.40	5.70	6.00	9.00	12.00	18.00	24.00	30.00	60.00
7	5.60	5.95	6.12½	6.30	6.65	7.00	10.50	14.00	21.00	28.00	35.00	70.00
8	6.40	6.80	7.00	7.20	7.60	8.00	12.00	16.00	24.00	32.00	40.00	80.00
9	7.20	7.65	7.87½	8.10	8.55	9.00	13.50	18.00	27.00	36.00	45.00	90.00
10	8.00	8.50	8.75	9.00	9.50	10.00	15.00	20.00	30.00	40.00	50.00	100.00
11	8.80	9.35	9.62½	9.90	10.45	11.00	16.50	22.00	33.00	44.00	55.00	110.00
12	9.60	10.20	10.50	10.80	11.40	12.00	18.00	24.00	36.00	48.00	60.00	120.00
13	10.40	11.05	11.37½	11.70	12.35	13.00	19.50	26.00	39.00	52.00	65.00	130.00
14	11.20	11.90	12.25	12.60	13.30	14.00	21.00	28.00	42.00	56.00	70.00	140.00
15	12.00	12.75	13.12½	13.50	14.25	15.00	22.50	30.00	45.00	60.00	75.00	150.00
16	12.80	13.60	14.00	14.40	15.20	16.00	24.00	32.00	48.00	64.00	80.00	160.00
17	13.60	14.45	14.87½	15.30	16.15	17.00	25.50	34.00	51.00	68.00	85.00	170.00
18	14.40	15.30	15.75	16.20	17.10	18.00	27.00	36.00	54.00	72.00	90.00	180.00
19	15.20	16.15	16.62½	17.10	18.05	19.00	28.50	38.00	57.00	76.00	95.00	190.00
20	16.00	17.00	17.50	18.00	19.00	20.00	30.00	40.00	60.00	80.00	100.00	200.00
21	16.80	17.85	18.37½	18.90	19.95	21.00	31.50	42.00	63.00	84.00	105.00	210.00
22	17.60	18.70	19.25	19.80	20.90	22.00	33.00	44.00	66.00	88.00	110.00	220.00
23	18.40	19.55	20.12½	20.70	21.85	23.00	34.50	46.00	69.00	92.00	115.00	250.00
24	19.20	20.40	21.00	21.60	22.80	24.00	36.00	48.00	72.00	96.00	120.00	240.00
25	20.00	21.25	21.87½	22.50	23.75	25.00	37.50	50.00	75.00	100.00	125.00	250.00
26	20.80	22.10	22.75	23.40	24.70	26.00	39.00	52.00	78.00	104.00	130.00	260.00
27	21.60	22.95	23.62½	24.30	25.65	27.00	40.50	54.00	81.00	108.00	135.00	270.00
28	22.40	23.80	24.50	25.20	26.60	28.00	42.00	56.00	84.00	112.00	140.00	280.00
29	23.20	24.65	25.37½	26.10	27.55	29.00	43.50	58.00	87.00	116.00	145.00	290.00
30	24.00	25.50	26.25	27.00	28.50	30.00	45.00	60.00	90.00	120.00	150.00	300.00
31	24.80	26.35	27.12½	27.90	29.45	31.00	46.50	62.00	93.00	124.00	155.00	310.00
32	25.60	27.20	28.00	28.80	30.40	32.00	48.00	64.00	96.00	128.00	160.00	320.00
33	26.40	28.05	28.87½	29.70	31.35	33.00	49.50	66.00	99.00	132.00	165.00	330.00
34	27.20	28.90	29.75	30.60	32.30	34.00	51.00	68.00	102.00	136.00	170.00	340.00
35	28.00	29.75	30.62½	31.50	33.25	35.00	52.50	70.00	105.00	140.00	175.00	350.00
36	28.80	30.60	31.50	32.40	34.20	36.00	54.00	72.00	108.00	144.00	180.00	360.00
37	29.60	31.45	32.37½	33.30	35.15	37.00	55.50	74.00	111.00	148.00	185.00	370.00
38	30.40	32.30	33.25	34.20	36.10	38.00	57.00	76.00	114.00	152.00	190.00	380.00
39	31.20	33.15	34.12½	35.10	37.05	39.00	58.50	78.00	117.00	156.00	195.00	390.00
40	32.00	34.00	35.00	36.00	38.00	40.00	60.00	80.00	120.00	160.00	200.00	400.00
41	32.80	34.85	35.87½	36.90	38.95	41.00	61.50	82.00	123.00	164.00	205.00	410.00
42	33.60	35.70	36.75	37.80	39.90	42.00	63.00	84.00	126.00	168.00	210.00	420.00
43	34.40	36.55	37.62½	38.70	40.85	43.00	64.50	86.00	129.00	172.00	215.00	430.00
44	35.20	37.40	38.50	39.60	41.80	44.00	66.00	88.00	132.00	176.00	220.00	440.00
45	36.00	38.25	39.37½	40.50	42.75	45.00	67.50	90.00	135.00	180.00	225.00	450.00
46	36.80	39.10	40.25	41.40	43.70	46.00	69.00	92.00	138.00	184.00	230.00	460.00
47	37.60	39.95	41.12½	42.30	44.65	47.00	70.50	94.00	141.00	188.00	235.00	470.00
48	38.40	40.80	42.00	43.20	45.60	48.00	72.00	96.00	144.00	192.00	240.00	480.00
49	39.20	41.65	42.87½	44.10	46.55	49.00	73.50	98.00	147.00	196.00	245.00	490.00
50	40.00	42.50	43.75	45.00	47.50	50.00	75.00	100.00	150.00	200.00	250.00	500.00
60	48.00	51.00	52.50	54.00	57.00	60.00	90.00	120.00	180.00	240.00	300.00	600.00
70	56.00	59.50	61.25	63.00	66.50	70.00	105.00	140.00	210.00	280.00	350.00	700.00
80	64.00	68.00	70.00	72.00	76.00	80.00	120.00	160.00	240.00	320.00	400.00	800.00
90	72.00	76.50	78.75	81.00	85.50	90.00	135.00	180.00	270.00	360.00	450.00	900.00
100	80.00	85.00	87.50	90.00	95.00	100.00	150.00	200.00	300.00	400.00	500.00	100.00

THE COST OF SMOKING.

The following figures show the expense of smoking two cigars and three cigars a day, at 5 cents each, and at 10 cents each, from the age of 20 to the end of each period of five years, up to the age of 70, 6 per cent. compound interest semi-annually being reckoned upon the money.

FROM THE AGE OF—	Two Cigars a Day at 5 Cents Each.		Three Cigars a Day at 5 Cents Each.	
	Principal.	Prin. & Int.	Principal.	Prin. & Int.
20 to 25 years	$ 182.50	$ 209.71	$ 273.75	$ 313.95
20 to 30 "	365.00	490.39	547.50	745.74
20 to 35 "	574.50	868.25	821.25	1,314.72
20 to 40 "	730.00	1,376.08	1,095.00	2,081.16
20 to 45 "	912.50	2,058.44	1,368.75	3,110.74
20 to 50 "	1,095.00	3,094.99	1,642.50	4,494.41
20 to 55 "	1,277.50	4,367.46	1,916.25	6,353.87
20 to 60 "	1,460.00	6,078.73	2,190.00	8,655.02
20 to 65 "	1,642.50	8,378.52	2,463.75	12,215.36
20 to 70 "	1,825.00	11,469.25	2,737.10	16,216.37

FROM THE AGE OF—	Two Cigars a Day at 10 Cents Each.		Three Cigars a Day at 10 Cents Each.	
	Principal.	Prin. & Int.	Principal.	Prin. & Int.
20 to 25 years	$ 365.00	$ 418.43	$ 547.50	$ 627.95
20 to 30 "	730.00	980.78	1,095.00	1,471.56
20 to 35 "	1,095.00	1,736.52	1,642.50	2,717.85
20 to 40 "	1,460.00	2,752.20	2,190.00	4,281.24
20 to 45 "	1,825.00	4,115.92	2,737.50	6,382.47
20 to 50 "	2,190.00	5,949.88	3,285.00	9,205.16
20 to 55 "	2,555.00	8,414.47	3,852.50	12,998.61
20 to 60 "	2,920.00	11,738.03	4,380.00	18,100.14
20 to 65 "	3,285.00	16,093.51	4,927.50	24,952.72
20 to 70 "	3,650.00	21,937.72	5,475.00	34,162.14

PRISONERS IN 1910.

Total Number in U. S.	136,472	New York	16,082
Whites	93,841	Pennsylvania	10,313
Negroes	41,729	Massachusetts	8,212
Other colored	902	Texas	4,412
Nativity Unknown	1,030	Illinois	7,025
Males	123,564	California	4,900
Females	12,006	Wyoming (Had the least)	287

Paupers in 1910—Alms-house paupers, 84,198. Males, 57,049; females, 27,149.

HOW WE SPEND OUR MONEY ANNUALLY.

Foreign Missions	$ 5,000,000	Flour	$ 345,000,000
Potatoes	110,000,000	Tobacco	515,000,000
Churches	125,000,000	Iron and Steel	560,000,000
Public Education	165,000,000	Meat	870,000,000
Boots and Shoes	335,000,000	Liquors	1,080,000,000

TABLES OF WEIGHTS AND MEASURES.

TROY WEIGHT.

24 grains make 1 pennyweight, 20 pennyweights make 1 ounce. By this weight gold, silver and jewels only are weighed. The ounce and pound in this are same as in Apothecaries' weight.

APOTHECARIES' WEIGHT.

20 grains make one scruple, 3 scruples make 1 drachm, 8 drachms make 1 ounce, 12 ounces make 1 pound.

AVOIRDUPOIS WEIGHT.

16 drachms make 1 ounce, 16 ounces make 1 pound, 25 pounds make 1 quarter, 4 quarters make 100-weight, 2,000 pounds make a ton.

DRY MEASURE.

2 pints make 1 quart, 8 quarts make 1 peck, 4 pecks make 1 bushel 36 bushels make 1 chaldron.

LIQUID OR WINE MEASURE.

4 gills make 1 pint, 2 pints make 1 quart, 4 quarts make 1 gallon 31½ gallons make 1 barrel, 2 barrels make 1 hogshead.

TIME MEASURE.

60 seconds make 1 minute, 60 minutes make 1 hour, 24 hours make 1 day, 7 days make 1 week, 4 weeks make 1 lunar month, 28, 29, 30 or 31 days make 1 calendar month (30 days make 1 month in computing interest), 52 weeks and 1 day, or 12 calendar months, make 1 year, 365 days, 5 hours, 48 minutes and 49 seconds make 1 solar year.

CIRCULAR MEASURE.

60 seconds make 1 minute, 60 minutes make 1 degree, 30 degrees make 1 sign 90 degrees make 1 quadrant, 4 quadrants or 360 degrees make 1 circle.

LONG MEASURE—DISTANCE.

3 barleycorns 1 inch, 12 inches 1 foot, 3 feet 1 yard, 5½ yards 1 rod, 40 rods 1 furlong, 8 furlongs 1 mile, 5,280 feet 1 mile, a knot, or nautical mile, 6,086.7 feet, or about 1.18 mile.

CLOTH MEASURE.

2¼ inches 1 nail, 4 nails 1 quarter, 4 quarters 1 yard.

MISCELLANEOUS.

3 inches 1 palm, 4 inches 1 hand, 6 inches 1 span, 18 inches 1 cubit 21.8 inches 1 Bible cubit, 2½ feet 1 military pace.

SQUARE MEASURE.

144 square inches 1 square foot, 9 square feet 1 square yard, 30¼ square yards 1 square rod, 40 square rods 1 rood, 4 roods 1 acre, or 160 square rods 1 acre, 43,560 square feet 1 acre, 100 square feet 1 square.

SURVEYOR'S MEASURE.

7.92 inches 1 link, 25 links 1 rod, 4 rods 1 chain, 10 square chains or 160 square rods 1 acre, 640 acres 1 square mile.

CUBIC MEASURE.

1,728 cubic inches 1 cubic foot, 27 cubic feet 1 cubic yard, 128 cubic feet 1 cord (wood), 40 cubic feet 1 ton (shipping), 2,150.42 cubic inches 1 standard bushel, 231 cubic inches 1 standard gallon, 1 cubic foot four-fifths of a bushel.

METRIC SYSTEM.

The unit of the Metric System is the meter 39.37 inches long, 1 kilometer= about ⅝ of a mile. The gram is the unit of weight, weighing 15½ avoirdupois grains; a kilogram weighs 2¼ pounds. The liter is the unit of measure of capacity and =.908 dry quarts, a hectoliter equal about 26 gallons. A hectare equals 2.47 acres.

MISCELLANEOUS TABLE.

12 things make	1 dozen.
12 dozen make	1 gross.
12 gross make	1 great gross.
20 things make	1 score.
196 pounds of flour make	1 barrel.
200 pounds of beef or pork make	1 barrel.
135 pounds of potatoes make	1 barrel.
280 pounds of salt make	1 barrel.
400 pounds of molasses make	1 barrel.
200 pounds of sugar make	1 barrel.
240 pounds of lime make	1 barrel.
100 pounds of fish make	1 quintal.
100 pounds of nails make	1 keg.
50 pounds of soap make	1 box.
20 pounds of raisins make	1 box.
2 pounds of cigars make	1 box.
20 pounds of soda make	1 box.
40 pounds of cheese make	1 box.
25 pounds of tobacco make	1 box.
32 pounds of tea make	1 box.
60 pounds of saleratus make	1 box.
25 pounds of chocolate make	1 box.
56 pounds of butter make	1 firkin.

CARRYING CAPACITY OF FREIGHT CARS.

	One Car-Load
Salt	100 to 150 bbls.
Lumber	13,000 to 20,000 feet.
Barley	300 to 400 bush.
Wheat	350 to 500 bush.
Corn	400 to 500 bush.
Potatoes	430 to 500 bush.
Oats	680 bush.
Rye	400 bush.
Cattle	20 to 35 head.
Hogs	70 to 80 head.
Sheep	80 to 100 head.
Hay	20 tons.
Coal	40 to 50 tons.
Stone	40 to 80 tons.
Gravel	27-35 cubic yds.

Tile all sizes 30,000 lbs. See page 342 for weight of tile.

There are 30,000, 40,000, 50,000, 60,000 and 80,000 lb. cars and on some of these commodities it is for the shipper to select the size of the car.

A CUBIC FOOT OF

	Pounds.
Common soil weighs	124
Strong " "	127
Loose earth or sand "	95
Clay "	135
Lead "	708¾
Copper "	555
Wrought iron "	486¾
Anthracite coal "	50-55
Bituminous " "	45-55
Clay or stone weighs	160
Cork "	15
Tallow "	59
Bricks "	125
Marble "	172
Granite "	165
Oak wood "	55
Red pine "	42
White pine "	30

WIRE NAILS TO THE POUND.

	Number to the lb.	Length in inches.
3 penny fine	778	1⅛
3 penny common	568	1¼
4 penny common	316	1½
6 penny common	181	2
8 penny common	106	2½
10 penny common	69	3
16 penny common	49	3½
20 penny common	31	4
40 penny common	18	5
60 penny common	11	6
8 penny fence	82	2½
10 penny fence	50	3

WEIGHT AND VALUE OF GOLD AND SILVER.

A ton of pure gold is valued at $602,799.21. The weight of a million dollars in gold coin is 3,685.8 pounds.

A ton of pure silver is valued at $37,704.84. The weight of a million dollars in silver coin is 58,929.9 pounds.

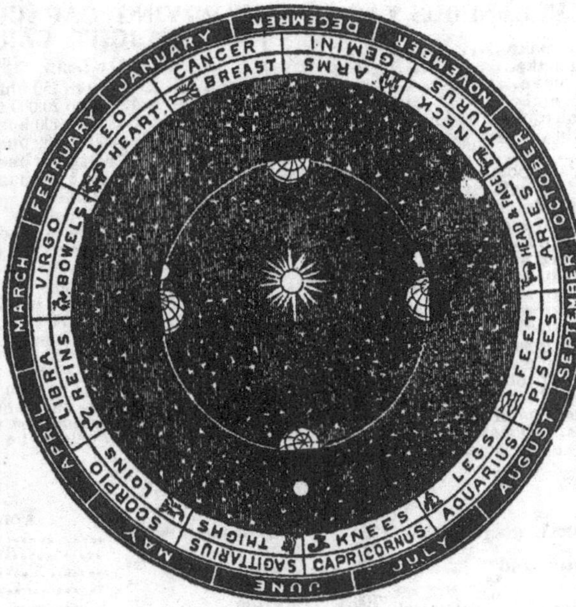

HOW TO FIND THE DAY OF THE WEEK FOR ANY DATE.

Rule.—Take the last two figures of the given year and add one-fourth of itself to it; add also to this the day of the month and the ratio of the month and divide the sum by 7, and the remainder will be the day of the week, 1 denoting Sunday, 2 Monday, 3 Tuesday, and so on, and when there is no remainder it is Saturday.

Ratio: For Feb., March and Nov. is 6; for Sept. and Dec. 1; for April and July 2; for May 4; for Jan. and Oct. 3; for Aug. 5, and for June 0.

Example: On what day of the week was John born if the date was Sept. 16, 1841?

Last 2 figures of the year 41.
Solution: 41÷4=10
Day of the month 16
Ratio 1

Total 68
68÷7=9 with 5 remainder.

Hence John was born on the 5th day of the week or Thursday.

N. B. The above rule is for the 19th century; for the 18th century add 2 before dividing by 7, and for the present century subtract 2 before dividing by 7. For leap years, subtract 1 from the ratio of January and February.

FAILURES, ASSETS, LIABILITIES AND NUMBER IN BUSINESS IN THE UNITED STATES YEARLY SINCE 1881.

Year	No. failures	Per cent. increase or decrease	Actual assets, millions	Total liabilities, millions	Per cent. assets to liabilities	Number in business	P. ct. fail-ing
1919....	5,515	—40.8	$55.3	$115.5	47.9	1,843,066	.29
1918....	9,331	—28.3	69.3	137.9	50.9	1,824,104	.51
1917....	13,029	—21.0	84.8	166.6	50.9	1,828,464	.71
1916....	16,496	—13.3	86.1	175.2	49.1	1,790,776	.92
1915....	19,035	+13.4	160.8	284.1	56.5	1,770,914	1.07
1914....	16,769	+15.2	197.2	357.1	55.2	1,749,101	.95
1913....	14,551	+5.3	159.0	292.3	54.3	1,718,345	.84
1912....	13,812	+9.2	98.5	198.9	49.5	1,673,452	.82
1911....	12,646	+9.2	102.0	188.1	54.2	1,637,650	.77
1910....	11,573	—2.3	94.2	188.7	49.8	1,592,509	.72
1909....	11,845	—15.6	69.3	140.7	49.2	1,543,444	.76
1908....	14,044	+36.8	168.4	295.9	56.9	1,487,813	.94
1907....	10,265	+9.3	287.9	383.7	75.0	1,447,680	.70
1906....	9,385	—5.9	63.1	127.2	50.0	1,401,085	.66
1905....	9,967	—4.3	65.0	121.8	53.3	1,352,947	.73
1904....	10,417	+6.5	75.7	143.6	52.7	1,307,746	.79
1903....	9,775	—1.9	84.1	154.3	54.5	1,272,909	.76
1902....	9,973	—6.3	50.4	105.5	47.7	1,238,973	.80
1901....	10,648	+7.4	61.1	130.1	46.9	1,201,862	.88
1900....	9,912	+2.8	60.1	127.2	47.2	1,161,639	.85

TOTAL RECORDED IMMIGRATION INTO THE UNITED STATES SINCE THE ORGANIZATION OF THE GOVERNMENT UP TO 1921 IS 33,728,221.

Year.	Immigrants.	Year.	Immigrants.	Year.	Immigrants.	Year.	Immigrants.
1830.	23,322	1853.	368,645	1876.	169,986	1899.	311,715
1831.	22,633	1854.	427,833	1877.	141,857	1900.	448,572
1832.	60,482	1855.	200,877	1878.	138,469	1901.	487,918
1833.	58,640	1856.	195,857	1879.	177,826	1902.	648,743
1834.	65,365	1857.	246,945	1880.	457,257	1903.	857,046
1835.	45,374	1858.	119,501	1881.	669,431	1904.	815,361
1836.	76,242	1859.	118,616	1882.	788,992	1905.	1,027,421
1837.	79,340	1860.	150,237	1883.	603,322	1906.	1,100,735
1838.	38,914	1861.	89,724	1884.	518,592	1907.	1,285,349
1839.	68,069	1862.	89,207	1885.	395,346	1908.	782,870
1840.	84,066	1863.	174,524	1886.	334,203	1909.	751,786
1841.	80,289	1864.	193,195	1887.	490,109	1910.	1,041,570
1842.	104,565	1865.	247,453	1888.	546,889	1911.	878,587
1843.	52,496	1866.	163,594	1889.	444,427	1912.	838,172
1844.	78,615	1867.	298,967	1890.	455,302	1913.	1,197,892
1845.	114,371	1868.	282,189	1891.	560,319	1914.	1,218,480
1846.	154,416	1869.	352,569	1892.	623,084	1915.	326,700
1847.	234,968	1870.	387,203	1893.	502,917	1916.	298,826
1848.	226,527	1871.	321,350	1894.	314,467	1917.	295,403
1849.	297,024	1872.	404,806	1895.	279,948	1918.	110,618
1850.	369,986	1873.	459,803	1896.	343,267	1919.	141,132
1851.	379,466	1874.	313,339	1897.	230,832	*1920	528,118
1852.	371,603	1875.	227,498	1898.	229,299		

* Figures for nine months only.

TENSILE STRENGTH OF MATERIALS.

Materials	Lbs.*	Materials	Lbs.*	Materials	Lbs.*	Materials	Lbs.*
Metals		**Metals**		**Metals**		**Woods**	
Aluminum castings	15,000	Cast iron	20,000	Nickel vanadium steel	99,700	Poplar	7,000
Aluminum sheets	24,000	Cast steel	60,000	Chrome nickel vanadium steel	129,100	Redwood	8,500
Aluminum wire	50,000	Wrought iron	50.000	Manganese steel (cast)	90.000	Spruce	14.500
Aluminum bars	28,000	Soft steel	58,000	Manganese steel (rolled)	140,000	White pine	15,000
Nickel aluminum	40,000	Carbon steel (not annealed)	75,000	**Woods**		Yellow pine	11.000
Aluminum bronze	70,000	Carbon steel (annealed)	80,000	Ash	14,000	Red fir	10,000
Manganese bronze	60,000	Carbon steel, oil tempered	85,000	Black Walnut	12,000	Yellow fir	12,000
Phosphor bronze	46.000	Nickel steel (annealed)	80,000	Beech	14,500	Teak	14,000
Tobin bronze	66,000	Nickel steel, oil tempered	90,000	Cedar	10,000	**Miscellaneous**	
Bronze gun metal	35,000	Rivet steel	53,000	Chestnut	10,000	Blue stone	1,400
Platinum wire (annealed)	32,000	Steel for bridges	60.000	Elm	13,400	Granite	600
Platinum wire (not annealed)	56,000	Medium steel	65,000	Hemlock	8,700	Limestone	1,000
Tin	3,500	Vanadium steel (cast)	70,000	Hickory	15,000	Marble	700
Gold (cast)	20,000	Chromium nickel steel	81,400	Locust	22,000	Sandstone	100
Silver (cast)	40,000	Chromium vanadium steel	100,000	Lignum vitae	11,000	Bricks (common)	200
Lead	2,000			Maple	10,500	Bricks (best hand pressed)	400
Zinc	5,400			White oak	14,500	Ordinary single leather belting	3,000
Brass (cast)	24,000			Live oak	13,000	Ordinary double leather belting	6,000
Copper (cast)	24,000					Cotton belting	6,000
Soft copper wire	35,000						
Hard copper wire	60,000						

Tensile Strength is the resistance of the fibres or particles of a body to separation. It is therefore proportional to their number, or to the area of its transverse section. The fibres of wood are strongest near the center of the trunk or limb of a tree. *Tensile strength in pounds per square inch.

INCOME TAX CHART

Based on the War Income Tax Law, and the Income Tax Law, as amended October 3, 1917

(Chart shows the tax payable by a married person, but does not take cognizance of the $200 exemption for each dependent child)

Net Income	Normal Tax: Old Law 2% on Excess of $4,000†	Normal Tax: New Law 2% Additional on Excess of $2,000§	Normal Tax: Total Normal Tax	Surtax Percentages: Old Law	Surtax Percentages: New Law Additional	Surtax Percentages: Total	Surtax: Amount subject to Tax	Surtax: Installment of Surtax at Each Rate	Surtax: Total Surtax **	Total Tax
$3,000		$20	$20							$20
4,000		40	40							40
5,000	$20	60	80							80
7,500	70	110	180		1%	1%	$5,000 to $7,500	$25	$25	205
10,000	120	160	280		2%	2%	7,500 " 10.000	50	75	355
12,500	170	210	380		3%	3%	10,000 " 12,500	75	150	530
15,000	220	260	480		4%	4%	12,500 " 15,000	100	250	730
20,000	320	360	680		5%	5%	15,000 " 20,000	250	500	1,180
40,000	720	760	1,480	1%	7%	8%	20,000 " 40,000	1,600	2,100	3,580
60,000	1,120	1,160	2,280	2%	10%	12%	40,000 " 60,000	2,400	4,500	6,780
80,000	1,520	1,560	3,080	3%	14%	17%	60,000 " 80,000	3,400	7,900	10,980
100,000	1,920	1,960	3,880	4%	18%	22%	80,000 " 100,000	4,400	12,300	16,180
150,000	2,920	2,960	5,880	5%	22%	27%	100,000 " 150,000	13,500	25,800	31,680
200,000	3,920	3,960	7,880	6%	25%	31%	150,000 " 200,000	15,500	41,300	49,180
250.000	4,920	4,960	9,880	7%	30%	37%	200,000 " 250,000	18,500	59,800	69,680
300,000	5,920	5,960	11,880	8%	34%	42%	250,000 " 300,000	21,000	80,800	92,680
500,000	9,920	9,960	19,880	9%	37%	46%	300,000 " 500,000	92,000	172,800	192,680
750,000	14,920	14,960	29,880	10%	40%	50%	500,000 " 750,000	125,000	297,800	327,680
1,000,000	19,920	19,960	39,880	10%	45%	55%	750,000 " 1,000,000	137,500	435,300	475,180
1,500,000	29,920	29,960	59,880	11%	50%	61%	1,000,000 " 1,500,000	305,000	740,300	800,180
2,000,000	39,920	39,960	79,880	12%	50%	62%	1,500,000 " 2,000,000	310,000	1,050.300	1,130,180
3,000,000	59,920	59,960	119,880	13%	50%	63%	On excess of 2,000,000	630,000	1,680.300	1,800,180

† Single persons, $3,000. § Single persons $1,000. ** Total Surtax is the total of the Installments for the Income considered.

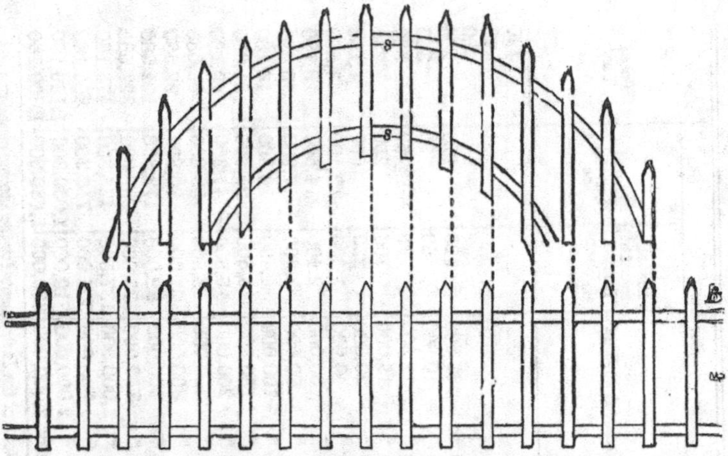

DOES IT TAKE MORE PICKETS TO BUILD OVER A HILL THAN ON A LEVEL?

Many arguments and discussions have taken place over this simple problem. It takes no more pickets to build over a hill than on a level. You can see from the above figure, that the number of pickets are the same by actual count. The curve lines represent the hill, and the lower lines the level ground. The dotted lines join the two, and they make the same fence over the hill, and are no farther apart than on the level.

DOES THE TOP OF A CARRIAGE WHEEL MOVE FASTER THAN THE BOTTOM?

This seems absurd, but it is strictly true, as any one may satisfy himself in a moment by setting up a stake by the side of a wheel and then moving the wheel forward a few inches. The accompanying illustration may make it still clearer. Let the wheel move from position held by Fig. 1 to position of Fig. 2. 1 has moved over a much greater space than 3, and consequently has moved faster.

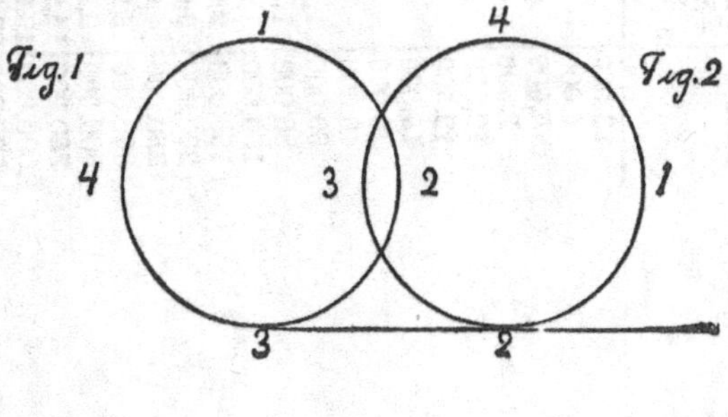

HE THAT REGARDETH THE CLOUDS SHALL NOT REAP.

USEFUL REFERENCE RULES AND ITEMS.

HOW TO WRITE YOUR NAME ON IRON TOOLS.

1. Melt a little beeswax or hard tallow and pour it on the iron at the place intended to be marked. After the wax or tallow cools take an awl or sharp piece of iron and write your name in it.

2. Pour a little nitric acid on the wax, where you have written your name, and allow it to remain a few moments. Then wipe off the wax, and your name remains indelibly marked as written in the wax.

3. Be careful and allow none of the acid to come in contact with your clothes or hands.

HOW TO WRITE YOUR NAME ON GLASS.

1. Apply beeswax and write your name as in the above.

2. Then instead of nitric acid, apply hydrofluoric acid and your name will remain permanently written on the clear surface of the glass.

HOW TO MAKE A HOLE IN GLASS.

Place a piece of stiff clay or putty on the part where you wish to make the hole. Make a hole in the putty reaching to the glass and just the size you want the hole in the glass. Pour a little molten lead into this hole and the piece of glass will drop out. This will not fail unless the glass is very thick.

COMMON NAMES OF CHEMICAL SUBSTANCES.

Blue Vitriol	Sulphate of Copper
Chalk	Carbonate of Calcium
Common Salt	Chloride of Sodium
Copperas	Sulphate of Iron
Water	Oxide of Hydrogen
Lime	Oxide of Calcium
Glucose	Grape Sugar
Soda	Bicarbonate of Sodium
Cream of Tartar	Bitartrate of Potassa
Epsom Salts	Sulphate of Magnesia
Oil of Vitriol	Sulphuric Acid
Potash	Hydrate of Potassium
Vinegar	Acetic Acid (diluted)
Spirits of Hartshorn	Aqua Ammonia

PAINTING RULES.

One coat, or priming, will take, per 100 yards of painting, 20 pounds of lead and 4 gallons of oil. Two-coat work, 40 pounds of lead and 4 gallons of oil. Three-coat, the same quantity as two-coat; so that a fair estimate for 100 yards of three-coat work would be 100 pounds of lead and 16 gallons of oil.

One gallon priming color will cover 50 superficial yards; white zinc, 50 yards; white paint, 44 yards; lead color, 50 yards; black paint, 50 yards; stone color, 4 yards; yellow paint, 44 yards; blue color, 45 yards; green paint, 45 yards; bright emerald green, 25 yards; bronze green, 75 yards.

One pound of paint will cover about 4 superficial yards the first coat, and about 6 each additional coat. One pound of putty, for stopping, every 20 yards. One gallon of tar and one pound of pitch will cover 12 yards, interchange the first coat, and 17 yards each additional coat. A square yard of new brick wall requires, for the first coat of paint in oil, ¾ pound; for the second, 3 pounds; for the third, 4 pounds.

A day's work on the outside of a building is 100 yards of the first coat, and 80 yards of either second or third coat. An ordinary door, including casings, will, on both sides, make 8 to 10 yards of painting, or about 5 yards to a door without the casings An ordinary window makes about 2½ or 3 yards.

HOW TO MIX PAINTS OF VARIOUS COLORS.

Buff—White, yellow ochre and red.
Chestnut—Red, black and yellow.
Chocolate—Raw umber, red and black.
Claret—Red, umber and black.
Copper—Red, yellow and black.
Dove—White, vermilion, blue and yellow.
Drab—White, yellow ochre, red and black.
Fawn—White, yellow and red.
Flesh—White, yellow ochre and vermilion.
Freestone—Red, black, yellow ochre and white
French Grey—White, Prussian blue and lake.
Grey—White lead and black.
Gold—White, stone ochre and red.
Green Bronze—Chrome green, black and yellow.
Green Pea—White and chrome green.
Lemon—White and chrome yellow.
Limestone—White, yellow ochre, black and red
Olive—Yellow, blue, black and white.
Orange—Yellow and red.
Peach—White and vermilion.
Pearl—White, black and blue.
Pink—White, vermilion and lake.
Purple—Violet, with more red and white.
Rose—White and madder lake.
Sandstone—White, yellow ochre, black and red.
Snuff—Yellow and Vandyke brown.
Violet—Red, blue and white.

The first named color is always the principal ingredient, and the others follow in the order of their importance. Thus in mixing a limestone tint, white is the principal ingredient, and the red the color of which the least is needed. The exact proportions of each color must be determined by experiment with a smaller quantity. It is best to have the principal ingredient thick, and add to it the other paints thinner.

DISTANCES, POPULATIONS AND TIMES OF FASTEST MAILS.

INDIA, CHINA, JAPAN AND AUSTRALIA MAILS.

Figures in parenthesis indicate number of days in transit from port of embarkation.

The Post-Office Department allows 6 days for transmission of mails from New York to San Francisco, and 7 days from New York to Vancouver, B. C., and Tacoma, Wash., and 9 days from New York to London.

Leave London, Eng., every Friday for Aden (11-13), Bombay (17), Colombo (18), Singapore (26), Hong Kong (33), Shanghai (38), Yokohama (44).

Leave San Francisco, Cal., about every 9 to 12 days for Singapore (31-35), Hong Kong (25), Shanghai (25-28), Yokohama (17). By Pacific Mail and Occidental and Oriental Steamship lines.

Leave Tacoma, Wash., about every 17 days for Hong Kong (25), Yokohama (16). By Northern Pacific Steamship Co.

Australia Mails.—Mails for West Australia are all sent via London.

Leave San Francisco, Cal., every 9 to 19 days for Honolulu, Sandwich Islands (7); and every 28 days for Auckland, New Zealand (21), Sydney, New South Wales (26). By Oceanic Steamship Co. Mails also leave Vancouver, B. C., on the 8th of each month, and must be marked "Via Vancouver."

POSTAL DISTANCES AND TIME FROM NEW YORK CITY.

As indicated by the Official Postal Guide, showing the distance by shortest routes and time in transit by fastest trains from New York City.

Cities in United States.	Miles.	Hours	Cities in United States.	Miles.	Hours
Albany, N. Y.	142	4½	Louisville, Ky.	854	34
Atlanta, Ga	882	24¼	Memphis, Tenn	1,163	40
Baltimore, Md	188	6	Milwaukee, Wis.	985	29¾
Bismarck, N. Dak	1,738	60½	Montgomery, Ala	1,057	30½
Boise City, Idaho	2,736	92½	Montpelier, Vt.	327	10½
Boston, Mass	217	7	New Orleans, La.	1,344	40
Buffalo, N. Y	410	11½	Omaha, Neb	1,383	43
Cape May, N. J	172	6	Philadelphia, Pa	90	3
Carson City, Nev	3,086	109	Pittsburg, Pa	431	13
Charleston, S. C	804	21¼	Portland, Me	325	12
Chattanooga, Tenn	853	32	Portland, Ore	3.181	114½
Cheyenne, Wyo	1,899	56	Prescott, Ariz	2,724	94
Chicago, Ill	900	24	Providence, R. I	189	6
Cincinnati, O	744	23½	Richmond, Va	344	11½
Cleveland, O	568	19½	St. Louis, Mo	1,048	29
Columbus, O	624	20	St. Paul, Minn	1.300	37
Concord, N. H	292	9½	Salt Lake City, Utah	2,452	71½
Deadwood, S. Dak	1,957	65½	San Francisco, Cal	3,250	124½
Denver, Col	1,930	60½	Savannah, Ga	905	26
Des Moines, Ia	1,257	37½	Tacoma, Wash	3.209	127
Detroit, Mich	743	25	Topeka, Kan	1,370	40
Galveston, Tex	1,789	56½	Trenton, N. J	57	2
Harrisburg, Pa	182	6	Vicksburg, Miss	1,288	50
Hartford, Ct	112	4	Washington, D. C	228	6½
Helena, Mont	2,423	89	Wheeling, W. Va	496	16½
Hot Springs, Ark	1,367	55	Wilmington, Del	117	5
Indianapolis, Ind	808	23	Wilmington, N. C	593	20
Jacksonville, Fla	1.077	31½			
Kansas City, Mo	1,302	38¼			

Distance in Miles of the Different State Capitals from Washington, the National Capital.

According to a compilation of the Postmaster-General, February 12, 1894.

Albany, N. Y.	373
Annapolis, Md.	42
Atlanta, Ga.	649
Augusta, Me.	615
Austin, Tex.	1,556
Baton Rouge, La.	1,179
Bismarck, N. D.	1,610
Boise City, Idaho	2,600
Boston, Mass.	444
Carson City, Nev.	2,898
Charleston, W. Va.	386
Cheyenne, Wyo.	1,763
Columbia, S. C.	490
Columbus, O.	487
Concord, N. H.	491
Denver, Colo.	1,743
Des Moine, Ia.	1,113
Frankfort, Ky.	604
Guthrie, Okla.	1,466
Harrisburg, Pa.	125
Hartford, Conn.	341
Helena, Mont.	2,295
Indianapolis, Ind.	643
Jackson, Miss.	1,011
Jefferson City, Mo.	1,019
Lansing, Mich.	661
Lincoln, Neb.	1,285
Little Rock, Ark.	1,064
Madison, Wis.	910
Montgomery, Ala.	824
Montpelier, Vt.	555
Nashville, Tenn.	770
Providence, R. I.	425
Olympia, Wash.	3,110
Phoenix, Ariz.	2,472
Pierre, S. D.	1,554
Raleigh, N. C.	299
Richmond, Va.	116
Sacramento, Cal.	3,022
St. Paul, Minn.	1,172
Salem, Ore.	3,104
Santa Fe, N. M.	2,006
Springfield, Ill.	835
Tallahassee, Fla.	872
Topeka, Kans.	1,204
Trenton, N. J.	169

Distances from New York and the Time it Takes Letters to Reach their Destination in Different Parts of the World.

To—	Miles.	Days.
Adelaide, via San Francisco	12,845	34
Alexandria, via London	6,150	13
Amsterdam, via London	3,985	8
Athens, via London	5,655	12
Bahia, Brazil	5,870	21
Berlin, via London	4,385	9
Bombay, via London	9,765	24
Buenos Ayres	8,045	26
Calcutta, via London	11,120	26
Cape Town, via London	11,245	27
Constantinople, via London	5,810	11
Florence, via London	4,800	10
Glasgow	3,375	8
Greytown, via New Orleans	2,810	7
Halifax, N. S.	645	2
Havana, Cuba	1,400	3
Hong Kong, China, via San Francisco	10,590	25
Honolulu, Sandwich Islands, via San Francisco	5,645	12
Liverpool, England	3,540	7
London, via Queenstown	3,740	7
Madrid, via London	4,925	9
Melbourne, Australia, via San Francisco	12,265	26
Mexico City by railroad	3,750	5
Panama	2,355	6
Paris	4,020	8
Rio de Janeiro	6,730	23
Rome, via London	5,030	9
St. Petersburg, via London	5,370	9
Shanghai, via San Francisco	9,920	25
Stockholm, via London	4,975	9
Sydney, via San Francisco	11,570	21
Valparaiso, via Panama	5,910	37
Vienna, via London	4,740	9
Yokohama, via San Francisco	8,725	20

DIFFERENCE OF TIME BETWEEN WASHINGTON AND OTHER PRINCIPAL CITIES OF THE WORLD AND LONGEST DAY AT PRINCIPAL PLACES.

12.00	o'clock	noon at	WASHINGTON.
12.12	"	P. M.	New York.
12.24	"	"	Boston.
12.27	"	"	Portland.
1.37	"	"	St. John (N. F.).
4.31	"	"	Lisbon.
4.43	"	"	Dublin.
4.55	"	"	Edinburgh.
5.07	"	"	London.
5.17	"	"	Paris.
5.58	"	"	Rome.
6.02	"	"	Berlin.
6.14	"	"	Vienna.
7.04	"	"	Constantinople.
11.01	"	"	Calcutta.
12.54	"	A. M.	Pekin.
2.48	"	"	Melbourne.
4.51	"	"	Auckland.
8.58	"	"	San Francisco.
9.40	"	"	Salt Lake.
11.08	"	"	New Orleans.
11.18	"	"	Chicago.
11.52	"	"	Buffalo.
12.00	"	noon	Lima (Peru).

	LONGEST DAY. Hr.	Min.
St. Petersburg...	18	38
Stockholm.......	18	35
Cape Horn......	17	34
Edinburgh......	17	32
Copenhagen.....	17	20
Dublin..........	16	52
Berlin	16	40
London	16	34
Paris	16	05
Victoria, B. C...	16	00
Vienna	15	56
Albany	15	20
Boston..........	15	14
Chicago.........	15	08
Ogden	15	05
Constantinople..	15	04
Naples..........	15	00
Pekin...........	14	58
Philadelphia.....	14	56
Washington.....	14	52
Cape Town......	14	20
Calcutta	13	24
Panama.........	12	34
Quito	12	00

The above is actual time, not *standard* time.

DISTANCES AND RAILROAD FARES FROM CHICAGO TO ALL THE PRINCIPAL CITIES OF THE UNITED STATES AND CANADA.

First-Class Fare Subject to Slight Changes.

(We aim to give the most direct route only.)

PLACES.	MILES.	FARE.	PLACES.	MILES.	FARE.
Akron..............O.	368	Multiply the number of miles by 3.6c and add 8% additional for war tax.	Dunkirk..........N. Y.	500	Multiply the number of miles by 3.6c and add 8% additional for war tax.
Albany...........N. Y.	838		Duluth...........Minn.	478	
Albuquerque......N. M.	1,391		Elgin...............Ill.	36	
Allegheny City......Pa.	467		Erie.................Pa.	452	
Allentown ....Pa.	916		Evansville..........Ind.	287	
Alliance.............. O.	385		Fall River.........Mass.	1,042	
Altoona...............Pa.	686		Fargo..............N. D.	645	
Annapolis...........Md	834		Fernandina ....Fla	1,083	
Atlanta...............Ga.	733		Fitchburg ....Mass.	954	
Atlantic City.......N. J.	886		Fort Wayne.........Ind.	148	
Atchison...........Kan.	556		Forest..................O.	239	
Augusta.............Me.	1,200		Fort Scott...........Kan.	557	
Augusta...............Ga.	905		Fort Worth.........Tex.	957	
Aurora ....Ill.	37		Frankfort............Ky.	368	
Austin ....Tex.	987		Freeport..............Ill.	114	
Bangor...............Me	1,263		Galveston ....Tex.	1.152	
Baltimore ....Md.	859		Galesburg............Ill.	164	
Battle Creek.......Mich.	164		Gettysburg...........Pa.	771	
Bay City...........Mich.	296		Grand Rapids....Mich.	215	
Bellaire................O.	469		Grenada.............Miss.	618	
Berlin ....Ont.	445		Green Bay..........Wis.	198	
Birmingham.........Ala.	652		Greenville..........Tex.	905	
Boston...........Mass.	1,004		Hamilton ....Can.	472	
Bridgeport.........Conn.	968		Hamilton............ O.	28[illegible]	
Buffalo ....N. Y.	523		Hannibal.............Mo.	329	
Burlington............Ia.	207		Harrisburg...........Pa.	716	
Burlington...........Vt.	1,095		Hartford..........Conn.	961	
Cairo..................Ill.	365		Hastings...........Neb.	638	
Canton ....O.	367		Haverhill ....Mass.	1,034	
Cape May..........N. J.	903		Helena ....Mont.	1,562	
Cedar Rapids.........Ia.	271		Hot Springs.........Ark.	693	
Charleston ....S. C.	1,103		Holly Springs.....Miss.	543	
Chattanooga.......Tenn.	595		Houston.............Tex.	1,102	
Cheyenne ....Wyo.	1,000		Hudson..............N. Y.	836	
Cincinnati..............O.	300		Indianapolis.........Ind.	183	
Cleveland..............O.	339		Iowa City.............Ia.	237	
Columbus ....O.	398		Ithaca..............N. Y.	666	
Council Bluffs.......Ia.	488		Jacksonville.........Fla.	1,083	
Columbia..........S. C.	837		Jackson.............Miss.	730	
Concord...........N. H.	963		Jackson ....Mich.	209	
Corsicana . ...Tex	975		Janesville...........Wis.	91	
Crestline ....O.	280		Jefferson City......Mo.	376	
Dallas................Tex.	760		Joliet..................Ill.	37	
Davenport..............Ia.	183		Kalamazoo.........Mich.	14[illegible]	
Dayton ....O.	265		Kansas City.........Mo.	489	
Decatur.................Ill.	170		Keokuk................Ia.	250	
Denver ....Colo.	1,118		Knoxville ....Tenn.	566	
Des Moines............Ia.	357		La Crosse.........Wis.	280	
Detroit.............Mich.	272		Lake Geneva .....Wis.	85	
Dover.................Del.	921		Lancaster.............Pa.	754	
Dubuque..............Ia.	188		Lansing............Mich.	2[illegible]0	

PLACES.	MILES.	FARE.
Leadville.........Colo.	1,169	Multiply the number of miles by 3.6c and add 8% additional for war tax.
Leavenworth.......Kan.	589	
Lexington...........Ky.	376	
Lincoln.............Neb.	552	
Little Rock........Ark.	628	
Logansport..........Ind.	116	
Long Branch........N. J.	914	
London................Can.	899	
Los Angeles ....Cal	2,266	
Lyons...............Ia.	137	
Madison............Ind.	269	
Madison............Wis.	138	
Macon...............Ga.	821	
Manitowoc.........Wis.	162	
Marquette........ Mich.	390	
Marshalltown........Ia.	288	
Memphis..........Tenn.	528	
Menominee........Mich.	265	
Milwaukee..........Wis.	85	
Minneapolis.......Minn.	420	
Moline...............Ill.	165	
Montpelier...........Vt.	1,224	
Montgomery........Ala.	793	
Mobile...............Ala.	973	
Montreal.......... Can.	837	
Muscatine............Ia.	211	
Nashville..........Tenn.	444	
Nebraska City......Neb.	498	
New York......... N. Y.	912	
New Haven........Conn.	915	
New Orleans.........La.	912	
Newark........ ... ...O.	865	
Newark............N. J.	905	
Newark............N. Y.	927	
Newport............R.I.	1,044	
Niagara Falls......N. Y.	513	
Ogden............Utah.	1,514	
Ogdensburg........N. Y.	788	
Oil City..............Pa.	498	
Omaha...............Neb	497	
Ottawa..............Can.	757	
Pasadena...........Cal.	2,255	
Paterson...........N. J.	969	
Pensacola..........Fla.	955	
Peoria...............Ill.	155	
Peru.................Ind.	132	
Philadelphia .... Pa.	822	
Pine Bluff..........Ark.	633	
Pittsburg.... ....Pa.	468	
Portland.......... Me.	1,114	
Portland............Ore.	2,488	
Port Huron.......Mich.	335	
Portsmouth.... ......O.	413	
Pueblo..............Colo.	1,107	
Pullman.... .. ..Ill.	14	
Quebec...............Can.	1,107	

PLACES.	MILES.	FARE.
Quincy...............Ill.	262	Multiply the number of miles by 3.6c and add 8% additional for war tax.
Racine...............Wis.	62	
Raleigh ....N. C.	1,154	
Richmond...........Ind.	223	
Richmond.............Va.	933	
Rockford ....Ill.	86	
Rochester..........N. Y.	550	
Rock Island...... ...Ill.	181	
Rome ....N. Y.	711	
San Antonio........Tex.	1,213	
Saginaw...........Mich.	283	
Sacramento.........Cal.	2.257	
Salt Lake City....Utah.	1,566	
Santa Fe..........N. M.	1,342	
Sandusky ....O.	307	
Savannah............Ga.	1,088	
San Francisco.......Cal.	2,411	
Seattle............Wash.	2,342	
Sherman............Tex.	871	
Shreveport ....La.	815	
Sioux City ....Ia.	510	
Springfield.......... O.	300	
Springfield...........Ill.	185	
Springfield........Mass.	935	
Spokane ....Wash.	1,914	
Steubenville ....O.	426	
St. Louis............Mo.	280	
St. Paul..........Minn.	410	
St. Joseph...........Mo.	469	
Syracuse..........N. Y.	673	
Tacoma..........Wash.	2,314	
Tallahassee.........Fla.	1,033	
Terre Haute.........Ind.	178	
Texarkana..........Ark.	773	
Tiffin...................O.	254	
Toledo ....O.	243	
Topeka.............Kan.	555	
Toronto,.............Can.	506	
Trenton.... ....N. J.	859	
Troy................N. Y.	826	
Urbana.... ....O.	267	
Utica...............N. Y.	725	
Vicksburg..........Miss.	761	
Vincennes...........Ind.	235	
Waco................Tex.	1,031	
Washington........D. C.	819	
West Point.........N. Y.	916	
Wheeling........W. Va.	475	
White Sul. Spgs...W.Va.	637	
Wilmington ....Del.	930	
Winona ....Minn.	306	
Winnipeg.....Manitoba	345	
Xenia ....O.	280	
Yankton ....S. D.	569	
Youngstown..........O.	398	
Zanesville ....O.	390	

THE PRINCIPAL CITIES OF THE UNITED STATES WITH A POPULATION OF 10,000 OR MORE ACCORDING TO THE CENSUS OF 1920.

Cities.	1920.
ALABAMA.	
Anniston	17,734
Bessemer	18,674
Birmingham	178,270
Dothan	10,034
Florence	10,529
Gadsden	14,737
Mobile	60,151
Montgomery	43,464
Selma	15,589
Tuscaloosa	11,996
ARIZONA.	
Phoenix	29,053
Tucson	20,292
ARKANSAS.	
Fort Smith	28,811
Hot Springs	11,695
Little Rock	64,997
North Little Rock	14,048
Pine Bluff	19,280
CALIFORNIA.	
Alameda	28,806
Bakersfield	18,638
Berkeley	55,886
Eureka	12,923
Fresno	44,616
Glendale	13,536
Long Beach	55,593
Los Angeles	576,673
Oakland	216,361
Pasadena	45,354
Pomona	13,505
Richmond	16,843
Riverside	19,341
Sacramento	65,857
San Bernardino	18,721
San Diego	74,683
San Francisco	508,410
San Jose	39,604
Santa Ana	15,485
Santa Barbara	19,441
Santa Cruz	10,917
Santa Monica	15,252
Stockton	40,296
Vallejo	21,107
Venice	10,385
COLORADO.	
Boulder	10,989
Colorado Springs	30,105
Denver	256,369
Greeley	10,883
Pueblo	42,908
Trinidad	10,906

Cities.	1920.
CONNECTICUT.	
Ansonia	17,643
Bridgeport	143,538
Bristol	20,620
Danbury (city)	18,943
Danbury (town)	22,325
Derby	11,238
East Hartford	11,648
Enfield	11,719
Fairfield	11,475
Greenwich	22,123
Hartford	138,036
Manchester	18,370
Meriden (city)	29,842
Meriden (town & city)	34,739
Middletown (city)	13,638
Middletown (town)	22,129
Milford	10,193
Naugatuck (borough)	15,051
New Britain	59,316
New Haven	162,519
New London	25,688
Norwalk	27,700
Norwich (city)	22,304
Norwich (town)	29,685
Orange (town)	16,614
Stamford (city & town)	40,057
Stamford (city)	35,086
Stonington	10,236
Stratford	12,347
Torrington (borough)	20,623
Torrington (town)	22,055
Wallingford	12,010
Waterbury	91,410
Willimantic	12,330
Windham	13,801
DELAWARE.	
Wilmington	110,168
DISTRICT OF COLUMBIA.	
Washington	437,571
FLORIDA.	
Jacksonville	91,558
Key West	18,749
Miami	29,549
Pensacola	31,035
St. Petersburg	14,237
Tampa	51,252
GEORGIA.	
Albany	11,555
Athens	16,748
Atlanta	200,616
Augusta	52,548

Cities.	1920.
Brunswick	14,413
Columbus	31,125
La Grange	17,038
Macon	52,995
Rome	13,252
Savannah	83,252
Valdosta	10,783
Waycross	18,068
IDAHO.	
Boise	21,393
Pocatello	15,001
ILLINOS.	
Alton	24,682
Aurora	36,397
Belleville	24,823
Berwyn	14,150
Bloomington	28,725
Blue Island	11,424
Cairo	15,203
Canton	10,928
Centralia	12,491
Champaign	15,873
Chicago	2,701,705
Chicago Heights	19,653
Cicero	44,995
Danville	33,750
Decatur	43,818
East St. Louis	66,740
Elgin	27,454
Evanston	37,215
Forest Park	10,768
Freeport	19,669
Galesburg	23,834
Granite City	14,757
Herrin	10,986
Jacksonville	15,713
Joliet	38,406
Kankakee	16,753
Kewanee	16,026
La Salle	13,050
Lincoln	11,882
Mattoon	13,552
Maywood	12,072
Moline	30,709
Murphysboro	10,703
Oak Park	39,830
Ottawa	10,816
Pekin	12,086
Peoria	76,121
Quincy	35,978
Rockford	65,651
Rock Island	35,177
Springfield	59,183
Streator	14,779
Urbana	10,244
Waukegan	19,226
INDIANA.	
Anderson	29,767
Bloomington	11,595
Clinton	10,962
Crawfordsville	10,139
East Chicago	35,967
Elkhart	24,277
Elwood	10,790
Evansville	85,264
Fort Wayne	86,549
Frankfort	11,585
Gary	55,378
Hammond	36,004
Huntington	14,000
Indianapolis	314,194
Jeffersonville	10,098
Kokomo	30,067
Lafayette	22,486
Laporte	15,158
Logansport	21,626
Marion	23,747
Michigan City	19,457
Mishawaka	15,195
Muncie	36,524
New Albany	22,992
New Castle	14,458
Peru	12,410
Richmond	26,765
South Bend	70,983
Terre Haute	66,083
Vincennes	17,160
Whiting	10,145
IOWA.	
Boone	12,451
Burlington	24,057
Cedar Rapids	45,566
Clinton	24,151
Council Bluffs	36,162
Davenport	56,727
Des Moines	126,468
Dubuque	39,141
Fort Dodge	19,347
Fort Madison	12,066
Iowa City	11,267
Keokuk	14,423
Marshalltown	15,731
Mason City	20,065
Muscatine	16,068
Ottumwa	23,003
Sioux City	71,227
Waterloo	36,230
KANSAS.	
Arkansas City	11,253
Atchison	12,630
Chanute	10,286
Coffeyville	13,452
Eldorado	10,995
Emporia	11,273
Fort Scott	10,693
Hutchinson	23,298
Independence	11,920
Kansas City	101,177
Lawrence	12,456

Cities.	1920.
Leavenworth	16,912
Parsons	16,028
Pittsburg	18,052
Salina	15 085
Topeka	50,022
Wichita	72,128
KENTUCKY.	
Ashland	14,729
Covington	57,121
Henderson	12,169
Lexington	41,534
Louisville	234,891
Newport	29,317
Owensboro	17,424
Paducah	24,735
LOUISIANA.	
Alexandria	17,510
Baton Rouge	21,782
Lake Charles	13,088
Monroe	12,675
New Orleans	387,219
Shreveport	43,874
MAINE.	
Auburn	16,985
Augusta	14,114
Bangor	25,978
Bath	14,731
Biddeford	18,008
Lewiston	31,791
Portland	69,272
Sanford	10,691
Waterville	13,351
MARYLAND.	
Annapolis	11,214
Baltimore	733,826
Cumberland	29,837
Frederick	11,066
Hagerstown	28,066
MASSACHUSETTS.	
Adams	12,967
Amesbury	10,036
Arlington	18,665
Attleboro	19,731
Belmont	10,749
Beverly	22,561
Boston	748,060
Braintree	10,580
Brockton	66,138
Brookline	37,748
Cambridge	109,694
Chelsea	43,184
Chicopee	36,214
Clinton	12,979
Danvers	11,108
Dedham	10,792
Easthampton	11,261
Everett	40,120
Fall River	120,485
Fitchburg	41,013
Framingham	17,033
Gardner	16,971
Gloucester	22,947
Greenfield	15,462
Haverhill	53,884
Holyoke	60,203
Lawrence	94,270
Leominster	19,744
Lowell	112,759
Lynn	99,148
Malden	49,103
Marlborough	15,028
Medford	39,038
Melrose	18,204
Methuen	15,189
Milford	13,471
Natick	10,907
New Bedford	121,217
Newburyport	15,618
Newton	46,054
North Adams	22 282
Northhampton	21,951
Northbridge	10,174
Norwood	12,627
Peabody	19,552
Pittsfield	41,751
Plymouth	13,045
Quincy	47,876
Revere	28,823
Salem	42,529
Saugus	10,874
Somerville	93 091
Southbridge	14,245
Springfield	129,563
Taunton	37,137
Wakefield	13,025
Waltham	30,915
Watertown	21,457
Webster	13,258
West Springfield	13,443
Westfield	18,604
Weymouth	15,057
Winchester	10,485
Winthrop	15.455
Woburn	16,574
Worcester	179,754
MICHIGAN.	
Adrian	11,878
Alpena	11,101
Ann Arbor	19,516
Battle Creek	36,164
Bay City	47,554
Benton Harbor	12,233
Detroit	993,739
Escanaba	13,103
Flint	91,599
Grand Rapids	137,634
Hamtramck	48,615
Highland Park	46,499

Cities.	1920.
Holland	12,166
Ironwood	15,739
Ishpeming	10,500
Jackson	48,374
Kalamazoo	48,858
Lansing	57,327
Marquette	12,718
Monroe	11,573
Muskegon	36,570
Owosso	12,575
Pontiac	34,273
Port Huron	25,944
Saginaw	61,903
Sault Ste. Marie	12,096
Traverse	10,925
Wyandotte	13,851
MINNESOTA.	
Austin	10,118
Duluth	98,917
Faribault	11.089
Hibbing	15,089
Mankato	12,469
Minneapolis	380,582
Rochester	13,722
St. Cloud	15,873
St. Paul	234,595
Virginia	14,022
Winona	19,143
MISSISSIPPI.	
Biloxi	10,937
Columbus	10,501
Greenville	11 560
Hattiesburg	13,270
Jackson	22,817
Laurel	13,037
Meridian	23,399
Natchez	12,608
Vicksburg	17,931
MISSOURI.	
Cape Girardeau	10,252
Carthage	10,068
Columbia	10,379
Hannibal	18,950
Independence	11 686
Jefferson City	14,490
Joplin	29,855
Kansas City	324.410
Moberly	12.808
Sedalia	21,144
Springfield	39,631
St. Joseph	77,939
St. Louis	772,897
MONTANA.	
Anaconda	11,668
Billings	15.100
Butte	41,611
Great Falls	24,121
Helena	12.037
Missoula	12.668

Cities.	1920.
NEBRASKA.	
Grand Island	13,960
Hastings	11,647
Lincoln	54,934
North Platte	10,466
Omaha	191,601
NEVADA.	
Reno	12,016
NEW HAMPSHIRE.	
Berlin	16,104
Concord	22,167
Dover	13,029
Keene	11,210
Laconia	10,897
Manchester	78,384
Nashua	28,379
Portsmouth	13,569
NEW JERSEY.	
Asbury Park	12,400
Atlantic City	50,682
Bayonne	76,754
Belleville	15,660
Bloomfield	22,019
Bridgeton	14,323
Camden	116,309
Clifton	26,470
East Orange	50,710
Elizabeth	95,682
Englewood	11,627
Garfield	19,381
Gloucester	12,162
Hackensack	17,667
Harrison	15,721
Hoboken	68,166
Irvington	25,480
Jersey City	297,864
Kearny	26,724
Long Branch	13,521
Millville	14,691
Montclair	28,810
Morristown	12,548
Newark	414,216
New Brunswick	32,779
Orange	33,268
Passaic	63,824
Paterson	135,866
Perth Amboy	41,707
Phillipsburg	16,923
Plainfield	27,700
Rahway	11,042
Roosevelt	11,047
Summit	10,174
Trenton	119,289
Union	20.651
West Hoboken	40,068
West New York	29,926
West Orange	15,573
NEW MEXICO.	
Albuquerque	15.157

Cities.	1920.	Cities.	1920.
NEW YORK.		Watervliet	16,073
Albany	113,344	White Plains	21,031
Amsterdam	33,524	Yonkers	100,226
Auburn	36,192	**NORTH CAROLINA.**	
Batavia	13,541	Asheville	28,504
Beacon	10,996	Charlotte	46,338
Binghamton	66,800	Durham	21,719
Buffalo	506,775	Gastonia	12,871
Cohoes	22,987	Goldsboro	11,296
Corning	15,820	Greensboro	19,861
Cortland	13,294	High Point	14,302
Dunkirk	19,336	Newbern	12,198
Elmira	45,305	Raleigh	24,418
Fulton	13,043	Rocky Mount	12,742
Geneva	14,648	Salisbury	13,884
Glens Falls	16,638	Wilmington	33,372
Gloversville	22,075	Wilson	10,612
Herkimer	10,453	Winston-Salem	48,395
Hornell	15,025	**NORTH DAKOTA.**	
Hudson	11,745	Fargo	21,961
Ilion	10,169	Grand Forks	14,010
Ithaca	17,004	Minot	10,476
Jamestown	38,917	**OHIO.**	
Johnstown	10,908	Akron	208,435
Kingston	26,688	Alliance	21,603
Lackawanna	17,918	Ashtabula	22,082
Little Falls	13,029	Barberton	18,811
Lockport	21,308	Bellaire	15,061
Middletown	18,420	Bucyrus	10,425
Mount Vernon	42,726	Cambridge	13,104
Newburgh	30,366	Canton	87,091
New Rochelle	36,213	Chillicothe	15,831
New York City	5,621,151	Cincinnati	401,247
Brooklyn	2,022,262	Cleveland	796,836
Bronx	732,016	Cleveland Heights	15,236
Manhattan	2,284,103	Columbus	237,031
Queens	466,811	Coshocton	10,847
Richmond	115,959	Cuyahoga Falls	10,200
Niagara Falls	50,760	Dayton	152,559
North Tonawanda	15,482	East Cleveland	27,292
Ogdensburg	14,609	East Liverpool	21,411
Olean	20,506	East Youngstown	11,237
Oneida	10,541	Elyria	20,474
Oneonta	11,582	Findlay	17,021
Ossining	10,739	Fremont	12,468
Oswego	23,626	Hamilton	39,675
Peekskill	15,868	Ironton	14,007
Plattsburg	10,909	Kenmore	12,683
Port Chester	16,573	Lakewood	41.732
Port Jervis	10,171	Lancaster	14,706
Poughkeepsie	35,000	Lima	41,306
Rensselaer	10,823	Lorain	37,295
Rochester	295,750	Mansfield	27,824
Rome	26,341	Marietta	15,140
Saratoga Springs	13,181	Marion	27,891
Schenectady	88,723	Martins Ferry	11,634
Syracuse	171,717	Massillon	17,428
Tonawanda	10,068	Middletown	23,594
Troy	72,013	Newark	26,718
Utica	94,156	New Philadelphia	10,718
Watertown	31,285		

Cities.	1920.
Niles	13 080
Norwood	24,966
Piqua	15,044
Portsmouth	33,011
Salem	10,305
Sandusky	22,897
Springfield	60,840
Steubenville	28,508
Tiffin	14,375
Toledo	243,109
Warren	27,050
Youngstown	132,358
Zanesville	29,569
OKLAHOMA.	
Ardmore	14,181
Bartlesville	14,417
Chickasha	10,179
Enid	16,576
Guthrie	11,757
McAlester	12,095
Muskogee	30,277
Oklahoma City	91,258
Okmulgee	17,430
Sapulpa	11,634
Shawnee	15,348
Tulsa	72,075
OREGON.	
Astoria	14,027
Eugene	10,593
Portland	258,288
Salem	17,679
PENNSYLVANIA.	
Allentown	73,502
Altoona	60,331
Ambridge	12,730
Beaver Falls	12,802
Berwick	12,181
Bethlehem	50,358
Braddock	20,879
Bradford	15,525
Bristol	10,273
Butler	23,778
Canonsburg	10,632
Carbondale	18,640
Carlisle	10,916
Carnegie	11,516
Carrick	10,504
Chambersburg	13,171
Charleroi	11,516
Chester	58,030
Coatesville	14,515
Columbia	10 836
Connellsville	13,804
Dickson City	11,049
Donora	14,131
Dubois	13,681
Dunmore	20,250
Duquesne	19,011
Easton	33,813
Erie	93,372
Farrell	15,586
Greensburg	15,033
Harrisburg	75,917
Hazleton	32,277
Homestead	20,452
Jeannette	10,627
Johnstown	67,327
Lancaster	53,150
Lebanon	24,643
Mahanoy City	15,599
McKeesport	45,975
McKees Rock	16,713
Meadville	14,568
Monessen	18,179
Mount Carmel	17,469
Nanticoke	22,614
New Castle	44,938
New Kensington	11,987
Norristown	32,319
North Braddock	14,928
Oil City	21,274
Old Forge	12,237
Olyphant	10,236
Philadelphia	1,823,158
Phoenixville	10,484
Pittsburgh	588.193
Pittston	18,497
Plymouth	16,500
Pottstown	17,431
Pottsville	21,876
Punxsutawney	10,311
Reading	107,784
Scranton	137,783
Shamokin	21,204
Sharon	21,747
Shenandoah	24,726
Steelton	13,428
Sunbury	15,721
Swissvale	10,908
Tamaqua	12,363
Uniontown	15.692
Warren	14,256
Washington	21,480
West Chester	11,717
Wilkensburg	24,403
Wilkes-Barre	73,833
Williamsport	36,198
Woodlawn	12,495
York	47,512
RHODE ISLAND.	
Bristol	11,375
Central Falls	24,174
Cranston	29,407
Cumberland	10,077
East Providence	21,793
Newport	30,255
Pawtucket	64,248
Providence	237,595
Warwick	13,481

Cities.	1920.
West Warwick	15,461
Woonsocket	43,496
SOUTH CAROLINA.	
Anderson	10,570
Charleston	67,957
Columbia	37,524
Florence	10,968
Greenville	23,127
Spartanburg	22,638
SOUTH DAKOTA.	
Aberdeen	14,537
Sioux Falls	25,176
TENNESSEE.	
Chattanooga	57,895
Jackson	18,860
Johnson City	12,442
Knoxville	77,818
Memphis	162,351
Nashville	118,342
TEXAS.	
Abilene	10,274
Amarillo	15,494
Austin	34,876
Beaumont	40,422
Brownsville	11,791
Cleburne	12,820
Corpus Christi	10,522
Corsicana	11,356
Dallas	158,976
Del Rio	10,589
Denison	17,065
El Paso	77,543
Fort Worth	106,482
Galveston	44,255
Greenville	12,384
Houston	138,076
Laredo	22,710
Marshall	14,271
Palestine	11,039
Paris	15,040
Port Arthur	22,251
Ranger	16,205
San Antonio	161,379
Sherman	15,031
Temple	11,033
Texarkana	11,480
Tyler	12,085
Waco	38,500
Wichita Falls	40,079
UTAH.	
Ogden	32,804
Provo	10,303
Salt Lake City	118,110
VERMONT.	
Barre	10,008
Burlington	22,779
Rutland	14,954
VIRGINIA.	
Alexandria	18,060
Charlottesville	10,688
Danville	21,539
Lynchburg	29,956
Newport News	35,596
Norfolk	115,777
Petersburg	31,002
Portsmouth	54,387
Richmond	171,667
Roanoke	50,842
Staunton	10,623
WASHINGTON.	
Aberdeen	15,337
Bellingham	25,570
Everett	27,644
Seattle	315,652
Spokane	104,437
Tacoma	96,965
Vancouver	12,637
Walla Walla	15,503
Yakima	18,539
WEST VIRGINIA.	
Bluefield	15,282
Charleston	39,608
Clarksburg	27,869
Fairmont	17,851
Huntington	50,177
Martinsburg	12,515
Morgantown	12,127
Moundsville	10,669
Parkersburg	20,050
Wheeling	54,322
WISCONSIN.	
Appleton	19,561
Ashland	11,334
Beloit	21,284
Eau Claire	20,880
Fond du lac	23,427
Green Bay	31,017
Janesville	18,293
Kenosha	40,472
La Crosse	30,363
Madison	38,378
Manitowoc	17,563
Marinette	13,610
Milwaukee	457,147
Oshkosh	33,162
Racine	58,593
Sheboygan	30,955
Stevens Point	11,371
Superior	39,624
Waukesha	12,558
Wausau	18,661
West Allis	13,765
WYOMING.	
Casper	11,447
Cheyenne	13,829

INFORMATION REGARDING YOUR LIBERTY BONDS

ISSUE	DATE OF ISSUE	MATURITY OF ISSUE	CALLABLE AT 100	CONVERSION PRIVILEGE	INTEREST PAYABLE
3½% **1st Liberty Loan** 1932-1947 Original Issue	June 15, 1917	June 15, 1947	On and After June 15, 1932	Conversion privilege has expired	June 15 Dec. 15
4% **1st Liberty Loan** 1932-1947 Converted	Nov. 15, 1917	June 15, 1947	On and After June 15, 1932	Convertible until privilege is terminated into 1st Converted 4¼'s 1932-1947	June 15 Dec. 15
4¼% **1st Liberty Loan** 1932-1947 Converted	May 9, 1918	June 15, 1947	On and After June 15, 1932	Not Convertible	June 15 Dec. 15
4¼% **1st Liberty Loan** 1932-1947 Second Converted	Oct. 24, 1918	June 15, 1947	On and After June 15, 1932	Not Convertible	June 15 Dec. 15
4% **2d Liberty Loan** 1927-1942 Original Issue	Nov. 15, 1917	Nov. 15, 1942	On and After Nov. 15, 1927	Convertible until privilege is terminated into 2d Converted 4¼'s 1927-1942	May 15 Nov. 15
4¼% **2d Liberty Loan** 1927-1942 Converted	May 9, 1918	Nov. 15, 1942	On and After Nov. 15, 1927	Not Convertible	May 15 Nov. 15
4¼% **3d Liberty Loan** 1928 Original Issue	May 9, 1918	Sept. 15, 1928	Not Callable	Not Convertible	March 15 Sept. 15
4¼% **4th Liberty Loan** 1933-1938 Original Issue	Oct. 24, 1918	Oct. 15, 1938	On and After June 15, 1933	Not Convertible	April 15 Oct. 15
3¾% 4¾% **Victory (5th) Lib. Ln.** 1922-1923 Original Issues	May 20, 1919	May 20, 1923	June 15 and Dec. 15, 1922	Convertible one issue into the other as long as outstanding	June 15 Dec. 15

(SEE OPPOSITE SIDE FOR TAX EXEMPTIONS OF VARIOUS ISSUES)

TAX EXEMPTIONS

An analysis of the total exemptions allowed shows that an individual, partnership (each member), association or corporation may, after January 1, 1919 (in addition to unlimited holdings of 3½% bonds of the First Liberty Loan and 3¾% Victory Liberty Loan Notes), hold an aggregate amount of $160,000 of Liberty Bonds, Notes, Certificates of Indebtedness and War Savings Stamps, issued after September 1, 1917, free from surtaxes, war profits and excess profits taxes, as follows:

UNDER THE SEVERAL LOAN ACTS

(Exempt as long as the obligations are outstanding)	
Aggregate holdings of First 4's, First 4¼'s (issues of May 9, 1918, and October 24, 1918), Second 4's and 4¼'s, Third 4¼'s, Fourth 4¼'s, Treasury Certificates of Indebtedness and War Savings Stamps	$ 5,000
UNDER FOURTH LIBERTY LOAN ACT	
(For a period of two years after the war, Exempt as to interest received after January 1, 1918)	
Fourth Loan Bonds subscribed for or purchased......	30,000
An amount of First 4's, First 4¼'s (issue of May 9, 1918, only), Second 4's and 4¼'s and Third 4¼'s, equal to 1½ times the original subscription to the Fourth Loan held at date of tax return, but not to exceed..........	45,000
3½% Bonds of First Loan Converted to 4¼% Bonds of October 24, 1918, issue..........	30,000
UNDER VICTORY LIBERTY LOAN ACT	
(For a period of five years after the war, Exempt as to interest received after January 1, 1919)	
Aggregate holdings of First 4's, First 4¼'s (issues of May 9, 1918, and October 24, 1918), Second 4's and 4¼'s, Third 4¼'s and Fourth 4¼'s......	30,000
(For the life of the Victory Loan Notes, Exempt as to interest received after January 1, 1919)	
A further exemption of bonds of the same issues in an amount equal to three times the original subscription to Victory Liberty Loan held at date of tax return, but not to exceed..........	20,000
	$160,000

NOTE.—Each member of a family owning such securities individually, each beneficiary of a trust, to whom the income of the trust is distributed annually or regularly, and each member of a partnership is entitled separately to the maximum exemption, so that, for example, a partnership with 10 members, each having a tenth interest, can hold an aggregate of $1,600,000 par value, exempt from surtaxes.

BOND INTEREST TABLE

INTEREST ON $1.000 FROM 1 DAY TO 6 MONTHS

Day	3½%	4%	4½%	5%	6%	7%
1	$0.0972	$0.1111	$0.125	$0.1389	$0.1667	$0.1944
2	0.1944	0.2222	0.250	0.2778	0.3333	0.3889
3	0.2916	0.3333	0.375	0.4167	0.5000	0.5833
4	0.3889	0.4444	0.500	0.5556	0.6667	0.7778
5	0.4861	0.5555	0.625	0.6944	0.8333	0.9722
6	0.5833	0.6667	0.750	0.8333	1.0000	1.1667
7	0.6805	0.7778	0.875	0.9722	1.1667	1.3611
8	0.7778	0.8889	1.000	1.1111	1.3333	1.5555
9	0.8750	1.0000	1.125	1.2500	1.5000	1.7500
10	0.9722	1.1111	1.250	1.3889	1.6667	1.9444
11	1.0694	1.2222	1.375	1.5278	1.8333	2.1389
12	1.1667	1.3333	1.500	1.6667	2.0000	2.3333
13	1.2639	1.4444	1.625	1.8055	2.1667	2.5278
14	1.3611	1.5555	1.750	1.9444	2.3333	2.7222
15	1.4583	1.6667	1.875	2.0833	2.5000	2.9167
16	1.5555	1.7778	2.000	2.2222	2.6667	3.1111
17	1.6528	1.8889	2.125	2.3611	2.8333	3.3055
18	1.7500	2.0000	2.250	2.5000	3.0000	3.5000
19	1.8472	2.1111	2.375	2.6389	3.1667	3.6944
20	1.9444	2.2222	2.500	2.7778	3.3333	3.8889
21	2.0417	2.3333	2.625	2.9167	3.5000	4.0833
22	2.1389	2.4444	2.750	3.0555	3.6667	4.2778
23	2.2301	2.5555	2.875	3.1944	3.8333	4.4722
24	2.3333	2.6667	3.000	3.3333	4.0000	4.6667
25	2.4305	2.7778	3.125	3.4722	4.1667	4.8611
26	2.5278	2.8889	3.250	3.6111	4.3333	5.0555
27	2.6250	3.0000	3.375	3.7500	4.5000	5.2500
28	2.7222	3.1111	3.500	3.8889	4.6067	5.4444
29	2.8194	3.2222	3.625	4.0278	4.8333	5.6389
30	2.9167	3.3333	3.750	4.1667	5.0000	5.8333
1 Mo	2.9167	3.3333	3.750	4.1667	5.0000	5.8333
2 "	5.8333	6.6667	7.500	8.3333	10.0000	11.6667
3 "	8.7500	10.0000	11.250	12.5000	15.0000	17.5000
4 "	11.6667	13.3383	15.000	16.6667	20.0000	23.3333
5 "	14.5833	16.6667	18.750	20.8333	25.0000	29.1667

FRACTIONAL EQUIVALENTS

ON BOND OF $1,000 DENOMINATION

	$
1/16%	= .625
3/16%	= 1.875
5/16%	= 3.125
7/16%	= 4.375
9/16%	= 5.625
11/16%	= 6.875
13/16%	= 8.125
15/16%	= 9.375
1/8%	= 1.25
3/8%	= 3.75
5/8%	= 6.25
7/8%	= 8.75
1/4%	= 2.50
3/4%	= 7.50
1/2%	= 5.00
1%	= 10.00

FOOD CONSUMPTION PER MAN PER YEAR.

(Pounds.)

	Average United States*	A. E. F. Ration†	Standard Budget Dept. of Labor‡	Japanese National Diet§
Meat	280	456	140	2.5
Fish	21	...	21	50.2
Eggs	33	...	30	2.1
Legumes	50	56	28	35.4
Bread and cereals	450	410	340	309.4
Vegetables	600	456	420	459.4
Sugar	120	73	63	14.1
Fruit	250	27	200	29.7
Other foods	100	50	33	...
Total excluding milk	1,904	1,528	1,275	902.8
Milk	760	12	500	2.2
Total	2,664	1,540	1,775	905.0

* Estimated by author from statistics of consumption of food in the United States. These figures include food wasted.

† From "America's Munitions," by Benedict Crowell, Government Printing Office, 1919, p. 438.

‡ From Monthly Labor Review, June, 1920, Volume X, No. 6, p. 3.

§ From "Standard of Living in Japan," by K. Morimoto, Johns Hopkins Press, 1918, p. 52.

RECENT LEGISLATION AND ITS EFFECT ON BUSINESS.

FEDERAL CHILD LABOR LAW.

Child Labor in the United States came to an end in August of 1917, according to act of Congress in August, 1916.

What the Law Accomplishes.—It prohibits interstate commerce in the products of any mine, quarry, mill, cannery, workshop or manufacturing establishment in which children under 14 years of age have been employed, or in which children between the ages of 14 and 16 have been employed more than 8 hours per day, more than six days a week, before six o'clock in the morning or later than seven o'clock in the evening.

The Children's Bureau was created April 9, 1912, in the Department of Labor to investigate and report upon all matters pertaining to the welfare of children.

These two agencies have done more than anything else to blot out one of the darkest pages in American industry.

THE INHERITANCE TAX LAWS.

Where Found.—Each State and Territory in the Union, with the exception of Alabama, District of Columbia, Florida, and South Carolina, has an inheritance tax upon the transfer of any property, real, personal or mixed, or of any interest therein, or income therefrom, in trust or otherwise, to persons, institutions or corporations, either by will or by intestate laws.

In Illinois.—The Illinois law provides the following tax where the transfer is to father, mother, husband, wife, child, brother, or sister, wife or widow of the son, or the husband of the daughter, or legally adopted children:

Up to	$ 50,000.00	tax of 1%
Next	100,000.00	tax of 2%
Next	100,000.00	tax of 3%
Next	250,000.00	tax of 5%

(Exemption $10,000.00)

In cases where the relationship is not so close, the tax runs from 3% up to 8%. (Exemption $500.00.) In all other cases the tax ranges from 5% up to 15%. (Exemption $100.00.)

The Clear Market Value of the property transferred determines the basis of the tax.

Federal Inheritance Tax.—Inheritances amounting to over $50,000.00 are subject to an additional Federal tax.

Safeguards.—Safe deposit companies, trust companies, corporations, banks or other persons having in possession or under control property belonging to a decedent are required to secure permission from the Secretary of State before opening safety deposit boxes or disbursing funds, and to furnish a list of such securities or funds in their possession or under their control.

Joint Checking Accounts and safety deposit boxes held in common also come under the requirements of the law.

WORKMEN'S COMPENSATION LAWS.

The United States and practically all of the States and Territories have passed laws providing compensation of employes for personal injury sustained while in the performance of duty. In other words, the government holds the employer responsible for the death or injury of his employes.

Insurance Policies.—Firms have the privilege of insuring themselves against liability and in case of accidents the insurance company stands the loss. In fact, any fair benefit plan will be accepted instead of the legal compensation required.

The formation of these benefit funds, with a consequent necessity for saving has been one of the most beneficial results of the compensation legislation.

The Amount of Compensation varies in the several States according to the rate of wage, the number of dependents, etc. In some States the amounts are fixed for death benefit, total disability and partial disability. In others the amounts are determined by the wage scale.

Compulsory Compensation Laws are in effect in the following States: Arizona, California, Hawaii, Maryland, New York, Ohio, Oklahoma, Washington and Wyoming.

Elective Compensation Laws.—The employer may elect whether he will provide and pay compensation according to the provisions of the act and thereby relieve himself from liability for the recovery of damages. Such laws exist in Alaska, Colorado, Connecticut, Illinois, Indiana, Iowa, Kansas, Louisiana, Maine, Massachusetts, Michigan, Minnesota, Montana, Nebraska, Nevada, New Hampshire, New Jersey, Oregon, Pennsylvania, Rhode Island, Texas, Vermont, West Virginia and Wisconsin.

THE FEDERAL FARM LOAN ACT OR THE RURAL CREDITS BILL.

Through act of Congress, July 17, 1916, farmers can now borrow money at low rates of interest in order to purchase land for agricultural purposes, to purchase equipment, fertilizers and necessary live stock, to erect buildings and improve the land or to liquidate existing incumbrances.

How the System Operates.—The law provides for a Federal Farm Loan Board, a Federal Farm Loan Bureau, twelve Land Bank Districts, and any number of Farm Loan Associations.

Ten or more farmers get together and form a farm loan association, which furnishes the Federal Land Bank in its district with farm loans for the purposes mentioned above. These loans bear a maximum rate of 6% interest, and run from 5 to 40 years on an amortization plan so that the entire debt is paid at maturity. No loan can exceed 30% of the land value and 20% of the value of the permanent improvements. No loan is made for less than $100.00 or more than $10,000.00 to any one borrower.

The Federal Land Banks deposit these loans with the Federal Farm Loan Bureau and issue Federal Land Bonds, bearing a lower rate of interest, not to exceed 1%.

The twelve Federal Farm Loan Banks are located at Springfield, Mass., Baltimore, Md., Columbia, S. C., Louisville, Ky., New Orleans, La., St. Louis, Mo., St. Paul, Minn., Omaha, Nebr., Wichita, Kans., Houston, Tex., Berkeley, Cal., and Spokane, Wash.

THE FEDERAL TRADE COMMISSION.

The Federal Trade Commission is a non-partisan commission created by act of Congress approved September 26, 1914, and is composed of five members appointed by the President. The term of office is seven years, and the members may have no other occupation during that time.

Powers.—The Commission has power (1) to prevent persons, partnerships or corporations from using unfair methods of competition in commerce; (2) to enforce certain provisions of the Clayton Anti-Trust law; (3) to conduct investigations, and (4) to require annual and special reports.

Hearings.—Headquarters of the Commission are in Washington, but hearings may be held in any city of the United States.

Benefits.—The Commission stands ready to aid and assist business men in all matters pertaining to credit, cash accounting and will furnish on request suitable forms, advice, and suggestions for the development of domestic and foreign trade.

THE TRANSPORTATION ACT OF 1920.

The Esch-Cummins Bill.

The main features of this bill are:

1. Power invested in the Interstate Commerce Commission to fix rates so that the railroads will earn an annual income equal to a "fair return" upon the aggregate value of their property used in the transportation service.

2. From March 1, 1920, to March 1, 1922, the Commission is to take as a "fair return" 5½% of the aggregate value and may allow an additional half of 1% for improvements and equipment. It is only for two years that the percentage is to be so fixed.

3. The Interstate Commerce Commission is to divide the country into "Rate Groups," and rates are to be uniform in each of these groups. The Commission may also adjust or modify rates which may be different in the different groups.

4. An arbitration board of nine members is to sit on labor questions. Three members represent the public, three the railroads and three the labor.

5. When the railroads' income exceeds 6% on the value of the property used for transportation, one-half of this excess goes to the Interstate Commerce Commission and the other half into a reserve fund to the credit of the road. The Commission is authorized to loan out the money it receives under this arrangement to those roads who desire to borrow and can furnish proper security.

A SCORE OF RAILROADS WITH NEW PRESIDENTS.

Name of Road	President in 1914	President Now
Atchison, Topeka & Santa Fe	E. P. Ripley	W. B. Storey
Atlanta, Birmingham & Atlantic	E. T. Lamb	B. L. Bugg
Chicago, Milwaukee & St. Paul	A. J. Earling	H. E. Byram
Chicago & North Western	W. A. Gardner	W. H. Finley
Chicago, St. Paul, Minneapolis & Omaha	W. A. Gardner	James T. Clark
Great Northern	Louis W. Hill	Ralph Budd
Lehigh Valley	E. B. Thomas	E. E. Loomis
Missouri Pacific	B. F. Bush	Harry Bronner
Nashville, Chattanooga & St. Louis	John Howe Payton	W. R. Cole
New Haven	Howard Elliott	E. J. Pearson
New Orleans Great Northern	H. I. Miller	A. C. Goodyear
New York, Chicago & St. Louis	W. H. Canniff	J. J. Bernet
Pere Marquette	In Receivership	Frank H. Alfred
Philadelphia & Reading	George F. Baer	Agnew T. Dice
Rock Island	H. V. Mudge	Charles Hayden
Seabord Air Line	W. J. Harahan	S. Davies Warfield
Union Pacific	A. L. Mohler	Carl R. Gray
Wabash	E. B. Pryor	J. E. Taussig
Western Pacific	B. F. Bush	Chas. M. Levey
Wheeling & Lake Erie	W. M. Duncan (Receiver)	W. M. Duncan

CAMPAIGN EXPENDITURES AND ELECTION RESULTS.

Year	Candidate	Campaign Fund	Electoral Vote
1860	Lincoln	$ 100,000	180
	Douglas	50,000	12
	Breckinridge	....	72
1864	Lincoln	125,000	212
	McClellan	50,000	21
1868	Grant	150,000	214
	Seymour	75,000	80
1872	Grant	250,000	286
	Greeley	50,000	...
1876	Hayes	950,000	185
	Tilden	900,000	184
1880	Garfield	1,100,000	214
	Hancock	355,000	155
1884	Blaine	1,300,000	182
	Cleveland	1,400,000	219
1888	Harrison	1,350,000	233
	Cleveland	855,000	168
1892	Harrison	1,850,000	145
	Cleveland	2,350,000	277
1896	McKinley	16,500,000	271
	Bryan	675,000	176
1900	McKinley	9,500,000	292
	Bryan	425,000	155
1904	Roosevelt	3,500,000	336
	Parker	1,250,000	140
1908	Taft	1,700,000	321
	Bryan	750,000	162
1912	Taft	750,000	8
	Roosevelt	325,000	88
	Wilson	850,000	435
1916	Hughes	2,012,535	254
	Wilson	1,400,220	277
1920	Cox	1,680,371	127
	Harding	4,022,580	404

HOW TO RECOGNIZE FABRICS.

How to tell a pure fabric from its counterfeit, as disclosed by the experts of the department of agriculture, may prove quite interesting as well as profitable to our readers—men and women alike.

A microscope is the most accurate means of distinguishing cotton and linen threads. Cotton fibers, under the microscope, have a ribbon-like appearance with many twists, and a broad, flat central canal; linen fibers are round, jointed and heavier than cotton.

If the fiber is without starch, oil makes linen translucent and cotton opaque. The finish must be washed out of highly finished material before the test can be applied. A comparatively simple test that, after some experience, enables you to distinguish between linen and cotton is called the "tearing" test. The linen weaves, in general, are more difficult to tear than the cotton weaves. The torn ends of the linen threads appear uneven in length, and the individual fibers of the threads are parallel; the torn ends of the cotton threads are more even in length, and the individual fibers are twisted in every direction. The sound of tearing linen is shrill; that of cotton, dull or muffled.

Another simple test is to touch a lighted match to the threads and then to blow out the flame and examine the burned ends. The cotton threads will have blunt ends, but the linen threads will have pointed ends.

An easy way of distinguishing between the highly sized and calendered cotton damask and true linen damask is to boil a sample. After having been dried and ironed, if it is cotton it will have a dull and somewhat fuzzy appearance; if it is linen, the luster and the smoothness will not be affected by the treatment. Mercerized cotton damask keeps more luster than untreated cotton, but less than linen.

Cotton and Wool.—Here is a safe, simple method of determining whether a piece of goods is made of wool or of cotton. Touch a lighted match to a thread. Cotton will burn freely with a flame, while wool will merely singe. A combination of the two results indicates that the goods is part wool and part cloth.

AUTOMOBILE DENSITY, UNITED STATES, 1920

State	*Number of Automobiles January 1, 1920*	*Population per Automobile (1920 Census)*
South Dakota	104,628	6.1
Nebraska	200,000	6.5
Iowa	363,079	6.6
California	477,450	7.2
Kansas	227,752	7.77
North Dakota	82,885	7.79
Nevada	9,305	8.3
Colorado	104,865	9.0
Wyoming	21,371	9.1
Washington	148,775	9.12
Oregon	83,332	9.16
Minnesota	259,743	9.19
Montana	59,324	9.23
Idaho	42,220	10.2
Wisconsin	236,290	11.1
Michigan	325,813	11.26
Ohio	511,031	11.27
Arizona	28,979	11.5
District of Columbia	35,400	12.4
Utah	35,236	12.8
Indiana	227,255	12.9
Vermont	26,807	13.1
Connecticut	102,410	13.48
Rhode Island	44,833	13.481
Illinois	478,438	13.6
Delaware	16,152	13.8
Missouri	244,363	13.9
New Hampshire	31,625	14.01
Oklahoma	144,500	14.03
Texas	331,310	14.1
Maine	53,425	14.4
Maryland	95,634	15.2
Massachusetts	247,182	15.6
New Jersey	190,873	16.5
Florida	55,400	17.4
Pennsylvania	482,117	18.1
New York	566,511	18.3
New Mexico	18,082	19.9
Georgia	137,000	21.1
South Carolina	79,143	21.3
North Carolina	109,017	23.5
Virginia	94,100	24.5
Kentucky	90,008	26.8
Tennessee	80,422	29.1
West Virginia	50,203	29.2
Louisiana	51,000	35.3
Arkansas	49,450	35.4
Mississippi	45,030	39.8
Alabama	58,898	39.9
Total	7,558,848	14.0

WHAT WE BOUGHT AND SOLD.

Our record breaking foreign trade is shown by the two tables below. The figures are from the United States Department of Commerce and include only the most important imports and exports. The reasons for many "shortages" may be found in these tables.

Imports	*1919–20*	*1918–19*
Animals, live	$49,136,672	$40,924,766
Articles returned	69,150,382	32,634,281
Art works	30,479,428	6,947,363
Breadstuffs	59,977,601	47,850,655
Chemicals, drugs, and dyes	177,969,520	150,225,186
Cocoa, crude	72,946,064	35,953,990
Coffee	310,701,872	143,089,619
Copper, crude	24,902,792	29,642,979
Copper, manufactured	65,106,842	84,931,967
Cotton, raw	156,918,719	37,633,612
Cotton, manufactured	111,874,821	34,762,723
Fertilizers	38,578,063	5,883,376
Fibers, cured	86,630,841	103,874,757
Fibers, manufactured	141,389,218	98,824,770
Fish	38,773,551	28,058,506
Fruits and nuts	124,773,197	68,234,657
Furs, undrest	103,772,044	37,965,713
Hides and skins	376,892,462	149,288,544
Rubber, crude	280,358,788	161,837,031
Iron and steel	37,423,289	24,306,839
Leather and manufactures	40,327,091	15,423,184
Meats and dairy products	42,424,105	60,445,083
Oils	195,141,567	144,621,251
Paper	63,407,279	46,551,731
Precious stones	114,019,472	52,367,057
Seeds	113,032,112	35,212,664
Silk, raw	454,573,638	217,517,484
Silk manufactures	87,728,181	29,349,198
Sugar	688,127,380	309,403,314
Tea	25,800,742	24,390,722
Tin, ore and pig	92,799,236	73,559,534
Tobacco, unmanufactured	78,164,290	66,329,689
Tobacco manufactures	13,274,307	9,983,622
Vegetables	46,569,851	33,687,305
Wood and manufactures	157,367,368	92,289,532
Wool, raw	212,848,568	224,414,983
Wool, manufactured	43,537,552	13,279,481
All imports	5,238,621,668	3,095,720,068

Exports	*1919–20*	*1918–19*
Agricultural implements	$36,724,902	$42,662,724
Animals	19,291,197	10,718,851
Breadstuffs	808,471,226	954,647,337
Automobiles	233,252,376	116,304,973
Cars	53,111,368	30,419,889
Chemicals and dyes	159,009,927	148,053,531
Coal, anthracite	40,667,538	30,927,815
Coal, bituminous	132,299,978	75,826,696
Coal, bunker	58,245,950	38,282,697
Cotton, raw	1,381,707,502	873,579,669
Cotton, manufactures of	364,036,786	232,206,566
Electric machinery	87,208,413	80,714,124
Explosives	28,215,657	122,730,877
Fertilizers	32,925,408	9,405,242
Fibers, manufactures of	28,720,545	35,014,942
Fish	42,178,071	37,219,828
Fruits and nuts	118,326,019	71,292,813
Furs and skins	38,883,097	14,612,015
Glass and glassware	25,906,621	21,898,185
Hops	17,716,222	2,333,850
Rubber manufactures	69,226,716	43,856,782
Iron and steel an	932,675,866	1,065,021,193
Leather	199,772,357	126,525,495
Shoes	78,064,947	50,506,986
Meats and dairy products	771,006,760	1,166,110,958
Naval stores	36,504,797	17,777,497
Oil cake	30,611,141	16,668,763
Oil, mineral	426,497,967	344,233,216
Oil, vegetable	96,225,582	59,057,820
Paper and manufactures	73,717,425	84,080,312
Paraffin	31,403,933	24,557,386
Photographic goods	23,707,316	16,943,127
Silk, manufactures of	26,945,293	22,354,895
Spirits and wines	30,224,313	12,911,178
Sugar, refined	131,771,308	81,569,660
Tobacco, leaf	271,940,888	189,894,417
Tobacco, manufactured	51,551,794	35,297,692
Vegetables	36,517,381	53,143,012
Wood and manufactures of	168,574,578	104,557,896
Wool manufactures	56,223,360	31,191,387
Zinc manufactures	26,984,162	24,526,166
All exports	7,950,429,180	7,081,461,938

Balance in our favor 1918-19 .... $3,985,741,870

Balance in our favor 1919-20 2,711,807,512

PRODUCTION IN THE UNITED STATES.

The United States has only about 6% of the world's population and 7% of the world's land. Yet this country produces approximately 25% of the world's agricultural products, 35% of the world's manufactured products, and 40% of the world's minerals. The following figures are compiled from an authoritative Wall Street journal:

Agricultural Products		Manufactories		Minerals	
Article	Percentage of World Production	Article	Percentage	Article	Percentage
Wheat	22	Woolens ...	22	Pig Iron..	50
Oats	35	Linens	25	Copper ...	56
Cotton	60	Cot. Cloth..	25	Petroleum.	60
Corn	80	Paper	45	Gold	20
Horses	25	Glass	25	Lead	40
Cattle	27	Shoes	36	Silver	40
Hogs	40	Steel	50	Coal	52
Dairy Prod.	25	Auto'biles..	85	Aluminum.	62

Our national wealth has increased from seven billion dollars at the time of the Civil War to more than two hundred and twenty-five billions today. The next wealthiest nation on the list is Great Britain with about eighty billion. From a debtor nation at the beginning of the war, with a trade balance of four billion dollars against us, we have become the chief creditor nation in the world, with a trade balance in our favor of billions of dollars.

RACES OF MANKIND CLASSIFIED

Table showing the different races of mankind divided into racial stocks, groups and peoples, with their distinctive complexions and numbers.

Race	Stock	Group	Peoples
Caucasian . . . (Numbering 880,350,000, Complexion generally white, but sometimes dark or brown.)	Aryan . . . . (Numbering 830,350,000 and supposed to have originated in Central Asia and to have migrated into India and Europe.)	Teutonic . . . (223,000,000)	Scandinavian: Danish, Norwegian, Swedish
			German
			Dutch
			English (Anglo-Saxon)
			Flemish
		Lettic . . . . . (4,000,000)	Lett
			Lithuanian
		Celtic . . . . . (9,250,000)	Scotch (part)
			Irish "
			Welsh "
			Armoric or Breton
		Slavonic . . . . (132,000,000)	Russian
			Polish
			Czech
			Bohemian
			Moravian
			Serbian
			Croatian
			Montenegrin
			Slovak
			Slovenian
			Ruthenian
			Dalmatian
			Herzgovinian
			Bosnian
			Bulgarian (part)
		Illyric . . . . . (1,500,000)	Albanian
		Armenic . . . . (3,000,000)	Armenian
		Hellenic . . . . (5,000,000)	Greek
		Italic . . . . . . (165,000,000)	French
			Italian (part)
			Roumanian
			Spanish
			Mexican, etc.
			Portuguese
		Iranic . . . . . . (22,000,000)	Persian
			Gypsy
		Caucasic . . . (10,000,000)	Caucasus peoples
		Euskaric . . . . (600,000)	Basques
		Indic . . . . . . (255,000,000)	Hindus, Mahrattas, etc.
	Semitic . . . . (Numbering 30,000,000, and supposed to be descended from Shem. Complexion dark or brown.)	Arabic	Arabians
			Bedouins
		Hebraic	Hebrew or Jewish
	Hamitic. . . . . (Numbering 20,000,000, and supposed to be descendants of Ham, second son of Noah.)	Egyptian. . . .	Coptic
		Lybian	Berber
			Lybian
		Abyssinian . .	Abyssinian
			Nubian
			Galla
			Someli

RACES OF MANKIND CLASSIFIED

Race	Stock	Group	People
Malay. . . . . . (Numbering 35,000,000. Complexion brown or yellowish.)	Malayan.	. . . .	Malays of Malacca and Sumatra
	Tagals.	. . . .	Tagals (of the Philippines)
	Javanese	. . . .	Javanese, etc. (of Java)
	Hova	. . . .	Hovas (of Madagascar)
	Dyak.	. . . .	Dyaks, etc. (of Borneo, etc.)
Mongolian. . . (Numbering 682,000,000. Complexion yellow or dark.)		Finic	Finnish, Lappish, Magyar, Bulgarian (part)
	Sibiric. . . . . (118,000,000)	Tartaric	Turkish, Cossac, etc.
		Japanese. . . .	Japanese, Korean
		Mongolic . . .	Kalmuk
	Sinitic. . . . . (564,000,000)	Chinese	Chinese, Siamese, Burmese, etc.
Ethiopian . . . (Numbering 150,000,000. Complexion black or brown.)	Negro.	. . . .	Senagambian, Dahomeys, Ashantis, etc.
	Bantu	. . . .	Bantus: Kaffirs, Zulus, etc.
	Papuan	. . . .	Papuans and Melanesians
	Polynesian	. . . .	Polynesian, Australian, Maori, etc.
	Negrito.	. . . .	Negrito
American Indian . . . . Aborigines of America (Numbering 25,000,000. Complexion red, copper-color or yellowish.)	North American .	Algonkian, etc.	Arapaho, etc.
		Aztecan, etc. .	Aztec, etc.
	Central American	Maya, etc. . . .	Lacandon, etc.
	South American .	Arawak, etc. .	Manoa, etc.

UNCLASSIFIED PEOPLES

Eskimos, etc., of the Arctic regions, numbering 40,000. Complexion, light brown.

Singhalese, of the island of Ceylon, numbering 2,000,000. Complexion, brown.

Hottentots and Bushmen, of Southwest Africa, numbering 117,000.

Total of all races and peoples, 1,931,850,000.

A COMPASS FOR SURVEYING LAND.

HOW LAND IS SURVEYED.

1. HISTORY. Thomas Jefferson and Albert Gallatin are supposed to be the authors of our system of United States land surveys.

2. TOWNSHIPS. The land is first divided into squares by lines, six miles apart. These squares are called *townships*, and a row of townships running north and south is called a *range*. Townships are given proper names but for the purpose of location, they are designated by numbers.

3. **Principal Meridians and Base Lines.** First the surveyors select some prominent object or point, and drawing a straight line, north and south, through this point, make what is known as the *principal meridian line.* Then drawing a line at right angles across the *principal meridian* they establish what is called a *base line.* Marks one-half mile apart are left on each of these lines throughout their entire length.

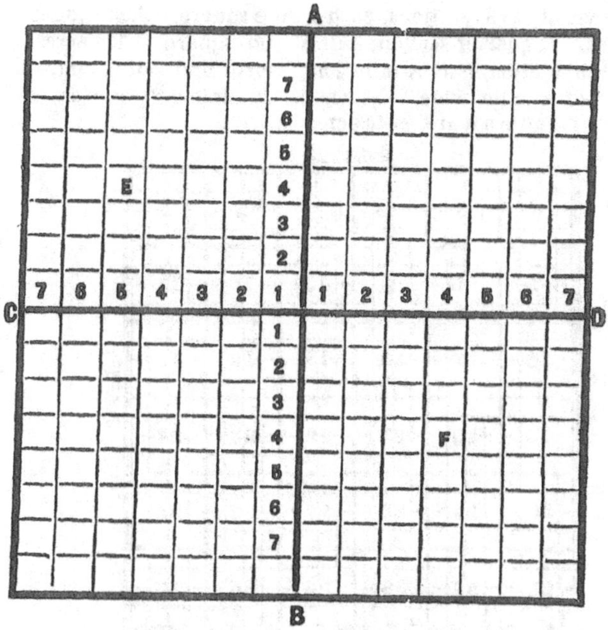

Illustration: A. B. = Principal Meridian. C. D. = Base Line. The numbers on the line A. B. mark the *township lines,* and the numbers on the line C. D. mark the *range lines.*

Range lines are run north and south six miles apart on both sides of the principal meridian and numbered as shown in diagram above. Township lines are run six miles apart, parallel to the base line and numbered as shown above.

Example: E. is in range 5, west, and in township 4, north, or 30 miles west from the principal meridian and 24 miles north of the base line (each square represents a township six miles each way). F. is in range 4, east, and is in township 4, south, or 24 miles east of the principal meridian and 18 miles south of the base line.

How to Locate Land and Read and Write Descriptions.

A Township is 36 sections, each a mile square. A section is 640 acres. A quarter section, half a mile square, is 160 acres. An eighth section, half a mile long, north and south, and a quarter of a mile wide, is 80 acres. A sixteenth section, a quarter of a mile square, is 40 acres.

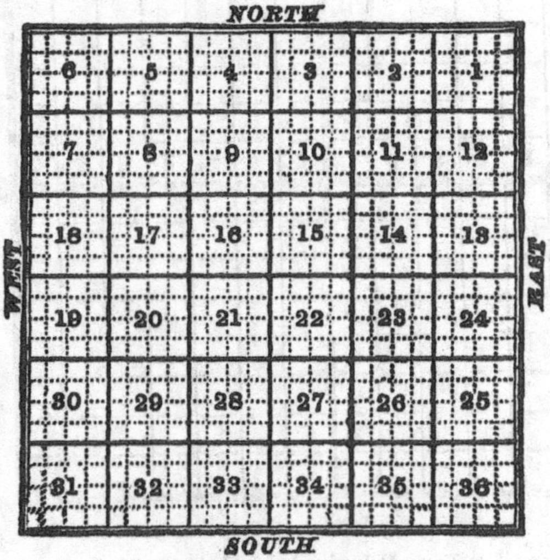

A TOWNSHIP WITH SECTION LINES.

1. United States survey ends with the location of the section lines. Marks are, however, made by the surveyors at the corners of the section and also half-mile marks between the corners. By these marks any piece of land may be accurately located.

2. Land is generally bought and sold in lots of 40 acres, or 80 acres, or 120 acres, or 160 acres, etc.

640 ACRES.

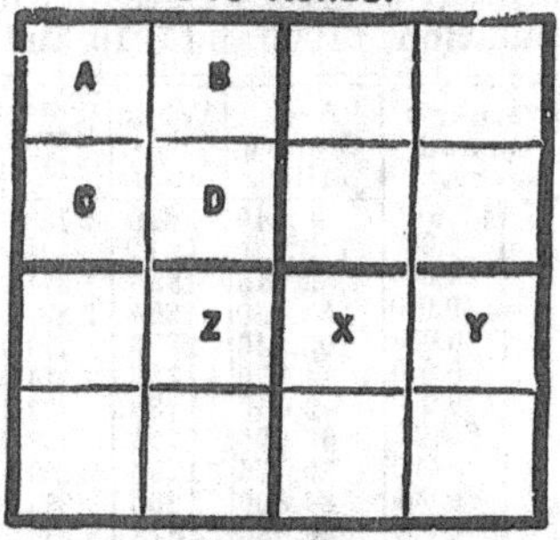

SEC. 25.

Example: Lots A. B. C. and D. taken together are one fourth of the entire section, and described as the N. W. ¼ of Sec. 25.

A. is described as N. W. ¼ of N. W. ¼ of Sec. 25.
C. D. is described as S. ½ of N. W. ¼ of Sec. 25.
X. Y. is described as N. ½ of S. E. ¼ of Sec. 25.
Z. is described as N. E. ¼ of S. W. ¼ of Sec. 25.

N. B.—Where the government surveys cannot be used, a full description has to be written out by the county surveyor.

STATES OF THE UNION.

Governors' Terms and Salaries, Areas, Dates of Admission, Thirteen Original States, Population in 1900 and 1910, and Electoral Votes.

States and Territories.	Governor's Term and Salary.		Area Square Miles.	When Ad-mit'd.	Population in 1910	Population in 1920	Elec. Votes 12 & 16
Alabama	4 yrs.	$7,500	50,540	1819	2,138,093	2,347,295	12
Arizona	2	4,000	113,020	1912	204,354	333,273	3
Arkansas	2	4,000	53,045	1836	1,574,449	1,750,995	9
California	4	10,000	158,360	1850	2,377,549	3,426,536	13
Colorado	2	5,000	103,645	1876	779,024	939,376	6
Connecticut	2	5,000	4,990	*1788	1,114,756	1,380,585	7
Delaware	4	4,000	2,050	*1788	202,322	223,003	3
Florida	4	6,000	58,680	1845	752,619	966,296	6
Georgia	2	5,000	59,475	*1788	2,609,121	2,894,683	14
Idaho	2	5,000	84,800	1890	325,594	431,826	4
Illinois	4	12,000	56,650	1818	5,638,591	6,485,098	29
Indiana	4	8,000	36,350	1816	2,700,876	2,930,544	15
Iowa	2	5,000	56,025	1846	2.224,771	2,403,630	13
Kansas	2	5,000	82,080	1861	1,690,949	1,769.257	10
Kentucky	4	6,500	40,400	1792	2,289,905	2,416,013	13
Louisiana	4	5,000	48,720	1812	1,656,388	1,797,798	10
Maine	2	3,000	33,040	1820	742,371	768.014	6
Maryland	4	4,500	12,210	*1788	1,295,346	1,449,610	8
Massachusetts ...	1	10,000	8,315	*1788	3,366,416	3 852,356	18
Michigan	2	5,000	58,915	1837	2,810,173	3,667,222	15
Minnesota	2	7,000	83,365	1858	2,075,708	2,386,371	12
Mississippi	4	5,000	46,810	1817	1,797,114	1,789.384	10
Missouri	4	5,000	68,735	1821	3,293,335	3,403,547	18
Montana	4	5,000	146,080	1889	376,053	547,593	4
Nebraska	2	2,500	77,510	1867	1,192,214	1,295,502	8
Nevada	4	7,000	110,700	1864	81,875	77,407	3
New Hampshire..	2	3,000	9,305	*1788	430,572	443,083	4
New Jersey	3	10,000	7,815	*1787	2,537,167	3,155,374	14
New Mexico	4	5,000	122,580	1911	327,301	360,247	3
New York	2	10,000	49,170	*1788	9,113,614	10,384.144	45
North Carolina ..	4	3,000	52,250	*1789	2,206,287	2,556,486	12
North Dakota ...	2	5,000	70,795	1889	577,056	645,730	5
Ohio	2	10,000	41,060	1802	4,767,121	5 759,368	24
Oklahoma	4	4,500	70,430	1907	1,657,155	2,027,564	10
Oregon	4	5,000	96,030	1859	672,765	783,389	5
Pennsylvania ...	4	10,000	45,215	*1787	7,665,111	8,720,159	38
Philippines	.....	15,000	....	.....	......	......	..
Porto Rico	4 ...	8,000	....	.....	......	......	..
Rhode Island ...	2	3,000	1,250	*1790	542,610	604.397	5
South Carolina ..	2	3,500	30,570	*1788	1,515,400	1,683,662	9
South Dakota ...	2	3,000	77,680	1889	583,888	635,839	5
Tennessee	2	4,000	42,050	1796	2.184,789	2,337,459	12
Texas	2	4,000	265,780	1845	3,896,542	4,661,027	20
Utah	4	6,000	84,900	1896	373,351	449,446	4
Vermont	2	2,500	9,565	1791	355,956	352,421	4
Virginia	4	5,000	42,450	*1788	2,061,612	2,306.361	12
Washington	4	6,000	69,180	1889	1,141,990	1,356,316	7
West Virginia ...	4	5,000	24,780	1863	1,221,119	1,463,610	8
Wisconsin	2	5,000	56,040	1848	2,333,860	2,631,839	13
Wyoming	4	4,000	97,890	1890	145,965	194,402	3
Alaska	4	7,000	531,410	.....	64,356	......	..
Dist. of Columbia.	.....	......	70	.....	331,069	437,571	..
Hawaii	4	7,000	....	.....	191,909	......	..
Total	.....	.....	3,557,010	.....	91,972,266	105,683,108	531

*Dates of ratifying constitution of original thirteen states.

NOTE—All have biennial sessions of legislature except Georgia, Massachusetts, New Jersey, New York, New Mexico, Rhode Island and South Carolina, where they are held annually, and in Alabama where they are held quadriennially.

ABBREVIATIONS.

Relating to Law and Government.

Administrator	Admr.
Advocate	Adv.
Attorney	Atty.
Against (*versus*)	V. or vs.
Alderman	Ald.
Assistant	Asst.
And others (*et alii*)	et al.
Clerk	Clk.
Commissioner	Com.
Committee	Com.
Common Pleas	C. P.
Congress	Cong.
Constable	Const.
County Court	C. C.
Co. Commissioner (or Clk)	C. C.
Court of Common Pleas	C. C. P.
Court of Sessions	C. S.
Defendant	Deft., Dft.
Deputy	Dep.
Department	Dep.
District Attorney	Dist. Atty.
His (Her) Brit. Majesty	H. B. M.
His (Her) Majesty	H. M.
His (Her) Roy. Highness	H. R. H.
House of Representatives	H. R.
Justice of the Peace	J. P.
Legislature	Leg.
Member of Congress	M. C.
Non prosequitur (he does not prosecute)	Non pros.
Member of Parliament	M. P.
Notary Public	N. P.
Parliament	Parl.
Plaintiff	plff.
Post-Office	P. O.
Post-Master	P. M.
Public Document	Pub. Doc.
Queen Victoria (*Victoria Regina*)	V. R.
Right Honorable	Rt. Hon.
Republic, Republican	Rep.
Solicitor	Sol.
Superintendent	Supt.
Surveyor General	Surv. Gen.

Ecclesiastical.

By God's Grace (*Dei gratia*)	D. G.
Church, churches	Ch., chs.
Clergyman	Cl.
Deacon	Dea.
Jesus the Saviour of Men (*Jesus hominum Salvator*)	I. H. S.
Jesus of Nazareth, King of the Jews (*Jesus Nazarenus Rex Judæorum*)	I. N. R. I.
Methodist	Meth.
Methodist Episcopal	M. E.
Protestant	Prot.
Protestant Episcopal	P. E.
Presbyterian	Presb.
Reformed, Reformation	Ref.
Roman Catholic	Rom. Cath.
God Willing (*Deo Volente*)	D. V.
Episcopal	Epis.
Evangelical	Evang.
Ecclesiastical	ecc., eccl.

Educational and Professional.

Bachelor of Civil Law	B. C. L.
Doctor of Civil Law	D. C. L.
Queen's Counsel	Q. C.
Dominion Land Surveyor	D. L. S.
Licentiate of Dental Surgery	L. D. S.
Privy Councillor	P. C.
Commander of the Bath	C. B.
Fellow Coll. of Accountants	F. C. A.
Fellow Royal Society	F. R. S.
Doctor of Divinity	D. D.
Bachelor of Laws	LL. B.
Doctor of Laws	LL. D.
Doctor of Medicine	M. D.
Bachelor of Arts	A. B.
Master of Arts	A. M.
Bachelor of Music	M. B.
Doctor of Music	D. M.
Doctor of Philosophy	Ph. D.
Bachelor of Philosophy	Ph. B.
Bachelor of Science	B. S.
Doctor of Science	S. D.
Civil Engineer	C. E.

BUSINESS ABBREVIATIONS.

Acct............Account.
Advtg............Advertising.
Agmt............Agreement.
Agt............Agent.
Amt............Amount.
Art............Article.
Atty............Attorney.
B. or *Bk*............Bank.
Bal............Balance.
Bbl............Barrel.
B. B............Bill-book or Bank-book.
B. Ex............Bill of Exchange.
B. P. or *Bills Pay*.Bills Payable.
B. R. or *Bills Rec*.Bills Receivable.
Bo't............Bought.
Bu............Bushel.
C, C't or ¢............Cent.
Cash............Cashier.
C. B............Cash Book.
Cer............Certificate.
Chgd............Charged.
Ck............Check.
Co............Company.
℅............In Care of.
C. O. D............Collect on Delivery.
Com............Commission.
Con. or *Const*............Consignment.
Cr............Creditor.
Cwt............Hundredweight.
D. B............Day Book.
Dep. B............Deposit Book.
Dft............Draft.
Dis............Discount.
Do. or *do*............(Ditto) The same.
Doz............Dozen.
Dr............Debtor.
Ds or *ds*............Days.
ea............Each.
E. E............Errors excepted.
e. g............For example.
E. & O. E............Errors and omissions excepted.
Ex. or *Exch*............Exchange.
Exp............Expense.
fav............Favor.
F. B. E............Foreign Bill of Exchange.
fi. fa............Cause it to be done. A writ of execution.
F. O. B............Free on board.
For'd............Forward.
Frt............Freight.
Ft or *ft*............Foot *or* Feet.
Gal............Gallon.
Guar............Guarantee.
Hdkf............Handkerchief.
Hhd............Hogshead.
Hund............Hundred.
I. or *Inv*............Invoice.
I. B............Invoice Book.
i. e............That is.
Ins............Insurance.
inst............(Instant) The present month.
Insol............Insolvency.
Int............Interest.
Invt............Inventory.
J. or *Jour*............Journal.
J. P............Journal page.
L. B............Letter Book.
lbs............Pounds.
L. F............Ledger Folio.
Mdse............Merchandise.
Mem. or *memo*............Memorandum.
Mols............Molasses.
Nat............National.
N. B............(Nota Bene) Take Notice.
Net............Without deduction.
O. I. B............Outward Invoice Book.
P. or *p*............Page.
Payt............Payment.
Pcs............Pieces.
Pd............Paid.
Pkg............Package.
Per. or *pr*............By the.
per ct............(Per centum) By the hundred.
P. & L............Profit and Loss.
P. O. D............Pay on Delivery.
Pr............Pair.
Prem............Premium.
prox............(Proximo) The next month.
P. C. B............Petty Cash Book.
Recd............Received.
R. R............Railroad.
S. B............Sales Book.
S. S............Steamship.
Shipt............Shipment.
ss............Sworn Statement.
St. Dft............Sight Draft.
Stg............Sterling.
Sunds............Sundries.
Tr. or *Trans*............Transaction.
ult............(Ultimo) The last month.
viz............(Videlicet) To wit; namely.
vol............Volume.
vs............(Versus) Against.
Yds............Yards.
$............Dollar.
¢............Cents.
£............Pounds Sterling.
d............Pence.
@............At, *or* to.
%............Per cent.
a/c............Account.
"............(Ditto) The same.
#............Number.
√............Check Mark.
1¼............One and 1 fourth.
1½............One and 2 fourths.
1¾............One and 3 fourths.

BUSINESS DICTIONARY.

A

Abatement.—A discount allowed for damage or overcharge, or for the payment of a bill before it is due.

Acceptance.—An assent and engagement to pay a bill or draft when due.

Acceptance for Honor.—An acceptance made after a bill has been protested for non-acceptance, for the honor of the drawer or any indorser.

Accommodation Paper.—A bill or note to which a party has put his name to accommodate another, who is to provide payment when due.

Account.—A written or printed statement of debits and credits in any business transaction.

Account Current.—A detailed statement of the transactions between parties for a certain period, showing the condition of affairs at the *current* or present time.

Account Sales.—A detailed statement of a commission merchant to his principal, showing his sales, the expenses attending the same, and the *net proceeds.*

Accountant.—A person trained to keep accounts.

Accrued.—Increase, or interest due and unpaid.

Acknowledgment.—A formal admission made before an officer.

Actionaire.—The owner of shares in a stock company, a stockholder.

Actuary.—A registrar or clerk. Generally applied to the manager of a life insurance company.

Administrator.—A person appointed to settle the estate of a testator, or to manage an intestate estate.

Admiralty.—The power that controls naval affairs in Great Britain. —**Courts of Admiralty.**—A court which decides questions of maritime justice.

Adulteration.—The debasing of an article or substance by spurious or less valuable admixture.

Ad valorem.—According to value.

Advance.—A rise in price, additional profits, stocks above par.

Adventure.—Goods sent to sea at the owner's risk, a speculation.

Adventure in Co.—Goods sent to be sold on joint account of shippers and consignee.

Advice. — Admonition, or suggestions offered, usually in regard to buying and selling goods.

Affidavit. — A written statement made upon oath.

Affreight.—To hire, as a ship, for transporting freight.

Agent.—One intrusted with the business of another, a deputy or factor.

Agio.—A term used to denote the difference between the real and nominal value of money.

Allonge.—A paper attached to a bill of exchange when there are too many endorsements to be contained on the bill itself.

Allowance—A deduction made, for instance, from the gross weight of goods.

Ambassador.—A minister employed by one government to represent it at the court of another.

Anker.—A common liquid measure, varying, in different European countries, from nine to ten gallons.

Antal.—A wine measure of Hungary, holding about thirteen and a half gallons.

Anticipate.—To be before in doing, or pay before due.

Appraise.—To set a value on goods or property.

Appurtenance. — Adjunct or appendage

Arbitration.—The hearing and decision of a cause between parties in controversy, by chosen persons.

Arbitration of Exchange. — The deduction of a proportional or *arbitrated rate* of exchange between two places through an intermediate place, to ascertain the most advantageous method of drawing or remitting.

Arrear.—That which remains unpaid though due.

Assay.—To subject an ore to chemical examination to find the amount of any metal contained in it.

Assess.—To fix a certain value for the purpose of taxation.

Assets.—The entire property of an individual or company.

Assignee.—One to whom something is assigned, usually one who receives property to dispose of for the benefit of creditors.

Assignor.—One who assigns an interest to another.

Assignment.—Placing property into the hands of assignees.

Association.—The union of a number of persons for some special aim.

Assume—To take on another's debts.

Attachment.—A seizure by virtue of a legal process.

BUSINESS DICTIONARY—Continued.

Attest.—To bear witness, to certify.

Attorney (Power of).—A written authority from one person empowering another to act for him.

Attorney in Fact.—An agent with full power.

Auctioneer.—One who sells goods at a public sale.

Auditor.—A person appointed to examine and settle accounts.

Avails. — Profits of property disposed of, proceeds of goods sold.

Average.—A proportional share of a general loss; also, a mean time of payment for several debts due at different times.

Avoirdupois. — Commercial standard of weight in United States and England.

B

Bail.—The security given for releasing a person from custody.

Bailee.—The person to whom goods are entrusted.

Bailor.—One who furnishes goods to another.

Bailment.—A delivery of goods in trust.

Balance.—The excess on one side; or what added to the other makes equality in an account.

Balance Sheet.—A statement in condensed form showing the condition and progress of business.

Ballast. — Any heavy material placed in the hold of a ship to steady it in the water.

Ballot.—A Swedish term signifying ten reams of paper; used also to designate a small bale or package.

Balsa.—A kind of float or raft used on the coast of South America for landing goods through a heavy surf.

Banco.—A commercial term used in Hamburg to distinguish bank money from common currency.

Banking.—The business of a banker, or pertaining to a bank.

Bankrupt.—An insolvent, one who is unable to pay his debts.

Bank Stock.—Shares in the capital stock of a bank.

Barratry.—An intentional breach of trust, particularly any fraud by the master of a ship.

Barque.—A three-masted vessel carrying no square sails on her mizzen mast.

Bazaar.—A word of Eastern usage, signifying a place of exchange or general market-place, a repository of fancy articles — especially of dress.

Beacon.—A signal or light for the guidance of mariners; usually erected and sustained by the government.

Bidder.—One who bids or offers a price.

Bill.—A name given to statements in writing; as goods; a note; a draft; a law not enacted; exhibition of charges.

Bill of Exchange.—A bill ordering one party to pay another a certain sum of money.

Bill of Lading.—Written statement of goods shipped with terms of delivery.

Bill of Parcels.—A detailed account of goods sold.

Bill of Sale.—A formal instrument for the transfer of goods and chattels.

Bills Payable.—Notes to be paid by a party.

Bills Receivable.—Notes to be paid to a party.

Board of Trade.—An association of business men for the advancement of commercial interests.

Bona Fide.—In good faith, in reality.

Bond.—A writing, under seal, binding a person and his heirs to fulfill certain obligations.

Bonded Goods.—Goods in charge of the officers of customs for the duties on which bonds are given at the custom house.

Bonds.—A premium or extra sum paid for a loan, a charter or other privilege.

Book-Debt.—An entry or charge on a ledger; called also an open account, in contradistinction to a written promise or note.

Bottomry.—A contract by which the owner of a ship pledges it as security for money loaned him.

Bottomry Bond. — A bond given upon a ship to secure the repayment of money borrowed.

Breakage.—An allowance made by the shipper or seller on certain descriptions of fragile goods.

Breach.—Violation of an agreement in contracts.

Breadstuffs. — Material for bread, grain, meal or flour.

Brief.—A paper containing the leading points in a lawyer's argument.

Broker.—A person who transacts business for another, commonly in stocks, money, etc., using the name of his principal.

Brokerage.—The fee charged, for transacting business by a broker.

BUSINESS DICTIONARY—Continued.

Bulls and Bears.—Persons engaged in the gambling transactions of the stock exchange. The bulls are personally interested in *tossing up* the prices of certain goods while the bears are fighting *to pull down* prices.

Bullion.—A commercial name for uncoined gold or silver.

C

Capital.—The stock employed in trade; the fruit of past labors saved.

Capital Stock.—Capital of an incorporated company.

Carat.—An imaginary weight that expresses the fineness of gold.

Cargo.—A ship's lading, or freight.

Cashier.—One who has charge of money and superintends the receipts and payments.

Centage.—A rate by the hundred.

Certificate of Stock.—A written instrument issued by a company certifying the number of shares the holder owns.

Certified Check.—A check which has been certified by the bank on which it is drawn, making the bank absolutely responsible for its payment.

Chancellor.—The chief judge of a court of chancery or equity.

Charter.—An instrument in writing from the sovereign power or legislature, conferring certain rights and privileges.

Charter Party.—A written agreement by which a ship is hired under specified conditions.

Chattel.—Personal property.

Choses in Action.—Things of which the owner has not possession, but merely the right of legal action, for possession, as notes, accounts, etc.

Choses in Possession.—Things in possession of the owner.

Circulating Medium.—Cash and bank notes payable on demand; the medium of exchange.

Clearance.—Permission from the custom house officer for a ship to sail.

Clearing House.—A kind of banking exchange for the convenience of daily settlements between banks.

Clerical Error.—An error in calculation or other accidental error on books or documents.

Coasting.—Sailing near land, or vessels trading between ports of the same country.

Codicil.—A supplement to a will.

Collaterals.—Pledges or security for loans of money, or other indebtedness.

Commerce.—The exchange of merchandise on a large scale.

Commercial Paper.—Bills of exchange, drafts or promissory notes given in the course of trade.

Common Law.—The unwritten law receiving its force from universal reception, as distinguished from statute law.

Commission.—The brokerage or allowance made to an agent or factor for doing business for another.

Cooperage.—Charges for putting hoops on casks or bales.

Compact.—A covenant or contract between different parties.

Company.—A number joined together to undertake some common enterprise.

Compound.—To adjust by agreement differently from the original terms, to settle by compromise.

Compromise.—A friendly settlement of differences by mutual concessions.

Consignment.—The act of consigning, as a charge for safe keeping and management, as goods, property, etc.

Consignee.—One to whom goods are intrusted.

Consignor.—The person who commits goods to another.

Consols—In England three per cent. annuities granted at different times, and consolidated into one stock or fund.

Consul.—A person commissioned to reside in a foreign country as an agent of the government.

Contraband.—Prohibited merchandise or traffic.

Contract.—To make an agreement, to covenant.

Copartnership.—A joint interest in business.

Counsellor.—A legal adviser.

Counterfeit.—To copy or imitate without authority, with a view to defraud; a forgery.

Countersign.—To sign, in addition to the name of a superior, that of the secretary or subordinate officer, as bank notes are signed by the president and countersigned by the cashier.

Coupon.—An interest warrant printed at the end of bonds, to be cut off when the interest is paid.

Court.—An official assembly legally met together for the transaction of judicial business.

BUSINESS DICTIONARY—Continued.

Covenant.—A formal contract between two or more parties.

Coverture.—The condition of a married woman, being considered as under the shelter and protection of her husband.

Credentials.—Testimonials, or certificates, showing that a person is entitled to credit, authority, or official powers.

Credit.—Trust given or received; mercantile reputation entitling one to be trusted; also the side of an account on which payment is entered.

Creditor.—One to whom money is due.

Credit Mobilier.—A name given to a joint-stock company in Paris, established in 1852, with exceptional charter privileges. The term has become familiar to intelligent persons in this country through the Congressional investigation of the Credit Mobilier Company of the Pacific Railroad.

Curb-Stone Brokers.—A term applied to a class of stock operators in New York, who do business on the sidewalk or pavement.

Currency.—That which circulates as a representative of value.

Customs.—Customary toll, tax, or tribute on imported or exported goods.

Custom House.—A building where duties are paid and vessels entered and cleared.

D

Damages.—A compensation to one party for a wrong done him by another, the estimated reparation in money for the injury.

Days of Grace.—Days granted for delay in the payment of a note, usually three after it is due.

Debase.—To lessen in value by adulteration.

Debenture.—A certificate given by the collector of the port of entry, to an importer for drawback of duties on imported merchandise, duties on which, when the merchandise is exported, are to be refunded.

Debit.—A recorded item of debt—the debtor side of an account.

Debt.—That which is due from one person to another.

Debtor.—The person who owes another either money, goods, or services.

Decimal.—Having a ten-fold increase or decrease. *Decimal fractions.* Having any power of ten for a denominator.

Deed.—A sealed instrument in writing used to transfer property.

Defalcation.—A diminution, deficit.

Defaulter.—One who fails to discharge a public duty, as to account for money entrusted to him.

Defendant.—The party sued in an action.

Deficit.—A deficiency; the difference between an account's statement of the assets and the assets themselves.

Del Credere.—A commercial term implying a guarantee of the solvency of the purchaser.

Delivery.—Giving money or goods to another.

Demand.—A peremptory urging of a claim, an exaction.

Demise.—To convey, to bequeath by will.

Demurrage.—Allowance for detention of a ship.

Deposition.—Testimony of a witness put in writing.

Depositary.—A trustee, one to whom something is committed for safe keeping.

Deputy.—One appointed to act for another, a representative or delegate.

Diplomacy.—The science of conducting negotiations between nations.

Disability.—Incapacity to do a legal act.

Discount.—An allowance or deduction made for the payment of money before it is due.

Discount Days.—The days of the week on which the directors of a bank meet to consider paper offered for discount.

Distress for Rent.—A landlord's taking personal property found on the land for rent due.

Dividend.—A percentage of profits paid to stockholders.

Divorce.—Dissolution of the marriage relation.

Donee.—The person to whom a gift or donation is made.

Donor.—One who confers anything gratuitously.

Dormant.—Silent partner, one who takes no share in the active business, but shares profit.

Dower.—Interest of a woman in the real estate of her deceased husband.

Drawback.—Money paid back on goods exported, a part or the whole of the duty charged.

Draft.—An order from one man to

BUSINESS DICTIONARY—Continued.

another directing the payment of money, a bill of exchange.

Drawee.—The person to whom a bill of exchange is addressed, the payer.

Drawer.—One who draws a bill of exchange, or an order for payment.

Dress Goods.—A term applied to fabrics for the garments of women and children, most commonly to those made of mixed materials, as silk and cotton, and silk and worsted, etc.

Due-Bill.—A written acknowledgment of debt; not transferable by mere endorsement.

Dun.—To press urgently the payment of a debt.

Duplicate.—A copy or counterpart of anything.

Duress.—Personal restraint, or fear of personal injury, or imprisonment. It nullifies all contracts into which it enters.

Duties.—A tax levied by the government on imported goods; money paid to the government on imports and exports.

E

Earnest.—A pledge, something given by the buyer to the seller to bind the bargain, and prove the sale.

Effects.—Goods, or personal estate.

Eleemosynary.—Founded by charity, or intended for the distribution of charity, as a hospital or college.

Ell.—An English measure of length, equal to 1¼ yards; the Scotch ell is $1\frac{1}{25}$ yards.

Embargo.—A detention of vessels in port, prohibition from sailing.

Embarrassment.—Perplexity arising from insolvency, or temporary inability to discharge debts.

Embassy.—The public business intrusted to diplomatic officers.

Engrosser.—One who buys large quantities of any goods in order to control the market.

Embezzlement.—To appropriate public money to private use by a breach of trust.

Eminent Domain.—The power of the State to take private property for public purposes.

Emporium.—A place of extensive commerce, a market place.

Endorse.—To endorse a note by writing the name on the back.

Entreport.—A bonded warehouse, a storeroom for the deposit of goods; a free port.

Equity.—A system supplemental to law, qualifying or correcting it in extreme cases.

Estate.—The degree, quantity, nature, and extent of interest which a person has in real property.

Estoppel.—A stop, a bar to one's alleging or denying a fact contrary to his own previous actions; allegation or denial.

Exchange.—Act of bartering; a bill drawn for money; a place where merchants meet; difference between the value of money in two places, or premium and discount arising from purchase and sale of goods.

Excise.—Taxes or duties on articles produced and consumed at home; internal revenue tax.

Execution.—A written authorization to enforce a judgment.

Executor.—The person appointed by a testator to execute his will.

Executory.—To be executed in the future.

Exports.—That which is carried out of a country, as goods and produce in traffic.

Ex Post Facto.—After the act.

Express.—A courier; also regular and quick conveyance for packages, etc.

F

Face.—The amount expressed on a note or draft.

Factor.—An agent who buys and sells in his own name, being intrusted with the goods, in this respect differing from a broker.

Facture.—An invoice, or bill of parcels.

Failure.—Becoming bankrupt, suspension of payment.

Fac-simile.—An exact copy or likeness.

Favor.—A note or draft is said to be in favor of the payee.

Fee Simple.—In the United States, an estate held by a person in his own right and descendable to his heirs.

Fiduciary.—In trust.

Finance.—Revenue, public money, income.

Financier.—One skilled in financial operations, a treasurer.

Firm.—A business house or company; the title used by a business house.

Firkin.—A measure of capacity; the fourth part of a barrel; or eight or nine gallons.

Fiscal.—Pertaining to the public treasury or revenue.

Fixtures.—The part of the furniture of a store or office, which is not

BUSINESS DICTIONARY—Continued.

movable, as gas pipes and burners, partitions, etc.

F. o. b.—Free on board; the bill or invoice with f. o. b. includes the transportation to the shipping port and all the shipping expenses.

Foreclose.—To cut off by a court judgment from the power of redeeming mortgaged property.

Forestall.—To buy goods on their way to market, intending to sell again at a higher price.

Forgery.—Fraudulently changing or making a written instrument.

Folio.—A page in an account book, sometimes two opposite pages bearing the same serial number.

Franc.—A silver coin used in France, equal to about nineteen cents.

Frank.—To exempt from charge for postage.

Fraud.—Injurious stratagem, deceit.

Free Trade.—The policy of conducting international commerce without duties.

Freehold.—Land held by free tenure, or in fee simple, subject to no superior or conditions.

Freight.—Merchandise being moved from one place to another; the price paid for carrying freight; also to load or burden.

Funded.—Turned into a permanent loan on which annual interest is paid.

Funds.—The supply of money or the capital.

G

Gain. — Advantage, acquisition, profit.

Garbled. — Drugs, spices or other goods which have been sorted or picked over and freed from impurities.

Gauging.—Measuring the capacity of casks, etc.

Gist.—The principal point of a question, the pith of the matter.

Go-between.—Agent for both parties.

Good Will.—The advantage accruing from a successful conduct of business; it is a property that may be transferred.

Grant.—A transfer of property by deed; a conveyance made by the Government.

Gross.—Twelve dozen; *gross weight;* weight of goods including dust, dross, bag, cask, etc.

Guarantee (or **Guaranty**).—A security or warranty given by a third party; one who warrants.

Guarantor.—One who promises for another's debt.

H

Habeas Corpus.—A writ to bring a party before a court, to prevent false imprisonment.

Haberdasher. — A seller of small wares, as thread, pins, etc.

Hand-book.—A book of reference; a manual.

Hand-money.—Money paid by the purchaser at the closing of a contract or sale.

Harbor.—A port or haven for ships.

Haven.—A port or shelter for ships; a harbor.

Hazardous.—Precarious, dangerous, uncertain.

High Seas.—The unclosed waters of the ocean outside the boundaries of any country.

Holding-Over.—A tenant's remaining in possession of the premises without the consent of the landlord.

Hollow-ware.—A trade name for camp and kitchen utensils made of cast iron or wrought iron.

Honor. — To accept and pay when due.

Husbandage. — An owner's or an agent's commission for attending to a ship.

Hypothecate. — To pledge for the security of a creditor.

I

Impolitic. — Wanting in prudent management; not politic.

Import.—To bring in from abroad.

Importer.—The merchant who imports goods.

Imposition.—Tax, toll, duty or excise prescribed by authority.

Impost.—A tax or duty imposed on imported goods.

Indemnify.—To recompense for loss, to reimburse.

Indenture.—A mutual agreement in writing.

Indorsement. — A writing on the back of a note.

Indulgence.—Extension of time of payment; forbearing to press for payment.

Inland Bills.—Drafts or bills of exchange drawn on a party in the same State as the drawer.

Insolvency.—Inability to discharge debts when due.

Insurance.—Indemnity from loss; the premium paid.

Installment.—Payment of parts at different times.

BUSINESS DICTIONARY—Continued.

Instrument.—A writing containing an agreement.

Interest.—Premium paid for the use of money.

Internal Revenue.—The part of the revenue of our Government which is collected in the form of internal duties.

Intestate.—Without a will; not disposed of by will.

In toto.—Wholly, entirely.

Inventory.—A list of merchandise made periodically for the purpose of knowing the quantity and value of unsold goods, in order to ascertain the condition of business.

Investment. – The laying out of money in the purchase of some species of property.

Invoice.—A written account or bill of merchandise bought; a bill of items.

J

Jettison. — Throwing goods overboard in case of peril to lighten and preserve the vessel.

Jointure.—An estate settled on a wife at the husband's death, for her life at least.

Joint Stock.—Stock held in company.

Joint Tenancy.—Joint occupancy; not so close intimacy as partnership.

Journal.—A book used to classify and arrange business transactions.

Judgment Note. — A note in the usual form, with the addition of the power to confer judgment if not paid.

Jurisdiction.—The power of exercising judicial authority.

K

Kilogram.—The French measure of weight equal to 2¼ lbs. avoirdupois, or 1000 grains.

Kiting or Kite Flying.—Exchanging checks on different banks for the purpose of obtaining the use of money for a single day.

L

Lame Duck.—A stockbroker's term for one who fails to meet his engagements.

Larceny.—Theft; taking personal property belonging to another.

Law-merchant.—The general body of commercial usages in matters relative to commerce.

Lay-days.—Days allowed for loading and unloading a cargo.

Laydown.—A phrase used to express the entire cost of a commodity, including transportation, etc., at a place remote from its production or purchase.

Lease. – Renting lands, etc., the written contract.

Legacy.—A gift, by will, of personal property.

Ledger.—A book in which a summary of accounts is preserved.

Lessee.—One who takes an estate by lease.

Letter of Attorney.—A writing by which one person authorizes another to act in his stead, commonly called power of attorney.

Letters of Credit.—A letter authorizing credit to a certain amount to be given to the bearer.

Liability.—Obligation; debts.

License.—A grant of permission by the authorities.

Lien.—A legal claim on property for debt.

Lieu.—Instead; in place of.

Liquidate.—To clear off; to settle; to pay as debts.

Lloyds.—A marine insurance association, or society of underwriters in London, deriving its name from the coffee house where it originated. The records of this society contain a complete history of the sea, so far as concerns the number of shipwrecks, collisions, fires, piracies, mutinies, etc.

Loan.—A thing furnished to another for temporary use, on condition that it be returned.

Long Price.– Price after the duties are paid.

M

Malfeasance.—Evil conduct; illegal deed.

Mandatary.—A person to whom a charge is given, or business intrusted.

Manifest.—An invoice of a ship's cargo.

Manufacture.—The process of reducing raw material into a form suitable for use.

Marine. — Relating to the ocean; nautical.

Maritime Law.—Law relating to harbors, ships, seamen.

Mark.—A weight of gold and silver used as a measure for these metals in Europe.

Mart.—A commercial center; a market place.

BUSINESS DICTIONARY—Continued.

Material Men.—Men who furnish materials for ships, houses, etc.

Maturity.—The date when a note or draft falls due or is payable.

Mercantile Law.—Law pertaining to trade and commerce.

Merchandise.—Whatever is bought and sold in trade.

Merger.—The absorption of a thing of lesser importance by a greater, whereby the lesser ceases to exist, but the greater is not increased. For instance, a note on which a judgment is recovered is absorbed by and merged in the judgment.

Metallic Currency. — Silver and gold coins forming the circulating medium of a country.

Mint.—The place where money is coined.

Misfeasance. — A trespass; doing improperly an act that might be done lawfully.

Mitigation.—The abatement of a judgment, penalty or punishment.

Monetary.—Pertaining to, or consisting in, money.

Money.—Coin; any currency lawfully used instead of coin, as bank notes.

Money-Broker. — A broker who deals in money.

Monopoly. — Sole permission and power to deal in any species of goods.

Mortgage.—To convey property for the security of a debt, the conveyance being void when the debt is paid.

Mortgagee.—One to whom a mortgage is given.

Mortgagor.—One who gives a mortgage.

N

National Banks.—Banking institutions, established in the United States under the provisions of an act of Congress, the object of which is to unify the currency.

Navigation. — The science of conducting vessels on the ocean.

Negotiate.—To transact business; to hold intercourse in bargain or trade.

Negotiable. — Transferable by assignment or indorsement to another person.

Net.—Clear of all charges and deductions.

Net Proceeds.—The sum left after deducting commissions or discount.

Non-Feasance. — An omission of what ought to be done.

Notary Public.—An officer appointed by the governor to take affidavits, acknowledgments, to protest bills and notes, etc.

Note.—A written or printed paper acknowledging a debt and promising payment.

Null.—Void.

O

Open Account.—A running or unsettled account with an individual or firm.

Open Policy.—An insurance policy covering undefined risks, which provides that its terms shall be definite by subsequent additions or endorsements.

Option. — A stockbroker's term for the privilege of taking or delivering at a future day a certain number of shares of a given stock at a price agreed upon.

Ordnance.—All kinds of large guns.

Ostensible Partners. — Those known to the public.

Ouster.—Turning out of possession any one entitled to it.

Out-Standing Debts. — Unpaid debts.

Overt.—Not covert, open, manifest.

Owe.—To be obliged to pay.

P

Panic. — A financial crisis among business men, generally the result of overtrading and speculation.

Par.—State of equality in value, equality of nominal and actual value.

Parol. —Oral declaration, word of mouth.

Partnership.—Union in business; business firm.

Par Value.—Face value or value named on certificate of stock.

Pass-Book. — A book in which a trader enters articles bought on credit, and then sends it to the creditor for his information.

Passport.—A document carried by neutral merchant vessels in time of war for their protection, also a government document given to travelers, which permits the person therein named to pass from place to place.

Pawn-Broker. — One who lends money on pledge or the deposit of goods.

Pay.—To make requittal, to give an equivalent for goods.

Payee.—One to whom money is to be paid.

Payer.—One who pays.

BUSINESS DICTIONARY—Continued.

Pigments.—Paints.
Pledge.—A pawn, personal property deposited as security.
Policy of Insurance.—The writing or instrument in which a contract of insurance is embodied.
Politic.—Well advised, adapted to its end.
Port of Entry.—A harbor where a custom house is established for the legal entry of merchandise.
Preferred Stock.—Stock taking preference over the ordinary stock.
Premises.—The thing previously mentioned; houses, lands, etc.
Premium.—The percentage paid for insurance; the excess of value above par.
Price.—Current value, or rate paid or demanded in barter.
Price Current.—A printed list of the prevailing prices of merchandise, stocks, specie, bills of exchange, rate of exchange, etc.
Prima Facie.—At first view or appearance.
Principal.—An employer, the head of a firm; a capital sum placed at interest.
Procuration.—A power of attorney; an instrument empowering one person to act for another.
Pro Rata.—A proportional distribution.
Protest.—A formal declaration, made by a notary, for want of payment of a note or bill of exchange.
Proxy.—A person appointed to represent and vote for another.

Q

Quarantine.—To prohibit a ship from intercourse with shore, when suspected of having contagious diseases on board.
Quasi.—As if, in a manner, in a certain sense.
Quo Warranto.—A writ by which the government ascertains by what warrant a corporation acts.

R

Rate.—The ratio or standard.
Real Estate.—Property in houses and lands.
Rebatement.—Deduction on account of prompt payment, discount.
Receipt.—An acknowledgment of payment in writing.
Reciprocity Treaty.—A commercial treaty between two nations securing mutual advantages.
Reclamation.—A claim made against the seller of goods which prove deficient or defective.
Refund.—To repay; to restore.
Release.—To give up a claim against a person or property.
Reprisal.—The act of seizing ships or property as indemnity for unlawful seizure or detention.
Resources.—Available means, funds.
Respondential Bond.—A pledge of a cargo at sea.
Retail.—Selling goods in small quantities.
Retainer.—The fee paid to a lawyer when engaging him.
Retire.—To take up one's note before due, to relinquish business.
Revenue.—Income, return; annual income of a nation for public uses.
Revenue Cutters.—Small vessels employed to aid revenue officers in the collection of duties, or to prevent smuggling.
Revocation.—The act of calling back, recalling some power or authority conferred.

S

Salvage.—A compensation allowed to persons for voluntarily saving a ship or her cargo from peril.
Seaworthy.—Fit for sea; a ship worthy of being entrusted with a cargo.
Sans Recours.—Without recourse.
Secondarily.—Applied to the endorser of a note or drawer of a bill, signifying that he is only conditionally liable, or liable if the maker and drawee fail.
Seize.—To take possession of, by virtue of a warrant or legal authority.
Seller's Option.—A term mostly confined to the sales of stocks, for a sale which gives to the seller the option of delivering the article sold within a certain time, the buyer paying interest up to delivery.
Shipment.—That which is shipped.
Sight.—Time of presenting bill to the drawee.
Signature.—The name of a person written with his own hand, signifying his consent to the writing above it.
Sinking Fund.—A fund set apart from earnings or other income, for the redemption of debts of government, or of a corporation.
Sleeping Partner.—One who shares the profits of a business without letting his name appear, or taking part in it actively.

BUSINESS DICTIONARY—Continued.

Slop-shop.—A store where cheap ready made clothing is sold.
Smuggler. —One who avoids the payment of duties by secretly importing goods into a country; a vessel engaged in smuggling.
Solicitor.—An attorney or advocate, the title of a person admitted to practice in the court of chancery or equity.
Solvency.—Ability to pay all debts or just claims.
Specialty.—A contract or obligation under seal.
Statement.—Usually a list of property, or resources and liabilities.
Statistics.—A collection of facts arranged and classified.
Statute.—A positive law, established by act of Legislature.
Stipend.—Settled pay or compensation for services.
Stipulation.—A contract or bargain.
Stock.—Money invested in business.
Stocks. — Property consisting of shares in joint stock companies.
Stock Broker and Jobber.—A broker who deals in shares or stocks.
Stoppage in Transitu.—The seller of goods upon credit resuming possession after their shipment before they get into actual possession of the buyer.
Sue.—To seek justice by a legal process.
Surcharge.—An overcharge.
Surety.—A bondsman, a bail, security.
Suspend.—To stop payment.
Suspense Account. —An account used to contain balances of personal accounts which may be considered doubtful.
Sutler.—An authorized vender of provisions, etc., to soldiers in camp or garrison.

T

Tacit.—Implied but not expressed.
Tally Man.—One who receives payment for goods in weekly installments.
Tare.—An allowance in weight for the cask in which goods are contained.
Tariff.—A list of duties to be imposed on goods imported or exported.
Tax.—A levy made upon property for the support of the government.
Teller.—An officer in a bank who receives or pays money.
Tenants in Common. — Persons holding lands, etc., by several and distinct titles, and not by joint title.
Tenant.—One holding property under another.
Tenement.—That which is held.
Tender.—To offer or present for acceptance.
Tenure. — The manner of holding property in lands.
Testator. — The person leaving a valid will.
Textile Fabrics. — All kinds of woven goods, generally restricted to piece goods.
Tickler.—A book containing a memoranda of notes and debts arranged in the order of their maturity.
Time Draft.—A draft maturing at a future specified time.
Tonnage.—The weight of goods carried in a boat or ship.
Tort.—Mischief, any wrong or injury.
Trade Discount.—An allowance or discount made to a dealer in the same trade.
Transact.—To perform commercial business, to conduct matters.
Transfer.—To convey right, title, or property.
Tranship. — To transfer merchandise from one conveyance to another.
Treasury. — A place where public revenues are deposited and kept.
Treasury Notes.—Notes of various denominations issued by the government, and received in payment of all dues, except duties on imports.
Tret.—An allowance to purchasers for waste of 4 pounds on every 104 pounds of weight after the tare has been deducted.
Trustee.—One who is entrusted with property for the benefit of another.

U

Ultimo or Ult.—Last month.
Uncurrent.—Not current, not passing in common payment as uncurrent coin, notes, etc.
Underwriter.—An insurer, so-called because he underwrites his name to the conditions of the policy.
Usage of Trade.—Custom, or the frequent repetition of the same act in business.
Usance.—Business custom which is generally conceded and acted upon.
Usury.—Exorbitant interest, formerly merely interest.

V

Valid. — Having legal strength or force.

BUSINESS DICTIONARY—Continued

Value.—Rate of estimated worth; amount obtainable in exchange for a thing.

Value Received. — Phrase used in notes and bills.

Vend.—To sell.

Vendee. — The person to whom a thing is sold.

Void.—Null, having no legal or binding force.

Voidable.—Having some force, but capable of being adjudged void.

Vouchers.—A paper attesting the truth of any thing, especially one confirming the truth of accounts.

W

Wages.—Hire, reward, salary.

Waiver.—The act of waiving; of not insisting on some right, claim, or privilege.

Wares.—Goods, merchandise, commodities.

Warrant.—A precept authorizing an officer to seize an offender and bring him to justice; also to insure against defects.

Warranty.—An agreement to make good all defects in an article sold.

Water-logged.—Said of a ship when she has received so much water into her hold by leakage as to become unmanageable.

Way-bill.—A document containing a list and description of goods sent by a common carrier by land.

Wharfage.—Fee or duty for using a wharf.

Wharfinger.—The proprietor of a wharf.

Wrecker.—One who searches for the wreck of vessels.

Wreck-Master.—A person appointed by law to take charge of goods, etc., thrown ashore after a shipwreck.

Writ.—An order of court.

DICTIONARY OF LEGAL TERMS.

Alibi.—In another place.

Alimony.—Allowance by court to wife from husband living separate from her.

A vinculo matrimonii.—From the bonds of matrimony.

Bequeath.—To give personal property by will.

Compos Mentis.—Sound mind.

Contempt.—Violation of rules or orders of a court of justice or legislative body.

Crime.—Violation of law punishable by the State.

Devised.—To give real estate by will.

Defeasance.—An instrument defeating the force of some other deed.

Disseized.—Unlawfully put out of possession.

Easement.—Privilege, like a way through another's land, water-course, etc.

Entail.—An estate limited in descent to a particular heir or heirs.

Escheat.—Falling of real property to the State.

Fee.—Hereditary estate.

Fee-tail.—Estate, limited to certain heirs by will of the first donor.

Fieri Facias.—Writ of Execution.

Heirloom.—Chattel descending to heir instead of going to administrator.

Investiture.—Giving possession.

Judicature.—A court of justice.

Jurisprudence.—Laws interpreting and applying them.

Leasehold.—Lease of land or tenements.

Lex Loci.—Laws of the place.

Mandamus.—Writ of superior court to inferior tribunal, etc., commanding performance of specified duty.

Moiety.—One-half of estate, goods or profits.

Non-age.—Under twenty-one.

Parcenary.—Holding lands and tenements in copartnership.

Particeps Criminis.—A helper of the criminal.

Replevin.—Recovering goods wrongfully taken.

Reprieve.—Warrant suspending execution of sentence.

Riparian.—Rights of water-courses.

Seisin.—Possession intending to claim freehold interest.

Vi et Armis.—By force of arms.

Writ of Capias.—Writ commanding officer to take the person.

ALPHABETICAL INDEX.

www.ingramcontent.com/pod-product-compliance
Lightning Source LLC
LaVergne TN
LVHW041206061126
851857LV00018B/1958
* 9 7 9 8 9 9 5 5 8 4 8 2 7 *